PREFACE

FIRE ON THE PRAIRIE is written primarily for the laymen and ministers of the United Methodist Church of Kansas. Included in the history is something of the story of the Methodist family in its larger outreach. It is hoped that historians will find the material accurate and the interpretations fair. The sub-title—Methodism in the History of Kansas—is important. The drama of Methodism is placed in a larger setting—with the background of the state, the nation and the total Methodist heritage forming a larger picture.

The book is not the work of any one person. Several years ago, in 1961, the two annual conferences of The Methodist Church in Kansas agreed to support the writing of a history of Methodism in Kansas. To begin the work as editorial writer, Dr. Roy L. Smith, famous native Kansan, was engaged to work under the guidance of the Editorial Board. Directing the work of this board through the years has been Dr. John Hoon, a long-time student of Methodism, especially in Kansas.

Death took Dr. Smith, after only a beginning. As a member of the board I was drafted to carry through the undertaking to its conclusion. To the entire board I owe a great deal—in planning and criticism of the manuscript in its two major revisions. It may be unfair, or not wise, to single out individuals, but two must be given special credit—Dr. John Hoon and Nyle Miller,

Executive Secretary of the Kansas State Historical Society. Through the latter other staff members of the Kansas State Historical Society have assisted in the reading and criticism of each chapter and in providing photographs. Dr. Hoon, as chairman, never failed in his encouragement, helpful criticism and organizational skill. Bishop W. McFerrin Stowe's introduction indicates his interest, concern and support since he came to Kansas in 1964.

A late entrant in the enterprise was the illustrator and designer of the book, Dolores Gwinn. In her work there is clearly demonstrated what a combination of artistic skill and creative imagination can do. Of inestimable value has been the assistance of Josephine Lafler, my secretary and later assistant to the president. In order to get the help of the Editorial Board, the individual chapters were mimeographed twice in addition to the typing of the total manuscript three times. Patience, skill and efficient management were called for. In the final stages Carolyn Arnpriester helped a great deal. Most of this secretarial service was the contribution of Saint Paul School of Theology Methodist.

The attractive design and the illustrations provided by Dolores Gwinn will commend the book to many, old and young. It is my hope that the whole story of the past will come alive, and not for the past only. My concern is more for the future. May the spirit and deeds of our fathers serve as an inspiration and give encouragement to daring adventures on the new frontiers of today and tomorrow.

Don W. Holter
November 1, 1968
Saint Paul School of Theology Methodist
Kansas City, Missouri

INTRODUCTION

It began as a tiny spark, but like a "fire on the prairie" it swept across the state until Methodism had touched the life of almost every person and every institution within the State of Kansas. This is the story that President Don W. Holter tells in this splendid account of "Methodism in the History of Kansas." Refusing the easier task of relating a sectarian story of the growth of a denomination, the author has dealt with the full sweep of the historical, sociological, political, and educational segments as they relate to the religious development of Kansas. It is a fascinating story of people and of events.

Doctor Holter is uniquely qualified for this large responsibility. He is the son of a Methodist parsonage in Kansas and has known personally many of the leaders of the Church who have helped shape its history. He received his undergraduate training at Baker University, and following his theological studies, continued his education, receiving his doctorate in the field of Church History. So he is a church historian and writes with the knowledge and ability of one who has acquired such training. By life and heritage he is, and has been, involved in Methodism in Kansas. This is an ideal combination.

The story that is told spans four centuries and includes the growth and development of Kansas from its early beginnings, through its days of difficulty and despair, to its present maturity and strength. The place that the Christian religion has had in these years of maturation is large, and the impact of the faith of the life of individuals is important. In such a study as this, multitudes remain nameless and must be passed over; but across these pages there walk those who, because of their unique ability and contribution, are described with clarity and vitality. These few become the representative of many, and behind each can be seen the faces of others equally dedicated and equally involved in living and sharing the Gospel.

The place of Methodism in the history of Kansas is nowhere more significant than in the establishment of the educational institutions of the state. The writer deals in detail with the story of the founding of schools and colleges from the establishing of the churches and institutions for the spiritual guidance and education of Indians to the present day, with special reference to the three Methodist colleges.

It is impossible to evaluate the significance of the people called Methodist—in their varied denominational expressions—upon the life of Kansas, but here is the account that better than any other, indicates how great this has been. Not only the people of one denomination are indebted to Doctor Holter for this fine work, but also all of those who are interested in the history of our state.

But especially in behalf of The United Methodist Church, we would express to this outstanding Methodist educator and minister great appreciation for his contribution to our Church in the writing of this, its story. We commend it to all readers, to the members of our denomination, and to anyone seeking to know more and appreciate more fully, the place of religion in the life and development of Kansas.

W. McFerrin Stowe
Bishop of The United Methodist Church
The Kansas Area

Dedicated to
my father and mother

Henry O. Holter, a native of Indiana, had his total ministry in Kansas—early in the Northwestern Kansas Conference, but the greater part was in the Kansas Conference. He was a delegate of the Kansas Conference to two General Conferences, 1920 and 1924. From Kansas Wesleyan University he received three degrees.

Lenna Mater Holter, also a native of Indiana, came to Kansas as a child with her parents. Her father, Daniel Mater, for a time a blacksmith on the Santa Fe Trail, north of the present site of Baldwin, was a loyal member of the United Brethren Church and served as a lay delegate to the organizing conference in Kansas. She was a graduate of Central College at Enterprise when it was a United Brethren school.

Always to them:
God reigned
Jesus Christ was the Lord of life
The Church was of God and would endure
    to the end of time
The Spirit was ever at work.

TABLE OF CONTENTS

GOLD, GLORY AND THE GOSPEL

A proud adventurer was at the end of the trail! It was more than eighteen months since he had marched out of the Mexican city, Compostela, at the head of the greatest army and entourage ever brought together by a white man in the new world. The dream he had long pursued was over. There was no gold to be found in the Seven Cities of Cibola or in Quivira. Where is the glory in shabby Indian villages?

The waving grass of the prairies indicated the passing of the wind. Likewise the dream of the noble Castilian was blown away. Nothing remained but the desolation of future disgrace when he returned to Mexico. In failure he turned from the endless plains to the south. It was the summer of 1541. Francisco Vasquez de Coronado had spent more than a month in the future area of Kansas after several months and hundreds of miles on a futile search.

1

Only 22 years earlier, in 1519, a conqueror who was to fire the imagination, ambition and cupidity of every Spaniard, left Cuba for Mexico. No outsider could have known that the year Hernando Cortez landed on the Mexican shore was in the cycle of the time the Aztecs expected the return of their god, Quetzalcoatl. Their messiah was to come from the east, he would be fair and with a beard.[1]

Amazing to the Spaniard and his followers, was the reception given by the people. Fabulous riches, precious stones, gold and silver jewelry, even gold and silver disks the size of wagon wheels, warm hospitality, and women were presented. The road to Mexico City was open to him. Slaves brought various articles:

They were of the most miscellaneous kind; shields, helmets, cuirasses, embossed with plates and ornaments of pure gold; collars and bracelets of the same metal, sandals, fans, panaches and crests of variegated feathers, intermingled with gold and silver thread, and sprinkled with pearls and precious stones; imitations of birds and animals in wrought and cast gold and silver, of exquisite workmanship; curtains, coverlets and robes of cotton, fine as silk, of rich and various dyes, interwoven with featherwork that rivalled the delicacy of painting.[2]

Only after Cortez had the Aztec emperor, Montezuma, under his control did the people realize this newcomer was an avaricious overlord and no returning god.

After a terrible struggle Cortez captured Mexico City and subdued an empire with a high civilization. The wealth of the country was unbelievable. There was enough for the conqueror and his band to "live like Kings," as he had always dreamed, and also enormous amounts of precious metals to flow back to Spain.

Not many years later one of the lieutenants of Cortez, Francisco Pizarro, and a small band duplicated this story in his conquest of the empire of the Incas. Again vast wealth came to a few and again the Spanish kingdom and the ruler, Charles V, received a tremendous financial reward.[3] Dreams of new conquests of new worlds were in the minds of every young Spaniard. Many new attempts were made to seek out new cities of wealth.

The Seven Cities of Cibola had been in the forefront of attention for many years. According to one legend, seven bishops had fled from Portugal during the Muslim invasion in the 8th Century and established the Seven Cities of Gold. The Viceroy of Mexico, Antonio de Mendoza, even sent out a small expedition to check on the claims. On his return, Friar Marcos, a Franciscan, had reported that he had not visited the cities, but from a hill had seen one of the cities and it surpassed the grandeurs of Mexico City.

For the conquest of Cibola the Viceroy and Coronado, whom he had chosen to lead the enterprise, collected the largest army or entourage ever assembled in the new world. There were 200 mounted Spanish cavaliers, 62 foot soldiers, 800 Indians, 1,000 Negro and native slaves and herds of horses, oxen, cows, sheep, droves of laden mules.[4] Possibly the cost was over two million dollars. Some say that Charles V contributed half of this amount. It was with high hopes they set out from Compostela in February of 1540 and headed north.

Cibola they conquered but it was only an Indian village in the area of the present-day New Mexico. There was a continuation of failures. They would have turned back but stories of a new land, that of Quivira, came to their attention. An Indian, called "the Turk," "because he looked like one," fabricated stories of a land of wealth to the north.[5]

All could not go but Coronado took a small band and left what remained of his company at Tiguex. Thus he came into the future Kansas only to find that he was again deceived. There was no gold, no settled people to exploit as in Mexico and Peru—therefore, no glory. The rest of his life was one of disgrace and imprisonment. On the journey Coronado passed the sites of the present Kansas towns of Liberal, State Line, Milner, Hayne, Archer, Arkalon, Kismet, Plains, Collano, Meade, Fowler, Advance, Minneola, Bloom, Kingsdown, Ford, Larned, Kinsley, Lyons and Lindsborg.[6]

But what of the gospel? Beginning with the first voyage of Columbus and continuing through all the expeditions of Spain a religious purpose was always written into the agreement. The cross and the sword went together! So it was with Hernando Cortez. Accompanying him and blessing his conquests were a small group of Franciscans. Indeed, the Mexican women could not be used as concubines by his men until they had been baptized into the Christian faith by the careful padres. Prominent also in the future conquest of Mexico were the pioneer efforts of many of the regular clergy. Often against the rapacious exploitation of the sword stood the power of the cross. Too often, however, the glorious goal of total conversion even though nominal blinded many missionaries to the immediate exploitation of the helpless.

In the adventure of Francisco Pizarro into Peru, there was a small group of padres who joined in the exploitation and blessed it. In fact it was the conversion of the Inca ruler by a padre that led to his being strangled by the Spaniards instead of being burned at the stake, as first ordered.[7]

Likewise, in the expedition of Coronado the men of the cross were represented. Most prominent of all was

3

Friar Juan de Padilla. He had come to the New World as early as 1529, had served well as a pioneer leader. It was with honor that he joined the mighty host as they set out up the western coast of Mexico for the famous Seven Cities. No great religious conquests were made along the way, but beginnings were made for future permanent establishments.

When Coronado's band left the area of the future Kansas, the conquistador wrote to Charles V as follows:

> The country itself is the best I have ever seen for producing all the products of Spain, for besides the land itself being very fat and black and being very well watered by the rivulets and springs and rivers, I found prunes like those of Spain and nuts and very good sweet grapes and mulberries.
>
> And what I am sure of is that there is not any gold nor any other metal in all that country, and the other things of which they had told me are nothing but little villages, and in many of these they do not plant anything and do not have any houses except of skins and sticks, and they wander around with the cows.[8]

Ironically, in his disdain, he could not know that under his very feet lay untold wealth in the form of oil and natural gas. In about 400 years, in 1961, this would be producing gas valued at $52,000,000.00 per year.[9] Nor could he know of the great salt deposits not far away. Also, as he stared at the endless prairie, he could not know that here would be the future "bread

FRIAR PADILLA MONUMENT NEAR LYONS

basket" of a nation of two hundred million people.

Friar Padilla wrote nothing. But when the advance band returned to Tiguex and the larger group were to leave for Mexico City he asked permission to return to work among the Indians of Quivira (Kansas). Permission was finally granted.

A little company did return. For a short time they did serve. When journeying further, however, they were set upon by a savage band of Indians. Friar Padilla was able to save his companions by remaining while they fled. Kneeling in prayer he received the Indians' murderous arrows.[10] The seed of the martyrs had been planted in Kansas soil! A monument to this noble friar stands south of Herington; other monuments are at Lyons and Council Grove.

BUILDERS OF EMPIRES

For a period of nearly two hundred years after the brief visit of Coronado there was little concern over this region on the part of Spain. There was little to draw them—no gold, no prospect of conversion, no settled people to exploit and no prospect of integrating the area in the already vast Spanish empire.

One contribution the conquerors made of which they were unaware—the horse. When we think of Indians it is next to impossible to imagine them apart from their ponies. When DeSoto and Coronado came the Indians knew nothing of this animal and at first thought of a man and a horse as one. From the expeditions of these two Spanish explorers and others came the beginnings of a large number of horses that later are found in North America. Some would say that they prospered here because the mid-west plains were very similar to the first natural habitat of the horse—on the plains of Asia, east of the Caspian Sea. They came to Spain by way of the Near East, Arabia and North Africa. To the plains Indian the horse gave a new lease on life—a new mobility, more power in warfare—and made them much more difficult to defeat and displace.[1]

The other essential animal was the buffalo, which roamed the prairies in herds of thousands. From them

the plains Indians secured all the necessities of life—fresh or "jerked" (dried) meat, tents, clothing, bedding, skin boats, and even fuel in the form of dung or "chips."

The flags of six non-Indian nations—Great Britain, France, Spain, Mexico, the United States and Texas—might have flown over a part of the territory of the present-day Kansas during the 18th and half of the 19th centuries, if all claims of nations had been accepted as valid. Two of the nations, Mexico and Texas, were not conscious of this small part of their holdings.

The continued tie with Mexico was maintained by the beginning of trade between Santa Fe and American pioneers. It began with the use of horses and oxen and grew rapidly after the introduction of wagons, especially after Mexico won its independence from Spain in 1821. Before that time Spain allowed no trade with any outside power; all goods from the Old World had to go through Spain and Mexico. Enterprising Americans soon found that goods taken by way of the Santa Fe Trail from Independence, Missouri, would reap a profit of six or seven hundred percent. In 1824, "80 men with 25 wagons, 150 pack horses and $30,000 worth of goods, made the journey that year, returning safely with silver and furs worth $190,000." Of the 800 miles to Santa Fe, 500 miles were in Kansas.[2]

Spain had an unrivaled claim to all the region in question, until the English claims which began with the settlement of Jamestown in 1607. Not only Virginia but other colonies laid claim to areas on the American continent from the Atlantic to the Pacific—with no idea of what they were demanding. No one took these various claims seriously, even as far as the Mississippi, but they were made. Later the British made a new bid for power in the Mississippi Valley.

The possibility of trade, especially in furs, drew the French into this region. Following the journeys of Marquette and Joliet and LaSalle, France dreamed of a vast inner empire joining Canada and the Gulf. To cultivate trade with the Indians came Bourgmont, in 1724, to what is now Kansas City. Later he traversed west as far as the area of today's Ellsworth, Kansas.

The struggle for supremacy among the European powers, in the middle of the 18th Century, had its counterpart in North America. The supporting wars in America were designated by different names, but they were part of the same struggle. The main contenders were England and France, but Spain played an important supporting role.

Just before the close of the Seven Year War (French and Indian War in America), 1756-1763, between England on the one side and France and Spain on the other side, France ceded Louisiana to Spain. At the close of the war France was eliminated from North America and the British were triumphant. The proud conquerors, like France earlier, dreamed of colonial possessions embracing Canada and the Mississippi Valley. What a new world empire was theirs—the older colonies on the Atlantic seacoast, the newly conquered territory already indicated and India, also won from France.

Part of the dream was shattered by the revolution beginning in 1775 by the "embattled farmers" and "the shot heard round the world." Not only did these rebels on the coast refuse to yield, but also through the leadership and forces of George Rogers Clark, made good their claims to extend American territory to the Mississippi River.

Soon therefore France came back into the American territorial struggle and the new ruler of France, Napoleon Bonaparte, proved to be an American benefactor. While Spain still possessed Louisiana, and particularly controlled trade on the Mississippi, American traders were pushing for trade concessions. Spain was ready to yield. About this time Louisiana was secretly ceded to France in a trade.

France and Britain were in a struggle. Britain had managed an effective naval blockade of the continent. Therefore, Napoleon could not retain control of his American holding and he also needed money. Imagine the surprise of the American diplomats, the ambassador to France and President Thomas Jefferson when Napoleon offered to sell not only the port at the mouth of the Mississippi but all of Louisiana.

After some haggling the greatest and most unusual real estate bargain was agreed upon. For a total of $15,000,000.00 the United States received an amount of land equal to its own size at the rate of 3¢ per acre. Someone said it was a highway bargain, the seller had no right to sell and did not control the land; the buyer had no right to buy and did so against his constitutional scruples. Napoleon said, "This accession of territory strengthens forever the power of the United States; and I have just given England a maritime rival that will sooner or later humble her pride." Needless to say, the United States Congress quickly ratified the illegal act of President Jefferson. A great portion of present-day Kansas was in this purchase.[3]

The final act in this drama came as a surprise to Mr. Jefferson but the vast region beyond the Mississippi had been in his thinking for a number of years. While American minister to France, he had planned an expedition for a man to explore the west by coming through Russia and to the west coast but the Russian Empress halted it after it was well on its way. Later, in 1792, he proposed to the American Philosophical Society that money be raised to explore the region from the Mississippi to the Pacific coast.[4]

Unknown to many is the fact that President Jefferson, in January, 1803, made a confidential recommendation to Congress of a plan to explore the Missouri to its source and thence to the Pacific. Congress approved and granted the money. The personnel of the leadership was chosen—Captain Meriwether Lewis, personal secretary to Mr. Jefferson, and William Clark as associate. All these actions took place while the area to be explored was under the control of Spain (or was it France?). The final consummation of the Louisiana Purchase reached Washington on July 1, 1803, only four days before Captain Lewis left Washington for Pittsburgh and west to the newly acquired territory.[5]

The main company of 45 led by Lewis and Clark, finally left St. Louis in May, 1804, and plunged into the vast unknown of the region west of the Mississippi. They made their way up the Missouri, across the mountains, on to the coast and then returned after more than two years on the way. On September 15, 1806, they were back at the mouth of the Kansas River. Eight days later they were back in St. Louis.[6]

Other expeditions were soon to follow. That of Zebulon Pike in 1805-1806 was especially important for Kansas, for he crossed the state. He was not impressed with the future prospects for he thought of it as becoming as famous as the deserts of Africa and doubted if many people could live there. He added:

But from these immense prairies may arise one great advantage to the United States, viz: The restriction of our population to some certain limits, and thereby a continuation of the Union. Our citi-

zens being so prone to rambling and extending themselves on the frontiers will, through necessity, be constrained to limit their extent on the west to the borders of the Missouri and Mississippi, while they leave the prairies incapable of cultivation to the wandering and uncivilized aborigines of the country.[7]

Another pessimist was the explorer, Stephen H. Long, who in 1819-20, travelled among the Kansas villages with the Indians, into Nebraska and on to Colorado. It was he who was responsible for the name "The Great American Desert" on his maps. It remained in the thinking of the American people for many years. After some description he said:

In regard to this extensive section of country, I do not hesitate in giving the opinion, that it is almost wholly unfit for cultivation, and of course uninhabitable by a people depending upon agriculture for their subsistence.[8]

Kansas was worthless for agriculture!

INDIANS IN TRANSITION

The morning of the fourth of June, 1823, was a turning point in the life of many Indians in the United States, especially those then living east of the Mississippi. Isaac McCoy was a missionary at the Baptist Indian Mission station at Carey, Michigan Territory. He had been reflecting on the discouragements and futility which were certain to attend all attempts at Christianizing the Indians in any region in which the white population was constantly advancing and from which the red man must in the future be moved.

On that day McCoy came to a definite and far-reaching plan of action:

At this time I formed the resolution that I would, Providence permitting, thenceforward keep steadily in view, and endeavor to promote a plan for colonizing the natives in a country to be made theirs, west of the State of Missouri, &c., and from that time until the present I have considered the promotion of this design as the most important business of my life.[1]

For this Scotch-Irish Baptist missionary, or for his wife, this was not the first relationship with Indians. When he was only 19, in 1803, he had married Christiana, daughter of Captain and Mrs. E. Polk. Before her birth her mother and three older children had been taken prisoners by the Ottawa Indians and held captive for several years in the region of the northern lakes. They were finally found by Captain Polk and brought back home.[2]

It is rather amazing that the daughter and her husband would later go as missionaries to these same Ottawa Indians. McCoy was commissioned as a missionary to the Indians by the Baptist Triennial Convention in 1818. During the subsequent six years and before this major decision of 1823, he had worked in Indiana and then in Michigan with the Potawatomi and the Ottawas. The major problem in working with the Indians was their contacts with white people. This ever-present and increasing difficulty between whites and Indians led to his decision of June 4, 1823.

His action on this resolution was immediate. He submitted his plan to Lewis Cass, Governor of Michigan Territory, and others, later to the Baptist Board of Missions. Soon he and others presented the proposal to the Secretary of War, John C. Calhoun, and subsequently to President James Monroe. Secretary Calhoun was immediately favorable and the President commended the plan in his message to Congress on March 30, 1824. It was not, however, until December, 1827, that Congress took any definite action. At that time an appropriation for a tour of exploration was made and the two men appointed for the task were Captain George Kennedy and Isaac McCoy.[3]

For several years following this initial tour, McCoy, although retaining his appointment as a missionary of the Baptist Board, was at various times in the employ of the government—making exploration tours and recommending courses of action.

Through his *Annual Register of Indian Affairs* McCoy furnished to the east information concerning the Indian Territory, especially the area which is now Kansas, descriptions of the territory, survey statements of the number of Indians in that territory, as to tribes, their location and other information.

To some people at the time, the purchase of Louisiana seemed a bad bargain. This point of view gained support after the exploration of the Pike expedition in 1806 and was confirmed by the statement of Major Stephen H. Long after his tour in 1819-20. What use could be made of "The Great American Desert"? "It was only a barrier or a borderland."

Beginning to come into the consciousness of the

government at Washington were the land hungry pioneers of the West—hunters, woodsmen and rough-and-tumble farmers. The government had been able to satisfy their desires by purchases from the Northwest Indians. Following the Battle of Fallen Timbers, in 1795 and in 1809, the Indians parted with 48 million acres which the government made available to the eager pioneers.[4]

In an attempt to halt the loss of their land the Shawnee war leader, Tecumseh, and his brother the Prophet, sought to weld all the significant tribes east of the Mississippi into a confederacy. Although they could command no great numbers—possibly 4,000 warriors in the area between the Ohio, the Lakes and the Mississippi, they were for a time irresistible in their movement of reform, regeneration and separation from the white man. Finally, Governor William Henry Harrison forced hostilities and the Indians were defeated at the battle of Tippecanoe. Harrison was a hero in the west. The British were blamed for the action of the Indians and another move toward the War of 1812 had been taken.[5]

Along with the desire of thousands to grab the lands of the Indians and get rid of them, were the sincere concerns of many to help the red man. President Jefferson wanted them to abandon hunting and take up agriculture. If they did, of course, they would not need as much land. The "Civilization Fund" established by the United States Congress in 1819, provided $10,000.00 annually for mission schools for Indian children. Roman Catholics and Protestants took action in response to the many requests on the part of the Indian tribes.

By the late 1840's the Congress was still appropriating only $10,000.00 annually, but private groups and the tribesmen themselves were pouring over $150,000.00 into schools which had sprung up.[6]

The first Methodist work with the Wyandots began as a part of this benevolent concern and the date, 1819, is important, as will be related later.

When the Baptist missionary, Isaac McCoy, proposed moving the Indians beyond the Mississippi it was prompted by the finest of motives. They needed land which would be theirs *in perpetuity*. To this end he gave his active and informed support. The lands west of the Mississippi and beyond the States of Missouri, Louisiana and the Territory of Arkansas were designated as "Indian Territory."

Here was a complete solution to the "Indian Problem," acceptable to white men with a conscience and to others who could see no other use for the land beyond Missouri. To the land-hungry pioneers, it would

13

open vast areas of rich land.

What of the Indians? With an exception or two they had kept their treaties made with the government! They saw no alternative, however, but to accept the new treaties being forced on them. Their people were being crowded. The association with the majority of white men was having an evil and disintegrating effect on their people. The promise of immediate annuities, the assurance of adequate tracts of land in perpetuity, and continual pressure finally won over the sad leaders.

The period beginning in 1825 and continuing for the next 20 years, was one of treaties and removal.[7] When President Andrew Jackson came into office in 1829, the pace was stepped up and the mass emigration was under way. An Indian removal bill was enacted on May 28, 1830. A special commission was set up and the position of Commissioner of Indian Affairs was created. In 1825, the Kansas and Great and Little Osage tribes were convened at St. Louis. After consultation and persuasion these tribes ceded to the government much of the present-day Kansas, especially in the eastern part, but retained reserves that were also large. The way was prepared for the coming of the red men from the east. More than 10,000 Indians were moved into this total Indian Territory.[8]

Our interest is with the emigrant tribes who came to the Kansas area. Among the first to agree to emigrate were some of the Shawnees near Cape Girardeau, Missouri, in a treaty late in 1825. About four years later some of the Delawares in Missouri and others in Ohio came to an agreement. As indicated before, President Andrew Jackson, a westerner, hurried the removals. Treaties followed with the Kickapoos, other Shawnees, Senecas, Ottawas, Wyandots, Potawatomi and others. The locations, in 1846, are indicated on the map.[9]

Later the story of the efforts of the various churches to minister to the indigenous as well as the emigrant tribes will be related. Before dealing with each of these missions it might be well to continue with the changes in our government's policy and the subsequent disposition of the Indians in Kansas.

All Indians understood that this new "land was to be theirs in perpetuity, or at least 'as long as the grass grew.' It began to wither in 1853." [10] The sad plight of the Indians was summed up well by Bishop O. C. Baker, in a letter from Kansas on January 29, 1857:

My Dear M.:

A strange providence has attended the red man. The Indians residing in the older states were assured by our government, that if they would remove to certain reservations, beyond the Mississippi, they should find permanent homes, and the faith of the Government was solemnly pledged, in their several treaties,

14

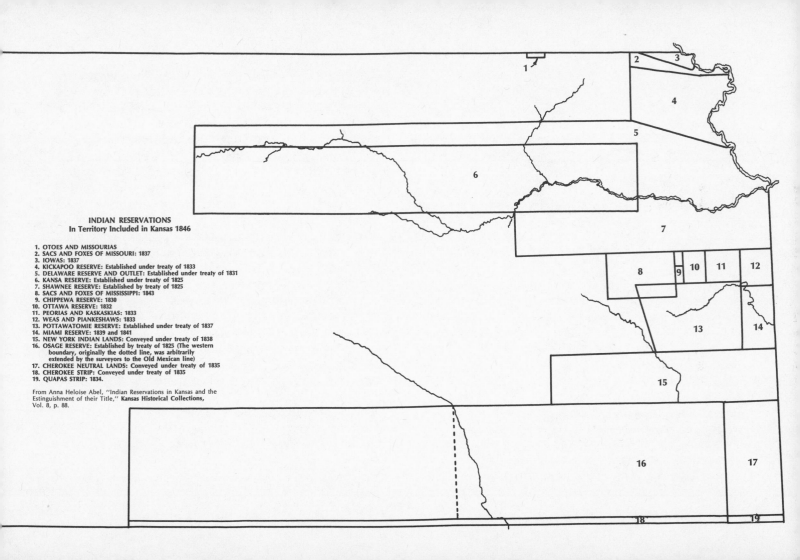

INDIAN RESERVATIONS
In Territory Included in Kansas 1846

1. OTOES AND MISSOURIAS
2. SACS AND FOXES OF MISSOURI: 1837
3. IOWAS: 1837
4. KICKAPOO RESERVE: Established under treaty of 1833
5. DELAWARE RESERVE AND OUTLET: Established under treaty of 1831
6. KANSAS RESERVE: Established under treaty of 1825
7. SHAWNEE RESERVE: Established by treaty of 1825
8. SACS AND FOXES OF MISSISSIPPI: 1843
9. CHIPPEWA RESERVE: 1830
10. OTTAWA RESERVE: 1832
11. PEORIAS AND KASKASKIAS: 1833
12. WEAS AND PIANKESHAWS: 1833
13. POTTAWATOMIE RESERVE: Established under treaty of 1837
14. MIAMI RESERVE: 1839 and 1841
15. NEW YORK INDIAN LANDS: Conveyed under treaty of 1838
16. OSAGE RESERVE: Established by treaty of 1825 (The western
    boundary, originally the dotted line, was arbitrarily
    extended by the surveyors to the Old Mexican line)
17. CHEROKEE NEUTRAL LANDS: Conveyed under treaty of 1835
18. CHEROKEE STRIP: Conveyed under treaty of 1835
19. QUAPAS STRIP: 1834.

From Anna Heloise Abel, "Indian Reservations in Kansas and the
Estinguishment of their Title," **Kansas Historical Collections,**
Vol. 8, p. 88.

to secure to them quiet and peaceable possession, and undisturbed enjoyment of the same, against the claims and assaults of all others. On such pledges, many tribes removed to the West some twenty-five years ago. Such removals greatly interrupted the missionary operations of the different churches, who had established missions among them, and were attended with many unhappy results to the Indians. They had not to be sure, many valuable improvements to leave behind, but there were the graves of their fathers, and cherished memories connected with their former homes. The chiefs generally used their influence to carry out the treaty stipulations with the government, yet many of the people revolted, and were forcibly removed to their assigned reservations. These removals were attended with many unhappy results to the Indians. They were not far removed from the snares of the white man. Their heavy annuities enticed many unprincipled men to follow them, and by gaudy, worthless wares, and poisonous liquors, to secure to themselves the government appropriations. Some devoted missionaries followed their people, and carried out the plan they had previously adopted for the moral culture of the Indians, and were the means of rendering them much aid. But many of the tribes went alone to their new homes and the moral influences which were thrown around them in their former residences, were soon destroyed. The white man is still building his cabin around him, and where can the red man go? There are no open, unappropriated fields suited to his wants and his habits. There is only one alternative for him, either to adopt the habits of civilized life, or to lie down in the grave.[11]

Some of the emigrant tribes had been in the "permanent" new locations only about 10 years when new agitation for another removal prompted the government to act. On March 3, 1853, the Indian Office was authorized to begin action for the re-cession of these same lands. The "Great American Desert" lands were now coveted by land-hungry, would-be settlers.

As a result, during 1854-55, a series of treaties were worked out with some 11 tribes. To make matters worse, the Kansas Territory was thrown open by the government in 1854, before all title changes were completed. Consequently, years were to go by before final clear titles could be obtained. Again the settlers crowded in with little respect for the rights of the Indians. Finally, in November, 1856, the government conducted its first public land sale. "Kansas, which was originally conceived as the red man's home, was rapidly becoming his grave. The causes of decay were many and universal: predatory white traders with their jugs of the "Great White Father's milk," disease, duplicity, the gold rush, the slavery controversy, the Civil War, and covetous land-hungry neighbors."[12]

Quickly all available land was taken up. More treaties with the Indians had to be made between 1859 and 1862. By now the railroads were in on the bidding. Vast areas were obtained: for example, the future Missouri Pacific bought 92,598 acres; the Atchison and Pikes Peak was able to buy 123,832 acres for

$1.25 per acre; and the Santa Fe purchased 340,180 acres for $1 per acre.[13] A number of individuals also profited greatly along with the railroads. A few obtained as much as 90,000 to 100,000 acres each. Often the individual settlers moved in, squatted on the land, and refused to move because speculators or railroads seemed to be favored.[14]

Another element was the discovery of gold in the Pike's Peak country. This news brought a flood of 100,000 prospectors across the plains into the western part of the Kansas Territory, now Colorado, in 1859.[15] They pushed their way into Indian lands nearby. Indian resentment flared and they were soon talking of war. Harsh action was taken by the whites and the many warriors went on the war path. Both red and white men were at fault. On November 29, 1864, occurred the terribly brutal Chivington Massacre of 450 unsuspecting Indians who thought they were under the protection of federal troops. Colonel J. M. Chivington, officer in charge, was a Methodist minister.[16]

This unwarranted action and the subsequent Indian response soon called forth the need for a consideration of our Indian Policy. Finally in March, 1867, there was introduced into Congress a bill "for establishing peace with certain Indian tribes now at war with the United States." It was passed quickly. A Peace Commission was established and they set out for the west in August, 1867.[17]

The Peace Commissioners agreed on two reservations for the plains Indians: Black Hills of Dakota Territory and in present-day Oklahoma, then Indian Territory. At a great council on Medicine Lodge Creek they met representatives of the Southwestern Tribes. The western land in Oklahoma was forced away from Creeks, Chickasaws, Choctaws and Cherokees and provision made for the newcomers from the western plains.[18] Other lands in eastern Oklahoma were secured for the emigrant and other plains Indians of Kansas and Nebraska. Led by the Wyandots, the superior tribes of Delawares, Shawnees and Ottawas early made it possible for their individual members to take their share of the tribal land in severalty.

Numerous treaties were signed by others throughout the 1860's and 1870's and many of the tribes moved to Oklahoma. Endless legal disputes resulted. Only about three or four of the 36 tribes remained. In the census of 1960 there were only 5,069 Indians in Kansas.[19]

One of the few bright spots in the story of the white man's relation to the Indian is that of the missionary efforts of many churches through the dauntless efforts of some great souls.

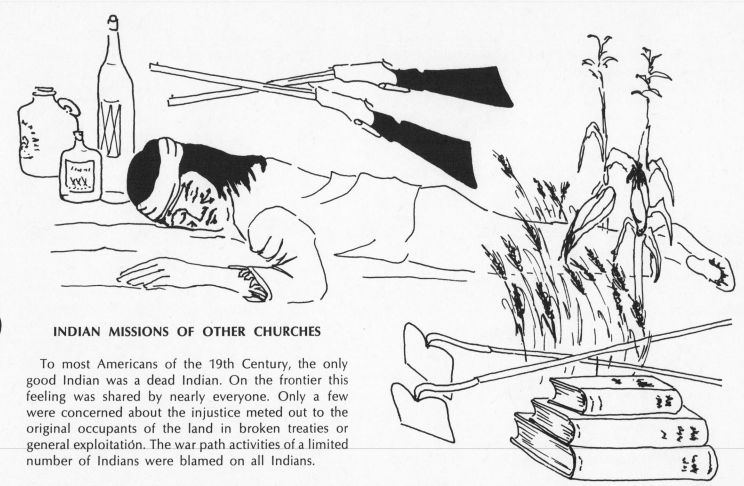

INDIAN MISSIONS OF OTHER CHURCHES

To most Americans of the 19th Century, the only good Indian was a dead Indian. On the frontier this feeling was shared by nearly everyone. Only a few were concerned about the injustice meted out to the original occupants of the land in broken treaties or general exploitatión. The war path activities of a limited number of Indians were blamed on all Indians.

18

Popular opinion seemed to follow the line of thinking concerning Indians expressed by Reverend J. S. Griffing, one of the earliest Methodist ministers to the whites in Kansas, in a letter of December 2, 1854:

I always supposed from descriptions given that they possessed much more native talent and genius than the whites and that it only needed education and religion to develop and refine these powers and they become a nation superior to the whites. But I have yet to see the first thing to give indication of this whilst on the other hand so far as natural intellect is concerned, unless I see something farther to change my mind, I should be inclined to place them below the blacks. Allowing them equal advantages. For nearly twenty years an untiring missionary effort has been exerted in endeavoring to civilize, christiainize and elevate the Indian. Schools have been established among them and the most philanthropic, talented and pious have been engaged in this noble work. Government seeing the great advantages that would accrue to itself has made large appropriations for the promotion of this object but discouragement and want of success seemed written upon almost every effort.[1]

Not many would have agreed with a missionary, L. B. Stateler, who had worked with the Indians for many years, when he said of them:

The Indian is as susceptible of religious influence as the white man. When he is stationary and has a permanent home, he is as easy to convert as his white brother—the surrounding influences being equal. And when an Indian is fully converted to God, I think that we may safely say that he is as stable and firm as the white man, or if there is any difference, he is more so.[2]

Before making a judgment as to the effectiveness of the numerous missions which were established among the Indians and prior to outlining those efforts it might be well to note several general conditions which thwarted the work of missionaries.

Although some of these were included in the previous chapter, a summary may be helpful. Among these are: (1) the degrading effect of liquor—this is a constantly recurring note in nearly all the reports; (2) the unsettled life of the Indians—their moving from east of the Mississippi to the west and settling for a time and then being removed again farther west or to another location; (3) the roving spirit—especially among the indigenous tribes; (4) the policy of the government in regard to money—the annual annuities tended to make the Indians lazy, shiftless and indifferent to work; (5) the trading activity with the whites—often lowering their regard for white men; and (6) the limited number of workers when compared with the tremendous undertaking.

Other Protestant denominations and the Roman Catholics were at work among the Indians along with the Methodists. Therefore, in order to see the activities of the latter group in a larger perspective, let us hurriedly outline some of the endeavors of other religious groups.

PRESBYTERIAN MISSIONS

Earliest to serve the Indians in Kansas were missionaries sent out by the United Foreign Missionary Society. This group, organized in 1817, by the Dutch Reformed, Presbyterians, and Associate Reformed, was later merged into the American Board of Commissioners for Foreign Missions (usually called the "American Board") in 1826-27. The latter Board had been established by the Congregationalists in 1810; later the Presbyterians and Dutch Reformed joined them. As a result of an exploring trip made by two agents sent out in 1819 by the United Foreign Missionary Society, a mission company of nine men and eight women was sent out in 1820 to establish a mission among the Osages of the Grand River and in March, 1821, a second company consisting of 25 adults and 16 children, led by Reverend William B. Montgomery, Reverend N. B. Dodge, and Benton Pixley, set out.[3] The Harmony Mission, as it was called, was located in what is now Bates County, Missouri. A school for the Indian children was soon begun and in August, 1823, a church of 20 members composed almost entirely of those in the mission family was organized. From this time on there was little to encourage the missionaries. The indifference of the Indian adults to their work along with their friendliness, their long hunting and predatory excursions, coupled with toil and hardships made it terribly difficult for the missionaries. The mission was finally given up in 1836.[4]

It was out of the Harmony Mission that the first mission in Kansas was established, probably late in September, 1824. The site was on the west side of the Neosho River, not far from the present town of Shaw in Neosho County. The Missouri Osages had been settling there a few years before and a larger number remained after the summer of 1823. The first missionaries, Reverend Benton Pixley and his family, had come to Harmony Mission in 1821, and after three years moved to Neosho. Another missionary couple, the Brights, joined them the next year.[5]

After only a few years of erecting permanent buildings, of attempting to conduct a school, of facing the opposition of white traders and the government agents, and experiencing the indifference of the Indians to civilized, settled life, the mission was closed. The reason for the traders' opposition is clear. If the Indians adopted a settled life and gave up hunting, the fur trade would be ruined. Apparently Reverend Pixley had good intentions but his methods were not conciliatory and after about four years it seemed wise for him to leave. His going spelled the end of the mission.[6]

Immediately after the schism in the Presbyterian Church, in 1827, the Old School branch withdrew their support from the American Board and organized their own Board of Foreign Missions to carry on distinctively Presbyterian work. One of the early missions established was that among the Weas in 1833. It was reported closed, however, in 1838 due to the fact that the Methodist stations among the Peorias and others were within 10 or 12 miles and could serve this small tribe, only about 200 in number, and were doing so.[7]

The work among the Iowas, Sacs and Foxes was of a much longer duration although it began later. Reverend Samuel Irvin, the Presbyterian missionary who was assigned to work among these Indians, gives the following description:

It was the 10th of April, 1837, when I first visited the Iowa Indians in what was then called the Platte Purchase . . . an important part of the State of Missouri. A year previous they had made a treaty with the government which obliged them to leave that country and take a new home in what is now the State of Kansas.

They numbered in all 830. They were a wild, warlike, roving people, and in a most wretched condition, depending mainly on the chase for subsistence. Their habitations were of the most frail and temporary kind. . . . Domestic animals, excepting ponies and dogs, were not among them. . . . With the men, war was the chief employment and great delight. . . .

The year after the Iowas moved to their new homes (in 1837) the government, under treaty stipulations, built for them five double log houses . . . also fenced and broke 200 acres of ground in ten-acre lots. The rails were soon used for campfires the houses, some of them, were occupied for a short time, but all were eventually abandoned. The doors, floors, windows, and all that could be were sold for whisky and trinkets, and the logs were finally burned. . . .

Under provisions of the same treaty, 100 head of milch cows and 100 head of stock hogs were delivered to them; also a large quantity of farming utensils. The cattle and hogs were soon devoured for food, and the farm tools were traded off for whisky and the like. . . . A water mill built by the government at a cost of $2800 was burned to ashes; whisky shops gathered around, and drunkedness prevailed to a fearful extent.[8]

Mr. Irvin moved to the new station in November, 1837, and Reverend William Hamilton arrived the following month. It is due to the untiring efforts, the consecration, and perseverance, of these two men, and their wives, that any results were obtained in the face of such difficulties.

During the first nine years the missionary work had to be carried on in the homes of the Indians, but in 1845 a boarding school to accommodate 75 scholars was erected with money from the Indian Department and the school annuities of $6,675.67 from the two tribes, Iowas and Sacs. The new building which was opened in the summer of 1848 was a stone and brick, three stories, 106 feet long and 37 feet in width. The Iowas responded enthusiastically and brought more children than the school could accommodate, but the Sacs declined to send any of their children and for several years seemed absolutely indifferent. During this time the Mission hesitated to fill up the school with others, and always hoped the Sacs would send their children.[9]

Mr. Hamilton left in 1853 to take charge of the Otoe and Omaha mission and Mr. Irvin retired from the mission in 1860, after 23 years of service. Irvin returned two years later, however, and stayed until the summer of 1864, when, because of his wife's health, he withdrew and was connected with the college at Highland.[10]

Presbyterian efforts among the Kickapoos were of short duration. To this tribe a missionary company of six led by Reverend William H. Honnell was appointed and reached their station in July, 1856. Buildings were erected, school opened the following December, but the irregular attendance of the scholars and the discouragements which attended the other missions caused the mission to close in June, 1860.[11]

ROMAN CATHOLIC MISSIONS

Earlier mention has been made of the martyr, Friar Juan de Padilla, who was associated with the Coronado expedition—"the first missionary to lose his life at the hands of the savages in the territory now comprising the United States."[12] When Roman Catholic missionaries next appeared in this region some three centuries later it was a part of the United States.

In 1820 the head chief of the Osage, Sans Neri, and some Indian companions called on the Roman Catholic Bishop, Bishop Du Bourg, residing in St. Louis. As a result, Father De La Croix paid two visits to the Osage in 1822 in Missouri and over into the village of the Little Osage on the Neosho. In Washington the following year Bishop Du Bourg proposed to Secretary John C. Calhoun the establishment of a seminary to train missionaries for the new territory. Calhoun approved the plan and allowed a grant of $800 per year. Such a school, under the Jesuits, was opened in 1824 under the supervision of Father Quickenborne, but the school only served until 1832. During this period, however, Father Quickenborne visited the Osage and his 17 baptisms on the Neosho in 1827 are "the earliest actually recorded for the territory that has since become the State of Kansas."[13]

Attempts of missions among the Kaws, in 1828, and the Kickapoos, in 1836, were made but without success. More permanent work was established among the 800 Potawatomi Indians after their move from Indiana in 1838 accompanied by Father Benjamin-Marie Petit to their new reservation. They were moved to Sugar Creek in 1839 and to the present site of St. Mary's nine years later.[14]

A year after their move to Sugar Creek the Jesuits opened a school. A subsidy to build a church came from the government and an annual grant also of $300. Good results were evident—in 1847 there were about 1300 Roman Catholic Potawatomi. The move to the future site of St. Mary's came as a result of the joining of another group of this tribe in Council Bluffs with that at Sugar Creek following a treaty in 1846. Here on the new location schools were opened in 1848 and a year later had an enrollment of 57 students.[15]

A new contact was made with the Osages. Consequently, a mission was opened in 1847 and schools were opened for Osage boys and girls. A year later the enrollments were 40 and 25 respectively and a church was built.[16]

A new day for Roman Catholicism in this region came in 1850 when John Baptist Miege was named "vicar apostolic with episcopal consecration and powers" for the territory east of the Rocky Mountains, except for the States of Arkansas, Missouri, Iowa and the Territory of Minnesota. He was consecrated a bishop in March, 1851, and journeyed to the St. Mary's Mission immediately and then on to the Osage Mission. Of the total 3,500 of the Potawatomi, about 1,500 were Roman Catholic and about 120 were in schools. Among the 7,000 Osage there were only 150 Roman Catholics and there were 80 in schools.[17] Bishop Miege described his missionary journey in the Indian country, in part, as follows:

We have no roads laid out in the Indian Territory except those which lead to Oregon, to California and to the different forts erected at intervals to keep the savages in respect and to protect the travelers from their dangerous vexations. If one leaves these well marked lines of communication, it is necessary to rely on the sun, the compass or a guide. The missionary, who must undertake a journey of several days needs a strong horse, a good blanket, a heavy line three feet long, and saddle bags in one side of which he puts the things necessary for Mass and on the other side a little bread, a bit of salt meat, and coffee. The coffee pot, axe, and two tin cups are entrusted to the guide. Equipped thus he trots, walks, or gallops across our immense prairies, as he wishes or the powers of his horse permit. . . .

You imagine, no doubt, that after a hard day's ride in the burning heat, to throw oneself on the grass and to sleep are one and the same thing. There you are wrong. Never is sleep more difficult for the traveler than at this moment. Squadrons of mosquitoes surround him, settle on him, harrass him, throw themselves at every unguarded point. It is a regular battle—a genuine massacre in which sighs and groans are as useless as slaps and puffs, which seem to have no effect other than to raise a sweat on the poor victim and to multiply the number of his enemies. There is only one defense: to cover your head with the blanket, to close every opening and resign yourself to the lesser evil that of sweating great drops until dawn comes to end the torture. . . .[18]

That he had no great missionary force under his command is noted in the fact that in 1855 when whites began pouring in he had only six priests.[19]

BAPTIST MISSIONS

In the summer and fall of 1830, Reverend Isaac McCoy made preliminary arrangements with the government for the establishment of Baptist missions among the "Shawanees," Delawares, Otoes, Omahas and Pawnees. It was not, however, until June 7, 1831, that Mr. Johnson Lykins, an old associate of McCoy's at the Carey Station, arrived to labor among the Shawnees.[20] He immediately began the erection of the necessary buildings, and after the arrival of Alexander Evans and Daniel French in 1832, a church was constituted and a school commenced. Lykins joined McCoy in visiting different sections of the Indian country during 1833 and 1834, and in arranging for future missionary operations. Meanwhile on October 2, 1833, Mr. and Mrs. Jotham Meeker from the Sault St. Marie mission arrived at the mission expecting to locate among the Ottawas who had migrated from Michigan but, inasmuch as the Ottawas were not yet definitely located, they remained at the Shawnee station and he engaged in printing.[21]

An alphabet was invented for some of the tribes and a great amount of time was spent in compiling elementary books which were printed on the press which Mr. Meeker brought with him:

The amount of printing for the year as stated by Mr. Meeker, February 10, 1836, is 6,600 copies of works in seven languages besides the English viz., the Shawanoe, Creek, Choctaw, Otoe, Potawatomie, Wea, and Ioway . . . besides a monthly newspaper, called Shawanoe Sun.[22]

The printing department was the most successful of all the activities of the Shawnee station and occupies an important place in their annual reports. The number of Indians belonging to the church was never large: eight in 1835; 19 in 1840; and 22 in 1847. The Boarding School could never boast of large attendance: 10 in 1841; and 16 in 1847.[23]

In 1856 the station was reported vacant. From this

time on little effort was made by the Baptists because many of the members of the church had moved away and the remainder were planning on moving. The report of 1862 states: "At Shawnee, there is little to encourage us in extensive effort." [24]

The Shawnee station served as a central point from which the missionaries moved out to minister to other tribes; the Shawnee station maintaining the general superintendence over them. In 1835, the Delaware station reported a school with 44 scholars, including adults, with Dr. Ira D. Blanchard as teacher; there was preaching among the Delawares by missionaries from the Shawnee station before the school was organized in 1833. This school was more successful than that at Shawnee, having in 1857 50 boarding pupils, and in 1860, 55. The missionary labor among the Delawares was carried by Mr. Blanchard and later it came under Mr. J. G. Pratt, who was first connected with the Shawnee station in 1837. The work was encouraging despite the indifference and hostility of some of the chiefs. Work was concluded when the Delawares, according to the treaty made in 1866, ceded a part of their territory to the Missouri River Railroad Company (later Missouri Pacific). [25]

Mention has been made of the coming of Mr. and Mrs. Meeker to the Shawnee station in 1833, and his work in the printing department. The Ottawa tribe experienced some difficulty in obtaining an acceptable location. For this reason Meeker's work until his settlement among them on June 18, 1837, consisted of occasional visits. A school embracing 26 scholars was opened in January, 1838. Mr. Meeker remained with this tribe until his death on January 12, 1855. He was successful as a preacher, having baptized 122 Indians, used the press to good advantage, and in addition to this, promoted temperance and industry. [26]

In accordance with a treaty, the Ottawa tribe divided up their lands among themselves and by 1865 most of the tribe had become citizens of the United States. [27]

FRIENDS MISSIONS

Like the Methodists, the Friends had carried on missionary activity among the Shawnees before their removal to the Indian Territory. The year following the formation of the Indiana Yearly Meeting, in 1821, work was begun among the Shawnees in Ohio at the Wapakoneta reserve and carried on until their final removal in 1832. [28] In 1833 the Indian Committee of the Indiana Yearly Meeting with the approval of the Ohio and Baltimore Yearly Meetings, sent a deputation of three Friends to visit the Indians on their new reservation. [29]

As a result of their report, plans were immediately made for the mission establishment. Buildings were erected, a corps of workers engaged, and work was begun in 1837. In this station more emphasis was placed on the instruction of the Indian children "in the doctrines and precepts of the Gospel."

For the first two years the attendance at the school had numbered only about 15 but this gradually increased until in 1848-49 there were 42 scholars in attendance. At this time there were only three of the children not Shawnees. It seemed necessary in the following years to accept children from other tribes. Consequently in 1861 there were 11 Shawnees, 10 Ottawas, four Senecas, two Wyandots, one Brotherton, and one Stockbridge in the school. After 1854 the missionary establishment was continued in an atmosphere of uncertainty caused by the events going on around about them. The government purchased a large part of their reservation in 1854, a scourge of cholera came in 1855 and three of the scholars died from it. The attitude of the Friends towards slavery was not a benefit to anyone living near the border of Missouri during the troublesome times following the opening of Kansas for settlement. The school had to be closed for a time on account of the cholera and again in 1856 because of threats of pro-slavery men from Missouri.

A special committee from the Indiana Yearly Meeting visited the establishment in 1861 and reported on the conditions, needs and prospects of the station.[30]

The school was closed in 1862 and re-opened in April, 1863, under a new arrangement whereby a contract was concluded with the government agent for each scholar. This brought prosperity to the school for a time and in 1864 76 students were in attendance, but this was an exceptional year. The mission continued, despite frequent closing, until 1870 when the affairs were finally brought to a close.[31]

A school for the Kaw Indian children was conducted for a few years by the Western Yearly Meeting. In the year of its organization, in 1858, the Western Yearly Meeting appointed a committee on Indian Affairs which conducted a school from 1863 to 1866; the expenses of this school were taken care of out of the school funds of the Kaw Indians.[32]

The work of the Friends with the Indians, however, was not concluded with the closing of these missions. Under President Grant's Peace Policy the various tribes of Indians were divided up into two superintendencies, the Northern and the Central. The Northern Superintendency was assigned to the Liberal Friends, and the Central Superintendency was assigned to the Orthodox Friends. The Northern Superintendency, in

Nebraska, comprised six agencies with an Indian population of about 6,000, while the Central Superintendency was made up of the Indians in Kansas and Indian Territory which included an Indian population of about 64,000. During the decade, 1869-79, in which this arrangement was in force, these branches of the Friends had the control over the secular and religious education of the Indians. Soon after the inauguration of President Hayes, in 1878, difficulties arose and the arrangement with the Friends was concluded.[33]

The value of the work of all these missions of the several churches is not easy to estimate. As indicated, some tribes were utterly indifferent to the devoted efforts of the missionaries and the government, while others responded with eagerness. Not enough can be said in commendation of the valiant and consecrated service of many missionaries who carried on in spite of the constant difficulties and discouragements which were always present.

WEST BUILDING—1839

EAST BUILDING—1841

REVEREND THOMAS JOHNSON

NORTH BUILDING—18—

5 METHODIST MISSIONS TO THE INDIANS IN KANSAS

Without much question, the most effective Indian mission of any church group in Kansas was that of the Methodists to the Shawnees. Beginning in 1830, under the leadership of Reverend Thomas Johnson, it continued largely with his guidance for a period of over 30 years. The work was discontinued in 1862.

Throughout the western frontier the name of Daniel Boone early became a legend. Neither he nor his family were Methodists. Nevertheless, it was due to Daniel Morgan Boone, the son of Daniel Boone, that the Methodists first became interested in serving the Indians in Kansas. The United States government in their treaties with the various tribes guaranteed them regular financial aid and especially money for schools. In addition, a Government Farmer who served as an agricultural adviser and a Government Blacksmith were also supported by the government for a tribe or a region. Morgan Boone was appointed as a Government Farmer in the western part of Missouri in 1826.[1]

It was a letter by Morgan Boone to his brother-in-law, Reverend Alexander McAlister, that prompted action on the part of Missouri Methodists. Government Farmer Boone urged the early establishment of a mission to the Indians of Kansas. Alexander McAlister, a leading member of the Missouri Conference, followed up the request by writing to Jesse Greene, the Presiding Elder of the Missouri District, whose region included the western frontier of Missouri. The letter is as follows:

Salurbia, April 2, 1830. Dear Bro. Greene:—I have just time to write a few lines by Bro. Peery, in which I wish to call your attention to the Caw Indians, on your frontiers. Col. Daniel Boon, who is the Government's Farmer among those Indians, married Mrs. McAlister's sister, which circumstance has led to a correspondence between him and myself and the Government Agent of those Indians. Boon is among them, perhaps thirty or forty miles from Fort Osage. He promises to do all he can for the support of a school among that tribe. The Agent also promises to assist, as far as he can, and informs me that the Caw Indians, according to the provisions of a treaty with the Government, have a considerable sum of money set apart to support schools among themselves, and the Agent advises us to get in there immediately and secure that fund, and improve it to their benefit. I think you might visit them, and know all about it soon, and perhaps get some pious young man to go and commence school among them before Conference. In haste, your obedient Servant, A. McAlister.[2]

Acting quickly, Presiding Elder Greene went to the Indian country. There he met George Vashon, the Indian Agent, Harmon Davis, the Government Blacksmith, some Indian leaders and possibly Boone. Agent Vashon had already requested the American Board (A.B.C.F.M.—Congregational, Presbyterian, Dutch Reformed) to begin a mission among the Shawnees. Already involved beyond their potential, the American Board declined. Now Agent Vashon made a similar appeal to the Methodists through Greene. Apparently at the latter's request, Mr. Vashon put the request in writing in part, as follows:

Indian Agency, near Kansas, July, 1830. Reverend Sir:—

I have the pleasure now to make the communication which I promised, when I had the happiness of conversing with you in my office, on the subject of establishing a mission for the instruction of the hapless portion of the human family entrusted to my care in this part of the agency. . . . And I now have the pleasure to inform you that I have this day been requested by Fish, a Shawnee Chief, alias Wm. Jackson, a white man, raised with the Shawnees, to make application for the establishment of a mission among them, for the education of their children, and I most earnestly solicit your attention to the subject.

Fish, the Shawnee Chief, has a son by the name of Paskal, who was put to school when he was a boy; he can speak english very well. He is a sober, steady, moral, good man. He has an Indian family, and is industriously employed in farming, and I think he would make the most efficient male interpreter that could be procured.

Having freely and fully communicated what appeared to my mind as necessary at this time upon this very interesting subject, permit me the privilege of offering up my fervent prayers to Almighty God for the influence and teaching of His Holy Spirit, to guide and direct the labors of all the human family. With sentiments of the highest respect and esteem, I remain, dear sir, Your most humble Servant, Geo. Vashon.[3]

About two months later, September 10, 1830, at the session of the Missouri Conference, the members voted to follow the suggestion of Morgan Boone, "to get in there immediately and secure that fund" for a mission not only to the Kansas (Caw) Indians but also to establish one for the Shawnees. To forward this endeavor the ministers formed themselves into a missionary society. The appointments made by Bishop Robert R. Roberts at the close of the Conference, included the following: "Shawnee Mission, Thomas Johnson; Kansas or Kaw Mission, Wm. Johnson." [4] From this time forward until their deaths, these two brothers, Thomas the older and William the younger, were largely identified with the welfare of their respective Indian tribes.

As indicated earlier, the Shawanoes or Shawnees were a historic tribe. As early as 1682 they had made a treaty with William Penn. About a hundred years later they settled in the valley of the Ohio and were allotted land by the United States contiguous to that of the Wyandots and the Delawares.[5] Some of their number, along with some Delawares, moved to the region of Cape Girardeau in Missouri in 1793. It was this Cape Girardeau group, Fish's band, now in Kansas, which immediately gave support to Thomas Johnson when he and Alexander McAlister, now Presiding Elder, came to the Shawnee reservation in Kansas at the end of November, 1830, to plan for the new mission.

Like other emigrant Indian groups from east of the Mississippi, the Shawnees had been in association with white people for generations. They were desirous of a settled life—homes, schools, agriculture, churches. Because money for a school was immediately available from the government, this was emphasized early.

The two-story double log house which was soon built near what is now Turner in Wyandotte County served as a home, a school and a church. The building which Johnson, the new missionary, put together largely by his own hands consisted of two rooms on the first floor, about 20 feet square and 15 feet apart. The covered space between being used as a hall. The upper floor provided sleeping accommodations for employees and occasional guests. One end of the main floor provided for the schoolroom and a chapel, and on the other end was a reception room and a living room for the missionary and his new bride. It was completed and ready for occupancy sometime late in the spring of 1831.[6] Early in the same year the Shawnee bands in Michigan reached an agreement with the government in Washington by which they ceded their lands in the east for holdings in the west. Thus the number of Shawnees on the reservations was enlarged and also the need for the school was increased.

Sometime during the late spring or summer of 1831, the school got under way and a short session was held only to be interrupted by the fact that Johnson had to return to Cape Girardeau to attend the sessions of the Missouri Conference of the Methodist Episcopal Church. He was scarcely out of sight of the reservation when an epidemic of smallpox broke out and deaths became a daily, almost an hourly, event. All activity at the mission came to an abrupt end as the school staff turned to the task of caring for the sufferers. When Thomas Johnson returned, in October, he found the Indians scattered, the reservation in disorder and the children dead or dispersed. It was not until late in December that classes could be resumed.[7] Late in July of the following year, 1832, however, he was able to report that a Methodist Society had been organized with 50 members and Chief Fish as the leading layman.

The year 1838 marks a new era in the life of all Methodist missions in Kansas. Before this an attempt had been made, or proposed, to have a school in each of the six tribes. With the encouragement of the Methodist Missionary Society and the promise of help from the government, the Missouri Conference agreed to establish "a central manual labor school." [8] As a result of the appearance of Thomas Johnson before the Missionary Society in New York on May 30, 1838, the Society pledged an amount, "not to exceed ten thousand dollars . . . for any one year." Payments were made by the Treasurer of the Society to Thomas Johnson: 1837-38—$4,737; 1838-39—$6,198.64; 1839-40—$12,270.57 (apparently for the mission and the Manual Labor School).[9] The government assistance was a gift of 2,240 acres of land. In addition, there was the Delaware Indian School Fund of $4,000 a year for 10 years as well as the Shawnee Fund of $1,500 for a similar period.[10]

The new site was about six miles from the original location, approximately six miles from the mouth of the Kansas River on the California Road, or Santa Fe and Oregon Trail. Work was begun early in 1839, brick kilns were put up, and soon two large buildings were erected. In the coming five or six years 16 buildings—blacksmith, wagon, and shoemaker shops, barns, granaries, sawmill, steam flour mill and tool houses—were built. That this was no small enterprise is indicated by the crop report for the first year—2,000 bushels of wheat, 4,000 of oats, 3,500 of corn and 500 of potatoes. On the farm were 130 cattle, 100 hogs and five horses.[11]

Imagine this daily schedule for a student's routine:

At five A.M. they were awakened by the ringing of a bell, when in summertime they performed light work about the farm until seven o'clock when they breakfasted, a horn being blown by way of signal before each meal. In wintertime their morning work, before eating, was confined to the preparation of fuel, milking the cows, some thirty or forty in number, and feeding the stock. At nine the school-bell summoned them to their studies, which were kept up, with a short interval for recess, until twelve N. They dined between twelve and one o'clock and then resumed their studies until four. Their hour for tea was six P.M. Their evenings were spent in the preparation of their lessons for the ensuing day until eight o'clock. They were then allowed to indulge themselves in indoor recreation until half-past eight, when they were sent to their dormitories for the night. The only religious services which were held during the week were the reading of a chapter of the Bible, followed by prayer, just before the morning and evening meals. Saturday forenoon was devoted to work and the afternoon given them as a holiday. Saturday evening was spent in the bath-room cleaning up for Sunday.[12]

The school was a success from the time of its opening in October, 1839, as is shown by the fact that 75 scholars were in attendance the first year; the number of scholars increased to 110 in 1843, and to 137 in 1845. The students coming from the various tribes—Shawnees, Delawares, Chippewas, Gros Ventres, Peorias, Potawatomi, Kansas, Kickapoos, Munsees and Osages—were taught the duties of the establishment; the girls were taught the domestic arts.[13]

In the church statistics of 1842 there are listed among the members at Indian Manual Labor School—10 colored, 33 whites and 37 Indians.[14] These 10 Negro children belonged to the slaves which Thomas Johnson brought into the territory to work at the mission.

In 1844 the Methodist missions in Kansas, together with the missions in the south part of the Indian Territory, were organized into an Indian Mission Conference. When the Methodist Episcopal Church was torn asunder in 1845, by the differences over slavery, all of these fell to the Methodist Episcopal Church, South. In 1847, Thomas Johnson returned as head of the school after an absence of six years and remained head of the mission until it was abandoned. In 1848, a classical department was organized, called in the Minutes, the "Western Academy." For three years Reverend Nathan Scarritt was in charge of this new department. The manual labor feature of the school was abandoned and only the classical feature continued after 1854; 122 scholars being in attendance in 1855, but only two tribes besides the Shawnees were included—Ottawas and Wyandots. The whole mission had to be abandoned during the Civil War and the last report of Thomas Johnson is that of September 6, 1862.[15]

After 1848 the Methodist Episcopal Church attempted to establish work among the Shawnees; a site on the Wakarusa River was chosen, buildings erected, and a school opened by Abraham Still. The work was carried on through the Platte Mission District of the Missouri Conference of which Mr. Still was the Presiding Elder. The work was hardly begun, however, when it was brought to an abrupt end because the mission premises were transferred to an Indian whose claim included this tract. Missionary activity was carried on among the Shawnees by the Methodist Episcopal Church despite these handicaps until the Civil War by such men as Thomas B. Markham, M. T. Klepper, J. M. Chivington, and the Indian preachers, Paschall Fish and Charles Ketchum.[16]

MISSION TO THE KAWS

When attention is turned to the Kaw or Kansas Mission we have an altogether different picture. It has been noted that in September, 1830, William Johnson was appointed as missionary to the Kansas Indians. This tribe was an indigenous one which McCoy estimated to be about 1,500 in number. In a letter of July 31, 1835, William Johnson wrote:

> I never before saw any part of the human family in so wretched a condition. They live chiefly in dirt houses. They cultivate only a small portion of ground, and this is done by the women with hoes. They do not plow. They have no fences. Their only dependence for meat is on the chase, and the deer have entirely disappeared from the prairie.[17]

KAW MISSION—COUNCIL GROVE

W. H. Goode described them later as:

an indigenous tribe, of rude, filthy habits, and seemingly almost untamable character, the lowest class of savages in the Territory.[18]

William Johnson spent two years with them and was then appointed to the Delawares and the Shawnees, but he returned to the Kaws in 1835. They erected mission buildings and he and his wife remained with the tribe until his death in 1842. Despite all his earnest efforts only one Indian convert appears in the reports and the school was never very successful. In 1844, Reverend J. T. Peery married the widow of William Johnson and the two of them returned to work with the Indians in 1845. Through a treaty the Kaws were moved to a new reservation near Council Grove in 1847; the mission work in their new location was carried on by the Methodist Episcopal Church, South through T. S. Huffaker and Henry Webster and was finally closed in 1854.[19]

MISSION TO THE DELAWARES

Missionary work among the Delawares began in 1832 when William Johnson and Thomas B. Markham were appointed to the mission and school. At the end of the first year they were able to report a membership of 27 Indians; the highest membership reported for any one year was 108 in 1844. Although the Indians patronized the Manual Labor School they were rather indifferent to the advantages of culture, and never took to agriculture despite the fact their land was probably the richest in all the reservations. In the separation troubles, they went into the southern branch of the church with the exception of a group led by Charles Ketchum who maintained a church attached to the northern branch. Among those who labored among the Delawares were Edward T. Peery, Learner B. Stateler, N. M. Talbott and John T. Peery.[20]

MISSIONS TO OTHER TRIBES

Soon after the removal of the Kickapoos to a tract around Fort Leavenworth, a mission was established among them in 1833, by J. C. Berryman. Its success was immediate as is shown in the report of 1834, when the members numbered 230. Although he had 90 scholars in attendance for the first year, the number in 1839, had dropped to 16, probably due to the influence of the prophet, Kenekuk, a Kickapoo Chief who taught a religion all of his own. This opposition seems to have been too strong for the mission. Although arrangements were made for the Kickapoo children to attend the Manual Labor School, few ever did and the membership in the church dropped from 264 in 1837 to 35 in 1843.[21]

In 1832, James H. Slavens was appointed to work among the four small tribes—Weas, Piankeshaws, Peorias and Kaskaskias—who were settled in the Osage River lands and whose total number McCoy estimated to be 540. N. M. Talbott served the mission from its second year until 1841; a school was established, two buildings were built. The largest number of students in the school seemed to have been in 1836 when 16 were in attendance, while the church reached its greatest number in 1837 when 55 were reported. Between 1841, when Mr. Talbott left to take charge of the Kickapoo station, and at the time when the mission was abandoned around 1845, it was conducted by Nathan T. Shaler, Thomas Hurlburt, Thomas B. Ruble and their assistants.[22]

Before the Potawatomi came to Kansas and while they were located in Illinois, some missionary work had been attempted by the Methodist Episcopal Church but it had been abandoned about 1830. The year of their arrival in Indian Territory, 1837, a mission was begun with Frederick B. Leach in charge at about the place where Osawatomie now stands. From this time until the removal of the Potawatomi to their new reservation in what is now Pottawatomie County, Kansas, in 1847-48, missionary work was carried on by E. T. Peery and N. M. Talbott in connection with the Peoria Mission. Finally Thomas Hurlburt and Thomas B. Ruble served in connection with the Chippewa, Peoria and Wea work.[23]

In the Missouri Conference appointments of 1832 the "Iowa and Sac Mission and School" are left "to be supplied" and very little work seems to have been done. In 1860 Richard P. Duvall began work among the "Sauks" and Foxes and continued until 1866 except for a time when he was in the army, 1862-63. He worked on their reservation at the present site of Quenemo. He had visions of an orphanage for Indian children at Baldwin City and the proposal was approved by the Conference, but was given up on account of lack of funds.[24]

THE SPARK FOR A SPREADING FLAME—

THE MISSION TO THE WYANDOTS*

John Stewart had come a long way when he arrived at the Wyandot reservation at Upper Sandusky, Ohio! Geographically, the place of his birth was far to the east in Virginia. Morally and spiritually, he had come even further. Only a short time back he had been a poverty-stricken drunkard. In between his nights of careless revelry he felt called to something higher but lost his hold again and again. In these times of despair he often contemplated suicide. Who would have thought that this would be the type of person to spark the beginning of the missionary movement among Methodists?

Little is known of Stewart's parents, except that they left him in Virginia when they moved west. He is usually called a free-born mulatto, but there was also some Indian blood in his veins in addition to white and Negro. The white blood was probably French, but he

had no idea as to the Indian tribe to which he was related.

On his way to join his parents in Tennessee he headed toward Marietta, Ohio. On his journey he was robbed of all his property and came to the Ohio city destitute. For a time he alternated between a state of shame coupled with a determination to reform on the one hand and intemperance and dissipation on the other. When sober he was a dyer by trade. The death of a friend shocked him into a new determination to follow the guidance of his prayers and his reading.[25]

---

* There are several ways of spelling the name of the Indian tribe —Wyandot, Wyandott and Wyandotte. Wyandotte is the official spelling of Wyandotte County. Wyandot seems the oldest and most acceptable spelling for the tribe and is the one used throughout except for the County.

Passing along the street in Marietta, he heard the sound of voices, in song and prayer. It was a Methodist prayer meeting. After some struggle of soul he entered. In spite of his prejudice against the Methodists, probably gained from his Baptist parents and his brother who was a Baptist minister, he agreed to attend a camp meeting. In September of 1814, Marcus Lindsey had been appointed to "Marietta Circuit." That fall, or a year or more later, he held a camp meeting near Marietta and it was to this gathering that John Stewart was induced to come. In response to the preaching and the call of Reverend Lindsey and after an all-night struggle he was converted and set upon his feet.

Renting a house, he resumed his trade. Soon he felt a call to preach but he resisted it. In the midst of a serious illness he promised to obey that call. Later in the fields while praying,

It seemed to me . . . that I heard a voice . . . praising God; and then another . . . saying to me, "you must declare my counsel faithfully." These voices ran through me powerfully. They seemed to come from a north-west direction.

Soon he set off for the northwest with an exhorter's license from the Marietta Church.[26]

First he visited a remnant of the Delawares at Goshen and stayed a few days. One evening after the Indians had danced vigorously and were quiet he took out his hymn book and began to sing. They were charmed by the melody and the spirit of the man. When he ceased, Johnny-Cake said in broken English, "Sing more." He sang more and exhorted them through an interpreter. All through his later ministry he mixed songs, prayers and exhortations. But this was not the ultimate place where he "must declare my counsel faithfully." On he went to the reservation of the Wyandots, and the home of the Indian sub-agent and interpreter, William Walker, Sr. At first Walker thought Stewart was a runaway slave, but he allowed him to tell his story. Walker's wife was,

a most amiable woman of good education, and half Wyandott. She possessed great influence in the nation; and this family became his hospitable friends, and the untiring friends of the mission . . . and all (wife and sons) became members of the church.[27]

One of the Huron tribes, earlier in Canada, the Wyandots had settled in Ohio sometime after 1650. The new American government placed them on a reservation, 19 miles by 12 miles. Religiously, they had been served earlier by Roman Catholic priests and before the War of 1812 by the Presbyterians.[28] Neither effort survived. The prospect was not too promising when the self-appointed missionary arrived at the Walker home. The year was 1816.

With the help of Jonathan Pointer, a Negro, as an interpreter, Stewart aroused a good deal of religious interest and even several chiefs were converted. Even his interpreter, Pointer, was converted in spite of his early opposition because he preferred a "religion that did not fit so close, but give him leave to indulge in sin." In the spring of 1818 some objections arose because Stewart with only an exhorter's license had solemnized matrimony and baptized several persons. Consequently, when he learned of a quarterly meeting of the Methodists at Urbana in March, 1819, he determined to attach himself officially to the Methodist Episcopal Church. Several of his red brethren accompanied him to the meeting presided over by Bishop Enoch George. Wisely, the ministerial brethren voted unanimously to license him after hearing the Wyandot converts "who gave a good account of his life and labors in the conversion of many of their nation." Several of the Local Preachers present offered to go to assist him.[29]

On August 7 of the same year, at the session of the Ohio Annual Conference at Cincinnati, a mission to the Wyandots was approved. This was the first official Methodist missionary to the Indians, but actually it was accepting responsibility for work already begun. As indicated in the Episcopal Address to the General Conference of 1820, by Bishop McKendree, one of the reasons for the organization of an official missionary society by the Methodist Episcopal Church was the need of the Wyandots. These Indians had sent an address to the General Conference requesting that missionaries be sent to them. Now in 1820 there was established an organization that was to have an important part in the years to come in the spread of the Gospel throughout the earth.[30]

For an additional four and one half years Stewart worked with the Wyandots along with the appointed missionaries, until his death of consumption on December 17, 1823. Needing a home when he was married in 1820, he was aided by Bishop McKendree who collected $100. With this money a 60 acre tract was purchased and a log cabin built. It was here that he was buried. Before the Wyandots moved to Kansas, however, they "gathered his bones and buried them on the south side of the Wyandotte Mission Church." The tombstone of this missionary is now a part of one of Methodism's national shrines. A part of the inscription on the stone is "Earth For Christ."

A succession of devoted missionaries from the Ohio Conference served the Wyandots from 1819 until 1843 when they left for the west. Charles Elliott, later an editor of the *Advocate,* was appointed in 1819 and reduced their language to writing. Much we know of these red men comes from James B. Finley, the Presiding Elder and Missionary from 1820 to 1828, and author of *Life Among The Indians*. In the four years just before their emigration, the missionary was James Wheeler. Fortunately he was able to accompany them to Kansas.

Not to be forgotten were laymen, whites and Indians. The eminent Henry Clay, after attending the Methodist General Conference in Baltimore in 1824, where he heard the Wyandot Chief Manoncue, pronounced him the greatest orator in the United States. Chief Between-the-Logs, Chief Scuteash and Squire Grey Eyes were early converts and remained faithful. The tribe was governed by a council consisting of a chief and six councilmen. At the time of the move west their chief was Francis A. Hicks. In the total membership of the tribe were many white men and women. Some authorities have estimated that when the Wyandots arrived in their new home the tribe was at least three-fourths white. This conjecture may be high, but through the generations these Indians had welcomed whites, French and English, many by adoption through capture or marriage. Among other emigrant Indians, especially the Shawnees, white leadership was evident and heartily accepted by the red men.[31]

As related in an earlier chapter, all Indian nations were pressured into leaving their lands east of the Mississippi. As land-hungry white pioneers moved west the demand for the Indian lands became more insistent as the years went by. The Wyandots held out longer than others but finally in 1843 they too were on their way. It was a sad farewell the last Sunday in their Church. James Wheeler preached again the funeral sermon for John Stewart, using Stewart's old interpreter, Jonathan Pointer. Squire Grey Eyes told of his conversion and then expressed the feeling of many when he said:

Farewell! thou temple of our God in which we have often worshipped. Farewell! thou graveyard where we leave the remains of our departed friends. Farewell! ye roads and paths where we and those we are leaving have often walked together.[32]

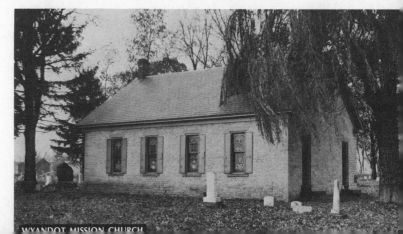

WYANDOT MISSION CHURCH

After some exploitation on the way, travelling by land to Cincinnati and then by boat to the mouth of the Kaw, they arrived. The journey took about three weeks in July, 1843. Of the total 700 emigrants about 200 were members of the Methodist Episcopal Church, including nine class leaders, three local preachers and several exhorters. Earlier in 1839, a delegation had gone to select a site for settlement. On arrival this site was adjudged unsatisfactory. Through the kindness of the Delawares and with the money from the federal government they purchased a new area of 39 sections or 24,960 acres from their close friends and neighbors of the old days in Ohio for $46,080. For improvements on their lands in Ohio, they were reimbursed by the government to the extent of $120,000.[33]

Another sad period was immediately ahead of them. Within the first three months while they were constructing new shelters in which to live, 60 of their number died. Nevertheless, their faith held. Regular religious services were held on the journey and during the days before a church was available. Late in January, 1844, Squire Grey Eyes challenged his fellow Methodists to join him in providing a "house for his soul." As a result, before most had their own homes constructed, they built, before the end of April, a good hewed-log house about 30 feet by 40 feet. During the next few months a school house and a parsonage were also constructed.[34]

The year 1844 opened a period of controversy in the total Methodist Episcopal Church and reverberations of this divisiveness were felt among all the missions to the Indians. The General Conference of 1844 had placed all mission work along the western border in a newly created Indian Mission Conference. In October of the same year, the new Conference held its first session near Tahlequah with Bishop Morris presiding. With impending division in the air, the members of the conference voted to adhere to the South, if division came. When the Plan of Separation went into effect in 1845, all missions in Kansas came under the control of the new Methodist Episcopal Church, South.[35] Thereby, in 1850 the missions in Kansas came under the control of the St. Louis Conference of the Southern Church. Meanwhile, the Missouri Conference of the Northern Church came into existence in 1848, and the Northern Church forced her way into the field again. Consequently, work in Kansas was included in the Platte Mission District from 1848 until 1853; the Kansas and Nebraska District was established in 1854, the North Kansas Mission District in 1855.[36] The Kansas-Nebraska Conference was authorized in 1856, and organized that fall. The Southern Church also went through similar moves: 1854—organization of the Kansas Mission Conference with two districts; the first session was held in 1856; it met annually until 1861, and then conference relations were abandoned until 1866.

The changes in control particularly affected the Wyandots. Their early missionary was a free-born mulatto, John Stewart of the Ohio Conference; their helper was Northern; their present missionary, James Wheeler was a free-state man; and many of the Indians felt strongly about slavery. Suddenly, they were under the control of the Southern Church. The situation held steady under the successor of Wheeler, Reverend E. T. Peery, but not after he left in 1848.

For the next eight years there was trouble. The Northern Church returned to the field and made claims. The Southern Church maintained that their action was in accord with the Plan of Separation, but the Northern Church had abrogated the Plan in 1848. In the same year the records of the Church were stolen. Also, at the end of the year Reverend James Gurley, of abolitionist tendencies, was sent to preach to the Wyandots by the Ohio Conference. Soon he was expelled by the Indian sub-agent. To this action the Bishops of the Northern Church objected strongly to the government at Washington and the agent was removed and the Northern Church recognized as an equal of other Christian groups. There was a division in the local church and both branches maintained services in separate buildings. Finally, both churches were burned to the ground in April, 1857.[37]

In 1855 the Wyandot nation made a treaty with the federal government and took their land in severalty and became individual citizens. Later, in 1867, some who did not take up their land in this way were provided for in a tract of land in the Indian country.[38]

The Northern branch of the Wyandot Church became Washington Avenue Methodist Church, now Trinity United Methodist Church of Kansas City, Kansas, and the Southern branch became the basis for the present Seventh Street United Methodist Church of the same city.

CONCLUSION

This chapter would not be complete without an additional word about a few key personalities and a reminder of the immense problems that were inherent in the total situation.

For some men missionary work was only a training period for later leadership. Mission work only claimed

NATHAN SCARRITT

Nathan Scarritt for three years, as head of the classical department or Western Academy of the Shawnee Station. He stayed in the vicinity of Kansas City, however, went into business and also served the Church. It was his family, or the Chick family, who gave the land for the school named for him, "The Scarritt Bible and Training School for Missionaries," now Scarritt College in Nashville, Tennessee. It began its work in Kansas City and remained in that city until 1924 when it was moved to Tennessee.

Few figures are more controversial and illustrate the confusion of loyalties more than John M. Chivington. This native of Ohio, born in 1821, was one of the five sons of Isaac Chivington. The father was one of those who fought with General William Henry Harrison against Chief Tecumseh at the Battle of Tippecanoe on November 6, 1811. Like his father and brothers, John

was a huge man, six feet four and one-half inches tall and weighed 260 pounds. Entering the Methodist ministry when about 20 years of age, he preached in Ohio, in Illinois, on to the Missouri Conference about 1845, and then as a missionary to the Wyandot Indians in 1853. Here as pastor of the Wyandotte City Church he worked with Indians and whites.[39]

The Masonic Lodge was one of his enthusiastic concerns throughout his adult life. Indeed, few men have done more pioneer work than he did for masonry. In Kansas he organized the first Masonic Lodge and was the first Master of the Lodge, No. 2, A.F. and A.M., Kansas City, Kansas. Later in Nebraska, in 1857, he helped organize the Masonic Lodge and even later, in 1861, he assisted in forming the Masonic Grand Lodge of Colorado and became the first Grand Master.

Due to a dramatic experience in Illinois, he became a life-long foe of slavery and a free-soiler, and was always militant about it. When serving in Platte County, Missouri, he was warned by a slave society not to preach in that county. As a response, he appeared in the pulpit, put two pistols beside his Bible, and announced, "By the grace of God and these two revolvers, I am going to preach here today!" He was not interrupted.

From Kansas he went on to Nebraska in 1856, be-

JOHN M. CHIVINGTON

came the Presiding Elder of the Omaha District of the Kansas-Nebraska Conference. To meet the rush of people to Colorado after the 1859 gold discovery, Bishop Baker, in 1860, appointed Chivington as Presiding Elder of the Rocky Mountain District of the Kansas-Nebraska Conference. When war came he went into the army and had a colorful career on the side of the Union.

Sad to relate, it is this same giant of a man who led the group of volunteers who perpetrated the awful Chivington massacre of over 450 Indians in November, 1864. The results of the investigation were not clear and Chivington was never court-martialed. He always stood by his action.[40]

43

Two men of greater stature were the Johnson brothers, Thomas and William, earliest Methodist missionaries to the Indians in Kansas. There is no information available concerning any previous training either brother may have had. Certainly, they were not school men but they were resourceful, faithful, ingenious, and endowed with a rare degree of managerial ability. They had had no technical training for their new responsibilities. William seems to have been a somewhat more scholarly turn of mind, for at the time of his death in 1842, it was said that he could preach fluently in at least ten different Indian languages and dialects. Thomas, had he been more politically inclined, might have become one of the outstanding political leaders of the State of Kansas. Before he died at the point of a gun in the hands of a ruffian, he had served as a member of territorial legislatures and was the administrator of the most successful educational and industrial institution in the territory, the Methodist Indian Manual-Labor School. It is a fact that he was a slaveholder and this was used against him with telling effect by the free-soilers from the north during the tumultuous times before the Civil War. As the chief Methodist figure in the territory and state for over 30 years, he cast the vote of the Methodist Church in favor of slavery, but as a determined opponent of secession he used his great influence in favor of the Union. When it became necessary for him to choose between the two branches of the Methodist Episcopal Church, he went with the South, reluctantly and with a divided mind. In spite of the fact that much evidence is lacking, it seems to be true that he was murdered on January 2, 1865, by border ruffians who resented his loyalty to the Union. Such were the tangled circumstances which characterized his last days and that of many others in this time of divided loyalties.

To the Johnson brothers and the many other effective missionaries who served in Kansas, a great debt is due. No more consecrated men ever labored under Methodist appointment than they. Their work was not lost. Many of the Wyandots, Shawnees and other Indians, served by other denominations, such as the Ottawas, took their share of land in severalty and became responsible citizens. The churches of the future were enriched by these missionary efforts although their subsequent fruitage is immeasurable.

As related in an earlier treatment, the 50 year period from about 1820 to 1870 was a time of change, uncertainty, movement and disillusionment for all Indians within the borders of the United States. The Plains Indian, roaming vast areas beyond the Mississippi, experienced an invasion of his hunting grounds. Not only was he forced to give up his land, but there was also the demand that he change his whole way of life. Of course, he was given money, educational opportunities and the offer of practical assistance through government farmers and blacksmiths. Along with these noble efforts came the white exploiter with his liquor and other means of extracting the annual money payments from the government. Needless to repeat, the plains red men did not respond in the way expected by the white man. He did not send his children to school and did not settle down to an agricultural life. He refused white civilization. Eventually many, in their frustration and final efforts to strike back, went on the warpath and were responsible for vicious, indefensible actions. This called forth the reprisal actions by the federal government to bring peace.

The picture from the standpoint of the emigrant Indians from the region east of the Mississippi is altogether different. Many were already far advanced in their ways. For many of them the actions of the whites were even more unjust and therefore more disillusioning. To them the forced movement brought removal from the lands of their forefathers and the journey west was actually "a trail of tears." Not all of the migrant tribes that came to Kansas took advantage of the "civilizing" efforts of the federal government—schools, agricultural help—but many did. The children in the missionary schools were sent by such interested Indian parents.

That the failure of the total relationship of whites with the red men is to be placed at the door of the white man is not fair or accurate. As indicated earlier, many Indians were lazy and irresponsible. Changes in ways of living are part of life, especially in a dynamic, new nation surging across a continent. New patterns of living were forced on all. Nevertheless, the treatment of the Indians is a sad page in the history of a great nation. Only the devoted, sacrificial efforts of a few men of God, some government agents and other laymen who felt called to serve, helps to remove some of the stain of guilt.

INHERITANCE

The inheritance of Kansas Methodism coming from the rise and development of the early Methodist Movement cannot be overlooked. Likewise the Methodist involvement in the impending slavery crisis which broke into open conflict as the state of Kansas was born must be traced in order to understand the bitterness of the early years in this new territory and state.

METHODIST ORGANIZATION AND "WAY"

Methodism in America is about 200 years old. By the time it arrived in Kansas Territory with work among the white settlers, its genius for meeting the needs of the frontier in a successful way was already proven on the earlier frontiers. Therefore, early Kansas Methodism was the beneficiary of methods out of the experience of other pioneers over a period of three-fourths of a century.

From the arrival of John Wesley's first appointed missionaries, the phenomenal growth of the followers of Wesley in America was a part of a surging expansion of a new nation. The sense of destiny that possessed the people of the new land was matched by a comparable belief on the part of Methodists in their

God-given mission: "To reform the nation, more particularly the Church; to spread scriptural holiness over the land." This wording of the purpose had come from Wesley. In the first Discipline—"Form of Discipline for the Ministers, Preachers, and other Members of the Methodist Episcopal Church in America"—it was restated in the Fourth Question: "What may we reasonably believe to be God's design in raising up the Preachers called Methodists?" The answer was: "To reform the continent, and to spread scriptural holiness over these lands." [1] A vast domain demanded no small response! Brave words from a mere handful of preachers!

Who could have imagined at the end of the Revolution, or in 1790, that the little nation of about four million people in an area of 800,000 square miles, would in the course of the next 160 to 170 years, expand to a land of nearly 180 million people scattered over a domain of over 3 1/2 million square miles. Only the growth of Methodism matched this dramatic march.

When John Wesley appointed George Shadford, the sixth missionary, to go to America, he wrote to him at the end of March, 1773, in part:

. . . I let you loose, George, on the great continent of America. Publish your message in the open face of the sun, and do all the good you can. . . . [2]

That these early missionaries and others "published" effectively is easily demonstrated. In 1776 there were only 4,921 members and 24 preachers; at the time of the Christmas Conference, 1784, the number of preachers had grown to 83 and the membership was 14,988. 89% were south of the Mason-Dixon Line. [3] In the first eight years of the life of the Methodist Episcopal Church the total membership grew to 65,980 served by 266 preachers. [4] At the time of the tragic division of the Church, in 1844, there were nearly 4,000 itinerant preachers ministering to over one million members. [5] When Kansas became a state, in 1861, the northern branch alone had expanded to a membership of nearly one million.

How can we account for this spread? The first thought would be Methodism's organization, and certainly it played no small role. In the beginning and until 1792 there was only one conference but it functioned in sections. Finally there were 17 of these sections which complicated the passage of conference action. In 1792, when the first General Conference met, the office of Presiding Elder was legalized although it had been used before. Four years later there were six annual conferences: Eastern (New England), Philadelphia, Baltimore, Virginia, South Carolina and Western. The latter conference included everything west of the Alleghenies until 1812, when the Western Conference was divided and was succeeded by the Ohio and the Tennessee Conferences. By 1840 there were 15 conferences west of the Alleghenies. Before 1812 every minister had a right to go to General Conefrence as a delegate but at that time by action of the General Conference of 1808 the controlling body of the Church became a delegated body—one delegate for every five ministers.[6]

Of more importance in the expansion of the new movement were the sacrificial efforts of the preachers including the bishops. Surely these ministers were not motivated by any monetary rewards for in the beginning, as established by the General Conference, they were allowed a pittance which amounted to $64 and travelling expenses per year but they seldom received the full allowed amount. Increases did not come rapidly: $80 in 1800, but a like amount was allowed for each of the few wives and small allowances for their children; in 1816 the salary was placed at $100; it was set at $200 in 1836, and in 1848 differences in salaries appear by authorized allowances for "table expenses" to be determined by the Quarterly meeting.[7] Of interest is the fact that in the early days bishops, even Francis Asbury, received the same salary as the preachers. Indeed, it was a brotherhood of poverty.[8] Asbury declared, "We must suffer with, if we labor for, the poor." [9] As indicated before, few of the Methodist ministers were married. If they did marry it often seemed necessary for them to locate because they could not have an established home and carry on the vigorous, wide-ranging, itinerate ministry. For example, in 1809, out of 84 preachers in the Virginia Conference, only three had wives. Likewise, the first four bishops were single.[10]

Not to be forgotten in the appeal of the Methodists to the frontier people of the new nation, was the "Methodist Way." Certain elements were a part of this vital religious movement, according to the late Dr. Wade Crawford Barclay.[11] With boldness the untrained preachers emphasized to the masses that religion was "a conscious, dynamic, verifiable experience," as Wesley taught. First, a sense of sin and a desire for deliverance was the way for anyone to begin. The Holy Spirit operated to convert the sinner and bring him into direct contact with God. Thereby, through Christ, his sins were forgiven and he became assured of his salvation.

The second is the experience of wholeness, or as Wesley phrased it, the experience of becoming not "almost Christians" but "altogether Christians." This the early Methodists insisted: That the experience of perfect love, equally with the experience of conversion, is a basic and central requirement of Christianity as an ethic of life.[12]

Other elements were fellowship and discipline. Every Methodist Society by its earliest definition was a "company of men having the form and seeking the power of godliness." The members of the Society were united to "help each other to work out their salvation."[13] Precisely and definitely stated this was the aim and purpose of organization. All in all, it was a people's movement, open to all—rich or poor, high or low— for the grace of God was available to all.

"The external husk of any religious movement," writes Rufus M. Jones, "is obvious and describable, the inner core is indescribable, and is missed by all except those who are initiated." The external peculiarities of the early Methodists—their methodical ways, their extemporaneous preaching, the emotional features of many of their meetings, their plainness of dress—in other words, "the external husk" of the movement, have impressed most secular writers. The distinctive experience, the immediate sense of God, the inspiration and strength which were the fruit of Christian fellowship, the new dynamic for living—these constituted the "inner core" of the Methodist movement. This inner core for a large proportion of the members was found in the meetings for which lay men and women were responsible—above all in the Class Meeting. In this fact again, is found evidence that Methodism was in reality a True People's Movement.[14]

Peter Cartwright, the famous Illinois frontier Methodist preacher and long-time Presiding Elder, described the early Methodists as follows:

The Methodists in that early day dressed plain; attended their meetings, faithfully, especially preaching, prayer and class meetings; they wore no jewelry, no ruffles, they would frequently walk three or four miles to class meetings, and home again, on Sundays; they would go thirty or forty miles to their quarterly meetings, and think it a glorious privilege to meet their presiding elder, and the rest of the preachers. They could, nearly every soul of them, sing our hymns and spiritual songs. They religiously kept the Sabbath day; many of them abstained from dram-drinking, not because the temperance reformation was ever heard of in that day, but because it was interdicted in the General Rules of our Discipline. Methodists of that day stood up and faced their preacher when they sung; they kneeled down in the public congregation as well as elsewhere, when the preacher said, "let us pray" . . . Parents did not allow their children to go to balls or plays; they did not send them to dancing schools; they generally fasted once a week, and almost universally on the Friday before each quarterly meeting.[15]

When we think of the frontier, our minds immediately turn to the camp meetings. Indeed, these were the most dramatic and spectacular of the evangelistic efforts. Although the camp meeting was never recog-

CAMP MEETING ADVERTISEMENT

nized as an official Methodist institution, in the Discipline or by any General Conference action, it was widely used. Throughout Methodism many became well-organized institutions. In 1811 Asbury estimated that between 400 and 500 camp meetings were held and the number had increased to 600 by his death in 1816.[16] Often they were characterized by emotional disturbances, as will be pointed out later in descriptions of those held in Kansas. This was true in some meetings held by Wesley and Whitefield in England and the English rejected them in the 19th century. Like Wesley, Asbury did not encourage abnormal emotional expressions, as indicated by his statement:

I feel life among these people—preaching and praying is not labour here; their noise I heed not; I can bear it well when I know that God and Christ dwells in the hearts of the people.[17]

More important than all else, as a human means or agency of evangelism, was the untiring, day-by-day, fruitful preaching and service of the Circuit Riders—in cabins, barns, rude chapels, by the grave-side or wherever a group, large or small, was gathered.

INVOLVEMENT IN THE SLAVERY CRISIS

Methodism in Kansas began in the midst of a national crisis. Indeed, the very creation of Kansas, in the Kansas-Nebraska Act of 1854, was one of the causes of America's own bloody war of 1861-65. The slavery controversy was bitterly raging when white settlers first came to Kansas.

The prelude to crucial events in the life of America, even today, may be traced back more than 350 years to a short span of a few days in 1619. It was July 30, 1619, in the choir of the church at Jamestown, in the new colony of Virginia, the first permanent English settlement in our nation. The 22 chosen representatives of eleven hamlets and plantations, elected by the vote of all men aged 17 and upward, met in the first legislative assembly in the New World,

To make, ordain, and establish all manner of orders, laws, directives, instructions, forms and ceremonies of government and magistracy fit and necessary for, and concerning the government, of this colony.

From that time forth, government of the people, however limited or thwarted, has been a fundamental principle of the English colonies and the United States.[18]

It was only a few days after this meeting that another event took place, also at Jamestown, that would be of similar significance to the future of our country. A Dutch ship brought 20 "Negars" who were sold to the planters to work in the tobacco fields.[19] Thus, almost together came the birth of democratic government and freedom and its very antithesis or enemy, human slavery. One can add interest, if not authority, to the significance of this early prelude, if note is taken of the Indian massacre of 347 whites less than three years later in the same colony.[20] The lengthened shadow of these three events hovered over Kansas, especially during its early days.

Slavery related to conquest is of ancient origin but slavery related to color of skin, as we know it in our history, was not very old in 1619. During the latter part of the fifteenth century the Portuguese, the competitors with Spain in the opening of the world to European knowledge and relationships, introduced slavery in a new form to Europe and the New World—Negro slaves from Africa. Quickly other countries of Europe—Holland, Spain, France, England—joined in the nefarious but profitable trade in human beings.

For almost a century slavery was unimportant in the colonies. Although New England ship owners were slave carriers and owed much of their wealth to trade in slaves, the slave was least profitable as a laborer in that area. Due to climate and soil the middle colonies were likewise not suited to plantation life. Slavery became the acceptable pattern in the South. The number

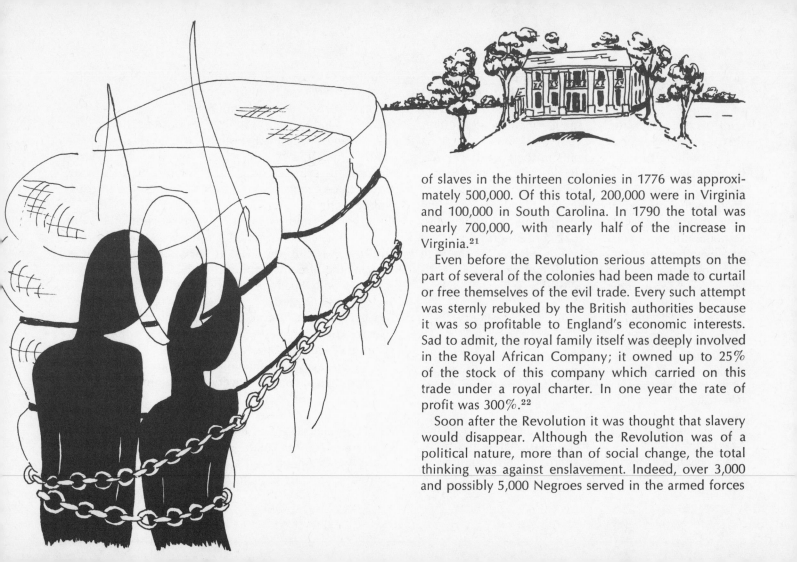

of slaves in the thirteen colonies in 1776 was approximately 500,000. Of this total, 200,000 were in Virginia and 100,000 in South Carolina. In 1790 the total was nearly 700,000, with nearly half of the increase in Virginia.[21]

Even before the Revolution serious attempts on the part of several of the colonies had been made to curtail or free themselves of the evil trade. Every such attempt was sternly rebuked by the British authorities because it was so profitable to England's economic interests. Sad to admit, the royal family itself was deeply involved in the Royal African Company; it owned up to 25% of the stock of this company which carried on this trade under a royal charter. In one year the rate of profit was 300%.[22]

Soon after the Revolution it was thought that slavery would disappear. Although the Revolution was of a political nature, more than of social change, the total thinking was against enslavement. Indeed, over 3,000 and possibly 5,000 Negroes served in the armed forces to win the freedom of the colonies from the mother country.[23] The outstanding leaders, including Washington, Jefferson, and Madison were on record against slavery.

However, a direct arraignment of the English king for forcing traffic in human beings on the colonies, in the first draft of the Declaration of Independence by Thomas Jefferson, was later eliminated.[24] Nevertheless, there was strong anti-slavery sentiment in most of the colonies and it was growing, especially in the North. In the Northwest Ordinance of 1787 the Congress prohibited slavery in the total area out of which the states of Ohio, Indiana, Michigan, Illinois and Wisconsin were later created.

What changed the situation? To no one event can we point but there was one invention that climaxed a series of other inventions—machine spinning and weaving in factories, for example. When Eli Whitney invented the cotton gin in 1793 he made it possible for one man to seed more cotton in a day than 50 workers had been able to do before. This also made short staple cotton economically valuable. All of this brought about an agricultural revolution in the South as the United States became the chief source of raw cotton in the world. In two years cotton exports increased six times. In 1832 the United States exported over three hundred million pounds of cotton, as compared with less than one-half million before the days of the cotton gin. The slave population of the cotton states increased from less than 150,000 in 1820 to more than 1½ million at the opening of the Civil War. Cotton was king! In the minds of many southern leaders the country could not get along without the export of cotton for this represented over half of our exports. To raise cotton, slaves were considered necessary.[25]

Economic determinism is not the whole explanation of the amazing change in the attitudes of the people, north and south, from 1787 to 1861. Concerned people gave serious thought to the fate of the Negro. The anti-slavery movement began about 1760 and Benjamin Franklin headed the first Anti-Slavery Society, organized in 1774. All the northern states provided for some constitutional or legal way of doing away with slavery. The American Colonization Society, established in 1817, had wide support in the South as well as the North.[26] Keep in mind, however, that these were not abolition societies—far from it! Other factors—industry, business interests—helped to sectionalize the North, while the agricultural change unified the South under the leadership of the cotton states. With the risk of oversimplification, the following chart may be helpful in clarifying the changes in the thinking of the people.

CHANGES IN ATTITUDES TOWARD SLAVERY

	Extreme Northern Radicals	North & South Moderates	Extreme Southern Pro-slavery
After Revolution	Evil To be eliminated	Evil	Evil No solution
1800-1830	Unmitigated evil	Necessary evil Support of possible solutions	Some good
1830-	Morally evil	Silence	Morally good
1845	Unchristian Abolition	Silence Uncertainty	Of Divine Origin Christian
1845-	Extreme abolition	Division	Thoroughly Christian
1861	No compromise	Separation of Methodist and Baptist Churches	No compromise
War	Religious and Righteous Cause—To eliminate		Religious and Righteous Cause—To retain

The attitude of Methodists toward the slave trade and slavery was very definite in the beginning. Later it was divided in accord with the above chart. Finally, the church was divided and the opinions, now diverse, were definite.

Among the first in England to denounce the slave trade was John Wesley. As early as 1774 he published "Thoughts On Slavery," in advance of the efforts of William Wilberforce.[27] Censure and ridicule were heaped on him in England but the pamphlet was republished in Philadelphia by Mr. Benezet. Soon after Mr. Wilberforce introduced the subject in the British Parliament and only six days before Mr. Wesley's death, Methodism's founder penned a letter to the leader of the anti-slavery forces. In the last letter of his life written on February 21, 1791, Mr. Wesley cheered the efforts of Wilberforce. He said in part:

Oh, be not weary in well-doing! Go on in the name of God, and in the power of his might, till even American slavery, the vilest form that ever saw the sun, shall vanish away before it.[28]

In the early conferences of preachers in America a forthright stand against slavery was taken. When the Methodist Episcopal Church was organized in 1784, the General Rules, prepared by Mr. Wesley for the English Societies in 1739, were adopted. Among these rules was one forbidding "the buying or selling the bodies and souls of men, women or children, with an intention to enslave them." This same conference also approved in the answer to Question Forty-two, a sweeping indictment against the whole system which is followed by six special rules designed to destroy slavery in the new church.[29]

In general the members complied with these rules, but there was immediate opposition in the South and the action was suspended. Now began the wavering from the first strong forthright position. In 1792 only the restriction in the General Rules was retained; four years later the opposition to slavery was strengthened. In 1800 two rules were added but only church officials were required to emancipate their slaves while preachers who became slave-holders must withdraw from the ministry or emancipate their slaves. Another change in 1804 exempted all members in North Carolina, South Carolina, Georgia and Tennessee from all such rules and slave-selling for all others is allowed with restrictions. As a result of the next General Conference action, each Annual Conference was authorized to form its own regulations but this was rescinded in 1820. In 1824 the section on slavery was amended for the last time until 1860 with three new paragraphs.[30]

Surprising from our perspective, the question of slavery was not brought before the Conference of 1832. The General Conference session of 1836 in Cincinnati was the most heated of any up to that time. Partly in response to appeals by fraternal delegates from Britain and Canada, a committee of three was appointed to frame a reply to the British and Canadian Fraternal Addresses and to draft the Pastoral Address to the Church. This latter document, signed by all the Bishops as well as the Committee and almost unanimously approved by the Conference, called attention to all the legal barriers against anti-slavery action and the dangers of agitation and then stated in part:

> These facts . . . constrain us as your pastors . . . to exhort you to abstain from all abolition movements and associations, and to refrain from patronizing any of their publications; . . .
> . . . we have come to the solemn conviction, that the only safe, Scriptural, and prudent way for us, both as ministers and people, . . . is wholly to refrain from this agitating subject, which is now convulsing the country, and consequently the Church, from end to end. . . .[31]

The Conference also voted disapproval of the actions of two New Hampshire delegates in addressing a local meeting of the Anti-Slavery Society.

Slavery was in the forefront in the quadrennial session of 1840. More than 10,000 members and at least 500 ministers had signed memorials. Only the New England delegates under the leadership of Rev. Orange Scott, however, were solidly abolitionist and in a definite minority. The brief and indefinite report from the Committee on Slavery advised the Annual Conferences to "adhere to the language of the Discipline" in their future action. No minority report was permitted. The Pastoral Address was mild and conciliatory.[32]

Before the 1844 General Conference assembled, threats of actions against free Negroes in Maryland in 1841-42 had stirred the church because many of those freed men were Methodists. In addition, the withdrawal of ministers and congregations from "a slave-holding" and "a slavery defending Church" made action necessary. Consequently, at the formation of the Wesleyan Methodist Connection of America opening on May 31, 1843, at Utica, New York, there were delegates representing some 6,000 members who had withdrawn from the Methodist Episcopal Church because of slavery.[33] The issue was drawn. The moderates must go with the abolitionists of the North or with the pro-slavery group in the South.

Imagine the tense concern a year later as the 180 delegates from 33 Annual Conferences gathered in New York on May 1, 1844. The delegates were overwhelmed by the large number of memorials and resolutions, both pro and con. Amazingly, the Episcopal Address did not even mention slavery.

As a result of the presentation of the case of Bishop James O. Andrew by the Committee on Episcopacy, a ten-day debate ensued. Bishop Andrew, six years earlier, had involuntarily become a slave-holder. There seemed no escape for either those of the North or of the South. Finally, the all-important resolution of decision was voted June 1, 1844, 111 for to 69 against:

Whereas the Discipline of our Church forbids the doing of anything calculated to destroy our itinerant general superintendency; and whereas, Bishop Andrew has become connected with slavery by marriage and otherwise, and this act having drawn after it circumstances which, in the estimation of the General Conference, will greatly embarrass the exercise of his office as an itinerant general Superintendent, if not in some places entirely prevent it; therefore,

Resolved, That it is the sense of this General Conference that he desist from the exercise of his office so long as this impediment remains.[34]

The great debate had been on a high level and there was real sorrow because no alternative to separation was apparent. A committee of nine was appointed on

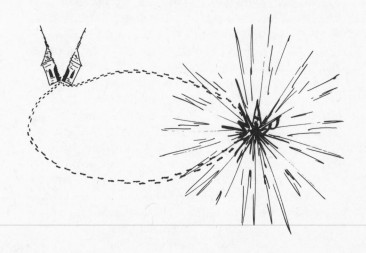

June 5, to draw up a Plan of Separation. It reported this plan on June 8, and it was adopted by the conference by a large majority. Thus, a separate church was authorized. The conference adjourned two days later. The southern delegates met the next morning and agreed to call a convention of the Southern Churches to meet at Louisville, Kentucky, on May 1, 1845.[35]

The division was a tragedy in itself. That it foreshadowed a greater separation to come between the States makes it even more stark from our vantage point.

BLEEDING KANSAS

"AD ASTRA PER ASPERA"—"To the stars through difficulties." This motto on the official seal of the State of Kansas was not chosen without due consideration of the beginnings of Kansas. Indeed, these words are freighted with meaning and catch up something of the lofty idealism which motivated many of the early settlers. Actually, the attention of the entire country, north and south, turned toward Kansas during the years following 1854. Without question, one of the major steps leading up to the Civil War was the struggle over Kansas—would it be free or slave? In this pre-war conflict the issue of slavery and its extension became clearly a moral, religious, and political problem with little ground for eventual compromise.

The moderates in regard to slavery and its extension, who comprised the majority of the country, were greatly relieved first in 1820, and again in 1850, when compromises were worked out between the two opposing groups holding extreme points of view. Pioneers continued to move west, however, and as a result new territories opened up. Therefore, the question of the extension of slave or free territory was still before the country.

When California was settled and came to the attention of the rest of the country the need for a rail connection was obvious. Which of three routes would it take? Should it go from Chicago, a middle way, or through the South? All of this had a relation to the future of Kansas. The squatter sovereignty doctrine proposed by the astute Senator Stephan A. Douglas of Illinois, in the Kansas-Nebraska Bill of 1854, appeased southern representatives and gained the support of Missouri Democrats for his northern route. The Kansas-Nebraska Act repealed the Missouri Compromise (this had provided that, except in Missouri, slavery was prohibited north of 36° 30'), and substituted "popular sovereignty." According to this new principle, the residents of each of the two territories were allowed to decide whether their state should be free or slave.

Even while it was before Congress, the reaction of many in the north was extreme. Numerous petitions from various groups of ministers and churches all over the north came to Congress opposing the bill. That of 3,050 New England ministers attracted the most attention.[1] Immediately militant plans were made to save Kansas, especially in New England. In response, many in the south and especially in western Missouri were frightened. Both extremes girded for action. The next five years were ones of turmoil, massacres, fighting and bitterness in eastern Kansas and western Missouri. This

59

affected not only that area but helped to bring the already existing sectionalism to a head. The widespread publicity given to Kansas by the press in the north and south was amazing. Emotions ran high. Indeed, to many the struggle which finally began in 1861 had seemed to be an "irrepressible conflict" several years before.

As soon as it became legal to do so, a swarm of land-hungry settlers hurried into the newly opened territory. Months before the final passage of the bill, hundreds of settlers collected along the border to wait until settlement was legalized. This number grew until it reached more than 20,000.[2] Although far greater, this waiting throng did not attract the attention of the country as much as those settlers sent out by the New England Emigrant Aid Company. Preceding this organization was that of the Massachusetts Emigrant Aid Association organized by Eli Thayer with a proposed capital of five million dollars. This plan was too pretentious and a revision was necessary. As a result, the New England Emigrant Aid Company was organized. The purpose of this organization was to aid the settlers on their way to Kansas, advise them as to eligible sites for settlement and to assist them after their settlement.

Clergymen were quite prominent in the early work of the company. A book called *Kansas and Nebraska: An Account of the Emigrant Aid Company*, was written by a young clergyman, Edward Everett Hale. In July, 1855, a "Circular of the Committee of Clergymen," written by 18 New England clergymen, was sent to all ministers in New England. In this circular the clergymen were urged to become life members of the New England Emigrant Aid Company and the work of the company for freedom, for religion, for education, and for temperance was stressed. Religious enthusiasm became a powerful motivating force in the raising of money for the enterprise. Dr. Henry Ward Beecher gave aid not only by speaking but also in helping to furnish the settlers with Sharpe's rifles; "Beecher's Bibles" became a synonym for these rifles and a "Beecher Rifle Club" was formed among the men of the New Haven Company. Horace Greeley, through the *New York Tribune*, became a propagandist for the enterprise. John Greenleaf Whittier's poem, "The Kansas Emigrants," added to the religious enthusiasm. The first and last stanzas of this poem are:

> We cross the prairie, as of old
>   The pilgrims crossed the sea,
> To make the West, as they the East,
>   The homestead of the free.
>
> We'll sweep the prairie, as of old
>   Our fathers swept the sea,

And make the West, as they the East,
The homestead of the free!

The companies of settlers sent out by the New England Emigrant Aid Company became the nucleus of the Free State Party with headquarters at Lawrence, Kansas.

BORDER CONFLICTS

In the well-known Kansas Conflict the Free State group was opposed by the so-called Border Ruffians of Missouri. All sorts of exaggerated stories were circulated in the north concerning the people of the Missouri border counties and their invasions into Kansas and no attempt was made to learn the truth of the situation. Nor was there any inclination to learn why the Missourians acted as they did. The people of the border counties in Missouri had heard of the five million dollar Massachusetts Emigrant Aid Association with its plan to colonize first Kansas and then Missouri and other states.[3] Heated editorials in western Missouri newspapers pointed out that this would mean the loss of slaves, Negro insurrections, and the final destruction of slavery in Missouri. To counteract the activities of the "abolition" societies of New England, secret societies were organized in Missouri. The pub-

licity given the Emigrant Aid Company from New England made it seem far greater than it was; nor did the Missourians realize that the great bulk of settlers who came were from states west of New England and New York. Exaggerations and false rumors were accepted as true by both north and south with very little question.

To understand fully the border difficulties it is necessary to keep in mind the already existing rivalry between the divided churches in Missouri. Ten years before the opening of Kansas and Nebraska for settlement both the Baptist and Methodist churches had divided over slavery. This had little effect on the Baptists inasmuch as they were all southerners or at least all connected themselves with the southern branch of the church.

This was not true of the Methodists. Although there were only a few of the members of the Missouri Conference that voted against joining with the Southern branch of the church, these men were able to maintain themselves until the re-organization of the Methodist Episcopal Church in Missouri in 1848. The great rivalry between the two Methodist churches begins with this date. Both branches claimed Missouri as a legitimate field. The larger Southern church looked on the Northern church as an intruder and treated it as such. When Northern Methodists moved into Missouri they

61

were advised to go into the Southern church for business and social reasons and were given to understand that they could have no status in the community if they belonged to the "abolition" church.[4] The members of the two churches differed in regard to political parties. Despite all such opposition, the Northern church was able to maintain itself, especially in the northern part of the State, and even enjoy a slow growth every year after its re-organization.[5]

The extent of the opposition to the Northern church is shown by the request of the people of Independence, Missouri, in 1855, that the Missouri Conference of the Methodist Episcopal Church be held elsewhere because of the excitement over slavery.[6] The appointed place of the conference was therefore changed from Independence to St. Louis. The feeling of the Missouri people against the Congregationalists was more intense than against the Methodists. Because of their abolitionist views the Congregational missionaries were not enthusiastically received by the people of Missouri.

It was this rivalry between the churches which had been going on in Missouri for several years before 1854 that was a part of the setting for the difficulties along the border when Kansas was opened for settlement. Coupled with this were the difficulties that had arisen over slavery in the Indian Mission work in Kansas. The Northern Methodists, Baptist and Friends felt that they had been discriminated against by a Democratic administration in the government treaties made with the Indians. The Northern Methodists also resented the action of the Southern church in regard to the Wyandot Indians. For the Missourian, on the other hand, the organization and work of the New Englanders in making Kansas a free state merely confirmed his opinion that certain churches were abolition organizations. The early success of the Methodist Episcopal and Congregational churches in Kansas must have made the situation even more intense. The two churches with the greatest abolitionary tinge and therefore the most disliked in the opening years of Kansas settlement were the leading churches.

The few years immediately preceding the Civil War were to see the establishment in Kansas territory of work by all the larger denominations. Many churches staged a race for Kansas. For some of these denominations it was their first attempt to do work of any kind in the region now called Kansas while for others it was a change in the type of work from Indian Missions to work among whites. Among the latter were the Northern Methodists, the Baptists, the Old School Presbyterians, the Friends, the Southern Methodists and Roman Catholics. Before attempting to trace the rise and development of some of the other denominations as well as the Methodists, it is necessary to know something of the conditions which existed at the time. Only in this way is it possible to understand the situation which the early religious leaders and churches had to meet.

POLITICAL AND SOCIAL CONDITIONS

Political activity in Kansas itself following the passage of the bill in 1854 until she was admitted as a State, January 29, 1861, was tortuous. Quickly two sides developed, each attempting to gain control. Territorial governors and legislatures came and went, several elections were held and constitutions were written and discarded. Finally, out of the Wyandotte convention of 1859 came the state constitution which was approved later that year. That constitution is still in use.

Out of the total population of 107,206, in 1860, there were 94,513 native-born Americans. Nineteen states furnished more than 500 each but the leading states from the standpoint of contributions to the population were Ohio with 11,617, Missouri with 11,356, Indiana with 9,945, Illinois with 9,367, Kentucky with 6,556, Pennsylvania with 6,463, New York with 6,331 and Iowa with 4,008.[7] From the six New England states came only 4,208. This is significant from a religious standpoint because it is natural to expect that the churches which were strong in those states which furnished the largest number of settlers would be the ones which would prosper in this new environment. That the larger number came from states bordering on the Ohio River shows the important part which river transportation played in the early settlement of Kansas.

For these Kansas settlers life was not as drab and uneventful as was usually the case on the early frontier. The first years were filled with excitement. The invasions of the Missourians were always in the thought of the settlers, especially those who were located near the Missouri border. The effect of such a life on church activities is shown by a letter from a missionary in Lawrence:

The whole time of my labor here has been filled with excitement & commotion of such character as to retard, if not entirely destroy, the influence of truth, but the past three months, more than any other time, seem worse than lost in a moral point of view. . . . It has seemed as though the sabbath was selected as the day for special excitements & not infrequently have the members of my congregation & even members of my church, left the morning service, to be called upon to go to the rescue of their brethren, attacked by the banditti who surround us. . . .[9]

63

Settlements such as Manhattan were not affected by the early border troubles because of their distance from Missouri, but the unsettled state of political affairs operated against the progress of religion. Even after warfare had died down there was still great excitement over elections:

> We have more caucusing, called conventions, and elections, than any other country in which I have ever lived. It would be a new thing under the sun, at least in Kansas, if we were to have a few months without a mass meeting, nominating convention, or some other call to collect the people together.[10]

During all this excitement over border warfare and elections it was necessary for the people to provide a place in which to live. Most of the settlers had spent all their money in removing to the new country and making some meagre improvements. They soon were to be faced with the necessity of paying for their land when it came into market. The description of a Kansas home, as given by Rev. S. Y. Lum, the first Congregational missionary in Lawrence, is typical:

> Perhaps you may feel an interest in knowing what sort of accommodations we enjoy here. My own house, which is said to be as comfortable as any, is entirely without a floor or wall; has nothing but bare "siding," and is so open, as to give us views of the country in almost every direction. . . . One small room has to serve us for bedroom, kitchen, sitting-room and study. . . .[11]

An early Methodist preacher, James S. Griffing, in writing to his fiancee, gives an added touch when he tells of hearing wolves around his cabin and of having nothing but a thin blanket for a door.[12]

One of the many things which made the erection of homes difficult was the lack of suitable excess timber. The available trees in Kansas bordered the Kaw River and the large streams and some of this was cottonwood which, as Horace Greeley said, "warps so when seasoned that it will draw the nails out of the side of a house." Some timber that could be used for boards was wonderful black walnut, but there was also some "small, short and gnarly oak." Although there was plenty of stone for building purposes, much of the lumber used for building had to be shipped in, sometimes coming from as far as New York. This absence of timber explains why mud was often used in the building of homes. For the building of churches it was also significant, since it meant that all churches cost more than the same buildings would have cost in a more wooded area. The lack of timber on the prairies west of the Mississippi made it necessary for the denominations later to organize societies to aid the churches. It was to meet this new need that the American Congregational Union, the Church Extension Committee, the Church Edifice Fund, and the Church Extension Society were later created. In this early day few of these organizations were in existence while others were not functioning as they did after the Civil War. Therefore, these early churches suffered from the lack of suitable places to worship. Log cabins without windows or floors, or sod houses or tents were often the only places for preaching.

The problem of feeding the large number of constantly arriving new settlers until they were able to produce some food by their own farming was tremend-

LAWRENCE
FIRST CONGREGATIONAL CHURCH

ous; and, as a result of the scarcity of all commodities, the cost of living in Kansas was higher than in the east.[13] Rents were, of course, higher in the river towns than any where else in the Territory and it was often difficult to obtain a house at any price.

MORAL PROBLEMS

All new enterprises seemed to invite speculation but land speculation was particularly prevalent in this newly opened region. Everyone was "buying up" land, corner lots, and interest in saw mills, or aiding in the building of a church to increase the value of property already held. This was a temptation for the early preacher who was having a difficult time in ekeing out a living. Richard Cordley, one of the early Congregational preachers, describes the situation in 1858 as follows:

I see too, it is very difficult for the ministry to keep their "hands off." Ministers, metamorphosed into keen speculators—are strewn all over the territory. I count 14 ex ministers of various denominations about Lawrence. Even some of those who are still in the service have "got one foot in"—and some are "almost all gone"— The transformation from a preacher to a speculator is gradual and unconscious. The preacher first seeks to get a *home of his own* which, of course, is proper. But he finds the word home in *Kansas* a very expansive term. It may mean a *log cabin* seven by nine— or a claim—a few town shares, a saw mill, etc. I am convinced that the efficiency of our ministerial force is reduced at least one half by this division of its energies.[14]

It was to prevent such a transformation that the American Home Missionary Society set down the iron-clad rule that its missionaries should not be engaged in any other activity than preaching the gospel. This weakness was prominent enough among some of the Methodist preachers to bring about the passage of the following resolution by the Kansas and Nebraska Annual Conference in 1860:

Resolved, That it is the sense of the members of this Conference, that they are decidedly and uncompromisingly opposed to any member of the Conference engaging in any secular pursuits which tends to injure the church, or his influence as a minister of the gospel; especially speculating in lands, or acting as land agents—running over the country hunting up corners, and vacant quarter sections of land, instead of preaching the gospel and being a man of one work. Carried by a vote of 39 ayes to 3 nays.[15]

The spirit of speculation also entered into the building of churches and the employment of ministers. The promoters of towns realized that the presence of churches and ministers would materially increase the value of the property. Lots were therefore generously supplied to any of the various denominations in order to have a church locate in the new town. It was always easier to get support for the first church building in any town. Consequently, there was a race between the various denominations to be the first to build a church.

Moral conditions on any frontier are never high and Kansas was no exception. Letters from the region are full of descriptions of the low moral condition in the towns. The missionary at Quindaro speaks of regular business being carried on on the Sabbath and says that "good morals are as little known among the boatmen as crystal drops in its turbid waters." He observes, however, that he is not sure that the people are any more wicked in Kansas but that "wickedness is less concealed everyone doing openly what he desires." [16]

In Wyandotte human life is held very cheap. . . . There have been several murders within a short time. . . . And worst of all none of these murders have been convicted or punished. No matter how public the crime, it escapes.[17]

Drinking, profanity, gambling, and Sabbath-breaking were the prevailing degrading forces against which the missionaries of the various denominations had to work.

Despite the prevailing presence of intemperance which seemed to accompany the excitement and unsettled conditions in the new communities the people in many of the towns were not unmindful of the great evil. To combat such a situation various societies were formed, temperance meetings held and definite action taken. In some places such as Quindaro and Tecumseh the people rose up in indignation and destroyed the saloons. In the latter case the missionary comments:

"The Lord has thus caused the wrath of man to praise him." [18] A further and more permanent step was taken by some of the towns when their town associations were formed. Such towns as Topeka, Manhattan and Emporia inserted articles in their charters which prohibited the selling or manufacturing of liquor in certain districts, while the Lawrence City Association forbade the selling of intoxicating liquor within the city limits.

The excitement caused by the border warfare was accompanied and followed by a great deal of political activity in the attempt to set up the new government. These two causes of unrest and uncertainy were beginning to die down when another disturbing element entered. This has been called "Pike's Peak Fever" or the "Gold Excitement." In the spring of 1859, all Kansas was in a turmoil caused by the great number of people on their way to "the land of gold." Rumors that gold had been found around Pike's Peak were everywhere current. It was estimated that no less than 1,000 people would go to the gold fields from the town of Leavenworth alone, and other towns suffered accordingly.[19] An idea of the extent of this migration from Kansas and states in the east, is given by C. E. Blood, of Manhattan, in a letter of April 22, 1859:

The road from Leavenworth to Fort Riley & on to Pike's Peak, passes in sight of my house. For four weeks not a day has passed but hundreds have been seen hurrying on to the land of gold. Many have gone with nothing but their carpet sacks; many with hand carts which they have to draw some 600 miles or more. Large numbers go with good outfits, with plenty of oxen or mules & covered wagons, tents provisions &c.[20]

DROUTH

Following the excitement of the "Pike's Peak Fever" came a catastrophe which far surpassed all others in its effect on all the people. The first emigrants had been in their new environment only a few years when the terrible drouth of 1860 descended not only on Kansas but also on the surrounding region. Its effect was greater in this newly settled region because of the utter lack of preparedness for it. The farming pioneers had been able to raise enough foodstuffs to care for their immediate needs but there had been no possibility of laying up a reserve and indeed, it was not thought necessary. Beginning in June, 1859, there was no rain of any consequence until 16 months later.[21] As a result, all crops were destroyed and even the wells and springs dried up. The only thing that saved thousands from starvation was the immediate relief sent from the east. Under the leadership of Thaddeus Hyatt of New York, the territory was organized into two districts and appeals made to the people of the east. The response was immediate and sufficient and the thousands who remained in Kansas were tided over the terrible period.

One missionary's description gives a view of the suffering in the interior:

The last has been a terrible season for Kansas. . . . The drain to the gold mines in the spring weakened us, but we should have recovered this fall. But the drouth has prostrated us completely. Many of our most reliable and worthy citizens are compelled to depend on charity for bread. Thousands of our people will starve unless they are aided from abroad. . . . One man came over one hundred miles to get bread and clothes. He left a wife and eleven children at home with only a bushel of cornmeal to last them until he returned. All the clothing they had was made out of an old wagon cover. He was dressed in . . . rags, but his conversation showed him to be a gentleman of refinement, and culture. . . . But his was only one case. Last week several men came here from Atchison, where they had been to get provisions. They had come from the south part of the territory. . . . The supplies at Atchison had failed and they were compelled to return empty to their hungry families. Their clothes were so ragged they had to be tied on with strings. . . . These are only specimens of what occurs daily . . . unless supplies come in more rapidly many of our people must starve. We can only meet the widespread demand by dealing out very small quantities at a time.[22]

Many people became discouraged and left for the west or back east and others remained because they were too destitute to leave. Some estimated that 30,000 left the territory during the drouth period. Confidence was restored in 1861 by a new and bountiful crop.

Such was the new territory into which the several denominations were sending their representatives.

METHODIST EPISCOPAL BEGINNINGS

One denomination to take early action looking toward religious work in Kansas was the Methodist Episcopal Church. Even before the final passage of the Kansas-Nebraska Bill this great church, through Bishop E. R. Ames, made plans for further work in Kansas and Nebraska territories.[23] W. H. Goode, a prominent leader in Indiana Methodism and earlier in Indian Mission work, was appointed as of June 3, 1854, by Bishop Ames to make a tour of the new region and report on the needs. Five days after his appointment Goode started for the field on his exploration tour. On this trip he visited the various Indian Missions in Kansas, preached at Kibbee cabin, located north of the present Baldwin, Kansas, on July 9, 1854, and proceeded north into Nebraska. A replica of the Kibbee cabin is on the Baker University campus in Baldwin, Kansas. Kansas Methodists claim that this was the

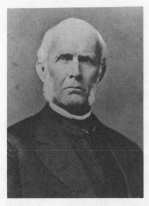

W. H. GOODE

DRAWING OF
KIBBEE CABIN

seven men selected by Goode were appointed to the work—James S. Griffing, J. L. Conklin, William D. Gage, T. J. Ferrill, J. H. Dennis and Charles Ketcham.[24] During the two years, 1854-56, the work was carried on under the Missouri Conference of the Methodist Episcopal Church. New men came to the field, new classes were organized in the new settlements and the whole region divided into three districts.

The General Conference of 1856 authorized the erection of a new conference to be called the Kansas-Nebraska Conference. The first session of this conference, presided over by Bishop Osman C. Baker, was held at Lawrence on October 23-25, 1856.[25]

OSMAN C. BAKER

first sermon among the white settlers in Kansas. As a result of the recommendations in his report, the new work was placed by the bishops under the care of the Missouri Conference.

At the session of this conference at Hannibal, Missouri, May 27, 1854, the Kansas and Nebraska Mission District was formed with Goode as Presiding Elder;

69

Our Conference at Lawrence was an occasion of deep interest. It was held in a tent, on the border of the town, where our people hold their regular worship. In the center of the tent was a stove, which rendered us quite comfortable. A table, placed on a low platform, served as a pulpit, and the seats, made of black walnut would be deemed really elegant if this timber were not abundant in that country. Between twenty and thirty preachers were in attendance. Some of them were aged and middle-aged men, who had filled stations of influence and responsibility in other conferences, and others were young and vigorous, with hearts strong to enter the work, and encounter the obstacles as they rise. Some ministers of other denominations were present, who sympathize with us in the great work of the world's salvation. . . .

Our conference love-feast was a session of deep interest, as it usually is on such occasions. Our tent was well filled. Some had come nearly forty miles to enjoy the religious services of the Conference. Squire Gray Eyes and his wife; Brother Curly Head, and Brother White Crow, of the Wyandot Mission, were present.[26]

The two Kansas districts reported a membership of 661 members, 66 probationers, 144 Indian members and 34 local preachers. At that conference nine preachers reported the work of 11 stations. The largest membership by a station was that of Wyandotte and Delaware with a total of 118 Indian members. Then followed Doniphan with 95 members, Osawatomie with 83, while Wolf River and Lawrence each had 80 members. Only three meeting houses were reported—at Lawrence, Wyandotte and Fort Scott. The 17 men appointed to the two Kansas districts at this first session show that the Methodists were attempting to supply all the important settlements such as Lawrence, Leavenworth, Columbus City, Oskaloosa, Topeka, Manhattan, Council City, Osawatomie and Fort Scott. At this first session the Conference took preliminary steps toward the founding of educational institutions.

During the next four years the denomination spread with unbelievable rapidity. The pioneer circuit-riders under the leadership of Presiding Elders such as L. B. Dennis, Abraham Still, W. Butt, James Shaw and Nathan Taylor, seemed to be everywhere. New preachers came to the territory, new classes were formed, new circuits established, new districts organized and the membership grew by leaps and bounds. At the last session of the Kansas-Nebraska Conference in 1860, the total membership in Kansas was reported as 2,997. Separate conferences had been authorized by the General Conference of 1860. Credit for such a numerical advance must be given to the untiring efforts of the circuit preachers who carried on despite all hardships.

SOUTHERN METHODISTS

The Methodist Episcopal Church, South, by virtue of the earlier extensive Methodist work among the Indians, was in a much more favorable position when this new territory was opened for white settlement. During the same month, May, 1854, that Bishop Ames made preliminary arrangements with Rev. W. H. Goode for Methodist Episcopal work in Kansas, the General Conference of the Southern Church created the Kansas Mission Conference. This conference was organized by Bishop Early at the session of the St. Louis Conference on October 24, 1855, with 14 members.[27] Two districts, the Lecompton and Kickapoo, were created and William Bradford and Nathan Scarritt appointed Presiding Elders. The first regular session of the Kansas Mission Conference was held in Kickapoo on September 12, 1856—one month before the organization of the Methodist Episcopal Conference. The total number of members reported at this session, 672, included 176 Indians and two Negro members. The appointments reporting the largest number of members in 1856 were: Fort Scott—100; Shawnee Mission—86, which included 82 Indians; Doniphan and Kickapoo—70 each; Pottawatomie—60; and Tecumseh Mission—33.[28]

With the great influx of settlers from the Northern states, however, the hope of the Southern church for any advance comparable to that of the Northern church was doomed. The life of the Southern circuit-preacher was not easy and his influence was limited. With admirable courage they maintained their work among the settlers from the southern states who were located in the towns as indicated below. Their greatest advance during any one year was the year ending in September, 1860. The reports showed that 569 members had been added to the rolls. There were now three districts—Lecompton, Council Grove and Leavenworth—and the total membership had increased to a total of 1,066. The largest full membership in the charges were: Doniphan—193; Grasshopper—83; Paris—79; Paola—78; Mt. Pleasant—72; Shawnee Reserve, Council Grove and Nimeha each had 62.[29] During the next conference year the Civil War began. Many of the members and preachers left the state, and, although a secret conference was held near Atchison in September, 1861, and appointments made, work was soon discontinued. It was resumed in 1866.

When taken separately, the accounts of the way in which denominations began their work in Kansas may not convey the intense rivalry which existed between the various groups in the small towns and settlements which sprang into prominence as a result of the rush of white settlers into the new territory. This competition is best seen in an individual town such as Lawrence or Leavenworth.

RELIGIOUS ACTIVITY IN LAWRENCE

The most important town in the early history of Kansas was undoubtedly Lawrence. This settlement, named for the treasurer of the New England Aid Company, Amos. A. Lawrence, became the headquarters of the company in Kansas, and the center of the Free-State Party. Its importance in the Kansas conflict is shown by the attitude which the Border Ruffians of Missouri had toward it. It was on Lawrence that the Missourians were anxious to vent their wrath and raids into Kansas reached their climax with the sacking of this Free-State stronghold. For the early settler this town was the immediate destination if he were from a Northern state. Here he could obtain knowledge of the territory, advice as to likely sites for settlement, supplies and temporary accommodations. For all these reasons Lawrence was important from a religious aspect. As noted by the earliest preacher in Lawrence:

This seems also to be the center of religious influence in the territory—at least all denominations deem it highly important to have a foothold here.[30]

One of the first denominations to gain a foothold was the Congregationalists. Their missionary, S. Y. Lum, was one of the first colonists to arrive. Soon after his coming in September, 1854, he organized the first Congregational church on October 15th. It was only a matter of weeks until two Baptist missionaries were in the field. Before the end of the year the Methodist pioneers, W. H. Goode and James S. Griffing, held services in Lawrence. Griffing, who had been appointed to the Wakarusa Mission, near Lawrence, by the Missouri Conference at Hannibal in 1854, organized a class in Lawrence early in 1855 but it soon disbanded. In May, 1855, a missionary of the American Unitarian Association, Ephraim Nute, arrived in Lawrence and immediately began to exert an important influence. In June the Baptist Church was organized, while in July the first permanent organization of Methodists was formed. The situation in September, 1855, is well expressed by S. Y. Lum:

Where, but one year ago I found but little over a hundred persons, just arrived in this unknown country, without shelter from the sun or storm, may now be found near 1,000 inhabitants. . . . 4 churches have been formed and another is in immediate prospect—these are—the Congregational, Methodist, Baptist, United Brethren & Unitarian. These divisions of evangelical christians, seems most unfortunate, where the whole united are so weak & will remove, much further off the time when the gospel can be sustained independent of foreign help, but it seems impossible to avoid it.[31]

The religious forces were increased in the fall of 1855, with the organization of the United Brethren Church by Rev. S. S. Snyder. For more than a year no other denomination entered into the competition. The warfare then going on undoubtedly accounts for this lull. Some indication of the success of the different denominations is given by the attendance at public worship. In October, 1856, it was estimated that the attendance ran as follows: Methodist, 250; Congregational, 180; Unitarian, 125; and Baptist, 30.[32] During 1857 and 1858 two more denominations became established in this city. The Protestant Episcopal Church began its endeavors in the summer of 1857 and the next year a parish was organized. During the summer of 1858 the Old School Presbyterian Church was formed. As a result, in a town of over 2,000 inhabitants, there were eight denominations struggling for prominence: Old School Presbyterian, Baptist, Methodist, United Brethren, Swedenborgian, Unitarian, Episcopalian and Congregational.

All of these churches were anxious to build as soon as possible and made noble efforts in this respect. The Congregationalists at first held services in the sleeping-room of the New England Emigrant Aid Company. The Methodists, in the spring of 1856, occupied a canvas tent in which the Kansas and Nebraska Conference was later organized. The Unitarians during the summer of 1855, held services in the open air. This group at Lawrence had an advantage over the other denominations because this particular church, under the leadership of Mr. Nute, was a special project of the American Unitarian Association and all their efforts in Kansas were centered around this one town.[33] During the three years, 1856-58, more than twelve thousand dollars were expended by the Association for work in Kansas. The corner-stone of the Unitarian Church was laid in February, 1856, but the building was not completely finished until the fall of 1857. Because of the lack of money the Congregational Church was not finished until late in 1862, although it was begun in the spring of 1856. A frame building was finished by the Methodists in 1858 and in the following year the Episcopalians completed a small stone building. In 1861 a correspondent, in speaking of Lawrence, said, "It has a population of 2,500. There are five respectable church edifices here: Catholic, Unitarian, Methodist Episcopal, Protestant Episcopal, and Congregationalist." [34] Despite all this rivalry there seems to have been a good spirit of co-operation between the denominations. The Unitarians allowed the Congregationalists and Methodists to use their church as soon as they could occupy it and a Union Sunday School was carried on.

THE CHURCHES IN LEAVENWORTH

Leavenworth was an altogether different town. It had been known in the east because of the army fort which was established many years before the territory of Kansas was opened for settlement by the whites. In regard to population it was far in advance of Lawrence. Horace Greeley, after visiting this city in 1859, wrote:

> Whether the three great cities of America are to be New York, St. Louis and Leavenworth, as one set of friends seem to think, or New York, St. Louis and Atchison, as another set assure, I do not pretend to decide.[35]

In the early days Leavenworth and Atchison were the two great centers of pro-slavery influence in the territory. Since Leavenworth was just across the river from Missouri it was controlled politically by the Missourians. Because of this fact the religious denominations which were favored by pro-slavery adherents were the first to establish churches in this busy city. The first two churches organized were the Methodist Episcopal Church, South and the Disciples of Christ, or Christian Church. The former appears on the minutes of the first organizing session of the Kansas Mission Conference as the Leavenworth Circuit, while the latter was organized in the summer of 1855. Although the Disciples as a denomination remained neutral on the slavery question, their church in Leavenworth was composed of people from the south with pro-slavery inclinations. Leavenworth was chosen as the field for the first Old School Presbyterian missionary, Rev. C. D. Martin. It was here that the first Old School Presbyterian Church in Kansas Territory was organized on January 1, 1856. Another "neutral" denomination entered the field with the coming of the Protestant Episcopal missionary, Rev. Hiram Stone, late in 1856. The first church of this denomination in Kansas was organized by this missionary on December 10, 1856.

It was necessary for the border warfare to subside before one of the "anti-slavery" denominations like the Methodist Episcopal Church could hope to do any permanent work in pro-slavery Leavenworth. Occasional preaching had been carried on from 1854 to 1857, but in the latter year the first appointment was made for Leavenworth.[36] In the same year a church was formed by the Presiding Elder, William Butt.

Before the opening of Kansas to white settlement in 1854, Bishop Miege, the Roman Catholic bishop, had little to do except oversee two Indian Missions. He even asked the archbishop at St. Louis for the care of St. Joseph, Missouri, "in order to have some occupation during the winter time." [37] As mentioned earlier, he had six priests under him.

When the emphasis of his work shifted from Indian to white he decided to move his residence from St. Mary's to Leavenworth. In 1855 his house was finished there and the building of a small frame church begun and was completed by the end of 1857. He entered into the life of Leavenworth—purchased a share in the town and soon had 23 lots in the city at a cost of $1,675, and paid $255 for 40 acres a mile from town. By the end of 1856 he had spent $11,000 in Leavenworth. During the first five years the money for the total work came from his savings of $9,000 and from grants from the Society for the Propagation of the Faith which totaled $29,000. A larger church in Leavenworth was soon needed because there were 600 Roman Catholics there.[38]

Little is known about the early priests. The first priest to be ordained in Kansas was Father Casimir Seitz. He was one of two Benedictines who came in 1857. The other was Father Augustine Wirth who was head of the Benedictine priory which was first located at Doniphan and then moved to Atchison when Doniphan declined. Atchison soon became an important Roman Catholic center—a church was built in 1858, enlarged the next year, and St. Benedict's College opened on October 1, 1859, with five students.[39]

By 1861 the bishop reported a total of 16 churches, 4 chapels, 23 mission stations, and 15 priests in the vicariate. Eight of the latter were devoting their time to the new settlements. During the first years there were not many Roman Catholics among the immigrants and those were "rusty." Part of the reason for reluctance in moving to Kansas was the Protestant involvement as well as the turmoil related to "bleeding Kansas." Added to this was the opposition to abolitionism and the threat of nativism. On the whole, Roman Catholics remained neutral in the early struggles over Kansas and slavery.[40]

Some idea of the success of the various denominations in Leavenworth is given by an estimate of the average number of attendants on public worship in 1858: Catholics, 600; Old School Presbyterians, 250; Christians, 150; Episcopalians, 150; Methodist Episcopal, South, 50; and Baptists, 50.[41] Organized religion was not as successful in Leavenworth as in other Kansas towns. Even with a population of 12,000 in 1860, there was no church in the city which was fully self-sustaining.

CONCLUSION OF A PERIOD

With the beginning of the Civil War the first period in the history of the churches in Kansas came to a close.

These first six years were crowded years. To the difficulties which accompany the establishment of new homes on a new frontier were added the great political activities, the Pike's Peak Fever, and the drouth of 1860. In the constantly changing scene the churches played an important role. Considering the denominations taken singly the most important place must be given to the Methodist Episcopal Church because of its greater numbers. The reasons for the greater numerical strength of the Methodist Episcopal Church may be given as: (1) the majority of the settlers came from the states where this denomination was particularly strong; (2) its early start in the field; (3) its organization was particularly fitted to meet the need of such a situation.

After a visit to Kansas early in 1861 the editor of the *Central Christian Advocate* spoke in glowing terms of the Methodist preachers of Kansas.

In general, we do not believe there is a more competent conference of ministers in the Methodist Church, either east of the Mississippi river to the Atlantic, or west of it to Pacific. We believe that Providence has collected here a company of ministers fully qualified to do a great work (of a peculiar kind, in doing which one of the old conferences would fail were they suddenly placed in their stead) . . . None but the enterprising men would enter on this work, and none others would stay, did they enter. . . . They are picked men. . . . Some were from Missouri, chosen out of those who refused to bow the knee in 1845. . . . Some came from Iowa, (a great pioneer school at that time for training men for the Kansas field). . . . New England and New York States furnished others, who were of the same mind with the reinforcements from Missouri, Iowa, Illinois, Indiana, Ohio and the Northwest. We were surprised at the selection of the men. . . .[42]

The lack of aid from the east militated against the prosperity of both the newer denominations and the small denominations. Pro-slavery tendencies doomed denominations like the Methodist Episcopal Church, South and the Old School Presbyterians to a slow growth, and in the case of the former, to extinction for a time. Taken as a whole, however, the religious forces had reason to be proud of their work during the days of Squatter Sovereignty in Kansas.

CIVIL WAR YEARS

Hardly had the border warfare ceased and Kansas time to enter the Union as a state, January 29, 1861, when the nation was plunged into a great sectional strife. The effects of this conflict were manifested with varying degrees of intensity in the different sections of this region. Some parts of Missouri were nearly depopulated and a vast amount of property destroyed in Missouri and Kansas while throughout the entire region war excitement took the foremost place in all endeavors.

Troubles between churches in the border state of Missouri began long before the outbreak of the Civil War and with its advent the rivalry was intensified and brought into open conflict. When the secessionists under General Sterling Price first gained control, northern preachers were driven out, threatened with hanging and their religious services broken up. With the advance of northern armies, however, the tide was turned and the southern preachers and church members persecuted. In the border counties along the river from Kansas City to Jefferson City, the "Bushwackers" were especially active.[1] (Bushwackers were free-booting guerillas who sympathized with the South and preyed upon and intimidated Northern supporters.)

In 1862 the pastor of the Christian Church of Kansas City, Missouri, thought it wise to leave, but the chief struggle in this city was between the two Methodist Churches. The Methodist Episcopal Church first attempted an organization in this young city in 1859 and applied to the Southern Church for the use of their building, but were denied and had to seek aid from the Presbyterians.[2] Four years later when the Union forces were in control, Reverend J. H. Hopkins of the Methodist Episcopal Church began to hold services in the edifice of the Southern Church, and gave out a public notice "that no disloyal person will be admitted." [3]

In Kansas City and Independence, Missouri, the Northern Church claimed and occupied the buildings erected by the Southern Church on the ground that the land on which they stood was deeded to the Methodist Episcopal Church. Hopkins advocated "taking possession of the entire ground in this part of the State, in the towns and cities" on the same basis.

The Southerners in Independence, Missouri, appealed to General John Pope, commander of the federal troops, who after investigation denied their claim. Undaunted by this refusal, the Southern women forced their way into the church, took possession and maintained a watch day and night until dispersed by the sheriff.

Numerous stories of atrocities perpetrated by the Northerners are told by W. M. Leftwich in his two volume work, *Martyrdom in Missouri,* while the northern angle is told with as much bias by Charles Elliott in his *History of the Methodist Episcopal Church in the South-West from 1844-1864.*[4]

Terrible is the story of the arrest and murder of Augustus H. F. Payne, a Disciple minister. The account by Payne's daughter relates that he was arrested despite his protection papers, and murdered by a detachment of Union soldiers and left in the brush three miles from his home. When the lieutenant in command was charged with the murder, he replied: "These preachers had more influence than any other class of men, and if they all had the benefit of a rope the country would be better off." [5] Concerning this period, one Methodist authority has said:

The situation in Missouri during the war is difficult to describe.

Nowhere were the churches more bitterly opposed to one another, and nowhere were greater cruelties and barbarities practiced in the name of the Church than in Missouri.[6]

In other sections, "Jayhawking," although supposedly directed against Southern sympathizers, became a disturbing factor to the northerners as well, because it was used as a cloak for "promiscuous stealing and midnight robbery." [7] (A Jayhawker was a free-booting guerilla who sympathized with the North and preyed upon and intimidated Missourians and Southern supporters.)

GUERILLA RAIDS

The greatest shock to Kansas settlers during the war was occasioned by the murderous guerilla raid on Lawrence by William C. Quantrill and his band in

WILLIAM C. QUANTRILL

August, 1863. Reverend J. Copeland, the Congregational missionary at Clinton, in a letter written only a few days after the tragedy, stated:

At present the all engrossing subject of thought & conversation is the guerrilla war, which has received a fresh impulse of late in Kansas. The late barbarous massacre, burning & plundering of Lawrence has aroused the people as with the shock of an earthquake; and this act will be terribly avenged on the murderers & their sympathizers in the border counties of Missouri . . . I have endeavored . . . to improve the solemn event by calling the attention of my congregations to the hand of God in the matter. . . .

The new church edifice at Wakarusa . . . was burned by the rebels on their retreat from Lawrence. . . . They also burned nearly every dwelling house on the road south of Lawrence for ten miles. . . . I was in Lawrence an hour or two after the marauders left. The best part of the town was in ashes & the dead even still lying on the ground in all parts of the town, some partially & some almost entirely consumed by the fire. I assisted in getting bodies out of the fire & in laying out the bodies of others endeavoring to speak a word of consolation here & there, to bereaved relatives, whose heart-rending cries & wails were heard in all directions. Eighty-five wives have been widowed & 240 children orphaned by this calamity.[8]

Among those killed was the United Brethren missionary, S. S. Snyder.[9] Several towns believed they were to be the next victims. The representative of the American Home Missionary Society at Emporia wrote:

It is well known that Emporia is among the doomed towns. . . . Of course I have joined the ranks for common defence. . . . There is hardly a man in this neighborhood that goes to bed without a loaded revolver or two or three rifles or muskets at his bedside —No prisoners now. O what a fearful time. It is reported that Quantrill is near our border with a thousand men. . . . Almost every town is guarded every night, pickets out, and men in camp their arms ready any moment.[10]

The people in Highland feared that they

may rise some morning to see our dwelling melting in the flames, and to feel the cold lead or steel of our demoniac enemies penetrating our vitals.[11]

While R. D. Parker in Wyandotte tells how he took his turn standing guard watching for "Quantrill's bloody band . . . prowling like beasts of prey along the Border."[12] In Lawrence the destruction of life and property caused many to leave. The loss to members of the Congregational Church, estimated at $250,000, nearly ruined the church.

The fear of Indians was another constant dread, for the pioneers felt that they "were situated between two fires, the Indians of the plains . . . & the Bushwackers of Missouri . . . equally barbarous & bloodthirsty."[13] Exaggerated rumors made some believe the fear expressed by Reverend G. C. Morse in 1861:

We are living in perilous times. . . . This state has been promised to the Indians if they would only exterminate the abolitionists. Thus you see, we are constantly exposed to attacks from the blood-thirsty savages, urged on by men only more ferocious.[14]

The ministers who, as shown above, were in the midst of the excitement were not exempt from military duty. The attitude of the ministers is explained by a Methodist minister in Lawrence, L. B. Dennis:

. . . the friends of liberty in this territory in the past are now the friends of the Union. . . . Yes, sir. One and all. Ministers and members; fathers and sons are saying: "Here am I. Send me" "Next to our God is our country." And some of us have lost the spirit of non-resistance so far, that we think we can serve God and our country at the same time. . . . This is no time for conservatism or neutrality, especially such as is basely termed "Armed neutrality." Why not say drunken sobriety?[15]

With this feeling concerning the conflict, it is not difficult to understand why a number of ministers became regular chaplains.

That there were mixed motives and confusion of loyalties among the people of western Missouri was not recognized by the free-state people of Kansas. To a lesser degree the same applied to the opposite situation for those in Kansas. The "Bushwackers" and "Jayhawkers" represented a small part of the population in either state. Unbelievable to most people in Kansas was the fact that many Missourians were committed to slavery and still loyal to the Union. Missouri never joined the Confederacy! The Reverend Thomas Johnson of the Shawnee Mission in Kansas was unique among missionaries in that he was a southern slave holder. On the other hand, on July 4, 1861, at a celebration near Turner in Wyandotte Couny, he condemned

the secession movement as unjustifiable, and stated in unequivocal terms that he should adhere to the flag of his country, that he had been indirectly for years in official relation with the government, enjoying its protection, and he owed to it fealty, love and support.[16]

MIXED MOTIVES—LOW MORALS

What can one say of "Jim" Lane, who was one of the first two senators from Kansas? Was he: democrat or republican?—hypocrite and/or Methodist?—statesman and senator or exploiter? As will be recounted in a later chapter, the United Brethren named their college for him. Stories of his religious experiences are many—a number involve the Methodists. Because his mother, he claimed, was a Methodist, he owed much to the Methodist Episcopal Church. She wanted him to be a preacher. At a Methodist Camp Meeting, near Lawrence, he pretended to give up chewing tobacco—

gave "up his last idol and surrendered his heart to the Lord." [17] Lane's Brigade's marching song, to a familiar tune, was:

I am a soldier of the boss,
A follower of Jim Lane,
And shall I fear to steal a hoss,
Or blush to ride the same?

"JIM" LANE

Depredations by Union soldiers in western Missouri, under Lane and others more vicious, opened the door for the horrible raid and massacre on Lawrence by Quantrill and his daring band. No other raids or actions earlier can condone this crime, but it does not stand alone. Partly in retaliation and to bring order, General Thomas Ewing, commanding the federal troops in the border region, issued the hated "Order No. 11" which brought about a mass banishment of population from four counties of western Missouri. To be noted is the fact that Quantrill was never accepted as a leader by any of the southern generals.

81

In 1862, Reverend J. D. Liggett of Leavenworth, after lamenting the lack of Bibles in the city, gives a lurid picture of the moral situation:

We have two theatres of a low order well patronized. Saloons and whiskey shops almost numberless. About 300 prostitutes; whose houses are very prominent and notorious, and one of which stands right in front of the Methodist Church, unmolested by Civil Authority. A very large proportion of our citizens are young men: Away from home and its restraints of well-organized and virtuous society. . . .[18]

In the neighboring town of Atchison, in the same year, "Drunkenness," says the Congregational missionary, "is so common that it is not considered a disgrace & brothels are frequented as openly as hotels," but the writer believed that "there are more than ten righteous here; although not more than one-tenth of the population attended any religious services."[19] In the following year, however, there was a moral and social advancement; brothels were closed and the temperance cause gained ground.[20] In the nearby town of Highland a sermon on the vices of youth met with a defiant response:

In preaching to the children on Sab. on the peculiar vices of youth, such as profanity, lying, stealing, drinking, etc. I mentioned that of using tobacco. The moment I touched upon that subject, a young man took out his pipe, filled it with tobacco, lighted a match, and deliberately went to smoking in my face. In another part of the audience (I have since learned) an old grandmother did the same, while two of her grand-daughters took from their pockets their plugs of tobacco, bit off a piece and went to chewing the delectable weed with infinite satisfaction to themselves.[21]

Despite the fact that Kansas, in its beginning, was the center of the national controversy and division over slavery, it obviously did not occur to our founding fathers that the Negro—and all women—should be treated equally with the white man when it came to voting. In the Wyandotte Constitution of 1859, the franchise was restricted to "white male persons" by a vote of 37 to 3.[22] The right to vote came to the Negro as a result of the Fourteenth Amendment to the United States Constitution, and to women in Kansas, through the state constitutional amendment of 1912.

EARLY WORK AMONG NEGROES

As indicated earlier in the story of the Shawnee Mission, there were a few Negro slaves brought in by the Reverend Thomas Johnson. Soon after the opening of the territory for white settlement, there were some Negroes who moved over from Missouri. As early as 1858 the Congregational missionary, S. D. Storrs, reported from Quindaro:

> Another great annoyance in this place is prejudice against colored children's attending our public schools. A majority are in favor of what is called the "Black Law" that forbids them attending schools with the whites. There are but few colored children in Quindaro, not enough for a separate school. They are well behaved and very anxious to learn. During the summer there has been no school that they could attend and Mrs. S. devotes a portion of her time every week giving them gratuitous instruction.[23]

As the war progressed many Negroes were liberated or escaped through the lines into territory occupied by the Northern armies. During the period from 1860 to 1865 more than 12,000 Negroes came into the state.[24] Many of these "contraband" Negroes came across from Missouri into Kansas and settled in the towns along the border, especially in Wyandotte, Lawrence, Atchison, Leavenworth, Topeka and Hiawatha. The Congregationalists, Baptists and Methodists immediately attempted to provide for their religious needs. The American Home Missionary Society supported the Negro preacher, Reverend Daniel Ellex, who organized churches in Lawrence, Topeka and Wyandotte, while the American Missionary Association gave partial support to a white preacher, Fox, who aided in establishing churches among the "blacks" at Wyandotte, Kansas City and Independence.[25] Since Lawrence was a well known town many of the Negroes came to that place; in 1862 there were 400, while a year later there were about 1,000.[26]

The Congregationalists organized the "contrabands" into the "Second Congregational Church" on March 16, 1862, and a year later had 23 members, all of whom had been slaves. A brick church had been erected and the congregation numbered 100 to 150.[27] The Methodist minister at Lawrence, in 1862, told of his extra efforts for the new Negro settlers:

> Many of the contrabands have heard that this is a place where they remain in safety, and so far they have. But it throws upon us a heavy burden, both morally and physically. The most of them have turned to our church for the instruction they so much need, both mentally and morally. Our Sunday School has run right up in a few weeks from forty, fifty and sixty, to one hundred and twenty or thirty every Sabbath. We have near sixty regular members of the M.E. Church, and they are doing remarkably well. At our late conference there were no provisions made for the accommodations of our colored friends, hence we have to manage as best we can. The congregation is so large we can not accommodate them comfortably.[28]

In the same year, 1862, in Lawrence, the African Methodist Episcopal Church was organized by Reverend J. M. Wilkenson, with 37 members. After meeting in public halls for four years they erected a stone building, and in 1872-73 they built again. In 1880 they had a membership of 207. Another Negro Methodist Church, St. Paul's, was organized in 1882.[29]

DECLINE OF CHURCH ACTIVITY

Since from the beginning of the war guerrilla raids, Indian raids and "Indian scares" were in the minds of all, it was to be expected that organized religion would make but slow progress. Due to the decrease in the number of people moving to the west, population in Kansas no longer increased so rapidly. The resources of the nation were being used to preserve the Union and it was necessary for denominational boards to curtail their activities. This retrenchment resulted in fewer missionaries and less money to aid religious work, not only in new fields but also in the established places. Receipts, in 1864-65, again reached the level of 1860, or surpassed it; there was still a lack of adequate laborers. Churches on the frontier suffered not only from the excitement of the period and the lower moral conditions but also from the loss of members. The enlistment of but a small number of male members into the army often spelled disaster for a small church and embarrassment for a larger church.

Although the population of Kansas was not increasing as rapidly as formerly, more than 32,000 additional settlers moved into the state during the Civil War years.[30] All denominations increased the number of churches and the number of members on their rolls but the most significant advances were those of the Methodists and Disciples. At the State Meeting of the latter denomination, in 1865, 79 churches reported a total membership of 3,020—an increase of more than 2,000 members and 59 churches since 1860.[31] Before the war the Disciples had been at a disadvantage because they had had little help from the east, but after 1861 this became an advantage. While other denominations faltered from lack of the accustomed aid, this group already conditioned to self-support, forged ahead on its own resources. A great portion of this membership increase was undoubtedly due to the emigration of a large number of people from western Missouri where the Disciples fellowship was unusually strong. Meanwhile, the Methodists were far from idle although their increase in membership was not as large as was that of the Disciples. The former church had been well established before the war and was, therefore, able to continue its progress with less help and to report an increase of more than 1,000 members during these years.[32]

SERVICE TO GERMANS

The large immigration of Germans into Kansas was to come in later years. Serving German people in these early years were the United Brethren led by S. S. Snyder, Josiah Terrel (in Missouri, but preaching at Fort Scott), William A. Cordwell and John S. Gingerish. Snyder came to Lawrence as early as October, 1854. The Kansas Mission Conference was organized on October 30, 1857, at Prairie City, south of Lawrence.[33] In 1860 the total membership was 928 with 23 ministers; five years later the membership showed only a small increase. The loss of the first missionary, Reverend S. S. Snyder, in the Quantrill massacre, was a severe blow. Another church serving the Germans was the Evangelical Association. Their representatives first began a class at Franklin, near Lawrence, before 1858. In August of 1858, Reverend M. J. Miller of the Evangelical Association arrived and began work among the estimated 3,000 Germans in Leavenworth but there were only three members with which to begin.[34] The Kansas Conference of the Evangelical Association was organized in 1864 at Leavenworth.

It was from the Illinois Conference that the first German ministers of the Methodist Episcopal Church came. In the appointments of that conference in 1859, on the Missouri District appear five places and ministers (Wyandot, Lawrence, Fort Riley, Leavenworth City and Columbus). Two years later, after General Conference action, when they are listed under the Kansas German District of the Kansas Conference there were six appointments in Kansas and five in Missouri—total membership in the district of 316, but only 121 in Kansas.[35]

METHODIST EPISCOPAL SITUATION, 1861

The statistics of a conference are always of interest and this is especially true of the earlier sessions of a new conference. In the reports of the Kansas Conference of the Methodist Episcopal Church in 1861, at Atchison, there are 25 churches with memberships totalling 60 or more in the seven districts, including the Rocky Mountain District.[36] The two largest churches in membership were Mountain City in the latter district and Oskaloosa, both with 200 members. Then followed:[37]

Holton	170	Leavenworth	118
Centropolis	150	Baldwin City	103
Garnet	140	Osage	100
Ottumwa	100	Denver & Auroria	78
Burlington	95	Atchison	70

Clinton	94	Seneca	70
Mound City	94	Fort Scott	69
Franklin & Shawnee		Fort Riley	67
Indians	92	Twin Springs	62
Humboldt	88	Prairie City & Minneola	61
Wyandot & Wyandot		Topeka	60
Indians	85		

Church buildings were not numerous nor very costly in comparison with later times. The most expensive were: Leavenworth—$8,000; Topeka—$4,000; Holton—$3,000; Atchison—$2,500; Lawrence—$2,000; Centropolis—$1,500; Oskaloosa—$1,200; and Humboldt—$1,200. In 1865 one of the Presiding Elders indicated that the salaries of preachers ranged from $500 to $900 per year. His own salary including house rent and moving expenses was fixed at $1,200.[38]

One method used to good advantage especially by the Methodists in Kansas was the camp meeting. The lack of adequate church buildings on the frontier made some other arrangement necessary and the primitive camp meeting was brought into use. "Protracted meetings" were often held by individual churches or several churches joined in an annual camp meeting. Two of the most famous Kansas camp meetings were those held at Baldwin and Topeka. Other meetings, although not as well known or as large, were held in several places in Kansas.[39] The following description of such a meeting is a reminder of those on an earlier frontier:

The last camp meeting which has just closed, was held near Ridgeway. . . . Old members that had attended hundreds of camp meetings in the South and West said that they had never witnessed such a display of power as was on Monday night. At the close of the sermon which was upon the subject of entire sanctification, a call was made for those who believed in it to come forth to the altar of prayer; whereupon every member of the church upon the whole encampment, fell upon their knees, those who had not fallen as dead men and women prostrate upon the earth; and oh! such cries and groans as ascended up for purity of heart and life, I have never seen nor heard, only read of it in the history of early Methodism.[40]

Congregational missionaries scoffed at these methods and one of them characterized it as "worship that cannot but disgust a crowd of intelligent sinners" while another described it as "noisy and ignorant."[41] Despite all ridicule and opposition this means was effective and beneficial under the existing circumstances.

When the Civil War days came to a close the religious pioneers of Kansas having been thoroughly tested were ready for the more glorious days to follow.

EARLY EDUCATIONAL ENDEAVORS TO 1880

Nearly every educational institution in Kansas during the early years owed its beginning to the efforts of some religious pioneer or some denominational group. In this development Kansas was following the lead and practice of earlier frontiers as far back as our colonial days. Indeed, until the comparatively recent rise of state colleges and universities, it was only the church that shouldered this responsibility. Usually the independent or state school has been a late entry in the field. To illustrate this early church leadership, mention only needs to be made of Harvard, Yale, Princeton, William and Mary, and Columbia as early examples.

One of the earliest concerns of Methodism was education. The establishment of a school, named Cokesbury, in honor of the first two general superintendents, was one of the first acts of the Methodist Episcopal Church. To Francis Asbury, John Wesley ridiculed the idea of the school being named for the two leaders of American Methodism in the following ungracious words:

. . . But in one point, my dear brother, I am a little afraid both the Doctor and you differ from me. I study to be little; you study to be great. I creep; you strut along. I found a school; you a college! nay, and call it after your own names! O beware, do not seek to be something! Let me be nothing, and "Christ be all in all!" . . . Thus, my dear Frankie, I have told you all that is in my heart. And let this, when I am no more seen, bear witness how sincerely I am

Your affectionate friend and brother[1]

The fact that this first school building burned soon thereafter, probably brought forth many interpretations. Not until 1830 or 1831 was Methodism in America to establish a permanent college—Randolph-Macon in Virginia or Wesleyan in Connecticut. Following this beginning, there were several established before Kansas was opened up for settlement. Other denominations were even more active in this regard than Methodists.

"The earliest settlers of Kansas . . . had no sooner driven down their tentpins than they began to talk of a college." [2] Amos A. Lawrence, the treasurer of the New England Emigrant Aid Company, was desirous that Kansas should have not only a college but also an adequate school system and contributed nearly $14,000 for the latter purpose and the establishment of Sunday Schools. In the years 1855-60 thirty colleges were incorporated.[3]

EARLY METHODIST EPISCOPAL EFFORTS

The Methodist Episcopal Church, however, claims to be the first to found an institution of a four-year college grade in the new territory. Other schools were chartered before Baker but they were not four year college grade schools. Nor did they take immediate action. At the first session of the Kansas and Nebraska Conference in 1856, the Committee on Education made the following report:

Your committee are of the opinion that the Kansas and Nebraska Conference should avail itself, through its members of the earliest opportunities to secure favorable sites for seminaries of learning or universities, under our own immediate management and control . . .[4]

On March 17 of the following year, a meeting of the Methodist Episcopal preachers in the Kansas Territory was held at Blue Mound to make preparatory arrangements for the location of a university. The action of this "preachers meeting" is related by one of the participants as follows:

Rev. L. B. Dennis was chosen chairman and Prof. Oakley, Sec'y. of the meeting. Business proceeded rather tardily on the first day, but at the adjourned meeting at Palmyra on the 18th, matters progressed, more speedily. Some excellent propositions were made by the different central places of the territory requesting the location of the University. . . . The friends of the cause around Palmyra seemed to open their hearts and purses a little the widest and were favored by having the University located there . . . they made a donation of eight hundred acres of land, and took stock in the association to the amount of twenty thousand dollars. Other bids ran high, viz.; Centropolis, Topeka, Lawrence, Blue Mound, Prairie City, etc.

The "naming" of the University was next taken up and with considerable unanimity it was decided to call it . . . Baker University. The fact that our beloved Bishop Baker visited us in times of such great danger . . . has greatly endeared him to those who formed the "little band" at the first session of the Kansas Conference.[5]

The action of this meeting was approved by the conference. The Kansas Education Association was formed, a charter for the Association obtained early in February, 1858, and a charter for the college on February 12, 1858. The construction of a stone building was begun before the session of the conference in 1858.[6] In the fall of 1858, Werter R. Davis, a professor and acting president of McKendree College, was elected president and on November 22, 1858, the first college in Kansas opened its doors with 20 students.[7]

BLUEMONT—KANSAS STATE UNIVERSITY

The founding of Manhattan, the establishment of the school that eventually became Kansas State University, and the beginning and growth of the Methodist Episcopal Church in that city, are all intertwined. Manhattan, as well as the state, owes a great debt to a few Methodist ministers and a layman—such as Rev. Joseph Denison, Rev. Washington Marlatt, Rev. C. H. Lovejoy and especially the layman, Isaac T. Goodnow.

ISAAC T. GOODNOW

The prelude to all this took place in New England at the end of 1854. Isaac T. Goodnow, a professor of English in Rhode Island and an anti-slavery advocate since 1840, and his brother-in-law, Rev. Joseph Denison, were together in Providence. There they heard a rousing lecture by Eli Thayer and talked with him after the meeting. "Fully believing that the rule of slavery or of freedom in the nation would be settled on the prairies of Kansas" they decided to emigrate. Goodnow went ahead of the company of 200, and selected the present site of Manhattan in the spring of 1855.

One of the dreams of Goodnow, Denison and Marlatt was the establishment of a great central college. To this end they secured a site of 160 acres and formed the "Blue Mont Central College Association" which was chartered February 9, 1858. By 1860 a building, library and apparatus were secured. To Professor Goodnow goes most of the credit for raising $15,000 in the east for this. On another trip he raised over $4,000 to help build the church. When the college opened in January, 1860, there were 59 students, with Rev. Marlatt as president or the principal teacher.[8] In light of later history, it is interesting to note that the charter of the Methodist school called for a classical college, but included the following provision:

The said association shall have power and authority to establish, in addition to the literary department of arts and sciences, an agricultural department, with separate professors, to test soils, experiment in the raising of crops, the cultivation of trees, (etc.) . . .[9]

The school was accepted by the Kansas Annual Conference in 1857, in spite of the known opposition of the presiding bishop, Bishop E. R. Ames—he arrived late for the conference and the favorable action had already been taken.[10]

The energetic Goodnow greatly desired the location of the State University at Manhattan. Through his efforts a bill to locate the school there and accept the offer of Blue Mont's building, library and facilities, was passed by both houses of the first legislature. It was vetoed by Governor Charles Robinson, who was committed to Lawrence for the university, or the capitol.[11] Manhattan supported Topeka for the latter. In 1862, however, after the passage of the Morrill land-grant act by the United States Congress, the offer was repeated, this time for an agricultural college. It was accepted by the State in the following year. With the gift of the early Methodist effort the present Kansas State University was established. Rev. Joseph Denison served as the first president for ten years.

EDUCATIONAL ACTIVITIES OF OTHER CHURCHES

Another state school, Kansas University, was established after three denominations—Presbyterian, Congregational and Protestant Episcopal—had failed in their attempts to found a university in Lawrence. The Presbyterians were the first to act. In 1859 they obtained a charter for "Lawrence University" and in September, 1859, the preparatory department was opened in the basement of the Unitarian Church.[12] Although the preparatory department lasted only a few months, the work on the erection of the building was continued until the drouth of 1860 stopped all activity. In the meantime, the Congregationalists endeavored to establish a school to be called "Monumental College," as a monument to those who had assisted in the victory over slavery.[13] A large sum of money was subscribed but the advent of the war caused the collapse of the enterprise; the Congregational college was later located at Topeka. About the same time, 1861, the Protestant Episcopal Church obtained a charter for "The Lawrence University of Kansas," and took over the claims of the Presbyterians, but the interference of the Civil War prevented much further work on the building and the project was given up.[14] Although the state university was located at Lawrence in 1863, it was not opened until 1866 because of the destructiveness and the resulting poverty which followed Quantrill's raid in August, 1863.

The founding of the State Normal School at Emporia (Kansas State College of Emporia), which was provided for by the legislature March 3, 1863, was largely the work of Rev. G. C. Morse, a Congregational missionary. As chairman of the board of directors, Morse not only employed the first principal but was the guiding spirit of the enterprise during its early years.

The first Presbyterian college in the state dates back to a school established at the Iowa and Sac Indian Mission. This school, under the name of Highland University, was granted a charter in 1858, but a college course was not included until 1870.[15]

Although a Congregational college was not opened until 1865, it had been under consideration since the meeting of the General Association of that denomination in 1857.[16] In 1858 it decided to locate the school in Topeka; it was changed to Lawrence in 1859, and then back to Topeka in 1860.[17] The drouth of 1860 and the war, caused the matter to rest until early in 1865. The name of the school was changed to Washburn College in 1868, following the donation of $25,000 by Deacon Ichabod Washburn of Worcester, Massachusetts.[18]

At the first meeting of the Kansas Baptist Convention in 1860, the committee of the two associations reported that it had secured a charter for a university under the name of "Roger Williams University." [19] The Ottawas were considering the establishment of a school at that time, and J. T. Jones, a delegate from the Ottawa Church, suggested that the Convention join the Indians in founding a school. As a result of the meeting of the representatives of the two groups, a treaty was entered into on June 24, 1862, whereby the Indians donated 20,000 acres of land in return for the education of their youth.[20] In 1865 a new charter was obtained under the name of Ottawa University, a temporary building was erected in 1866, and the school opened for one year. It was not until 1869, however, that a permanent building was completed and the school re-opened. Four years later a separation of the white and Indian interests was affected.

Like other denominations, the United Brethren were concerned for an educated ministry and laity. One of their authorities has stated:

During the first twenty-five years of its existence, Kansas Conference had the honor of establishing three institutions of learning. They also suffered the chagrin of seeing the first of these schools fail miserably. The remainder were in later years forced to merge with other institutions.[21]

At the first session of Kansas Mission Conference, a first step toward the establishment of a school was taken. As a result, moves were made toward a seminary at Fremont, but this effort did not come to any successful end.

The next move by the Conference was made in the year 1864-65. Solomon Weaver, president of a school in Iowa, was persuaded to come to Kansas and initiate a United Brethren school. The place selected was Lecompton because of the empty buildings available there. This town had been for a time the capitol of the Kansas Territory. The new trustees and the new president, Weaver, obtained the Rowena Hotel, a former inn, and converted this sizable building to school purposes. In 1865 they received, as a gift, the old capitol building foundations and the 13 acres of the capitol ground.[22]

It was decided to name the school for the largest donor. From the prominent James Lane, they received $2,000 and the promise of much more in the future, and the school was therefore named Lane University. No more than the original gift was ever received, however.

The first year there was a term of only three months, and during the early years the student body averaged 121 for college and preparatory work.[23] A regular university course was offered with nine departments. Between 1867 and 1882 there were 20 graduates and they received degrees as follows: B.S.—2; M.S.—13; M.A.—4; and M.D.—1.[24] In 1876-77 there were five professors and 105 students. It was not until 1882 that the college building, on the foundations of the old capitol, was completed.

The college had scripture reading, singing, and prayer in its daily chapel, which all students were required to attend. All students were required also to attend the school's Sunday church services, except students excused to attend other services. The students were invited and urged to attend the weekly prayer meeting. The college encouraged preparation for the ministry by offering free tuition to students of any denomination who desired to become ministers. Students for the ministry were required to present authorized credentials.[25]

The later history of Lane University and the story of Gould College, at Harlan, Kansas, will be told in a subsequent chapter.

Among the short-lived colleges that had a unique career was Ottumwa College. In 1862, under the supervision of the Kansas Education Association, the Methodist Episcopal Church laid the cornerstone. Soon thereafter, however, there was a Christian Church revival meeting and when many of the Methodists became members of the Christian Church the college was taken over also. After a year or two the school closed. It was reorganized again in 1872, opened in the fall of 1873, but only temporarily due to a fire.[26]

BAKER UNIVERSITY

The story of Baker University is one of more lasting interest. Its first president, Werter R. Davis, M.D., was a versatile person as proven by his various activities. After serving Baker for four years, 1858-62, during which time he was chaplain and member of the Wyandotte Convention which framed the State constitution, he became a chaplain in the army. During the war he was commissioned colonel of the 16th Regiment of Kansas Volunteers and after the war was commandant of Fort Leavenworth. Later, he campaigned against the Indians. Following his military exploits, he served as a Methodist Presiding Elder and pastor. He was the father-in-law of a more famous man, William Alfred Quayle.[27]

Old Castle, Baker's first building which is still standing, served as the only building for several years until 1871. In the first catalogue the cost of tuition is announced as $8 per term (a year consisted of three terms) in the college department. The regulations were even more strict than those of Lane University:

**OLD CASTLE AND
HISTORICAL TABLET**

Punctual and regular attendance at recitation, at public college exercises, at prayer and at church, and observance of study hours are required of every student. Unladylike or ungentlemanly conduct, disrespect toward the faculty, irreverence at church, noise in rooms on the Sabbath, writing upon or otherwise defacing the college building or furniture, using profane language, wearing firearms or other weapons, visiting circuses or theatres, card-playing, keeping intoxicating liquors in the room are strictly forbidden.[28]

A later catalogue of 1865 stated:

The college has a library of about 300 volumes. It has geographical and scientific maps and charts. It has good compass and chain, a compound microscope, magic lantern, and other apparatus. Also a considerable variety of geological specimens.[29]

All was well in 1867-68 with 13 in the college and 143 in the Preparatory Department and a library of 2,000 books. In the following year, however, came the "College Rebellion." In the *Excerpts of Minutes of Board of Trustees* in the fall of 1868, are these terse words:

At a meeting of the Board of Trustees, December 22, 1868, the action of the Faculty was overruled and the students reinstated. Pres. Rice and wife resigned, also some of the Board. Trustees transcended their power. Prof. Satchwell was elected to the Chair of Mathematics, and salary to be $1000.00, and Dr. Davis was elected Pres. until Conference.[30]

This mystery is cleared up by Albert R. Robinson in a statement made in 1908-09 concerning his two years in Baker, 1867-69. In regard to the latter year he wrote:

In the fall of 1868, the school had grown considerably and some new teachers were employed. . . .

The petty regulations about rising at 5 A.M., study hours at 1 and 7 P.M., retiring at 9 P.M., exactly how and when the young should mend their stockings and lingerie, and the proper distance to sit away from gentlemen callers; these began to be rather irksome. The students petitioned that these rules be modified, but were only met with a regular tirade of criticism, to put it mildly, morning after morning in chapel. Finally six of us got up and left chapel one morning during one of these tirades.

We were promptly suspended, but staid in town and interviewed all the Trustees we could get hold of. In two or three weeks we got a meeting of the Trustees and were reinstated. The President and most of the teachers resigned as they naturally would.

This is an episode that I have always regretted. It did us no good and the school a decided harm.[31]

The relation of the Kansas Education Association and Baker was not always clear or helpful. The Association was formed originally to manage all of the educational efforts of the Methodist Episcopal Church in Kansas. For example, Hartford Collegiate Institute, a preparatory school, and Ottumwa College were under its supervision, as well as other efforts. In later years it was retained as a holding company for the benefit of Baker because of the unusual tax-exemption privileges in the charter. During the early years it was not always clear as to what group controlled the school; was it the Association or the Trustees?

The darkest days of Baker were in the early 1870's. Notes which had been given by the Trustees to a professor, were sold to a man who brought suit in court to collect. As a result of a court order, college property was auctioned off for small amounts to raise $580! The Trustees appointed a special Investigating Committee and a like investigation was carried on by the Kansas Annual Conference.[32] Also, offers and suggestions for moving the school were made—Olathe offered $50,000. The conclusion came at the Annual Conferences in 1874, when the Commission reported to each conference:

They had looked carefully over the records and books of ten years, and their report was an able showing of the history of the college. Many had confidently expected that fraud would be found, but they were of the opinion that mistakes, not frauds, had crippled Baker University. It had been unfortunate in its connection with the Kansas Educational Association. They were also of the opinion that its location was good, and should not be changed.[33]

In spite of the grasshopper invasion of 1874, good

times returned under the leadership of President Joseph Denison, former president of Kansas State Agricultural College, 1874-79, and President W. H. Sweet.

OTHER EDUCATIONAL CONTRIBUTIONS

Before concluding the consideration of Methodism and education in early Kansas, mention must be made of the additional contributions of certain Methodists to other educational efforts in addition to colleges and preparatory schools. White as well as Indian children were included in the first free school established on July 1, 1844, at Wyandotte. The second such school was that of the Methodists at Council Grove, begun by T. S. Huffaker in May, 1851. Most of the early schools, after 1854, were voluntary and not supported by the city or state. Each of the earliest constitutions, however, called for a state system of education.

Especially to a Methodist layman, Isaac T. Goodnow, the people of Kansas owe a great debt. This promoter of Manhattan, Bluemont College and Kansas State Agricultural College, was also a great driving force behind public school education. Late in 1862 he was elected State Superintendent of Public Instruction and re-elected in 1863.

When the Kansas State Teachers Association was organized, September 29 to October 1, 1863, the man elected as the first president was Isaac T. Goodnow. Two of the vice presidents were Dr. Werter R. Davis, formerly of Baker, and Rev. Joseph Denison, then President of Kansas State Agricultural College. These two Methodists also served on the executive committee of five.[34]

By 1880 no college or university in Kansas was firmly established. Most of the 30 colleges incorporated, 1855-1860, had failed. The two state universities were still small. The Presbyterians with Highland, the Congregationalists with Washburn, and the Baptists with Ottawa, had laid permanent foundations. The United Brethren effort at Lecompton in Lane University, would later be merged with another school. The Methodists made an auspicious start at Bluemont in Manhattan which was turned over to the state. In Baker University they made a permanent establishment that was to have a great future.

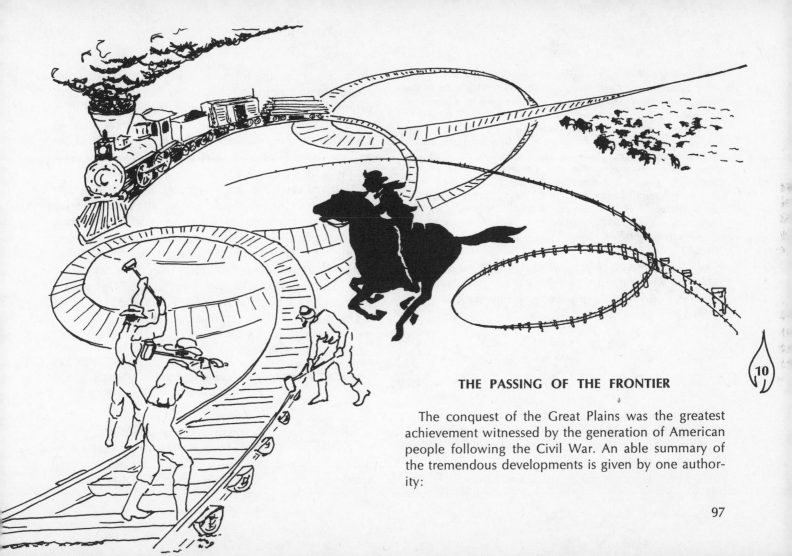

THE PASSING OF THE FRONTIER

The conquest of the Great Plains was the greatest achievement witnessed by the generation of American people following the Civil War. An able summary of the tremendous developments is given by one authority:

97

The roaring vitality, the cascading energy of the American people in the post-war years are nowhere better illustrated than in the history of the West. The generation after the Civil War witnessed the most extensive movement of population in our history; a hundred per cent increase in the settled area; the rapid social and economic development of this population from primitive conditions to contemporary standards to civilization; the final disappearance of the wild Indian; the rise and fall of the mineral empire and of the cattle kingdom; the emergence of new types of agriculture and of economic life articulated to the geography and climate of the High Plains and the Rocky Mountains; and the organization of a dozen new states with a taste for social and political experiments.[1]

The government census returns for the years 1860-1880, showed the unusual growth of population in Trans-Missouri during the years following the great conflict:[2]

	1860	1870	1880
Missouri	1,163,489	1,712,295	3,168,380
Kansas	107,206	364,399	996,096
Nebraska	28,841	122,993	452,402

One of the main reasons for the great influx of settlers was the passage of three federal laws during the Civil War: The Homestead Act, the Morrill Land-grant Act, and the Pacific Railway Act which gave the Central Pacific and Union Pacific, and later others, princely domains. According to the first act, each actual settler could obtain a farm of 160 acres by living on and cultivating the land. The Morrill Land-grant Act gave each state 30,000 acres of land for each member it had in Congress for the endowment of colleges of agriculture and mechanical arts. The Railway Bill gave the Union Pacific and Central Pacific, in addition to loans, ten sections of land per mile through all territories traversed, and ten sections within all states. Lesser amounts were given to other railroads.[3] The total amounts of public land given were as follows: Union Pacific—20 million acres; Central and Southern Pacific systems—24 million acres; Santa Fe—17 million acres and Northern Pacific—44 million acres. (This represents an area given almost as large as Texas.)[4]

This period in the west might well be called the railroad era. In Kansas in 1865 the state had only 71 miles of track in use. By 1870 this total had risen to 1,234, and by 1880 it reached 3,104. In 1890, Kansas had 8,763 miles, but after that date the increase was almost imperceptible.[5]

The future of most towns in the west was dependent on the location of railroads while many cities owed their existence to them. The railroads not only became arteries of commerce, but by selling land they induced people to settle, thus increasing the overall trade.

So dependent were towns on the location of railroads that the uncertainty of their coming and operation were a source of continued apprehension. A missionary at Oswego explains the situation thus:

> One of the greatest hinderances to the progress of religion in these new towns is the uncertainty of their permanence.
>
> In almost every instance the growth and prosperity of them depend on their securing a railroad. When a town is started with this idea in view by the exaggerated statements of unscrupulous speculators, immigrants rush to the place from all parts of the country expecting to make a fortune in a short time. For the first year or two if the town continues so long, business is lively, done under the stimulous of excitement; and fabulous prices are paid for "corner lots."
>
> Everything goes on swimmingly until fears are entertained that the anticipated railroad will fail them. . . .⁶

The railroad was partly responsible for the different types of towns. This was aptly described in 1870 by the Congregationalist agent in Nebraska:

> It is doubtless exceedingly difficult for the friends at the East . . . to understand the demands and the hopes of the various church enterprises set on foot. . . . I propose to classify our different stations & describe each class. . . .
>
> I. The Prematurely Old.
>
> Churches and places with this peculiarity are decidedly western. To look upon them causes much the same sensation as the sight of wrinkles on a baby. . . .
>
> II. Fever and Ague Towns.
>
> By this term I would designate those places which have regularly in alternation growth and stagnation. . . . The occasion of their peculiar condition is owning mainly to the movements of R.R. companies or to the influx of emigration and the lack of these influences. The R.R. officials determine upon some temporary work to be performed. Men are sent to do it, rents immediately advance, buildings are at once erected, mechanics are therefore plenty. Grocers and dry goods men come in swarms and thrive. Soon the work is done the traders fall to eating one another, the town becomes decimated. . . .
>
> III. Towns healthful and vigorous.
>
> These are at once most desirable and most discouraging, most hopeful and most difficult. Success tends to irreligion. . . . Public Spirit will build a church to save a decaying village when the pastor of a thriving town appeals in vain for funds. . . .
>
> IV. Infant Enterprises.
>
> . . . Last year there were 5,000,000 acres of land uninhabited which are now being entered as homesteads. . . . Towns of six months . . . build a home each day. . . . Yet these new fields are as expensive as they are important. . . .⁷

The Indian wars of the late 1860's added to the excitement and uncertainty in the settlers' advance toward the western parts of Kansas and Nebraska.

Partly due to the often bungling policy of the government the Indians were often "on the warpath," and military campaigns against them were necessary to bring about a return to peace.

After the Civil War, Kansas, for the first time, enjoyed a period of comparative quiet and prosperity despite the grasshopper scourge of 1874. The most notable achievement of the religious forces was the work under the leadership of the Presbyterian missionary superintendent, Timothy Hill, during the decade following the reunion of 1869. The results of Hill's organizing and executive abilities are shown in his report of 1880:

> If we go further back . . . and take the minutes of 1870, we find there were seventy-three ministers, eighty-nine churches, and 3,762 members. In 1880 there were one hundred and seventy-four ministers, two hundred and seventy-four churches, 11,259 members. . . . In 1870 . . . we had one member . . . to every one hundred and thirty persons. In 1880 . . . one member to every eighty-eight persons.[8]

Some of this advance was made at the expense of the Congregationalists, who were not able to maintain the strong position they had acquired in the opening years of Kansas settlement.

The disastrous effects of denominational competition was emphasized in letters from different parts of the state—Highland, Manhattan, Emporia, Topeka, Leavenworth and Neodesha.[9] The competition of Presbyterians and Congregationalists in the west finally resulted in a fraternal conference by the two missionary boards, but no definite accomplishments were achieved. At an early date the General Association recognized that the itinerant system best met the needs of the west and in 1867 they suggested to the American Home Missionary Society a change to some such system.[10] Of course the chief reason for Congregational difficulties was that fewer emigrants came from the states where that denomination was strong.

Other churches—Methodist Episcopal, Baptist and Disciple—all surpassed these two denominations in the increase of membership, and by 1880 they were the unquestioned dominant groups. In a former chapter attention has been called to the comparative failure of the Baptists in Kansas during the years preceding 1865. Although the American Baptist Home Mission Society in 1873 admitted that "in no State have your Board accomplished less as compared with what needed to be done," there was a rapid advance in the years just preceding 1880.[11] In 1866 less than 1,000 members were listed while in 1880 the total was nearly 18,000.[12] During the same period the Disciples added about the same number.

The scarcity of timber in Trans-Missouri and the difficulties which such a condition caused have been noted. Many of the churches erected on the treeless plains would never have been built had not the larger denominations created national societies to alleviate the situation. The first denomination to provide such an organization was the Old School Presbyterians. In 1843-44 a national Church Extension Committee was created and during its first eight years of existence it aided in completing 281 church edifices. During the period, 1856-70, this committee assisted 241 churches in Trans-Missouri alone: Kansas, 29; Missouri, 57; Nebraska, 6; and Iowa, 112.[13] A similar organization, the American Congregational Union, was one of the important results of the Albany Convention of American Congregationalism in 1852. From its beginning the Congregational Union's main task was "the payment of 'last bills' after needy churches have done all in their power to provide themselves with buildings." [14] Two years after the above action of the Congregationalists, the Baptist Home Mission Society created a Church Edifice Fund to lend and donate money to struggling churches. Practically all the Baptist Churches erected in the west in this early period were aided by this fund.[15] It was not until 1864 that the Methodist General Conference took similar action in creating the Church Extension Society. During the 16 years following its establishment the society aided 382 churches in Trans-Missouri with loans amounting to $77,075 and donations of $87,896.63.[16] Without the aid of such national organizations these denominations could never have been as successful as they were in the newly settled regions.

Before the close of this period (1880), a new wave of homeseekers was sweeping into the region. Attracted by the great opportunities pictured in the publicity material issued by the railroads, the states and private companies, a large number of immigrants from the Scandinavian countries, Germany and Russia came seeking the "promised land."

A picture of the numerical standing of the larger denominational groups in 1880 is given in the following table: [17]

	Missouri	Kansas	Nebraska
Methodist Episcopal (1879)	33,795	33,744	11,230
Baptist	95,967	17,648	4,855
Disciples	65,950	20,000	6,300
Presbyterian (U.S.A.)	10,976	11,532	4,340
Congregational	3,963	6,428	6,300
Methodist Episcopal, South	55,864	2,952	111

"EXODUSTERS"

During this period before 1882, African Methodist Churches were organized in Leavenworth, 1861; Topeka, Olathe, Paola and Atchison, 1868; Council Grove, 1871; Hiawatha, 1872; Holton and Garnett, 1874; Parsons, 1876; and in the following years at Junction City, Fort Scott, Girard, Wichita, Oswego, Chetopa, Burlington, and Osage City.[18] The Reverend John Wilkenson organized the churches in Topeka and Atchison, as well as the one at Lawrence. One of the largest of the A.M.E. Churches was at Wyandotte City, organized in 1880. Two years later it had a membership of 275.[19]

The greatest movement of Negroes began in 1878. The removal of federal troops from the South during the late 1870's frightened many Negroes into moving North. Further lured also by the false promise of "forty acres and a mule," nearly 20,000 Negroes came to Kansas in four years. In 1870 the Negro population in Kansas was 17,108 but in 1880 it was 43,107. In these years emancipated Negroes, known as "Exodusters," flocked to Kansas. One of the leaders of the emigrants from Tennessee was Benjamin (Pap) Singleton who styled himself as the father of the exodus and claimed that he led more than 7,000 from Tennessee. His main colonies were at Dunlap, Singleton and Nicodemus.[20]

BENJAMIN "PAP" SINGLETON

102

Beginning in 1879, 7,000 Exodusters came to Topeka alone, by boat up the Missouri to Kansas City, Missouri, and Wyandotte, Kansas, mostly from Mississippi and Tennessee. In 1880 Negro residents were 31% of the population of Topeka. About 3,000 remained in Topeka and settled in "Tennesseetown." Large numbers were encouraged to settle in other places in Kansas.[21]

FOREIGN IMMIGRATION

In 1860 there were already more than 12,000 foreign-born people among the population of 107,000 in Kansas. Of this 12,000 a little more than a fourth were Germans and nearly one-half were born in Great Britain or Ireland. In the next ten years the German element increased four times and by 1880 they numbered over 28,000.[22] In addition, the 8,082 Russians listed that year were largely Teutonic and not Slavic in origin. (They were the Germans who had gone to Crimea after 1783 and moved from Russia due to discrimination under Tsar Nicholas I, 1825-1855, a slavophil ultra-conservative.)

GERMAN METHODISM

Germans in eastern United States, and especially the followers of Carl Shurz, had a great interest in the early struggle in Kansas. Many Europeans had left their homelands after the revolutions of 1848 because of their concern for democratic freedom and a struggle against autocracy.

Methodist work among the German element was never numerically strong, but that group has made an unusual contribution as they have become a part of Methodism and given up their separate identity.

The starting point for Germans in Kansas was Leavenworth. In 1855 Rev. Carl Langer was in that city, having received as his appointment—"Kansas and Nebraska (Leavenworth City)."[23] The first German Methodist church building in Kansas was consecrated in Leavenworth August 29, 1858.

The 1859 and 1860 appointments and reports of the Missouri District of the Illinois Conference include, in addition to Leavenworth: Wyandot, George Shaz, 29 members; Lawrence, John Miller, 28 members; Fort Riley, Charles Stuckemann, 38 members; Columbus, August Meche, 8 members.[24] The list of preachers is entitled "New Powers in our borders." Church property at Wyandot in 1860 was valued at $1,500. From 1860 to 1864 this total work was under the direction of the Kansas German District, Jacob Feisel, Presiding Elder.

The General Conference of 1864 responded to the

requests of the German preachers, supported by others, to separate the German work from the English Conferences. As a result, three conferences were authorized: The Central German, the Northwest German, and the Southwest German. The work in Kansas was thereby a part of the latter conference, which convened for its first session, September 29, 1864, in St. Louis. Fourteen years later this conference was divided into two conferences, by authority given in 1876. Kansas work was in the new West German Conference which included Nebraska and Colorado, and the western part of Iowa and Missouri.[25]

Mention has already been made of the earliest German churches. The Wyandot church continued to grow, erected a building in 1866, ($4,000) and by about 1880 had 147 members; the church at Topeka was organized in 1870, and a building was erected the next year ($3,000).[26] Several German Methodist families moved to Wichita in 1876 and they applied to the Presiding Elder for a preacher. Rev. P. W. Matthaei was sent to them and the first meeting was held in a schoolhouse (Emporia Avenue and Third Street), in May, 1876. He soon had a small class.

However, other denominations also turned an eye to the promising fields. So it happened on one Sunday morning that the other half of the schoolhouse (for it was divided by a partition-wall, but had only one vestibule) was moved into by another denomination. The preacher took a position in the hall and when anyone wanted to go to the Methodist side he said: "You don't want to fall from the faith, do you?" But it didn't work. Brother Mathai carried off the victory, and the other preacher had to move out. Brother Mathai now made himself efficient in missionary work, not only in the city of Wichita where he was a resident, but also in the surrounding area. They say of him even today that no German family lived within a circumference of 100 miles whom he did not know. At one time he preached at ten different places in seven different counties.[27]

During the next year Matthaei was stationed in Wichita and in the succeeding year took in 78 members. In 1878 the first church building was erected. Calvary

P. W. MATTHAEI

CALVARY METHODIST CHURCH

Methodist Church, as it is known today, has had an illustrious career. To be noted is the fact that 20 young men have come into the Methodist ministry out of this one church, including Raymond E. Dewey, George W. Richards and Franklyn Edwards. The son of P. W. Matthaei, the first minister, and the grandson, Paul Matthaei, have also served as Methodist ministers in Kansas.[28]

UNITED BRETHREN

The growth of the United Brethren work in Missouri and Kansas made it seem wise to establish a new conference. Therefore, at their General Conference of 1869, provision was made for creating the Osage Conference in addition to the Kansas Conference. At their 1871 session they decided not to establish a college of their own and "acquiesced" to the biblical institute at Dayton agreeing to help support it as soon as possible.

Other resolutions adopted . . . included those decrying spiritualism . . . abandonment of the use of tobacco by ministers, and one saying that ministers should not sell tobacco. . . .[29]

As a visitor to the conference, along with Bishop Dickson, the presiding officer, came the agent of the denomination's publishing house, Rev. W. J. Shuey.

He and the Bishop roomed together in an early day Kansas home.

. . . on retiring to their room one night, speaking of the Conference, Bishop Dickson was heard to heave a sigh, and say, "Small potatoes." Shuey heaved another sigh, and echoed, "Few to a hill." [30]

By 1881 the total membership of the United Brethren Conference was given as 3,312—quite an increase over the 894 represented by the "small potatoes" in 1871. At this session the report to the Conference from Union Biblical Seminary indicated that it had an annual deficit of $4,500. In response they voted that they could not see "the propriety and certainly not the economy of employing three professors besides the president at an aggregate salary of $4,200 per year." [31]

Comparative figures of 1857 and of the totals for the four United Brethren conferences in 1882 are interesting:

	1857	1882	
Ministers	8	147	(1/3 local)
Appointments	27	465	
Members	196	7,427	
Sunday Schools	5	180	
Sunday School Scholars	172	6,133	
Meeting Houses	0	39[32]	

METHODIST PROTESTANT

Early endeavors of the Methodist Protestant people in Kansas go back to the late 1860's. The Rev. Samuel Young tells of the long journey of a colony of Methodist Protestants from West Virginia that began early in 1860. This group of sixty built a flat boat on a river and on it erected residences. Down two rivers to the Ohio River they floated and on to its mouth, and up the Mississippi to the Missouri River. They were then towed up the Missouri River to Kansas City from which point they made their way by land to Olathe, in Johnson County. Here they settled, organized a Methodist Protestant Church, and erected a house of worship. Their pastor, Rev. Young, followed them to Kansas.[33]

About 1867, under the leadership of the Rev. Moses Jared, a missionary, efforts began shaping up for a permanent church organization in Kansas. Apparently the first conference was held in either 1868 or 1870. Methodist Protestant statistics for Kansas in 1877, included the following: 37 itinerant ministers, 32 unstationed ministers, 1,542 members, one church and one parsonage ($1,440).[34] By 1880 there were two conferences—Kansas and North Kansas—and the membership had grown to 2,000 in the former and 593 in the latter conference and the total number of preachers was 47.[35]

EVANGELICAL ASSOCIATION

Several eastern conferences of the Evangelical Association came alive to the needs of the German people in Kansas in the year 1858. In that year the Illinois Conference sent the Rev. G. Berner and the Rev. G. G. Fleischer to Kansas. As indicated earlier, Fleischer began his work at Franklin. During the same year, the Ohio Conference sent out the Rev Michael J. Miller and the Rev. Philip Porr (the latter was assigned to western Missouri but itinerated around Hiawatha). Brother Miller began his efforts in Leavenworth but soon extended them widely to include Atchison, Lawrence, Monrovia, Grasshopper Falls (later Valley Falls). The first church building was at Holton, with R. Dubs as pastor.[36]

In accordance with the action of the General Conference of the Evangelical Association in 1863, the Kansas Conference was established. The following year the appointments for the Kansas Conference and its one district were as follows:

Kansas District—M. J. Miller, P.E.
Leavenworth and Lawrence—J. F. Schreiber
Humboldt—P. Fricker

Holton—S. W. McKesson
Arago and Rock Port—C. Berner and J. Scherer
West Kansas Mission—to be supplied.[37]

At the first session of the Kansas Conference which was held in Leavenworth, beginning May 26, 1865, scarcely 200 lay members were reported. By 1880, there were 25 congregations organized into two districts, and in 1900, the membership was nearly 5,000.[38]

FREE METHODISTS

Much of the leadership of the Free Methodists in early Kansas came from a former minister of the Methodist Episcopal Church, the Rev. C. H. Lovejoy. He had been identified with the Kansas Conference of the Methodist Episcopal Church in its earliest pioneer days, at Manhattan, Baldwin, and elsewhere. By 1867, however, he was a leader in the Free Methodist Church.

In that year a "Missouri and Kansas District" was named, with C. H. Lovejoy as chairman and Lawrence was the one appointment in Kansas. Three years later a "Kansas and Missouri Conference" was established by the General Conference of the Free Methodist Church and the first session was held in March, 1871. The total membership in Kansas and Missouri was only 463.[39] Finally, in 1882, two conferences in Kansas—Kansas and West Kansas—were established. There were 29 preachers and 414 members in the former conference, and 10 preachers and 382 members in the latter.

METHODIST EPISCOPAL CHURCH, SOUTH

The war brought to an end the Kansas Mission Conference, 1855-1861. Little could be accomplished by this group during the war years. In January, 1866, four of the former preachers, including Nathan Scarritt, met at the old Shawnee Mission. At the request of these men and others, the territory of the old Kansas Mission Conference was divided between the St. Louis Conference and the Missouri Conference. Two districts were formed—Kansas City and Leavenworth—one in each of the conferences. In 1867 the membership for both districts was estimated to be 943, including 62 colored.[40]

The 1870 General Conference of the Southern Church authorized the Western Annual Conference to "include the States of Kansas, Nebraska, Colorado and the Territories of Wyoming, Montana and Idaho, and any other territory east of the Rocky Mountains and west of the Missouri State line not included in other conferences. Journal of General Conference of

107

1870, pp. 296 and 346." [41]

In the reports of this first session the two districts reported a total of 1,535 members. The membership of the larger churches or circuits in the St. Joseph District was as follows: Oskaloosa Circuit—187; Wyandotte Circuit—150; Holton Circuit—124; Leavenworth Circuit—106; Leavenworth Station—104 (E. R. Hendrix, later a bishop, was the preacher); Nebraska Station—99; and Troy circuit—77. The Kansas District had fewer appointments but larger memberships: Council Grove—180; Shawnee circuit—175; "Leavenworth Col. Dist."—133 colored members; and Paola circuit—64. [42] In the Western Conference five years later, 1875, the total membership had increased to 2,359, and in 1880 the total was 3,063, including 111 members in the Nebraska Station. [43]

METHODIST EPISCOPAL

The late 1860's and the 1870's were years of tremendous growth for the Methodist Episcopal Church. By the end of the war in 1865, the denomination had over 4,000 members to report, even though the Colorado Conference had been organized the year before out of the Kansas Conference. By 1873 the number had grown to nearly 19,000. As a result of this growth, a new conference, South Kansas, was authorized by the General Conference and began its activities in 1874. Four years later the new conference had 16,633 members and the mother conference 12,418 members. [44]

Not always known or admitted by the self-sufficient conferences of today is the fact that the churches of their conferences were in the beginning the recipients of missionary giving from the older areas. This has been true of nearly all Methodist work on any frontier at home or abroad, both in the past and today. This missionary help was certainly beneficial during the first twenty years of Methodist life in Kansas. In the annual reports of Domestic Missions appropriations, the following amounts were indicated: for Kansas and Nebraska in 1857—$10,000; in 1858—$9,500; 1859 and 1860—$9,000 each year; for Kansas alone: $7,900—1865; $12,500—1866; $14,000—1867; $10,000—1868; a little less from 1869 to 1874, but still $9,000 for the two conferences in 1875. [45]

RESPONSE TO HARDSHIPS

Crises were the usual order of the day in Kansas. The conflicts of the 1850's were succeeded by the drouth of 1860 and the Civil War. In less than ten years there was another surprising blow—the grasshopper plague. In August, 1874, literally millions of the pests swept over Kansas. One witness described the situation as follows:

The sides of the house and the walks were covered with them. They flew up like a swarm of bees at one's step. They had the most voracious appetites of any living thing. One or two would begin on a melon; as the place grew larger others came, and the melon would soon be eaten down to a shell. Onions and beets were a luxury to them, but my husband saved ours by turning a furrow over them. The corn was destroyed down to the stalk, and farmers began cutting to save it for fodder. The crop was a poor one anyway that year, for lack of rain. The grasshoppers stayed so long that they destroyed the newly sowed fields of wheat. . . . We could get mosquito netting at that time, and we had the windows and doors screened. The netting went, like other things, down the throats of the pests, and I had to keep the windows closed. It was difficult even to save the clothes on the line; anything on the grass would surely go. When the "hoppers" went they left destruction over the state.[46]

More than 30,000 residents were in dire need. Nevertheless, a sense of humor did not fail them.

It is said that in the midst of that overwhelming disaster, when the pests were six inches deep in the streets, the editor of a certain local paper confined his comment on the situation down to a single line, which appeared among the trivial happenings of the week: "A grasshopper was seen on the court-house steps this morning."[47]

Following the grasshopper plague, people in the east responded to the call for help from Kansas with food, supplies and money. An example of such action was the case of the United Brethren preacher, George Gay, who wrote to Michigan friends after the invasion, describing the plight of the people.

A carload of goods—fruits, potatoes, clothing—and $75 in cash was received. Father Gay invited the nearby families to share. Clothing was hung on clothes lines and families filed past and made selections that would fit their needs. Altogether, $9,500 in goods and money was received by this conference.[48]

Missionary barrels were a common practice and a means of assisting needy preachers and their families. Some good things were sent, but not always. Following the receipt of such a barrel, a Congregationalist missionary wrote, in part:

... there are three nice dress coats *all* quite small for me—though I *can* wear them. ...

Then nine (9) vests are rather more than my share—especially as I cannot wear one of them except as it is enlarged or made over.

Besides a jaunty little "love of a bonnet" for my tall and rather large wife, there were nine (9) hats for our two girls—most of them very nice. ...[49]

REVIVALS AND CAMP MEETINGS

Effective in Kansas as they had been on earlier frontiers were revivals and camp meetings. Some were union efforts, such as the one in Manhattan in 1867, in which four denominations joined:

... the four pastors of the churches uniting preached alternately every evening for about three weeks, & prayer & Inquiry meetings were held every afternoon.
The Methodist Church has received on probation about 125. ... From fifty to sixty others will probably unite with the other churches, as the fruits of this revival.[50]

The response to Methodist meetings, however, was not always favorable, as indicated in two letters in the summer and fall of 1866:

The Methodists have held a protracted meeting in the village, just closed, in which they gathered into their church about forty new members. ... Their meetings were the most objectionable of all the religious meetings I have ever witnessed, exceeding noisy and disorderly. The Methodists here take into their membership all who express a desire to "get religion."
The Methodists have had one of their iron-clad preachers here who has held meetings every eve nearly the whole quarter & has got up a large amount of spurious excitement. Many of the young men who have usually attended our service have for the time attended these meetings—"to see the circus," as they express it. This brushwood burning of the sensibilities is about over & they are generally coming back to our meeting. ...[51]

That the Methodists promoted the revivals and usually profited more is seen in the Congregational minister's account of the revival in Olathe in mid-winter, 1870-71:

This city has been blessed with an extensive revival during the winter and our church shared the visitation of the Spirit. The work commenced in the Methodist Church. ... We never had the crowd; that was always attracted to the more exciting scenes at the Methodist Church. ... The influence of the revival in the town is very great. Religion has been the prevailing topic of conversation, anybody could be approached. Everybody expected to be approached on the subject. The liquor traffic, which had become a terrible scourge here received a damaging blow and we have strong hope of putting an end to it at the Spring elections. You will have some notion of the extent of this work when you consider that three churches held meetings daily through mid-winter, that more than 200 have professed conversion—one hundred and seventy joining the Methodist Church alone.[52]

A number of camp meetings were held in various places, according to accounts in the issues of the *Central Christian Advocate*. In 1866 one was held at Winchester and another at Hiawatha. A minister in Hiawatha described the meeting there and closed with an interesting comment:

. . . The power that overshadowed the people was so great that some fell like dead men, and lay in this situation for nearly an hour. . . . I have received in the church up to this time 44, and most of them were converted. . . .[53]

For a dramatic result, note this meeting held by a United Brethren minister, George Gay, at Mulvane, Kansas, in 1872:

. . . A desperado, McKinney by name, decided to break it up. He put on his guns with the boast that he was going to be good for twelve of them at the meeting. Arriving at the church, he seated himself in the back of the church. Gay was warned of the man and was told of his reputation and his intentions. He answered that he would preach that night if the devil himself were in the pews. He preached and after the sermon McKinney left without a word or malicious act. The next night he came again, taking a front seat. When the altar call was given, he was the first one at the altar, asking that the Lord forgive "as big a rebel as ever lived."

After his conversion, McKinney felt called to preach. He went to Winfield and preached in the streets. He was picked up for being a nuisance, and was placed in jail. Since the jail was on the main street, he preached through the window. Some of the citizens

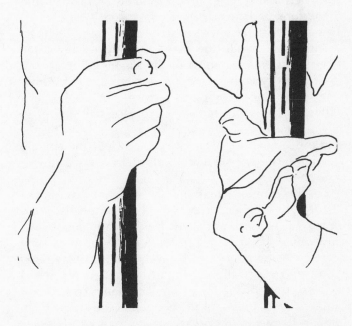

heard him, obtained his release, and started a tabernacle. During the meeting which followed, between 300 and 400 were converted. This was the beginning of Winfield United Brethren Church.[54]

Annual camp meetings became popular because of the desire and the need for social fellowship. It was an occasion which people looked forward to during the year because it was an opportunity to renew old friendships and meet new settlers from "back east." The church service came as a relief from the past week's work, while the camp meeting usually came after the strenuous labors of the summer. The service itself often served as an important link for the homesick settler since it was one element not wholly new. Although divine worship was often necessarily informal, it was similar to that "back home"; the same hymns and the same order of worship were used. The church, being the center of the life of its members, was therefore cherished.

On this frontier where political questions were constantly demanding consideration, where the satisfaction of even simple economic needs was nearly impossible, and where moral standards were easily lowered, only a vital religion could live. That the various denominations, and especially Methodists, supplied that need was attested by their growth and their consequent influence in the lives of the people. In the life of these early settlements the preacher, as a part of the community, had a fundamental task to perform. To combat the discouragements, failures, privations and loneliness he attempted to bring joy, hope, encouragement and faith. Amid the precarious and constantly changing scene the minister attempted to turn the thoughts of the sturdy pioneers toward that which is eternal and changeless.

CARRY A. NATION

ENTERPRISE SALOONS SMASHED
BY CARRY NATION—1901

TEMPERANCE AND PUBLIC MORALS

The Methodists of Kansas have had definite ideas on temperance and other moral questions, as they did on slavery and political issues. That these matters were of great concern is quite evident both in the record of their individual lives and in the official stands taken by the Church locally and in the Annual Conference.

113

Before the settlement of Kansas, on the earlier frontiers west of the Alleghanies,

incredible quantities of whiskey were consumed, everybody, women and preachers included, drinking the fiery liquid. A bottle was in every cabin—to offer it was the first gesture of welcome, to refuse unpardonable incivility. All used tobacco, chewing, smoking, snuffing; and corn-cob pipes in the mouths of women were a not uncommon sight. Men were quick to fight and combats were brutal. Profanity was general and emphatic.[1]

For a time Abraham Lincoln clerked at a store in New Salem,

. . . where everybody came on Saturdays to trade, gossip, wrestle, raffle, pitch horseshoes, run races, get drunk, maul one another with their fists, and indulge, generally, in frontier happiness, as a relief from the week's monotonous drudgery on the raw and difficult farms.[2]

Confirming this is a statement by Peter Cartwright, famous circuit rider and presiding elder of the Methodist Episcopal Church in Ohio, Indiana and Illinois for fifty years just prior to the settlement of Kansas:

From my earliest recollection drinking drams, in family and social circles, was considered harmless and allowable socialities. It was almost universally the custom for preachers, in common with all others, to take drams; and if a man would not have it in his family, his harvest, his house-raisings, log-rollings, weddings, and so on, he was considered parsimonious and unsociable; and many, even professors of Christianity, would not help a man if he did not have spirits and treat the company.[3]

Methodism's founder, John Wesley, took a strong stand on temperance and other moral questions, just as he had on slavery. Indeed, he was ahead of others. As early as 1743, he inserted into the General Rules for the guidance of his societies one rule which prohibited "drunkenness, buying or selling spiritous liquors, or drinking them, unless in cases of extreme necessity." Not only did he make a rule but he enforced it. In one year he excluded seventeen members from one of his societies for drinking and retailing spiritous liquors.[4] In dealing with the scarcity of food in a pamphlet in 1773, he again condemned the making and use of this "liquid fire" when he wrote:

Why is food so dear? The grand cause is because such immense quantities of corn are continually consumed by distilling. Add all the distilleries throughout England, and have we not reason to believe that little less than half the wheat produced in the kingdom is every year consumed, not by so harmless a way as throwing it into the sea, but by converting it into deadly poison, that naturally destroys not only the strength and life, but also the morals, of our countrymen.[5]

In the new world, the conference of 1780 and 1783 asserted an attitude similar to that of their founder. The latter conference forbade the members to "manufacture, sell, or drink any intoxicating liquors." [6] At its beginning, the Methodist Episcopal Church adopted Wesley's rule on temperance. Only six years later, however, similar to the action on slavery, the rule was relaxed with the elimination of the words, "buying and selling." The discipline of the United Brethren Church in one article, provided in 1814 that "every member shall abstain from strong drink and use it only on necessity as medicine." [7]

Attempts were made to restore the original prohibition in the 1830's and again in 1844, but with no success. State and national temperance societies were organized early, and by 1833 one national group had over one million members.[8] Finally, in 1848, Wesley's original rule was restored by the General Conference of the Methodist Episcopal Church by an overwhelming vote.

In Kansas, the interest of Methodists in temperance in any organized way, goes back to the temperance society formed by the Wyandots as early as 1844-45. The motivation for this came as the response to the action of a number of intoxicated Indians through whose negligence a prominent member of the tribe lost his goods in the Missouri River. The society at one time had forty members.[9]

Little time was lost by the new government of the Kansas Territory in trying to control the liquor traffic with Indians. An early act prohibited the selling, giving or bartering of liquor to any Indian or reservation, unless directed by a physician. The penalty for violation was a $200-$500 fine and a prison term of one to six months. For the same purpose a new law was passed later in March, 1862, by the new state government. This provided for a fine of $50-$500 and/or a term of three to twelve months. It passed both houses unanimously.[10]

In the early free state towns official action was taken toward prohibition. This was true of Topeka, Emporia, Ottawa, Baldwin and Lawrence. The latter city was the leader due to the urging of the Congregational and Methodist clergy and church members. There was probably more liquor in towns settled by Southerners, but the first anti-liquor act of March 8, 1855, was passed by a pro-slavery body. To the surprise of many today the manufacture of liquor was an early Kansas industry —there were three or four breweries in Leavenworth by the end of 1857.[11] Of course, some may have insisted that liquor was needed—a pint or quart—to neutralize the effects of a rattle snake bite.

The concern of Methodist ministers in regard to liquor and tobacco is clearly seen in the reports of the Committee on Temperance approved by the Kansas and Nebraska Annual Conference in the early years, 1856-1860, and of the Kansas Conference, 1861.[12]

The first resolve of the Committee on Temperance in 1856 was: "That we give king alcohol no quarters within our bounds." Tobacco came in for condemnation in 1857 as

a baneful poison unnatural to the human system, destructive to health and often to life . . . we will hereby recommend to all members and probationers of the Conference to desist from the use of it.

In 1858 it was recommended: "that our efforts among the people shall be directed to the passage and sustaining of prohibitory liquor law in our Territories" and in regard to tobacco we: "cannot but regret that any of our ministers or lay members should indulge in the use of the vile and poisonous 'weed.'" At the first session of the Kansas Conference, 1861, it was urged: "That Christians carry their temperance principles to the ballot box with them."

The Civil War and its accompanying uncertainties stimulated the use of liquor and there was a loss in the membership of temperance organizations nationally. There was a phenomenal increase in the capital in-

vested in the manufacture of liquor in the United States during the succeeding years 1860-1900: 1860—over $28 1/2 million; 1870—over $66 1/2 million; 1880—$118 million; 1890—nearly $270 million; and 1900—over $450 1/2 million.[13]

To meet the demands of the liquor threat there was a renaissance of the temperance movement late in the sixties and in the seventies. Established organizations increased their memberships. For example, the Independent Order of Good Templars, after a drop during the war, rose from a membership of nearly 76,000 in 1865, to 168,548 in 1866, and to 433,000 in 1873.[14] In 1869 the Prohibition Party was organized to be followed in 1873 by the Woman's Temperance Crusade. Later the same year came the formation of the Woman's Christian Temperance Union with Frances E. Willard, a Methodist, at its head. Within twenty years there were W.C.T.U. local organizations in every state and territory.[15]

Methodist response was likewise forceful. The General Conference of the Methodist Episcopal Church in 1868 voted:

We hail every legal measure to effectually restrain and extirpate this chief crime against society, and trust the law of prohibition may yet be the enactment of every State, and of the National Congress and be successfully executed throughout our republic.[16]

FRANCES E. WILLARD

H. D. FISHER

Reverend H. D. Fisher, Methodist minister, presiding elder and army chaplain, proposed an action of significance in 1867, as president of the Kansas State Temperance Society. He offered the first resolution to a convention in any state

memorializing the legislature of the State of Kansas to submit the question of legal prohibition by constitutional amendment and enactment to a vote of the people . . . but it failed by a small vote." [17]

Chaplain Fisher was ten years ahead of his time.

Although temperance occupied the center of the moral stage at this time for the Methodists, there was an awareness of other issues. Their concern over popular amusements is seen in a report approved by the Annual Conference at Emporia in 1872:

Your committee, believing that many popular amusements, generally practiced at the present time, are vitiating and destructive in their moral influences, and in direct opposition to spiritual growth, beg leave to report as follows:

Resolved, That it is the sense of this Conference that the practice of card-playing for amusement has a pernicious tendency, and should be banished from all our homes and social circles.

Resolved, That the base ball club, the social dance, whether in the parlor or the public hall, all tend to dissipate the mind and are detrimental to virtue and religion, and in many instances positively injurious to health of the body, and should be discarded.

Resolved, That horse racing, whether on the race track, the highway, or the fair grounds, is contrary to the spirit of the Gospel and should not be tolerated by a Christian community.

Resolved, That every preacher be instructed to read this report to his congregation and to preach on the subject. [18]

Opposition to tobacco began to take legal form in the church. First, the conference requested ministers and laymen to desist from its use. Finally, in 1874, the Conference requested the Bishops not to transfer in "any man who habitually used it, unless he will cease its use in a reasonable time." Also passed was the resolution: "That we will not admit among us on trial, or to membership, or elect to orders, those who use it, unless they will cease its use within a reasonable time." [19] Four years later it was required that "candidates for admission into the Conference be free from the habit. . . ." [20]

The late 1870's saw the build-up of the determination not only to enact a prohibitory law, but to make it legal by constitutional amendment. Many churchmen were worried about the growth of drinking across the nation partly due to the increased immigration of Europeans. Many favored national legislation. This was true of the United Brethren Church, the Evangelical Association and the Methodist Protestants. By 1872 there were two distilleries and forty-six breweries in Kansas.[21] This cannot be blamed wholly on the "wild west" because the famous Dodge City was not founded until 1872.

In some towns there were unusual reactions to the saloons. For example, there was the response of a Methodist preacher in Newton:

The citizens of Newton did not like bloodshed and gun battles, nor the things which seemed to cause them—cattle men, gamblers, and saloons.

The first reaction to the saloons and cattle men came in 1871 from a Methodist minister, the Reverend M. M. Haun who lived on his claim between Newton and Sedgwick City. He preached the first sermon in Newton from a beer barrel pulpit. The minister selected the Golden Rule saloon as the first place to hold a service. . . .

The Reverend Haun asked the owner for permission to preach in his saloon at 8 p.m. and when he arrived that night he found he had to pass the bar in order to take his position. As he passed the bar he was offered a drink but politely refused.

The cowboys and gamblers were quite respectful and the service went through to its end as though it were conducted in a real church—this is discounting the swearing which coincided with the "amen" of a prayer because someone in the back of the room had lost at the faro table, the barking of the coons, and a dog fight which took place.

Following the final hymn several of the cowboys whipped out their six-guns, and took off their hats. They used the guns as persuaders to get the "congregation" to contribute to the collection-plate-hats.

The minister accepted the collection to which everyone had been forced to contribute, turned down another drink and left.[22]

Dramatic were the activities of the Independent Order of Good Templars, The Murphy, or the Blue Ribbon movement, the Woman's Crusade, the W.C.T.U., the churches and the mass meetings at the Bismarck Grove or Camp Ground near Lawrence. Also of great importance was the influence of John P. St. John, a temperance advocate, who was elected governor in 1878.

A joint resolution for the legislature was drafted which called for a constitutional amendment. It was presented and passed the Senate without much trouble, but was about to fail in the house by one vote for the required two-thirds majority. George W. Greever from Wyandotte County changed his vote in a dramatic gesture of loyalty to his new wife's belief and the issue was put to the people. His wife, a former school teacher, was a member of the Methodist Episcopal Church.[23] In this victory the influence of the churches was significant and the Methodists played an important role. One of the strongest leaders was Reverend J. E. Gilbert, pastor of the First Methodist Church of Topeka. On January 4, 1879, he preached on "What ought the State Legislature to do in Behalf of Temperance." As a result of a follow-up meeting, weekly union meetings of several churches were held with out-of-town speakers participating.[24]

During the rest of 1879 and until the election in the fall of 1880, mass meetings at Bismarck Grove were held. For example, on August 17, 1879, there were nearly 12,000 people in attendance and nine days later there were 25,000. The auditorium held only 5,000 people but the speakers spoke several times to crowded houses. Quite important were the activities of the W.C.T.U. and its leaders—Mrs. Drusilla Wilson, the State president, and the National president, Miss Frances E. Willard. The latter spent April and May of 1880 in Kansas. Of importance was the work of Governor St. John.

In the midst of the struggle the Kansas Annual Conference enthusiastically supported the pending constitutional amendment, and "we heartily endorse the position and record of Governor J. P. St. John on the temperance question and thank him for his public efforts in behalf of prohibition in Kansas. . . ."[25]

When the votes were in, the amendment had carried by nearly 8,000 votes. Kansas was the first state to pass a constitutional amendment although Tennessee and Maine had earlier prohibitory laws. Not until 1948 was the Kansas amendment repealed.

119

Not long after the effective date of prohibition, in May, 1881, it was discovered that liquor was still available, for drug stores could sell alcohol for medicinal purposes and did a profitable business in supplying the needs of people.

The New York *Tribune* pointed out in November, 1886, that in Osage County, 215 different reasons had been cited by patrons for purchasing alcohol including 'a bilious headache,' 'dry stomach,' 'congestion of the lungs,' and 'for making a mixture to wash apples against rabbits." The saloons soon reappeared in large numbers as did also the patrons.[26]

There developed a strange situation—wide open saloons in a prohibition state. One result of this dilemma was the remedial action of Carry A. Nation, famous destroyer of saloons, who began her crusade in June, 1899. Before this, however, there were many developments which are less well-known but nearly as dramatic as those of the hatchet-swinging or stone-throwing crusader from Medicine Lodge.

That prohibition was on trial was obvious to all. That it would be ridiculed, lied about and sabotaged was also evident and immediately experienced. Attempts were made to strengthen the law, but the enforcement of it was not easy. At the same time that prohibition was stirring up the state came the political and financial turmoil that contributed to the rise of Populism. This financial turmoil changed the political climate and prohibition became a secondary issue with the old political parties. The Republican Party now fighting for its very life in Kansas, did not have the militant defenders of prohibition as in the days of Governor J. P. St. John. As will be indicated in another place, the Methodists officially, in their Minutes of the Annual Conferences, ignored the political and financial happenings of the day, except in regard to prohibition. On this issue they were very excited and determined to hold the line. Throughout the 1880's they reiterated their stand and urged national legislation. In 1882 the Kansas Conference said:

That we decry the truth of all that class of statements spread broadcast over the East to the effect that more liquor is consumed now than before the passage of the law, and believe that a fairer statement would be that the subversion of law and order has been sought by the liquor interests, who, although they have not failed to use every device of money, argument and deception, have steadily lost ground. Fraud, subornation of perjury, threats of violence, and violence performed, are among the weapons used against temperance and temperance people.[27]

In 1887 the South Kansas Conference expressed gratitude to the present legislature for strengthening the prohibitory law and giving women the right to vote in municipal elections.[28]

On July 16, 1890, the Kansas Temperance Convention with over 3,000 delegates gathered in Topeka. The mass meeting in front of the State House was attended by 12,000 people. They set forth the temperance situation in Kansas, urged national prohibition, protested against "original package saloons" and then went on to take pride in the effects of nine years of prohibition in Kansas: An increase of 191,363 children of school age; a gain of 100% in assessed valuation of property; the addition of over 5,000 miles of railroad track; a decrease in the percentage of convicts in prison;[29] a gain of 90% in field crops; live stock, 88%; manufacturing, 159%; churches, 103%; school property, 43%; church property, 164%.[30]

A threat is seen in the action of the Methodists in 1892 when the Kansas Annual Conference resolved:

That the great political party to which the State is indebted for its prohibitory law can hope for the continued support of the Christian element only so long as it shall continue to be loyal to the interest of prohibition. If, in the present emergency, it shall refuse longer to maintain its fidelity to this supreme question, it will but invite and deserve defeat at the hands of a disappointed people.[31]

Often individual towns took action against the saloons or the "jointists." For example, in Vermillion under the leadership of the Methodist pastor, M. G. Hamm, late in 1892, it was decided to do something about the saloons which had been open for two years. A meeting of the business men was called and a temperance league organized with 36 prominent men enrolled. Surprisingly Hamm says:

The jointists came into the meeting and declared they had quit business and would not resume it. We have a quiet town now. Every joint is closed. An active temperance league stands ready to prosecute the first violation of the law. Sunday hunting, gambling, playing at cards and all games of chance have been suppressed.[32]

Even more astonishing was the action taken in Fort Scott against the mayor, P. C. Hesser, on January 23, 1899. He was publicly expelled from the Grace M. E. Church because he made no effort to close the saloons. His wife was the president of the local W.C.T.U.[33]

Not to be forgotten in the dramatic events before the Carry Nation exploits in Wichita, is the action, involving Methodists, in Winfield, Kansas. Operating in Winfield in disregard of the law were a half dozen joints, or saloons, in spite of the opposition of the six evangelical churches of the town. Toward the middle of February, 1899, a student in what is now Southwestern College, Ernest Hahn, was stirred by the sight of a barrel of whiskey on the platform of the railroad station. After smashing it open with an ax he ran into a saloon and ordered them to shut down at once. One of the owners hit him with a billiard cue and he retreated. His fellow ministerial students, when they saw the lump on his head, determined to avenge the insult. Several windows of the saloon were broken that night, but more important, the next morning some 500 students and others gathered in the First Baptist Church to plan a raid. They turned toward the saloon, now defended by the two owning brothers with shotguns. Two women raiders were shot, the owners fled, and the saloon was wrecked. Two other saloons immediately closed.[34]

That night the liquor forces retaliated. The United Brethren Church was invaded, sixty stained glass panes broken, the organ and pulpit hacked with axes, and they left a note threatening the life of the pastor. The town armed for the fight with guards posted at the Methodist college and all the churches. The saloon group also armed. That night shots were exchanged, the Baptist church attacked, and houses set on fire. The next morning two small cannon were set up in the business section, clergymen carried revolvers, and armed farmers came to town to help. The mayor finally brought peace and all the saloons closed.

Actions such as these, but less violent, took place throughout the state. Following the methods and example of Carry Nation, about 1,000 of the 1,500 saloons were warned to close their doors and approximately thirty towns in eastern Kansas were free of drinking places.[35]

In Topeka, as in Wichita, Carry Nation made news with her exploits. The leader of the temperance group in the capitol was Dr. T. J. McFarland, pastor of the First Methodist Church, but he was ably supported by other evangelical ministers, such as Reverend S. C. Sobentz, of the United Brethren Church. On the first visit of the crusader, there was no immediate need for violent action because out of a mass meeting of 3,000 came an organization of 1,000 church men, divided into companies of 100 each. The saloon-keepers retreated and the "joints" were closed.[36] Later, the battle was joined again. Carry Nation was arrested, brought to court, found guilty and fined. Dr. McFarland protested strongly and the judge fined him $10 for contempt. The Methodist preacher said, "$10 does not begin to express the contempt I have for this court." The judge raised it to $100. Friends of Dr. McFarland quickly brought in ten checks of $10 each, signed by prominent men in Topeka; the judge tore up the checks and dismissed the case.[37]

State and county officials were severely criticized for their complacency by the W.C.T.U. and other temperance organizations. Imagine the prominence given to an article in the *Baker Orange*, the school student publication, written by Harry Stanley, the governor's son, in which he criticized the governor and supported Carry Nation.[38]

In 1905, when the battleship, *U.S.S. Kansas* was to be christened, Governor Hoch, a Methodist, suggested that Kansas crude oil be used instead of champagne. On August 12 of that year when it was launched, Miss Ann Hoch, the governor's daughter, broke a bottle of water from the John Brown spring over the bow.

Rumor has it that the superstitious sailors gave it a second christening with champagne. Nearly two years later recruiting officers claimed it was difficult to get a full crew for the *U. S. S. Kansas*. To navy men, "No ship is lucky unless she touched wine before she touched water." On April 23, 1909, U.S. Marines balked at duty on the ship because of the water christening. Finally, the captain with due ceremony christened it with champagne.[39]

With no hesitation the Methodists continued their pressure toward better enforcement of prohibition. They were pleased with the law of 1909 which forbade the sale of liquor for medicinal purposes. Finally, on February 23, 1917, Governor Arthur Capper signed the "Bone Dry Law" while 150 legislators sang, "How Dry I Am." [40]

Although temperance held the center of the stage for churchmen in their demand for higher moral standards, there were other concerns. Mention has been made of the fight against tobacco on the part of many and especially Methodists. Finally, in 1909, the legislature barred the sale of tobacco and cigarettes to minors,[41] and for the period, 1917-1927, the sale of cigarettes or cigarette paper was prohibited.[42] In the second year of this period, 1919, Lorraine E. Wooster, State Superintendent of Public Instruction, indicated that she would revoke the certificates of school teachers who used tobacco.[43]

Other minor actions are of interest but of less importance. In 1886 the legislature ruled against hunting on Sunday; in 1898 a Methodist Bishop urged a campaign against the gum-chewing habit; for playing cards and checkers on Sunday, five men were arrested in Topeka in 1908; during the Kansas Methodist Conference in Topeka in 1915, Reverend Bernard Kelley advocated a law against riding in automobiles on Sunday.[44]

From the view point of many years later some of the positions taken by the earlier Methodists may seem narrow and legalistic. Before coming to any quick judgment, however, it would be well to remember the conditions of their day. The immorality, corruption, crudities and harshness of frontier life seemed to demand a severe moral response. In the apt summary of a great authority on the American frontier, Dr. William Warren Sweet, "the churches were the moral courts of the frontier." The concern of our fathers was for firm foundations for the new state.

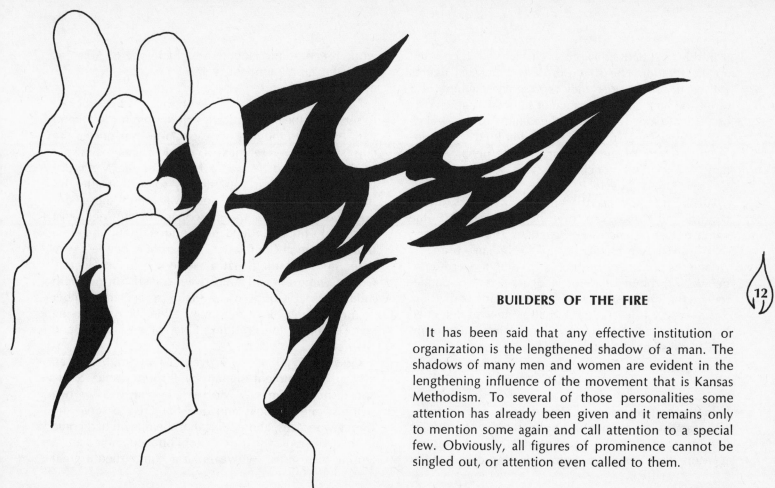

BUILDERS OF THE FIRE

It has been said that any effective institution or organization is the lengthened shadow of a man. The shadows of many men and women are evident in the lengthening influence of the movement that is Kansas Methodism. To several of those personalities some attention has already been given and it remains only to mention some again and call attention to a special few. Obviously, all figures of prominence cannot be singled out, or attention even called to them.

125

In this treatment a few great characters will be lifted up. In addition, the shadows of two unusual figures will be traced because they represent something of a variety of personalities, strange or surprising, which may be used of God. To be sure, the witness of the strange ones was unique but also to be admitted is the unusual character of the situation and the people whom they served. The concluding story will be that of William Alfred Quayle.

For the first 30 years of Methodism in Kansas (Indian country and Kansas Territory), beginning in 1830, the name of prominence was Reverend Thomas Johnson —an outstanding missionary to the Indians, primarily among the Shawnees. In the early conflict over Kansas he was a prominent political figure with sympathies toward the South. As with others in this time of division, this man was a slaveholder but also one who defended the Union. He lost his life by an assassin's bullet probably because of his outspoken Union sympathies.

WILLIAM H. GOODE

In three states—Kansas, Nebraska and Colorado— one man was the pioneer for Methodism in establishing "Outposts of Zion," as he, William H. Goode, termed it. More than ten years before he was called to his work in Kansas and Nebraska he had gone to Arkansas to be the superintendent of the Fort Coffee Academy, near Fort Smith.

Of interest is the fact that both this and his later call to service in the new territories were from the Reverend E. R. Ames. On the first occasion Ames was one of the corresponding secretaries of the Missionary Society; at the later time he was a bishop of the Methodist Episcopal Church. It was said by some that after his tour of duty in Arkansas Goode was one of those seriously considered for the episcopacy of the Methodist Episcopal Church. Indeed, at one time during the elections at General Conference, he had only one less vote than Ames. Desiring that a western man be elected, Goode withdrew and Ames was elected.[1] In northern Indiana W. H. Goode was a highly respected member of the conference. At the time he left for Arkansas he was serving as the Presiding Elder of the South Bend District.

On April 27, 1843, he arrived at Fort Smith with an official appointment signed by Bishop Joshua Soule and Bishop Thomas A. Morris. The plan was for two schools, one for boys and one for girls, to serve the Choctaw Indians, about 20,000 of them, who had come from Mississippi. The boys' school opened immediately. During his tour of two years he accomplished a great deal for the Indians and the school was in an excellent condition when he was transferred back to Indiana.[2]

Even before the passage of the Kansas-Nebraska Bill, three of the bishops of the Methodist Episcopal Church, including E. R. Ames, met to plan for the potential work in the new area. Again an appeal went to Goode, then pastor in Richmond, Indiana, to go back to the frontier of Kansas and Nebraska in a new role of explorer.

The request from the bishops was written on May 15, 1854, and on June 8, Goode left for Kansas, having accepted the appointment for one year. July 5 found him in Kansas Territory. It was during the trip that he reports the occasion of his first sermon in Kansas:

The succeeding day being the Sabbath it was determined to ride to a settlement that was being formed in the "Big Timber," and try to collect a congregation for public worship. Accordingly we set out at an early hour, our company being now enlarged by the accession of Dr. Still, Friend Mendenhall, the teacher from the Quaker Mission, and several others, making a party of considerable size. A prairie ride of some fifteen miles through the tall grass, at times almost hiding man and beast from sight, brought us to "Hickory Point," a place since rendered famous in the history of Kansas by the deeds of blood with which it has been connected. We stopped at the cabin of a man named "Kibbee," originally from Parke county, Indiana, a large, athletic fearless frontier's man. . . . The structure was a rude one, newly erected, to which we received a cordial, backwoods welcome. Little expection was had of a ministerial visit; but our host and one or two others volunteered their services to go out and invite the settlers to assemble for preaching. By about noon the company was collected, and there in Kibbee's cabin I opened my commission by preaching from Matthew xxiv, 14; being, so far as I knew, the first sermon preached under an regular appointment to the white settlers in Kansas. . . . Part of the congregation, after assembling, were called away to protect some young stock from the wolves. . . .[3]

The needs of the region, as he saw them, called for four mission circuits, two in Kansas and two in Nebraska, and to be supplied from the Missouri Conference; over the work should be a superintendent. Very quickly he was transferred to the Missouri Conference and appointed the superintendent! Goode's new "district" included the area from Arkansas to the Canadian line, and from the borders of Missouri and Iowa to the Rocky Mountains. "To this field I was sent with only three adjutors, one of these an aged grey-haired man, and another a stripling just admitted." [4] (John H. Dennis and his son, Baxter, from Iowa.)

Other early workers were: Reverend A. L. Downey; Reverend Isaac F. Collins, from Arkansas; Joseph Denni-Dennison and Charles H. Lovejoy from New England; Reverend Hiram Burch, from Illinois; David Hart, a young Englishman; and James S. Griffing.[5] The latter was Goode's first assistant and admired him very much, as he indicated in a letter to his fiancee.[6]

Some days they would travel nearly the whole day without seeing a house. At one time Goode wrote: "That night I passed in a house, having slept out for the twenty-one preceding." Another time he wrote:

> From this place we went to Lawrence, where we held the second quarterly meeting for Wakarusa mission. Our place of service was the hotel, a long sod-building, thatched with prairie-grass, the one great room serving as dining-room, parlor, and dormitory, a table with bench-seats reaching from end to end, and a line of double bunks stretching the same length, with sleeping accommodations. Here also we organized a society with respectable members and fair prospects.[7]

At the first and organizing session of the Kansas & Nebraska Annual Conference, at "Lawrence City, Kansas Territory, Oct., 23rd A.D., 1856" it was "Br. Wm. H. Goode" who read the list of members:

L. B. Dennis	Wm. H. Goode
Wm. Butt	I. F. Collins
Charles H. Lovejoy	W. D. Frye
Abraham Still	John W. Taylor
Joseph Denison	John M. Chivington
Thomas J. Ferrill	Benjamin F. Bowman
	J. T. Cannon.[8]

In 1857 the pioneer Goode served as presiding officer of the Kansas-Nebraska Conference for one day, and again in 1859 due in each case to the late arrival of the Bishop. He was appointed Presiding Elder of the Nebraska City District in 1857 and to the same position for the Omaha District in 1858. In 1860 he was elected a delegate to General Conference, the first at which Kansas & Nebraska were represented. For a time he took an interest in a possible seminary or university at Oreapolis, Nebraska. His pioneering interest turned him toward Colorado and on June 28 and July 8, 1859, he along with Jacob Adriance held sessions in Denver. A week later Goode preached at Central City and the following day, July 11, he organized a church of 45 members, then went on the next Sunday to Golden City where he preached in a gambling tent and another church was organized. Another church, now Trinity, was organized in Denver on August 2.[9]

Indiana, Kansas, Nebraska and Colorado owe much to this intrepid, dynamic man of God—explorer, missionary, organizer and great soul. A visitor, the editor of the *Central Christian Advocate,* said of the men he recruited:

> . . . Here are strong-minded men. . . . They are also laborers. . . Here are literary men. . . . Here are pioneer men, who carry their beds with them in their blankets and wolf-skin coats and surtouts,

who can sleep on the snow on the Rocky Mountains, or on the bleak prairie, and ride fifty or more miles without the sight of a house, or human dwelling of any sort, and without road or blaze on trees, to serve as guides to their appointments. Now just look at this royal artillery, and ask, Are not these the men for the Work?[10]

EDUCATORS

In regard to education, only two individuals will be singled out for special consideration—Isaac T. Goodnow and Werter R. Davis. Some attention was given to the former for his singular work in Manhattan in an earlier chapter on education. Without doubt, his work, as an organizer and money-raiser, was the most significant in the foundation of the town of Manhattan and of Bluemont College, as well as the establishment of the state school, now Kansas State University, in Manhattan with the gift of the Bluemont property. To this Methodist layman also must go a tribute for his contribution to public school education—as State Superintendent of Public Instruction, 1862-64, and as first president of the Kansas State Teachers Association in 1863.

Serving with Goodnow as vice-presidents of the Kansas State Teachers Association were two other Methodists—Reverend Joseph Denison and Dr. Werter R. Davis. The former was another key person in Manhattan and the first president of the new school, serving for nine years. During his subsequent ministry he served as president of Baker, 1873-1879, presiding elder and pastor. He was a delegate to the General Conference in 1864 and 1880.[11]

WERTER R. DAVIS

Werter Renick Davis, M.D., 1815-1893, the first president of Baker University, was an educator, orator, soldier, preacher, as well as a medical man. The parents of this native of Ohio were of two denominations. According to his son-in-law, William A. Quayle, he had a favorite phrase: "paternally he was an Episcopalian, maternally a Presbyterian, but by the grace of God a Methodist."

WERTER R. DAVIS

129

His college work began at Kenyon College, continued with an M.A. from Indiana State University, and concluded with an M.D. from the College of Medicine and Surgery in Cincinnati. In his early ministry in West Virginia, he was imprisoned because of his anti-slavery opinions, and then returned to Ohio. In 1844 he was transferred to the Missouri Conference and after a few years in a pastorate in St. Louis, was elected a professor in McKendree College in Illinois and acted as president in 1858. He was elected to the presidency of Baker and arrived in Baldwin, September 1, 1858, to establish the new school which opened November 22, 1858, with 20 students in attendance—all in the preparatory department.[12]

While president, Davis served as chaplain of the Wyandott Constitutional Convention and was a member of the first House of Representatives. After four years as president he resigned to become a Presiding Elder but in a short time he enlisted in the army. During the war he served as chaplain and later, in 1864, as colonel of the Sixteenth Kansas Volunteer Cavalry Regiment, and for a time as Commandant at Fort Leavenworth. Later he returned to the ministry and again served as Presiding Elder. Three times he was a member of the General Conference and was a delegate to the First Ecumenical Conference, in London.[13]

LOCAL PREACHERS

Among the influential people in the establishment of the church were the local preachers. Two of these in the early northwest of Kansas were unique. In that day others in that region may have been of more influence in conference affairs—such as Reverend W. A. Saville, Reverend J. P. Ryan and Reverend James Boicourt[14]—but they did not attract as much attention as two others, Reverend R. P. West and Boston Corbett.

Toward the close of 1863, R. P. West, a Virginian, settled in the Republican Valley, taking a homestead near Belleville. Soon thereafter this Methodist local preacher, a good singer and a fluent speaker, was working in the counties of Cloud, Republic, Clay and a part of Washington. In appearance he was always a surprise—sometimes in overalls and an old black coat with a rip in one of the back seams, while on other occasions he wore a plug hat. His sermons were salty and down-to-earth—in one he talked of the evil of disturbing landmarks. Of course he was a character and was often caricatured as "Reverend Romulus Pintus Westlake." One of the most famous stories about him is that of a pioneer wedding he performed out in a grove. He followed up the ceremony with an exhortation about training up children and then nearly turned the occasion into a wedding revival. He asked about others in the crowd who might want to be married—two couples came forward! Fortunately, a justice of the peace arose and called attention to the legal requirements necessary.[15]

BOSTON CORBETT

A better known figure was that of Boston Corbett, an occasional Methodist preacher, who came to Kansas in the late 1870's, and acquired 80 acres of land about ten miles from Concordia. He was a poor man, a hatter by trade, and unmarried. Immediately he built for himself a dug-out about 12 ft. by 15 ft. with a dirt floor. In this simple dwelling was only a home-made bedstead, a chair or two, an old musket, a rifle and a well-worn Bible.[16]

Soon after his arrival he associated himself with the Methodist Episcopal Church. Here was a shouting brother, interested in evangelism, who would preach with a revolver in his pocket or a brace of pistols dangling from his belt. He was known as an expert shot—he used to lie in the open field and shoot hawks as they flew by overhead. The only living thing dear to him was a black pony, "Billie." People would come to hear him and listen because of his famous background—but even his lectures usually ended in a sermon.

John Corbett was born in England in 1832. He took the name of "Boston" after he was converted in Boston, Massachusetts. He volunteered in the Civil War and for a time was a prisoner in the infamous Andersonville prison. After the assassination of President Abraham Lincoln he volunteered from his army company to go in a group to hunt down the assassin, John Wilkes Booth. In a tobacco barn Booth was cornered. It was Corbett who fired the fatal shot at Booth. He always maintained that the bullet struck Booth in the same place in the head that the assassin's bullet had entered the head of President Lincoln—for God directed it!

But Corbett was no hero. In order to save a fellow soldier whom the assassin was ready to shoot, he had fired against orders to take Booth alive. The end of the affair saw Corbett in disgrace, because the government authorities wanted to make a spectacle of Booth. In disgrace, therefore, he had come to Kansas.

The closing years of his life were also unusual. In 1887 he came to Topeka and was a door keeper in the house of representatives and an object of curiosity as he wore his pistols. Tragedy resulted from a session of the legislature. When they came to the prayer, it seemed a mockery and blasphemy to Corbett. From his position in the balcony he drew his gun and ordered them all out of the room. Quickly the police took him and he was tried for insanity, convicted and sent to the Insane Asylum. The county attorney who got the verdict was a young lawyer, Charles Curtis, years later the Vice-President of the United States. From the mental institution Corbett escaped and no one knows where he went, or anything of his later life.[17]

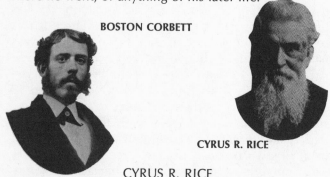

BOSTON CORBETT

CYRUS R. RICE

CYRUS R. RICE

For nearly 50 years, 1855-1904, Father Rice, as he was familiarly called at a later time, was a strong and active participant in the life of Methodism in Kansas. He began his service in Kansas when the Kansas Mission Conference of the Methodist Episcopal Church, South was organized at the tenth session of the St. Louis Conference at Springfield, Missouri, October 24, 1855. As a probationer, having been admitted on trial the previous year, he was appointed to Potawatomie.[18] Until he transferred back to the St. Louis Conference in 1861 he served the Southern church at Fort Scott, Tecumseh, Shawnee Reserve, and Olathe.[19]

This native of Tennessee had graduated from a medical college but never practiced medicine. Rather, to the distress of his father, a physician and surgeon, he turned to the Methodist ministry in 1854, soon after his graduation.[20]

During the Civil War he served as a Union Scout. When the war closed he brought his family back to Kansas and joined the Methodist Episcopal Conference at Topeka in 1865. Immediately he assumed a position of leadership, serving as the Presiding Elder of the Emporia District, 1866-69, and again in the same office, 1880-84.

Few men have organized more churches as the following list indicates: First Methodist Church, Wichita, 1866; First Methodist Church, Eureka, 1867; others he claimed were Independence, Eldorado, Augusta, Marion, Chetopa, Baldwin, Hartford, Americus, Pleasanton, Burlington, Ottawa, Douglas and Burlingame.[21]

He retired in 1904 but remained vigorous and answered his 50th conference roll call in 1915. Two of his sons followed him in the ministry, the Rev. E. T. Rice and the more famous Dr. Merton S. Rice. Father Rice died in 1920, after a vigorous ministry.[22]

WILLIAM ALFRED QUAYLE

The greatest preacher to come out of Kansas was William Alfred Quayle, dramatically characterized by his protege and biographer, Merton S. Rice, a fellow Kansan, as "The Skylark of Methodism":

I saw a skylark spring from the furrow of a field, and with its strange circling climbing flight, wing its fascinating way into the very concealment of the sky above me, while it thrilled my soul with the melody of its song. For that reason, as I have watched this fascinating friend of mine, starting from his humble place soaring to the heights of genius, and leaving the world aflood with his song, I have chosen to call him THE SKYLARK OF METHODISM.[23]

WILLIAM ALFRED QUAYLE

During a journey of a couple across the country on their way to Colorado where the man was to engage in mining, a baby was born to them but the mother died. This was the entrance of William Alfred Quayle into the world at Parkville, Missouri, on June 25, 1860. The miner father left the baby with the brother of the mother, Edward Gill, a Methodist preacher in Kansas, and continued on to Colorado. Not only did the boy never know his mother, but he never knew where she was buried; his father was never a great influence in his life afterwards. The boy always thought of himself as an orphan. As a boy of 13 he was sent to another Methodist preacher, Reverend James Boicourt. After the death of this pioneer preacher in northwest Kansas, Bishop Quayle wrote:

He was all man. To think that a little lad could be so impressed that in all those years a Christian minister's character has stayed with him like a beatitude. . . . He lived a great and sinewy gospel. . . . He has passed into the immortal minstrelsy of my heart and the heart of many another.

No mean thing or selfish thing ever peeked around the corner of his life. He lived out in the open prairie of soul where you could see him from sky to sky. . . .[24]

Young Quayle's first book was a copy of an almanac. The King James version of the Bible was the second book of influence. Next came a copy of Shakespeare which he carried with him even while plowing—he went up the row with "Hamlet" and back with "King Lear." The night he was converted, in response to a farmer preacher in a little schoolhouse, he came forward and bowed his head on a dictionary. This was the fourth book. He always was enamoured of words and fond of reading the dictionary. He said of it, "It is a little disconnected, but very interesting."[25]

As a boy he lived on a farm near Auburn, Kansas, and went to the country school. At 14 years of age he came to Baker University. For his board and room he worked on a farm near Baldwin. As a practice he went to bed at nine and got up at one o'clock to study in the quiet. Early he joined a literary society and eventually became the representative of the college in the state oratorical contest, using an original oration on John Milton. Surprising to many, he did not win the contest because one judge gave him last place. The judge was confident that there was plagiarism involved because it was too good for a college student. Needless to say, the material was Quayle's own and is an early manifestation of his literary ability and individuality. 1885 was the year of his graduation from Baker in a class of six.

Soon after graduation he married the daughter of the former president of Baker, Dr. Werter R. Davis.

From the Kansas Conference his first appointment was Osage City, Kansas. There the people took up a collection for the young couple—for him it meant a new outfit which included a Prince Albert suit and a slick hat. Later, on the train from Lawrence, Quayle appeared in a shining silk hat much to the distress of the well-known conductor. The latter called in the train crew to sit on the hat. Always afterwards Quayle wore a soft hat.

After a short time in the pastorate he was back at Baker occupying the chair of Greek Language and Literature. Within three years, when he was not yet 30 years of age, he was elected president and inaugurated in 1890, only five years after graduation.

Baker could not hold him for long. After four years the great Independence Avenue Church in Kansas City pursued him and there he had an effective ministry. There followed a period in Indianapolis and then back to Kansas City at the Grand Avenue Temple, and later to St. James Church in Chicago. In 1908 he was elected a bishop.

As a bishop he was unique. He always spoke of his "arena" instead of his area. Many stories are told of his exploits in this high office. On one occasion an episcopal colleague presented a thoroughly regimented schedule for his preachers, and the suggestion was for others to use it as well. The Kansas maverick upset it all by indicating that there was one serious omission in the schedule—"no time for a man to spit." In one of his cabinets he had a very aggressive district superintendent who struggled to get only the best men under his care. During the illness of one cabinet member the opportunist unloaded all of his "lemons" on the sick brother. Bishop Quayle went along in apparent agreement, but when he read the appointments he simply switched the district superintendents from one to the other district.

All through his pastorates and his episcopacy he was an avid collector of Bibles; the collection is now famous and is housed at Baker University. In addition, he was a writer—more than 20 books and numerous articles. Also, he was a voluminous, rapid reader of books.

As a preacher or lecturer he had few peers. One of his friends, in a bit of poor verse, said:

> When Quayle spoke,
> The brooks their silv'ry way
> Went singing to the lakes,
> And life's dull drudgeries
> Took on Transfiguring light,
> The blood that sluggish lay,
> Stirred, leaped and ran;
> Ambition's waning hope

Flushed and stood up,
Prophets were born,
New sermons sprang to life,
The stooping shoulder lifted hopefully,
Dulled eyes reflected the return of day,
Men, wearied with the exactions of their lot,
Felt the rebuke of their awakened souls,
And turned with strange new zest,
Not to the task tedious,
But to the "Task Golden."
And God came nearer to our mortal clay,
Touched our poor eyes to glories here and there—
When Quayle spoke.[26]

Some idea of his philosophy of preaching is caught in these excerpts from one of his most popular books, "The Pastor-Preacher." [27]

To be interesting is no sin: to be prosy is no sign of depth of thought or piety of life. The sin is in being uninteresting with so thrilling a gospel as it is each pastor's office to present. The charm of high destiny is on the message, and the mercy of heavenly help.

This is not a plea for sensationalism. Only weak men are sensational. The preacher who knows the art of preaching will never need to be sensational. He will be inspirational. This is a plea for dealing squarely with a message which has not its like this side of heaven, and in all its relation has not its like inside of heaven. . . .

.   .   .   .

. . . It is muddy preaching that is mistaken for deep preaching. And thought clearly grasped by a preacher and presented clearly to his auditors will render any such thought intelligible. People are brainier than the conceited preacher has comprehended. They have about as much brains as he has, and not infrequently more. Let him treat their brains democratically and use his own, and illumine his argument by light brought from all luminaries from earth, heaven, history, poetry, fiction, soul experience, the by-paths and tears of his own wonder and knowledge of God, and his own wonder and knowledge of man: and words will smile and weep and ache and bleed and battle like a sword and trumpet like the tempest. . . .

.   .   .   .

. . . But the preacher as orator has all these themes. He lights his torch at all their fires, and then has a torch lit not by their flaring lamps, but at the sun, which sun is Christ. The preacher has all they had, and more—and more, aye, gloriously more! No interest vital to the world which he does not touch. He stands at the center of a circle whose entire rim is fire. Glory envelops him. He is a prisoner of majesty. . . .

If he had one fault it was the danger of mimicry. Like a contemporary, Dr. Frank Gunsaulus, he had the temptation to be an actor. Often it was said that he was an orator rather than a preacher. Of his appearance he was negligent. His red hair was usually uncombed and his clothes unpressed. On one occasion, at a dinner, his attention was called to gravy on his tie. He replied, "When I wear gravy, that's where I always wear it." Another time he appeared for a lecture in the South in a dishevelled state. The reason for this was that he had sat up all night in a coal car in order not to disturb the brakeman who was sleeping in the caboose. Audiences, however, soon forgot his appearance as they were caught up in his words and his spirit.

In his appearances at conferences or churches few lecturers could surpass him as he opened up the resources of great literature, history and drama, especially Shakespeare. Never to be forgotten was his lecture portraying Napoleon and the emptiness of selfish glory, or his dramatization of "King Lear" and the sin of ingratitude. Jean Valjean out of "Les Miserables" came to life on the platform and the entire audience struggled with Jean as he lifted the heavy weight from the body of a man. The problem of the conflict of justice vs. mercy became incarnate in the struggle of the French police-inspector, Javert; and the redeeming power of love, even with a criminal, was made manifest in Quayle's retelling of Victor Hugo's masterpiece. Most listeners, young and old, were lifted out of themselves and saw life from a new dimension as this man of God roamed the pages of the Bible, great literature and history, and related it to everyday living. The latter ability came from the fact that he knew and loved people and they responded to his spirit of love and compassion joined with greatness of soul. During the 1920's it was no uncommon sight on a street corner in Baldwin, Kansas, to see a group of people—young and old, rich and poor—gathered around and talking to a red-haired man sitting on the curb. "Willy" Quayle was home for a visit!

The Skylark of Methodism died in Baldwin in 1925, and was buried there. When he came to die and could no longer speak, he still communicated the request that the verse he was pointing to in his Bible, I Thessalonians 2:4, should be put on his tombstone—"Allowed of God to be put in trust with the gospel." These words had been the "driving impulse of his whole ministry." [28] There was triumph in his departure!

These are a few of the "Builders of the Fire"—the fire that was and is Methodism in Kansas.

NOTE: To the writer of this history, the life of the late Bishop Quayle is of real personal interest for several reasons. On the campus of Saint Paul School of Theology Methodist is a wonderful maple tree planted in 1929 in honor and memory of Bishop Quayle, a friend of the Kansas City National Training School, the institution of which Saint Paul is the successor. In addition, the writer was a student at Baker when the presence and memories of the beloved bishop were very real in Baldwin and attended the funeral. Even earlier, his lectures and preaching are a vivid memory. During one of the years when Dr. Quayle was president of Baker, the writer's father was a student there.

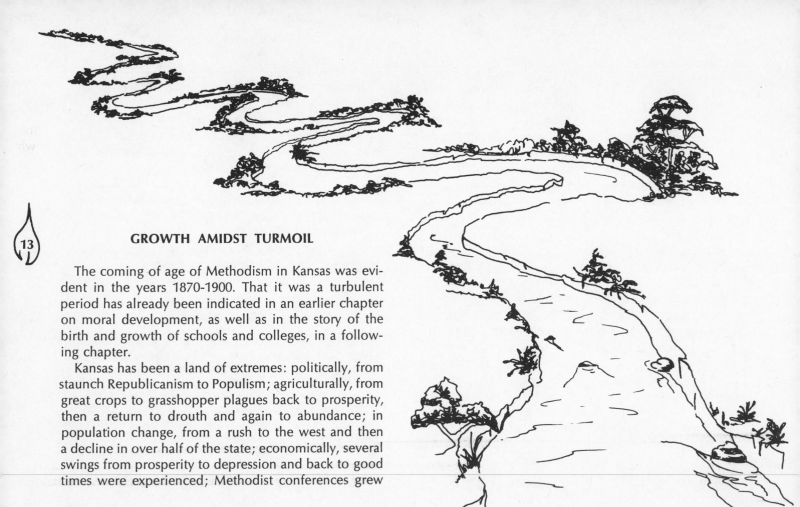

GROWTH AMIDST TURMOIL

The coming of age of Methodism in Kansas was evident in the years 1870-1900. That it was a turbulent period has already been indicated in an earlier chapter on moral development, as well as in the story of the birth and growth of schools and colleges, in a following chapter.

Kansas has been a land of extremes: politically, from staunch Republicanism to Populism; agriculturally, from great crops to grasshopper plagues back to prosperity, then a return to drouth and again to abundance; in population change, from a rush to the west and then a decline in over half of the state; economically, several swings from prosperity to depression and back to good times were experienced; Methodist conferences grew from one conference in the late 1850's which included Nebraska and Colorado, to four in Kansas alone late in the 19th century, and then back to three in 1914, and finally to two in 1939; at the same time membership was growing. Amid difficulties and constant change it was not always easy to see the stars. Yet there remained a vigor in all phases of life.

SOCIAL CONDITIONS

A traveler through Kansas in 1870, H. Ashton, in correspondence to the *Christian Advocate* (April 28, 1870), went into ecstasies about the state:

Its fertility is unsurpassed. Bottom lands have produced fifteen successive corn crops with no sign of exhaustion. We called upon a farmer five miles south of Topeka, who said, "Three years ago we took this land—knew nothing about farming—had a boy to sod-plow for corn and plant the corn under the sod, and did nothing more till we husked it, and gathered forty bushels to the acre; the next year seventy-five bushels to the acre. The peach trees were raised from the seed three years ago, and last year we sold $175 worth of peaches." A farmer received a premium at Topeka, proving that his yield of corn last year was 130 bushels to the acre. Here and there unimproved lands are covered with wild fruits of all kinds—plums, grapes, berries, etc. etc.

Kansas farming is easily done—no stones, or bogs, or stumps. The farmer rides, cattle and machinery toil. Many went to Kansas three years ago ignorant of farm life, with but little capital, who are now independent.

Its climate. No country has a more healthful climate. . . . The winters are so short and mild. The summers are hardly ever oppressive, its heat is so tempered with strong cool winds.[1]

He then goes on to show that the rainfall, for May through August, was higher in Kansas in a ten-year period, than in 21 other states, including most of the middle west.[2] Then follows a description of several cities: Topeka with 10,000 in population and eleven churches, of which the Methodist is the largest with 850 members, is outstanding; Leavenworth, numbering 35,000, "a very dull place . . . Religion is equally low —it even touches zero."[3]

In a final paean of praise he speaks of Kansas as the poor man's home:

We would say in conclusion to the hundreds and thousands of families who are swarming our cities, and are full of anxiety about the rainy day, but find it impossible to provide for it, you may find your desired goal by seeking a home in Kansas, and in two to five years, with ordinary toil and intelligence, you may have a comfortable independence, be the owner of a large farm, etc., for the great questions asked by those seeking such a home—healthy climate, cheap lands, good society, schools, churches, etc., and ready markets, are all fully met by the State of Kansas. Land can be bought at $1.25 and upward, per acre; first-rate roads, no mud, and nearly a thousand miles of railroad and others being constructed at the rate of a mile per day. Go to Kansas.[4]

Descriptions like this and advertising by railroads and others, brought thousands of settlers to Kansas in the 1870's and the 1880's as homesteaders. In spite of the grasshoppers and the depression in the seventies, it was boom time in the eighties. In the ten-year period prior to 1890, railroad building increased by 5,421 miles, in excess of need. Eastern capital flowed into the state. Later, in commenting on the period, an official said:

> Most of us crossed the Mississippi or the Missouri with no money but with vast wealth of hope and courage. . . . Haste to get rich has made us borrowers, and the borrowing has made booms, and booms made men wild, and Kansas became a vast insane asylum, covering 80,000 square miles.[5]

Late in the 1860's and 1870's the cattle industry boomed. It was found that Texas longhorns driven north across the unfenced public domain could be fattened on the way and soon the "Long Drive" to a shipping point in Kansas or beyond became a regular event. According to one estimate, four million cattle reached Kansas between 1867 and 1880.[6]

In the years just after 1880 the rainfall in the western third of the state was far above normal. It was assumed that this "part of the great American desert" had changed. In the course of about three years the population in the western third of the state increased from 41,664 in 1885 to 148,125 in 1887. Disaster then struck Kansas and especially western Kansas. In 1892 in this same area, there were 86,360 people and a further decrease of 10,000 occurred by 1896. The population of the entire state declined from 1,514,778 in 1887 to 1,448,811 in 1891.[7] Sixteen cities in the eastern half of the state suffered a loss of more than 45,000 people—Leavenworth lost 15,000 and Wichita, 13,000.[8]

What caused this "bust" after the boom? Much of it is summed up in three words—lack of rainfall! Beginning with the season of 1887 and continuing for ten years, with the exception of two years, there was insufficient rain to produce a good crop. In the hope that the next year would bring relief, the farmer borrowed money at rates from six to eighteen percent and mortgaged his land. In Kansas in 1890, there was a mortgage for every two adults. Who was to blame? The farmer blamed the railroads, trusts, middlemen, moneylenders, bankers and the government. Many who stayed on and suffered through were a discontented group ready for political and economic revolt.[9]

POPULISM

The Populist uprising was more virulent in Kansas than anywhere else in the agricultural belt of the midwest through which it raged. One writer later described it as follows:

The upheaval that took place . . . can hardly be diagnosed as a political campaign. It was a religious revival, a crusade, a pentecost of politics in which a tongue of flame sat upon every man, and each spake as the spirit gave him utterance.[10]

This purple passage tells only part of the story, however. That the movement was strong in Kansas is attested by the fact that in the first organization meeting of the People's Party in Cincinnati, of the 1,417 delegates, 407 came from Kansas.[11] Also interesting is the prominence of women: Mrs. S. E. V. Emery of Michigan, the critic of the existing financial system; Mrs. Anna L. Diggs, effective speaker; and the most famous, Mary Elizabeth Lease of Wichita, who is said to have urged the farmers: "What you farmers need to do is to raise less corn and more Hell." [12]

Well-known to the students of Kansas political history is the success of the Populist Party in the elections of 1890, 1891, and 1892, the legislative war of 1893 and the election of 1896. Although the Populists attracted a lunatic fringe and were short-lived, they advocated many measures of merit:

The Populists advocated parcel post, postal savings, rural delivery, equal suffrage without regard to sex, workmen's compensation, eight-hour labor law, interstate commerce commission, government control of corporations, initiative referendum and recall, income tax, direct election of senators, Australian ballot system, primary elections, civil service reform, laws against importation of Chinese labor, government control of transportation and telegraph, regulations of organization and control of banks, factory inspection and numerous other things that we now take for granted.

One of the main pleas of the Populists was for government loans to farmers and home owners. . . . (Likewise they advocated) old-age pensions, and job insurance. . . .[13]

For a time, in a reform effort, they attracted

. . . tens of thousands of native Americans, immigrants, ex-Republicans, ex-Democrats, Catholics, Protestants, Knights of Labor, single-taxers, and plain farmers of every description. . . .[14]

Without question Methodists were involved in this movement although the majority probably remained as Republican supporters. It is significant that Methodist Church papers, such as the *Central Christian Advocate* and the *Annual Conference Journals,* remain nearly silent throughout the period of unrest. Sometime earlier a correspondent had commented on the Grange:

"The Grange" appears to be on the rampage—sweeping down all parties before them in every direction. Just how much good or evil they are likely to accomplish it is difficult to determine. It is very questionable whether it is the more excellent way of promoting reforms to arrogate themselves all the virtue in the country, and to seek the subversion of all parties, and carry out these much-desired reforms behind a curtain, under the most solemn oaths of secrecy. I see they are out with a complete ritual embracing songs, lectures, prayers, funeral services, etc. and are living in anticipation of meeting in "the great grange above." What a meeting that must be—none but honest farmers there! Would it not be well to consider and inquire about the propriety of dispensing with our old time-honored burial services before dispensing with "the benefits of the clergy" and going so far as to institute a heaven exclusively for the "patrons of husbandry." I fear that will develop the fact that these immaculates have tasted the apples of Eden as well as the rest of us. "Let the light enter." [15]

Later in a rather long "Report of Committee on State of the Country to the Kansas Conference," March 5-10, 1890, in the consideration of

causes which lie within the realm of political action . . . it is the duty of the church to call the attention of the powers that be to existing evils . . . your committee would refer but to the following. . . .

Then follows a list including: "Wrongs being suffered by our colored brethren in the South . . . growing influence of the Romish church," the need for support of the public schools, a resolute stand against lotteries, and preservation of morals at the military posts. [16] There was no word about the Populists.

A criticism of the Populist governor, or wonderment, was expressed in one item in the *Central Christian Advocate* on February 22, 1893, which suggested that the people

. . . must grieve that partisan bitterness, bickering, and difficulties have brought the State to the borders of civil war. There were two or three days last week when at any hour a single reckless, foolhardy man, by one shot from a gun, might have precipitated disturbances which would have cost hundreds of lives. It is not for us to attempt to arbitrate between the conflicting Houses in the divided Legislature; nor to determine questions which require patient and wise discrimination and legal investigation, and a spirit of the utmost fairness, in order to their conclusion. But surely it is evident that the Governor of any State ought not to make any threats until he is sure that justice requires them to be made, and that the means are within his reach to carry them out; it is clear that he ought not to call out the militia until the civil power has exhausted its ability to keep the peace and further the ends of law and order; and that he ought not to assign to the volunteer forces of the State any task which he has good reason to believe they will not execute. [17]

One year later, in 1894, the "Committee on the State of the Country" of the Kansas Conference was concerned with "emigration" of foreigners, Roman power, and free schools. The report concludes:

> Third—Our times tend to further turbulence and disorder, extreme partizanship and the multiplication of secret organizations. While we believe in the largest liberty in all political and social affairs we would counsel extreme deliberation in matters of political faith and insist that no question of government or society and no affiliation with secret orders be permitted to destroy interest in the kingdom of God on earth or introduce dissensions or weakness into the visible church. Our business is not more to save souls than to keep them saved. To this end we must support the various institutions of the church with marked liberality, be careful in all public matters to preserve the welfare of the whole people, moral, social and political, and to keep ourselves unspotted from the world.[18]

The South Kansas Conference, in the same year, passed the following resolution:

> Resolved: That in view of the appalling distress and disaster occasioned by strikes, lock-outs and reductions, we instruct our Secretary in our behalf to memorialize the executive of our State, and our legislature immediately upon its assembling, to enact a law establishing a proper board or boards of arbitration with jurisdiction to settle all disputes between employees and employers.[19]

These are the nearest and only approaches to the turmoil of those days on the part of official Methodism in Kansas, or in the issues of the *Central Christian Advocates*.

METHODIST EPISCOPAL CHURCH

In an earlier chapter the story of the organization, in 1856, of the earliest conference, the Kansas and Nebraska, was told. Subsequently, after Kansas and Nebraska were separated, the Kansas Conference was established, March 21, 1861. Three years later the Colorado Conference was formed out of the Kansas Conference. Ten years later it seemed wise to divide the Kansas Conference into two conferences. In March, 1874, the South Kansas Conference held its first session at Fort Scott. It continued as a separate conference until the unification of the Kansas and South Kansas Conferences in the spring of 1914.[20]

The Northwest Kansas Conference was authorized in the spring of 1882, and its first session was held the following year, March 15-19, at Beloit. Not long after the separation of the Kansas Conference into two conferences, came the organization of the Southwest Kansas Conference, largely out of the South Kansas Conference. The first session of this new conference was March 8-12, 1883, at Winfield. From the joining of the Northwest Conference and the Southwest Conference came the Central Kansas Conference with the latter's first session at Salina, October 5-9, 1939.[21]

The obvious reasons for the establishment of the

new conferences were the slowness of travel and the rapid growth of the church—in members of the conference, in churches, and total membership.

METHODIST EPISCOPAL GROWTH IN KANSAS

	1873	1886	1890	1894
Ministers in Conference	144	379	420	512
Probationers in Conference	41	57	76	95
Local Preachers	272	519	458	488
Members of Church	15,083	49,200	68,638	78,640
Probationers	3,791	12,320	11,763	14,863
Churches	79	518	653	813
Value $277,500		$1,265,465	$1,464,343	$1,980,484
Sunday Schools	226	670	733	1,050
Officers and Teachers	1,935	7,392	8,585	12,689
Scholars	14,187	53,720	61,342	83,281[22]

These statistical tables tell an interesting story. For example, the number of members of the Kansas Conference which covered the entire state in 1873, was 144. In 1886 the number of conference members in all four conferences was 379, and 141 in the Kansas Conference alone. In total membership there is also an amazing growth—from 15,083 in 1873 to 49,200 in 1886. The total membership in the South Kansas Conference alone, 15,488, was about the same as the total state membership in 1873; and membership in the Kansas Conference, 14,890, was nearly equal to the former state total. That it was a church building period is very clear—in 1883 there were 79 churches, while in 1886 the total number of Methodist churches in all the state was 518 (189 in the South Kansas Conference and 172 in the Kansas Conference).

In light of crop failures and the resultant economical difficulties and the decline of population during the time of these statistics, it would be expected that membership would not increase. Also church building should have stopped or shown a decline, to say the least, especially in western Kansas. The facts do not show this, however. In both of the two western conferences, during 1886-1894, the number of churches practically doubled, from 94 to 180 in the Southwest Conference, and in the Northwest Conference, from 63 to 123. Even more surprising are the contributions to missions during the drouth and mortgage problem era. The total contribution to missions from Kansas in 1886, was $13,599, and in 1894 the amount was $21,462. Even in the western conferences there were increases during these difficult days.[23]

The spirit of the Methodists is shown in the following excerpts from the reports on the State of the Church to the Annual Conferences, in 1894 and 1895:

The wonderful prosperity of the church in the Northwest Kansas Conference during the past year calls for gratitude in every heart and praise from every tongue.

Although there has been a failure of crops, there has been no failure of the grace of God. The revival fire which was kindled under the labors of Dr. Keen at the last conference has been burning through the year and 3,231 souls have been converted. "Praise the Lord, O my soul." Also, the grace of God has reached the pocket books of the people and the hard times has not stopped church building. During the year thirteen new churches have been built and dedicated, on which there was paid about $28,000, and old church debts have been paid to the amount of $9,000.

Notwithstanding the financial depression and failure of crops: for the past two years, which has, to a great extent, retarded church building and needed repairs, we feel to return thanks unto Almighty God that the spirituality of the church has moved steadily on, until multiplied hundreds have been converted and consecrated unto God. And though we have met with so much discouragement on account if the above mentioned failures, yet a number of churches have been built, needed repairs have been made, and a good percentage of our indebtedness canceled. For this we thank God.[24]

The minister suffered along with his people during this period following the collapse of the boom. Most churches could not pay salaries in full. In the Garden City District of the M. E. Church, for example, 14 churches paid less than $100 for their year's support and some dropped below $50. Many more paid less than $200. Fuel was scarce but the territory offered a meat supply for the hunter—ducks, geese, antelope, rabbits and prairie chicken and prairie dogs (called "prairie squirrel") were eaten.[25] Help did come from the east, in the form of coal and clothes, in response to the appeals.[26]

Later in 1894, eastern Kansas Methodists also organized to help their brethren in the northwestern part of the state. A "fuel fund" was started in the Atchison District and all but three churches responded with contributions in cash. In addition to fuel, there were gifts of clothing, flour, apples and potatoes.[27]

A comparison of Methodism with other large denominations in the state is seen in the following table of the statistics. Among the smallest groups the number of organizations was as follow: Swedenborgian—one; Hebrew—four; Universalist—six; Spiritualist—nine.

Denominational Statistics for Kansas—1896

	Members	Property
Congregationalists	12,597	$ 531,900
Presbyterians	24,935	1,900,700
Baptists	27,604	799,899
Lutherans	28,135	624,660
Christians or Disciples	34,737	498,401
Roman Catholics	72,051	1,309,950
Methodist Episcopalians	101,600	2,322,890[28]

UNITED BRETHREN

The story of the United Brethren during the earliest

days of Kansas history has been summarized earlier. In 1882 they were divided into four conferences— Kansas, Osage (later Neosho), Western and Arkansas Valley (later in 1905 the Southwest). In 1914 they were all joined into one, the Kansas Conference, for the state. By the latter year, compared with 1882, the following statistics are of interest for the entire state.

	1857	1882	1914
Ministers	8	147	185
Fields of Labor	8	100	137
Membership	196	7,427	18,915
Meeting houses	0	39	214[29]

Early in the 1880's the United Brethren throughout the church faced the burning issue of secret orders. Through the pages of *The Religious Telescope* a nationwide essay contest on secret orders was conducted. In some of the publications of the church, Masons, Odd Fellows, and members of other orders were placed by some writers in the same category as drunkards and narcotics addicts. The United Brethren in Kansas urged the General Conference to retain the secrecy law unchanged.

In the General Conference of 1889 at York, Pennsylvania, the radical opponents of the secret societies, led by Bishop Wright, broke with the church and established the United Brethren Church, Old Constitution. The home of the seceders in Kansas was at Lecompton. However, the separation movement did not have much success in Kansas. There were attempts to take over some property but without success.[30]

Like others, the United Brethren suffered in the lean years of the early 1890's with the drought and resultant crop failures. Only the Northwest Kansas Conference kept pace in church construction. Too little help was received from the mission boards. There was some truth in the statement: "The United Brethren converted them; the Methodists put them into church." Also lacking were adequate and well-trained men in the ministry. That their demands of pastors were high is evidenced by the following statement by Bishop Weekley in 1898: [31]

In quite a number of instances a supply of some sort could have been found, but we insisted upon it that no man at all was preferable to half a man. It is possible for a circuit or station to die with some degree of respectability without a pastor, but when it goes down to its grave under management, or rather mismanagement, of a half-hearted, inefficient minister, its last end is full of bitterness and disgrace.

In addition to the lack of help from mission boards and the inadequate supply of trained ministers was a third weakness. Indicated by one historian as crucial was the mistake of the United Brethren in the field of education. Witness the story in a later chapter of Gould College, Lane University and Campbell College, and finally Kansas City University.[32]

METHODIST EPISCOPAL CHURCH, SOUTH

Shortly after the close of the Civil War, the Methodist Episcopal Church, South resumed its activities in Kansas but without much success. The Western Annual Conference was organized in 1870, but in 1883 there were only 26 ministers, 35 local preachers, 31 charges and a membership of 2,722. In the reports two years later there were only three stations listed: Atchison—64; Council Grove—90; and Wyandotte—53. The largest circuits were: Holton—25; Talmadge—129; Leavenworth—229; Council Grove—231; Paola—140; Walnut Valley—163; Fairview—136; and Kinsley—108. The highest total membership was 3,549 which they achieved in 1892. Membership declined from that year on until 1904, when the membership was 2,688 with only 21 charges, 24 ministers and 11 local preachers. The next year the conference at its 36th Session, meeting at Kansas City, Kansas, with Bishop E. R. Hendrix, presiding, memorialized the General Conference that "what remains of our work be attached to the Southwest Missouri Conference as the Western District of that conference." Twenty men were appointed to the Western District.[33]

METHODIST PROTESTANT CHURCH

Immediately after the end of the war in 1866, the Methodist Protestants organized the Kansas Mission Conference and functioned in connection with the Missionary Board of the national church until 1871 when the conference became self-sustaining. By 1880 there were two conferences—Kansas and North Kansas. Writing in 1877, one of the early preachers, Daniel Young, said,

The first Conference that I attended in this State was in the fall of 1868. Three preachers only, besides myself, were present, Moses Jared, the missionary, Nelson Burgess and Brother Crane, and three delegates, all told. . . . At the session of 1870, we had several accessions to the ministry. Here we cut loose from dependance on the Board of Missions, to live on our own resources. Eight of us preachers entered into a bond, pledging ourselves to venture out, in old Methodist style, to make our Conference live by its own exertions. From that date we have prospered. We now (1877) have over seventy traveling and local ministers, and 1,503 members reported at last session.[34]

The tenth session of the Kansas Conference, held at Ottawa in 1880, was an important meeting for the Methodist Protestants. Of interest is that one of the 60 ministers, the Rev. J. Davis, a Negro serving at Spring Hill in Johnson County, asked for a leave of absence, after "soul searching remarks, concerning his labor among his own brethren." [35]

In the Methodist Protestant statistics in 1880 the 60 ministers reported to the Kansas Conference a total of 1,737 members in 28 appointments and a total property evaluation of $5,000; the North Kansas Conference reports indicated 23 itinerant ministers, 14 unstationed ministers and 593 members. [36] At this session of the Kansas Conference 34 persons, including two women, were appointed to churches and circuits.

Through the 1880's the number of appointments and the membership remained about the same but the property evaluation rose to $25,100 in 1887; the number of ministers listed dropped to 46. [37] From a statistical standpoint Methodist Protestants in Kansas reached their highest point in 1899 when they recorded a total membership of 3,039 and 36 charges. [38]

Like other Methodists the Methodist Protestants took a firm stand in 1880 in regard to tobacco as follows:

Resolved, That the use of tobacco in any form is second only to that of intoxicating liquor in its pernicious effect upon its devotees, and that it should be discontinued as an evil existing in our church, seeing that it purloins money from the support of the gospel, as well as prostrates the senses. [39]

The conference was just as determined in regard to liquor:

Resolved, That we, the members of the Kansas Conference, do heartily endorse and will earnestly support the proposed amendment to the State constitution, prohibiting the manufacture and sale of alcoholic liquor within the State of Kansas, save for medicinal, mechanical and scientific purposes. [40]

The Methodist Protestants were not only firm in regard to liquor and tobacco, but also in their position on sabbath observance. Not only should Christians refrain from all secular business and "visiting for pastime" but: "We hereby condemn all gaming on the Sabbath, such as playing ball and croquet, pitching quoits etc. which are a waste of time." [41] The next year they indicated their desire for prohibition of "running of trains, opening and handling of Sunday mails and publishing Sunday papers." In addition, Sabbath laws should be enforced like "any other criminal laws." [42]

That Methodist Protestants still maintained their historic opposition to an episcopal form of church government is seen in the presidential report in 1891.

"Aristocratic forms of church government," the president said, "cannot continue among a people of republican spirit and principles," and then he declared: "The voice of true patriotism, loyalty to the church of Christ and devotion to the principles that bind us as a common brotherhood, cry out against episcopacy." [43] Nine years later the presidential report calls attention to the fact that the Methodist Episcopal Church had admitted equal representation in General Conference "thereby admitting that the principle that gave rise to the existence of the Methodist Protestant Church was right." [44] But, he goes on, the work of the Methodist Protestant Church is not done yet for, "The work of reform must continue until Episcopacy shall loose its alien head and Methodism shall be re-united in the grand principle of a liberal government." [45]

One of the most effective evangelists among the Methodist Protestants in the Kansas Conference was Mrs. Eugenia F. St. John. In the year, 1890-91, she held nine meetings which resulted in 580 conversions and the next year she reported not only 302 conversions but also 400 pledges in regard to drinking and 500 similar pledges to refrain from tobacco. [46] That she was respected by her colleagues in the ministry is shown by the fact that in 1892 she was elected as a ministerial representative to the General Conference. The following year the Kansas Conference by a unanimous, standing vote rejected an overture from the General Conference which would have forbidden the ordination of a woman as an elder or a woman serving as a representative to General Conference. [47] Consistent with this stand for woman's rights in the church was the endorsement by the Kansas Conference in 1893 of an amendment to the Kansas Constitution which would grant equal suffrage to women. [48]

A new way of encouraging the raising of money for missions was tried by the Methodist Protestants in 1895. The conference decreed that in the future any pastor neglecting the meeting of missionary requirements by his local church would not be passed as to character. [49]

FRONTIER MINISTERS' PROBLEMS

On the frontier the minister often received his pay in food. One minister would accept no money for a wedding, but would receive food if it were offered. One couple paid in black-eyed peas while another promised a peck of beans on Sunday but never delivered. [50] Of course, in 1890, a bushel of corn sold for only about 10¢. [51]

That the ministers were not overpaid is emphasized by Reverend M. T. Long writing from Benton, Kansas, early in 1894. According to his calculations from the *Minutes of the Southwest Kansas Conference* of 1893, there were 39 "station preachers" who received over $750 per year. The other 96 received an average of only $458, including rent, and unlike farmers they could not grow their butter, eggs, meat, flour and fruit. He continues: [52]

Certain books and papers he must have; and he must move, too, nearly every year. He is required to attend conference every year, and this, with district conferences, Epworth League conventions, and other gatherings which it is expected he will attend, run his railroad expenses up considerably.

If he has a cow, he must hire pasture and buy food which added to the cost of moving her, makes it of doubtful economy to keep her. He must keep one or two horses, keep a buggy and harness in repair, and all of this must come out of that little five hundred dollars, besides his grocery bill, before wife can talk about a new carpet, or daughter can have a music lesson, or children have the necessary school books. . . . Now to summarize we have groceries, $300; rent at least $50; horse and buggy, $45; moving, $25; books and papers, $20; railroad expenses, $10. This alone leaves but $50 for clothing, schoolbooks, table and bed-linen, and an almost innumerable number of other items of household expense. Many a pastor and wife spend hours together in trying to solve the impossible problem of getting the greater out of the less. But it cannot be done; and so wife fixes over the old hat, and daughter goes without her music, and the boy goes to school in the old suit, and all this, too, when crops are good and all is paid in.

Going to conference in 1880 had its problems, as Reverend R. N. See relates: [53]

Sunday before Conf. I broke my buggy in a snow drift and went on horseback to the appointments, leaving the buggy in the drift. The roads were so bad that I got another horse and a wagon to go to Conference at Concordia. It got dark before we got to the river and we were about an hour in the ice water to the horses sides in finding the road, water was a mile wide and I did not know the way; the wagon was sometimes partly afloat and we could not tell where the river was and could make no one hear. When we finally got to the river we found the water was up to the floor of the bridge and running like mill race and the bridge tied up so as to prevent any one attempting to cross, and no one in sight or hearing and we could not stay here, and dare not go back so I left Mrs. See to hold the team, and I crossed the bridge to see that the planks were all safe and then untied the farther end of the bridge, so as to have nothing in the way if anything should break in crossing, so I could make a run and get across, for I knew I had a team that would take us over if any team could, and there was danger of the ice taking the bridge any moment, went back and drove on with whip in hand. I drove over safely, to a hotel, and we put on dry clothes and rested till morning. I found afterwards where only for a jump by the horses we would have been drowned, at least it seemed so.

Even in the year 1893 the life of the settlers in western Kansas was not easy, as indicated by Reverend William T. Ward: [54]

Our first Christmas dinner together in Kansas was served in a one-room dugout. This particular dugout, about 12 x 18 feet in size, was built on level ground. Dirt had been excavated to a depth of approximately 4 feet and sod with half-window openings in it had been laid up around the excavation to a height of about 3 1/2 feet. Over this was a box-car shaped roof covered with sod. The dirt in the bottom of the excavation formed the floor. The single entrance was at the south end of the room where dirt had been dug out of the wall wide and deep enough to permit putting in the steps. Just inside the entrance in the corner to the right as one entered the room was a cupboard; two beds occupied the far corners; and the cook-stove the remaining one. The table stood in the middle of the room. The meal was cooked with cow chips, that is, dried dung, a successor to buffalo chips, a common fuel in those days. The menu was: salt pork, water gravy, mashed potatoes, bread (No butter or spread), and dried peaches. The fare was plain, but the welcome was such as to grace any Christmas table anywhere.

There were no roads save some very short stretches close to the town. Beyond the towns we traveled trails, and if the ruts got too deep for travel, we simply drove on the sod at the side of the old trail, thus making a new one. These trails were not made by any set rule, rather they were matters of convenience. If we wished to go northwest, we struck out over the prairies northwest, and likewise, for any other direction we might wish to take. If the trail already made did not suit our convenience we were free to make a new one. If we came to a wire fence some settler had stretched about the land he wished to graze, the posts generally being far apart and usually carrying only a strand of wire, I would get out of the buggy, step on the wire and wife would drive across. When conditions were otherwise it was a simple matter to pull a staple or two, cross over, and replace the wire. . . . We always carried a compass with us in those days. This was a safeguard against the possibility of being lost upon the prairie in the darkness of the night, or possibly caught in a fog which occasionally settles upon the vast plains.

A log church, built in 1877, at Lyle, the first church in Decatur County, was rather primitive.[55]

It was about 16 by 20 feet in size. Built from local timber, out along the Sappa Creek. A fireplace was used for heat, and along on each side and ends were little brackets nailed to the wall, where the candles and later on small lamps were placed for the lighting. There was one window on each side, a wooden door facing the east, dirt floor and seats were made from split logs with holes bored in the ends where small posts were driven into the holes, making the legs. The seats had no backs. A post was set in the ground where the pulpit would be, and for a top a soap box was used and it had a cloth cover. A crude, ill furnished church, but you could say for it that it was much better than the homes that most of the settlers live in.

Of unusual benefit to the Methodists on the frontier was the work of the Church Extension Society. In a review of the Society's work in Missouri and Kansas from the beginning, a writer in 1897 pointed out that of the 761 churches erected during that period in Kansas, 744 had received aid one or more times. Nearly $66,000 was paid into the treasury of the society during these years, but the net received in contributions was nearly $80,000 and loans of over $20,000.[56]

METHODISM IN TOPEKA

Two of the greatest churches of Kansas—First Methodist of Topeka and First Methodist of Wichita—were founded early and became "Mother Churches" for their respective cities. Methodism came to Topeka in 1855 at the beginning of things with the Rev. J. S. Griffing as pastor. At that time Topeka was only a village and even five years later, in 1860, it had only 769 inhabitants. From the Town Company the Methodists received six lots in 1856 on Quincy Street, between Fifth and Sixth Streets. They could not start building however, until 1860, because the lots were occupied by fortifications against the "border ruffians." [57]

When the building was finished in 1867, and earlier, it was known as the Quincy Street Methodist Episcopal Church. The move to Sixth and Harrison came in 1880 when a new building was begun and the name changed to First Methodist Episcopal Church in 1882. In 1908 the church had a membership of about 1,300. By this time there were ten other Methodist churches in Topeka with a total membership of 3,200. These were:

Kansas Avenue on the north; Lowman Chapel on the west; Euclid Avenue on the southwest; on the south, Walnut Grove; on the east, Parkdale; Seward Avenue on the northeast; and out in the suburb of Oakland, the Oakland Methodist Church. In addition, there were two Negro congregations and one German congregation.[58]

METHODISM IN WICHITA

In May, 1870, the first Methodist class in Wichita was organized in a livery stable at the corner of Third and Main Streets. During the next winter they worshipped in the Presbyterian Church, with W. H. Zellers as their first minister. The first little church, 32x52 feet, was dedicated December 5, 1872. The population of the town then was only about 500. The Rev. C. R. Rice had a vital part in this early period.

Two families—W. B. Smiths and their daughter, Emma, who married Hiram Imboden—were key people from the beginning. At a benefit concert for the church, arranged by Mrs. Imboden, two of the leading numbers were given by a saloon keeper and a gambler.[59] A large addition to the building was made in 1877. Probably because of the stand of the church against saloons, the church was burned to the ground in 1884, but rebuilt in the same year at a cost of $28,000. In 1907 it had a membership of about 1,200. One-time governor of the State, W. E. Stanley, served as the first superintendent of the Sunday School and continued in that post for 20 years.[60]

The charter members of the next four churches to be organized in Wichita came from this "Mother Church." West Wichita began in 1879 with a society of 15 members with services in a storeroom on West Douglas. In 1886 they built as "The First Church of West Wichita" on the corner of Dodge Avenue and Burton. The church that became "Trinity" in 1906, was begun a year earlier. In the latter year it had 210 members. Emporia Avenue Church had its beginnings in a class organized in 1885. Also out of First Church, in 1887, came the beginning group which resulted in St. Paul's in the northern part of the city. About 1904 the need for a church on College Hill was apparent to First Church members and in 1907 work was started in that area. The Harry Street Church came out of the Emporia Avenue Church in 1906.[61]

Thus, in 35 years, while Wichita was growing from a town of 500 to a city of over 40,000, Methodism organized six churches with a membership of 2,500 and property valued at $155,000.[62]

At the end of 50 years of white settlement and progress, 1854-1904, Methodism launched into the twentieth century with real strength. No other denomination was so well represented in all parts of the state as Methodism. Much had been demanded not only of the first pioneers, but also from those who came later. Only hardy souls could have weathered the drouths, the economic turmoil and the political turbulence of the last quarter of the 19th century in Kansas. By the grace of God and their faith in Him, they found the strength to endure and conquer.

THE COLLEGES—THE MIDDLE PERIOD
1880 TO THE DEPRESSION

To the Methodist Episcopal Church, South, the Methodist Protestants and the United Brethren of Kansas, all adventures in higher education in Kansas have been quite disappointing in so far as permanent results are concerned. Auspicious beginnings were made by all three; the latter two groups then united their schools. But in the early 1930's the denominations had given up and regretfully were out of the higher educational field. Between 1880 and the 1930's, the

154

Methodist Episcopal Church opened two new colleges —the present Southwestern College and Kansas Wesleyan University—and Baker University became more firmly established. Along with this main story are the unsuccessful attempts—by the Methodist Episcopal Church, South, to found a college at Oskaloosa and by the United Brethren to establish schools to serve special areas, such as Gould College and Central College.

MARVIN COLLEGE

In 1876 the township of Oskaloosa in Jefferson County, Kansas, proposed to the Western Conference of the Methodist Episcopal Church, South, the establishment of a "school of high grade" at Oskaloosa. The town offered to lease a building which had cost $15,000 to the church for one dollar a year for 99 years.[1]

The property was accepted by the conference and a committee appointed to take care of legal matters, employ teachers and open the school at once. Under the name, "Enoch Marvin College Association," a charter was secured and the contract with the township closed.

The services of the Rev. N. E. Coltrane of Trinity College, North Carolina, were secured and in August, 1878, the school opened. After only two months the head of the school left abruptly without notice to anyone. The next principal secured was the Rev. J. S. Smith of the Missouri Conference. A term of five months was completed. At the conference session of 1879 Smith was appointed to Marvin College and the Rev. J. W. Faubion appointed as Agent to travel for the school; the Rev. G. J. Nunn was appointed as assistant.

That the school appeared to be on the road to success was indicated in the year, 1880-1881, when there were 100 students enrolled and the total proceeds of the school reached $1,500—"a sufficient amount to meet the demands of the teachers." Within the year, however, everything was changed.

The Dallas Female College in the North Texas Conference made a proposition to at least the principal and the assistant and they went to the Texas school in the fall of 1881. The school carried on only through the first term and then was closed. At the 1882 session of the Western Conference the Board of Trustees reported the necessary discontinuance of the school. The report closed as follows:

We deem the loss of the school a calamity to the Church in the Western Conf. Its life was brief & brilliant & died for want of fostering. We recommend that the Conf. concur in the action of the Board of Trustees. We recommend to our people the schools of our church in Missouri.

155

GOULD COLLEGE

As early as 1870, Harlan, Kansas, was eager for a college. Not until 1878, however, when the Reverend Isaac Williams became the minister of the United Brethren Church at Harlan did any action take place. A stone building was erected during 1881 and 1882. Hoping to attract a substantial gift, the college was named "Gould College" for Jay Gould, the wealthy railroad entrepreneur of New York, who owned part of the Union Pacific which on its way through Kansas crossed Smith County in which Harlan was located. It was a sad day for the promoters of Gould College when Jay Gould sold his interest in the railroad to the Missouri Pacific.[2]

During its first year, 1881, the school had 72 students, only six of whom were in the college department in spite of the fact that only two years were required to finish an A.B. or B.S. degree. Due to financial difficulties and low enrollment—there were only 17 students in the last year—the school failed to open in the fall of 1888.[3]

CENTRAL COLLEGE

Central College of Enterprise, Kansas, was established by the Northwest Conference of the United Brethren Church only ten years after Gould College opened. The property of a business school was acquired and classes began in 1891 with 147 students in attendance. The largest enrollment in the history of the school, 303, came the second year, but only 47 were in the college department.[4] Lane University supporters resented Central College as a competitor and the total life span of Central was only five years.

LANE UNIVERSITY

As related in an earlier chapter, the United Brethren established a school at Lecompton, in 1865, and named it for the well-known Senator James Lane who contributed to the school a total of $2,000. During the years 1867-1882, Lane University graduated 20 students. In the year 1876-77 there were five professors and 105 students; five years later the college building, on the foundation of the old capitol, was finished.

During its entire life at Lecompton, Lane University was plagued by two inadequacies, students and financial support. Each year an appeal was made to the conference to assist with each of these needs. In addition, the school was poorly located. Lecompton, after an early flash of prominence, declined and its population dropped from 7,000 to less than 700.[5] This affected local support and the need to make a change was soon obvious to the board of trustees. Not too far away, at Holton, was Campbell University which they arranged to buy for $17,000 and the movable property of Lane was moved to Holton. Thus ended the ambitious 37 year career of Lane University. It is remembered today because the parents of the former president of the United States, Dwight D. Eisenhower, first met there as students.

CAMPBELL COLLEGE

The merged school, Campbell College, named for its chief benefactor, Allan B. Campbell, began with a good financial and property foundation. It had an 11 acre campus, a college building, a dormitory, classroom equipment, and a $100,000 bequest from the late Mr. Campbell. In addition, the citizens of Holton offered $10,000 if the United Brethren would raise $40,000 for the school over a period of five years. Thereby, from these three sources an endowment of $150,000 would be assured. Until another merger and the next move in 1913, the school operated in Holton. With a new president, J. W. Bonebrake, M.A., and 492 students the school began its first year, 1902-03, with

high hopes for the future. About one half of the students were in the preparatory department.

Toward the end of this Holton period, the United Brethren and the Methodist Protestants as denominations were enthusiastic about uniting into one united church on a national basis. In harmony with this spirit in the two groups and the expectation of national union, the North Kansas Conference of the United Brethren Church in its session of October, 1912, was happy along with the other conferences, to favor the offer of the trustees of Kansas City University (Methodist Protestant) to unite the two schools on its campus in Kansas City, Kansas. The graduation of 1913 was the culmination of the activity of Campbell College. The new school would be under the joint control and ownership of the two denominations.[7] The Campbell president, T. D. Crites, and some faculty went to Kansas City, and others to York College in Nebraska. The united school opened in the fall of 1913 with 150 students, evenly divided between the preparatory and college departments.

KANSAS CITY UNIVERSITY

A Congregationalist, D. Samuel Fielding Mather, a descendant of Cotton Mather, was responsible for the

157

founding of Kansas City University at 33rd and Parallel Avenue, Kansas City, Kansas. This long dream of Dr. Mather finally came to fruition on September 10, 1894, when the school was incorporated under the auspices of the Methodist Protestant Church. Only about a year before his death, at 84, he bequeathed his property, valued at $215,000, to the school. Another donor of prominence was Mr. H. J. Heinz of Pittsburgh, Pennsylvania. The college functioned as a Methodist Protestant school from 1896 to 1913. When the United Brethren and the Methodist Protestants became joint owners and operators of Kansas City University in 1913, they both focused their educational attention and efforts here.[8] This school thus became the successor of other earlier endeavors in addition to Lane and Campbell—Gould College of Harlan, Central College of Enterprise and Avalon College of Avalon, Missouri.

In addition to the main degrees of A.B. and B.S., a variety of other degrees were conferred, including three master's degrees and five doctoral degrees: M.D., D.Mu., Ph.D., and two honorary degrees—L.L.D. and D.D. Oratory and medicine and surgery were popular the first year, 1897-98, with 82 enrolled in the former and 79 in the latter. In 1916-17, there were 245 in oratory, and a year later medicine and surgery enrolled 138. The School of Theology attracted only 37 in the year of its highest enrollment, but it was hoped the school would soon produce better educated ministers.[9] Some of those in oratory may have been headed for the ministry.

Compared with other similar institutions, the university's disciplinary policy was not very strict. It is described as follows:

The discipline of the University will be such as will be calculated to develop the disposition of self-control among students. The regulations will be few and simple, and will be such as will appeal to the student's self-respect and sense of responsibility.

The School's catalogs indicate that this disciplinary attitude was continued through the University's years. The catalog of 1929-30 lists a few additional regulations: The use of profanity, liquor or tobacco about the campus were forbidden; the organization and maintenance of fraternities and sororities by the students was prohibited; in-subordination and other violations automatically removed the student from the college community. Students were required to attend chapel.[10]

Another change came in 1926. In that year the Methodist Protestants because of financial problems decided to withdraw from the enterprise. The school thereby came under the sole control of the United Brethren after payment to the other group for its equity. The next six years were not happy ones. The school gradually lost its academic rating and was plagued as well with financial difficulties. When the depression struck, the school was $95,000 in debt, as reported to the United Brethren General Conference in 1932, nearly $30,000 of this amount to the Methodist Protestants. Tragically, the United Brethren lost their property—the Commerce Trust Company foreclosed on a mortgage of $33,000 and sold the property to the Augustinian Order of the Roman Catholic Church.[11] The church realized nothing out of the whole transaction. Some things, such as the library, equipment and academic records, were moved to York College in York, Nebraska, while other material was sold. Of this endeavor a United Brethren historian said in part:

It was born with high hopes; it lived its time with lofty ideals; but in failing to command the support of those whom it served; it slipped out of their hands. It served its day and its people. It built ideals and character into the lives of many persons.[12]

ONE CENTRAL UNIVERSITY FOR METHODISM

During the first 30 years following 1854, Methodism concentrated its main concern for collegiate education at Baldwin. With the spread of the church to the southwest and northwest, and the formation of the new conferences in 1883, came a desire on the part of the people in the new regions for new separate colleges to serve them. It was the need to give consideration to the total problem of collegiate education that prompted an attempt at joint action by the four conferences. In each of the four Kansas Annual Conferences in 1884, there was appointed a committee of three ministers and two laymen to meet together "to agree upon a plan of educational policy for the four Conferences in this State, said convention to meet in Emporia, June 11, 1884."[13]

The following year came the report from this group:

We recommend that this Conference adopt the resolution of the joint educational Committee of the four Kansas Conferences, which met at Emporia, Kansas, June 10, 1884, which reads as follows:
Whereas, We feel thankful to our Heavenly Father for the great prosperity of the Methodist Church in Kansas; and
Whereas, We are willing to put forth all our energy to advance every interest of our church, spiritual, intellectual, and material; therefore
Resolved, That we are in favor of an educational policy for our church that shall include the whole state; that shall rise above all local and sectional wishes, interests or claims; that shall unify and harmonize all our efforts in the line of education for having one, and but one, central University, to be such, in fact for the entire state; that it be suitably located, having ample grounds and buildings, and sufficient endowment; that it be managed by the "Kansas Educational Association of the M.E. Church," provided said Association shall, by its laws, permit its Trustees to be elected as fol-

lows: six by each of the patronizing conferences, and six by the Association; that in connection with this University, and under the general control of said Educational Association but having their local boards of Trustees, thereby established such Seminaries or Acadamies as each Conference may direct; that we recognize Baker University as the College of the Methodist Church in Kansas, and will endeavor, this Centennial year, to give it such financial aid as shall make it a grand institution, and we do this confidently, for in any event it will be an important factor in the educational system of our church in the state, and because it is now fulfilling a want that cannot otherwise be supplied.[14]

From the actions of the two new conferences, Northwest and Southwest, in these same two years, it would seem that they did not take the joint recommendation in regard to "one central University" as in any way binding. Both conferences proceeded to take action to establish colleges of their own at the same time.

SOUTHWESTERN COLLEGE

In consideration of the report of the joint committee of the four conferences the Southwest Conference, in 1885, voted to approve the report in the main but amend it so that each conference could establish "institutions of full college grade and powers."[15] They also created two committees: one of nine members to constitute a board of trustees "to procure a charter for an institution of learning of full college powers to be known as the Southwest Kansas College"; the other committee of seven "to secure an accessible location which would be assured large and permanent patronage and support, not less than twenty acres of land, a building fund of not less than $15,000 to be provided by citizens and corporations."[16] Immediately the city of Winfield went beyond the requirements and offered 40 acres of land and $60,000 and, in addition, the stone for the building, free use of water for the work, as well as all the hardware and lumber at cost.

Only a little more than a year later, September 3, 1886, a small faculty and 43 students came together with the President, John E. Earp, in North Hall, "shining garishly new." Another building, Ladies Boarding Hall, and the president's residence were ready for the fall of 1888. The first commencement was held on June 3, 1889, when a class of three was graduated. It was reported to the Conference in 1890:

A great revival of religion among the college students had been held and fully nine-tenths of the students were converted and became actively religious.

In the entire four years not one student has been summoned before the faculty for discipline. . . .[17]

A new president, Milton E. Phillips, who came in

1890, found much to be done. For example, the library was nearly non-existent. On their 25th wedding anniversary, in 1892, the president and his wife gave a reception for everyone—students, towns people, patrons and the conference—to which all guests were asked to bring a book. In this "selective" way the library grew as hundreds of guests came. Fortunately, money and checks were also given.[18] That year, 1892-93, Southwest Kansas College had the largest enrollment in any of the denominational schools of the state —a total of 613.

Then came the panic of 1893 which was preceded in Kansas by the earlier turmoil resulting from the drouth, foreclosures, and people moving out. In 1894, President Phillips resigned, a new president stayed only a short time, many of the faculty left and in 1895-96 the school was at its lowest ebb. One of the tragic sights witnessed by the members of the annual conference which met at Winfield in 1896, was that of creditors with moving trucks backed up to North Hall removing furniture and equipment. To save the school William C. Robinson, one of its benefactors, bought up the mortgages and received a deed to the school.

Many solutions in regard to the future of the school were offered. One plan was to move it to Wichita; another suggested asking the Oklahoma Conference to join in the school's support; new names were suggested, such as "Epworth" and "Cokesbury." (The name was changed to "Southwestern College" in 1908.) Nevertheless, the school opened in the fall of 1896. The faculty had leased the school and operated it for two years without a deficit, but faculty members received salaries ranging from only $30 to $50 per month. Tuition was $30 per year, rooms were $1 per month for each student, and board was as low as $1.10 per week. During these lean years more than half of the campus had to be sold—down to 15 acres. The academic rating was in serious jeopardy.

The arrival of Frank E. Mossman to begin his term as President, 1903-1918, marked the dawn of a new day for Southwestern Kansas College. The people of Winfield responded with $25,000, the Southwest Kansas Conference and the alumni rose to the challenge for additional support and new buildings were erected. By the fall of 1916 the efforts of all resulted in a successful campaign for $678,000. During the years of the presidency of Dr. Albert E. Kirk, 1919-1928, this unusual academic and financial advance continued. The following three years saw a decline, however, and the school lost its accreditation.

KANSAS WESLEYAN UNIVERSITY

". . . we believe that it is the duty of our people to give earnest and hearty support to institutions of learning under the supervision of our own church. . . ." These are words from the report of the Committee on Education to the first session of the Northwest Annual Conference, at Beloit, March 15, 1883. That this was partly in support of Baker University is true, but a subsequent report of a Special Committee definitely looked toward a school for their own conference. It called for the location of a college, appointment of a board of trustees, and securing a charter.[19]

Out of the next year came the call for joint action on education by all four conferences, but, as noted in relation to the action of the Southwest Kansas Conference, the report of the joint committee in 1885 resulted in no supporting action. Indeed, both of the new western conferences utterly ignored it and each moved ahead with its own college. The Northwest Kansas Conference in 1885 ordered the board of trustees of the new school to proceed. The name of the school, "Kansas Wesleyan University," was adopted and a charter from the state was secured during that year.

The choice of location was soon narrowed to Salina, with the promise of 15 acres of land and $25,000 for a building. Of interest is the fact that the leader of the Salina group was a member of the Protestant Episcopal Church, Mr. A. M. Claflin. During the first part of 1886 the administration building was completed except for the basement which was finished with student, trustee and faculty labor (one trustee was on crutches for two years as a result of an accident on this painting job). This was the only building for 17 years.[20]

The doors of Kansas Wesleyan opened to students on September 15, 1886, with a faculty of 11 and the total enrollment added up to 121, excluding duplication: two in the college, one of whom was a senior transfer student; 61 in the preparatory department; 25 in music; 20 in business; nine in the normal department; and a training school of 27. Mr. Henry M. Mayo, the senior, was the sole graduate in the spring of 1887, and the next lone graduate was in 1891. That there were only 14 graduates in the first five years indicates how much of the enrollment was in departments other than the collegiate; often over half of the student body were in the preparatory department.

Slow growth was experienced in the later 1880's and the 1890's which was a time of crop failures and social and financial dissent, especially in western Kansas. The needs of Kansas Wesleyan were the same of those of Southwestern—money and students. Indebtedness grew, to $13,000 in 1903, and continued to plague the school through the first two decades of the new century.[21] The school was accredited, however, for a time, 1916-19.

Hopes ran high in the early 1920's. A new president with great dreams, Larkin Bruce Bowers, came in July, 1919. At the next Annual Conference the Committee on Education expressed a new determination:

... The University Senate has now fixed a rule that by 1925 we must have a half million interest earning endowment. .... In view of all this we heartily endorse the campaign for $600,000 for building, equipment and endowment, launched recently and hope that it may be carried to completion as speedily as possible. ...[22]

Later the goal of $600,000 was raised to $1,000,000 in a "Victory Memorial Campaign." With real satisfaction, President Bowers reported early in 1922, that more than the latter amount was pledged. However, only $100,000 in net cash had been realized in 1922; the remainder was in pledges. As they dreamed in 1919 they could not know of the effects of the depression of 1921-22 on the whole agricultural area—real estate values shrank, price levels declined. As a result, pledges remained unpaid and all collections were difficult. Neverthless, still in high hopes, the trustees went ahead with the buildings for which only a part of the money needed was in hand. Financial problems delayed finishing the Hall of Pioneers for eight years and the School had an embarrassing indebtedness at the time of the dedication in 1930.[23]

In 1930 the prospects looked good, but there were soft spots. The total enrollment was approximately 900, including 283 in the Liberal Arts College; there were 34 faculty members and nine in administration; the total operating budget was almost $125,000, but the yearly deficit was almost $9,000; the total indebtedness was over $87,000; and an attempt to achieve accreditation had recently failed.[24] Along with most other schools, Kansas Wesleyan was not ready to face the depression of 1930's.

BAKER UNIVERSITY

In an earlier chapter something of the spirit of Baker was caught up in the story of the Skylark of Methodism, William Alfred Quayle. He first came to Baker as a student in 1874 and after graduation returned as a professor in 1887; then followed his term as president, 1890-94. In 1887 the enrollment for the fall term was 386. This compared very well with that of other schools in Kansas that year: University of Kansas—482; Kansas

163

State Agricultural College—472; State Normal School, Emporia—875; Ottawa—215; Bethany—340; and Highland University—91.[25] Like the other Methodist colleges, Baker had a large number of students in the preparatory, normal and commercial departments as well as in the liberal arts college. For example, in the year of 1894, out of a total enrollment of 500, only 130 were in the college department.[26]

In the year, 1887, football, in a primitive form, was first introduced into Baker athletics. Indeed, the introduction of football to western colleges occurred on November 22, 1890, when Baker played Kansas University at Baldwin—Baker won 22 to 9. Six days later Baker defeated Washburn 32 to 0, in the first game at Topeka.[27] The years 1892-93, were great football years for Baker. Merton S. Rice, later a famous Methodist preacher and biographer of W. A. Quayle, was captain of the team in 1892. In 1893 these scores are recorded: Baker 28—Missouri 0; Baker 14—K. U. 12; Baker 10—Nebraska 10; Baker 4—K. U. 0; Baker 32—Denver 0.[28]

The next year at the session of the Kansas Conference, the following action was taken:

We are pleased to know that a military department, through the wisdom of the president, has finally been established at Baker. We consider it a healthly and gentlemanly exercise for the young men of the institution. Upon the question of foot ball, we believe with the executive committee of the board of trustees, that the physical risk of the participants in the game, as now played, the danger is greater than should be, and that the game should not be permitted hereafter at Baker, unless the rules of the game be so changed and modified as to prevent what is usually called "mass plays" or "flying wedges," wherein most of the serious accidents to members of other clubs have occurred.[29]

Despite these objections a football team was organized that fall.[30] One further athletic note of April 26, 1902: "Forty men at Baker University were suspended for watching a women's basketball game. Admission had been denied everyone except the faculty and newspaper men."[31]

When President Quayle left in 1894 he was succeeded by another young man of only 33 years of age, Lemuel Herbert Murlin. He served a longer time as head of the school than any other president, 17 years, 1894-1911. Later he served as president of Boston University for 14 years, and after that in the same role at DePauw for three years. During Murlin's presidential term new buildings were erected, the financial situation improved, academic standards raised and enrollment increased. Indeed, in 1907 Baker ranked seventh among the 50 Methodist colleges in the United States in both total enrollment, 999, and in the college department,

506.[32] There were 30,000 volumes in the library. From the earliest Baker was approved by the University Senate of the Methodist Episcopal Church, accredited by North Central Association in 1908 and was on its first published list. It was later approved by the Association of American Universities in 1926, and three years later by the American Association of University Women.[33]

During President Murlin's tenure there was an attempt made by some people in Topeka to get Baker moved to their city. Real impetus was given to this effort when Mrs. Eliza Chrisman of the capitol city left $100,000—$150,000 for a "Methodist University" in Topeka. Baker authorities decided not to move but the money was claimed for Baker by the Kansas Annual Conference. After 12 years of litigation during which Kansas Wesleyan claimed a share, the matter was finally settled out of court and Baker got the estate.[34]

Without much question, the days of greatest national prominence for Baker University came on September 22-23, 1911, on the occasion of the inauguration of President Wilbur Nesbitt Mason. The presence of the President of the United States, William Howard Taft, and his address on Sunday afternoon, on World Peace, was the highlight. Also present were the two Kansas senators, Bristow and Curtis, Governor Stubbs and two

PRESIDENT WILLIAM TAFT
AT BAKER—1911

congressmen. Dr. Francis J. McConnell, then president of DePauw, and later a bishop of the Methodist Episcopal Church, preached in the morning service.[35]

The administrations of President Wilbur N. Mason, Samuel E. Lough and Wallace B. Fleming witnessed two large financial drives which resulted in increased endowment and new buildings. In 1930, Missouri Wesleyan College merged its educational work with that of Baker.

165

For all educational institutions the 1930's were difficult years financially. Baker was no exception as indicated in this excerpt from Baker's report to the Kansas Conference in 1934, but there is also a note of hope:

The budget for last year was balanced. This was made possible by the fact that all employees of the college were cut twenty-five per cent and that later they took a second cut of from ten to twenty-five per cent more. Notwithstanding these sacrifices it will be exceedingly difficult to balance the budget of the current college year. . . .

Our college had completed seventy-five years of service for the Kingdom of God. The present year is being celebrated as the Diamond Jubilee Year.[36]

The same report spoke for all Methodist colleges when it affirmed:

. . . The making of a better civilization for which the multitudes are yearning will require leadership trained according to the finest intellectual standards and developed with equal care as to Christian character. The leaders of the new day must be men of God if we are not to continue repeating the tragedies of the past.[37]

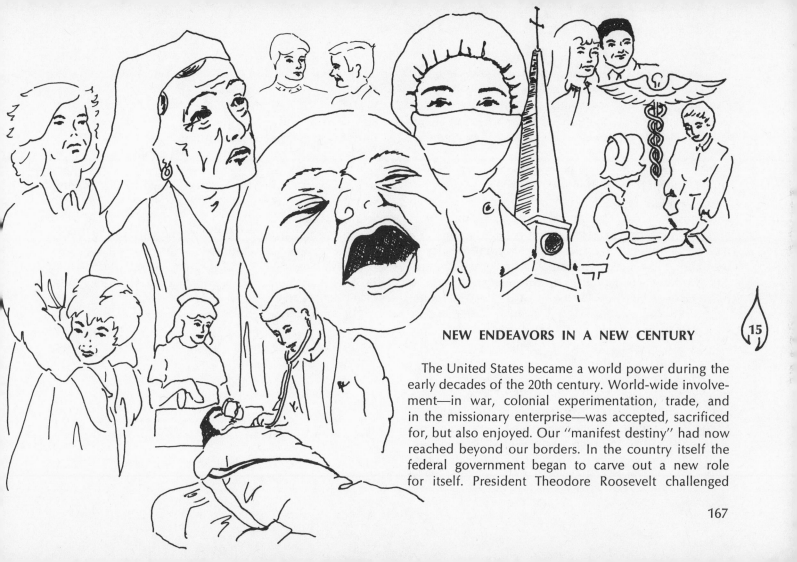

NEW ENDEAVORS IN A NEW CENTURY

The United States became a world power during the early decades of the 20th century. World-wide involvement—in war, colonial experimentation, trade, and in the missionary enterprise—was accepted, sacrificed for, but also enjoyed. Our "manifest destiny" had now reached beyond our borders. In the country itself the federal government began to carve out a new role for itself. President Theodore Roosevelt challenged

167

Wall Street, the federal income tax was voted and national prohibition was inaugurated. After we fought "to save the world for democracy" we hurried back to "normalcy" and isolation which spelled the doom for President Woodrow Wilson's dream of our country's involvement in the League of Nations.

In the first third of the century the country experienced a mixture of unbounded confidence in the future, development of a social conscience in the churches, Machiavellian as well as idealistic endeavors in world politics, extension of suffrage to women, "a noble experiment" in national prohibition, the rise of the labor movements, industrial strife, prosperity, recession, Ku Klux Klan, and uncontrolled expansion in business—all followed by the great depression of the 1930's. Kansas was involved in all of this and had its own manifestations of each. Obviously, the church and its members were active participants in all the changes and in the turmoil. However, the Methodist Church was vocal and actively involved overtly in only two crises—World War I and prohibition. Methodists, at every Annual Conference, spoke out boldly in regard to the liquor traffic. Tobacco, especially cigarettes, ran a close second as an object of their regular castigation. That members were involved on one side or the other of the other developments is to be assumed, but official records tell nothing or little of this concern or participation.

During the last decade of the 19th century many people over the nation had despaired of Kansas. The rampant growth of Populism and its seizure of power in the state were a threat to the establishment. Some felt that the need "to civilize Kansas" was of great importance. Making this widely known to the country was the famous editorial of William Allen White in his *Emporia Gazette*, August 15, 1896, entitled "What's the Matter with Kansas." This was no mild article but a vitriolic attack on Kansas—its political leadership, economy and the blind followers.[1] The editorial was broadcast by the Republicans as a campaign document in the fall of 1896.

The state soon righted itself, in the opinion of the Republicans, and a new day was at hand. A Methodist paper joyfully reported this in 1905 under the title "Happy Kansas":

F. D. Coburn, secretary of the Kansas Board of Agriculture, who knows more about that State than any other citizen, said to an interviewer: "Kansas is probably the most prosperous State in the Union. It has had a succession of large crops of wheat, corn, oats and hay that have brought good prices; their hogs and poultry have been in great demand, while their dairy products have grown enormously in volume and value.

In 1904 the total value of the farm products of Kansas was $208,406,365, and if you add the assessed valuation of live stock, it will bring the total up to nearly $370,000,000. Last year we had $51,000,000 worth of animals sold for slaughter, $9,000,000 worth of hay, nearly $8,000,000 worth of poultry and eggs were sold by our farmers, $7,000,000 worth of butter, and so on. From 1895 to 1898 we raised 199,260,222 bushels of wheat; from 1900 to 1904 we raised 381,504,953 bushels. The wheat crop alone of the past five years paid our farmers more than $250,000,000 and their other crops brought them a corresponding amount. That is the reason they are so contented." Hundreds of millions of dollars of mortgages have been paid off and the farmers now have over $110,000,000 in the banks.[2]

Ten years later, in 1915, in a similar report from the Board of Agriculture for the past 20 years, Kansas had increases: 9% in population; 400% in value of crops; 200% in live-stock, eggs and horticulture; 300% in manufacturers; and 400% in mineral output.[3]

During the intervening years, however, had come a jackrabbit invasion early in 1912, and another grasshopper scourge in the summer of 1913. A vivid glimpse of a glorious sense of humor that helped some Kansans face tragedy is seen in the reporting of the invasion,

January 1—Heavy snows had brought "invasions" by hungry jackrabbits. At Hugoton a man took a picture of 422 eating at a rick of feed. . . . The Hutchinson *News* declared they were knocking down the weak, wobbly cattle and eating their oil cake and hay. "A dozen farmers are missing," said the *News*, "rabbits have carried them to their dens in the sandhills. In Reno and Stevens counties jacks carrying bags of human scalps demanded ten-cent bounties from county clerks." . . . In Ford county rabbits destroyed 10,000 catalpa trees and barked cottonwoods along the Arkansas river to a height of two feet above the snow. . . . The Cimarron *Jacksonian* said Jim McNamara went out one day to feed his stock and saw a herd of jackrabbits coming over the divide. He had a sack of corn chops with him and as soon as he saw the rabbits he started toward the house to get his rifle. There was a hole in the sack, and the corn ran out in a stream, making a trail about 400 yards long to the house. As he reached the house the rabbits swooped down on the corn. As they were all in a perfect line with their heads to the ground, he sighted his rifle, "guaranteed to kill a bear a mile away." He let fly and killed every rabbit in the herd. There were 942 in the pile.[4]

The same spirit is exhibited in regard to the grasshoppers:

A Barton County farmer said they were so big that his chickens ran for shelter thinking they were hawks. A Ness County man said it was nothing to see one or two grasshoppers tugging against a steer for a stalk of corn.[5]

Our chief concern in this chapter is with new movements or new institutions within the total life of the church and especially the Methodist Episcopal Church. Our purpose is to trace the growth and developments of these hospitals or other institutions during more than 60 years although our major story is carried through only a third of the century.

THE EPWORTH LEAGUE AND INSTITUTES

One of the important new endeavors was the Epworth League as the national youth organization of the church and the subsequent development of the Epworth League Institute. The young people's organizations of the Methodist Episcopal Church actually go back to the Church Lyceum, in 1872, or more particularly to the Young People's Methodist Alliance, in 1883. The latter was organized at the Des Plaines Camp Ground near Chicago, by Doctor and Mrs. Lowry. The Alliance soon had 500 local societies and two full-time representatives. A year after the organization of the Alliance came the establishment of the Oxford League, in 1884, by Bishop J. H. Vincent. In 1887 two other groups—the Young People's Christian League in Boston and the Methodist Young People's Union in Detroit—were formed to coordinate and consolidate existing local societies.[6]

The actual birth of the Epworth League can be dated on May 15, 1889. The day before there gathered in Cleveland, Ohio, representatives of several youth organizations within the Methodist Episcopal Church seeking to establish one organization. Among the names considered for the new organization were "Wesley League," "Christian League," "Oxford League," and "Wesleyan League." After much prayer and discussion it was agreed on the second day to accept "Epworth League." Also accepted were: the colors—the white ribbon with the scarlet thread running from end to end to signify "Purity through the atonement"; the Maltese cross as the badge; and the motto, "Look Up, Lift Up." [7] It was not long before the new organization became an integral part of the total life of practically every church and became an item to be reported at Annual Conference. A central office was established in Chicago.

As an outgrowth of this new youth organization effort came the Epworth League Assemblies and Institutes. Northwest Kansas Conference, about 1899, began an assembly, held between Cawker and Downs at Lincoln Park. In 1902 they attracted 1,500 to 6,000 daily with an auditorium seating 3,000. "In all of these assemblies the special and predominating feature is how best to do

the work of the Epworth League in the local church." [8]
Undoubtedly other assemblies patterned after Chautauqua programs, or in connection with them, were held earlier but the first official institute held under the direct management of the Central Office of the Epworth League was held at the Des Plaines Camp Ground, near Chicago, in the summer of 1906, with an enrollment of 150. A year later three were held—at Lakeside, Ohio; Lake Geneva, Wisconsin; and Winfield, Kansas —with a total enrollment of over 800.[9] Six months before the institutes of 1908 more than 2000 registrations had been received by the Central Office.

The institute at Winfield was held on the grounds of the Chautauqua Assembly on Island Park on Timber Creek. The advertised total expense for the week was no more than $10. More than 500 registrations had been sent even six months before the 1908 institute which exceeded the 1907 institute enrollment of 300. The effectiveness of the 1907 institute was indicated by the fact that out of the 300 in attendance there were 12 young men who volunteered for the ministry, 22 young men and women who offered themselves for work in foreign mission fields, and 20 young momen who volunteered for deaconess service, while "about two hundred joined in consecrating themselves to return to their homes for service as earnest as they would give

in the heart of any foreign land." [10]

In 1910 the General Secretary of the Epworth League, the Rev. Edwin M. Randall, D.D., planned a series of Institutes to be held in succession from June 20 to August 28: Mount Herman, California; Bonner Springs, Kansas; Lake Minnetonka, Minnesota; Byron Camp Ground, Wisconsin; Cazenovia and Sea Cliff, New York; and Mountain Lake Park, Maryland. As indicated, the Winfield institute was moved after three years. The institute at Bonner Springs, July 11-17, advertised unlimited tenting facilities: 10x12 ft. tent—$4; cots—50¢ each; double blankets—40¢ each; pillow with slip —15¢; double sheet—15¢. Meals were offered at the rate of $4.50 for 21 meals. The ten faculty people brought in were involved in the following courses: General Epworth League Methods, Spiritual Work, Bible Study, Mission Study, Christian Stewardship, Christian Social Service, Temperance and Christian Citizenship, Social and Literary, Junior Work and Music.[11]

Three years later the Central Office sponsored two Institutes in Kansas—one at Baldwin and the other at Salina.[12] During the succeeding years changes were made. They became graded on three age levels and the total number of classes grew immensely. In 1934 the Institute at Winfield had a registration of 1,008 and an attendance of nearly 1,300 while the Baldwin Institute reached its highest enrollment in the summer of 1939, when there were 1,002 paid registrations and more than 70 classes offered during the week.[13]

THE RIGHTS OF WOMEN

Kansas women have always been an independent, forward-looking group. As early as 1861, women won the right to vote in school elections—an action prior to that of any state except Kentucky. After 1887 they could vote for any city or school official or school bonds in any first, second or third class city. This was extended to public bond improvements in 1903. The Methodist Protestant Church was more open to the participation of women, even as clergy, than other denominations. In 1912, however, came the big triumph when woman's suffrage was achieved, eight years prior to the 19th amendment to the United States Constitution.[14]

This success came as a result of a strenuous campaign dating back to 1879 in Lincoln, Kansas, with the organization of the "Equal Suffrage Association" and the subsequent state organization in June, 1884. Many groups joined in this effort from that date to 1912. The following verse to be sung to the tune of "Auld Lang Syne" appeared in the Burlingame *Enterprise* on October 3, 1912:

> If a body pays the taxes
> Surely you'll agree
> That a body earns the franchise,
> Whether he or she.

In the final drive Jane Addams from Hull House, Chicago, and Dr. Anna Howard Shaw, president of the National American Women's Suffrage Association, both conducted speaking tours in Kansas for the suffrage cause. The women won by a margin of over 15,000 votes, and the amendment to the state constitution was adopted.[15]

Similar rights were not always granted early in the church. Women were not seated in the General Conference of the Methodist Episcopal Church until 1904 although the admission of lay delegates to the General Conference was granted in 1872. The admission of women to the highest conference of the church had a long, stormy history. Women were elected but they were not allowed to be seated. Even the famous Frances E. Willard was chosen in 1888 but not allowed to serve. A non-Methodist has commented on this: "She was admitted, in marble, to Statuary Hall in the capitol building in Washington, but not to the Methodist general conference." [16]

172

BETHANY HOSPITAL AND DEACONESS HOME

Bethany Hospital and Kansas City National Training School came out of the desires of two groups. Five Kansas City physicians were eager to establish a mission hospital. At the same time, through the inspiration of an address on the Deaconess Movement by Mrs. Lucy Rider Myer, in Topeka, in 1889, some women determined to establish a Deaconess Home in Kansas City. The two groups decided to establish a Deaconess Hospital.

The new enterprise was chartered, March 8, 1892 under the name "Hospital and Training School for Deaconesses and Nurse Deaconesses." [17] At first it was located in a cottage at 312 Washington Avenue, Kansas City, Kansas, with a 12 bed capacity. It was controlled by a board of nine trustees, two-thirds of whom must be members of the Methodist Episcopal Church. The superintendent-nurse was Miss Annie Deutsche, a graduate of Mrs. Lucy Rider Myer's training school of Chicago (Chicago Training School that later joined with Garrett Biblical Institute).

To the Kansas Conference, meeting at Baldwin, March 1-6, 1893, came a request from the trustees for the adoption of Bethany Hospital by the conference. During the ten months previous to the Annual Conference, 64 patients had been treated at the small cottage hospital with the donated help of ten physicians in Kansas City, Kansas and Kansas City, Missouri. In addition, 140 persons had received treatment in a free dispensary. When Bethany was formally adopted by the Kansas Conference it had assets of $1,287.97. The action of the conference at the 1893 session was:

Resolved: That we adopt Bethany hospital, including the deaconess' home and training school, as the institution of this Conference.

Resolved: That we pledge the trustees of Bethany hospital our influence, prayers and hearty support.

Resolved: That we welcome to our various charges any representative of this institution and assist them in raising funds for the same. [18]

Miss Annie Deutsche, not only a graduate deaconess but a graduate nurse, served as superintendent of the hospital and director of the nurses from the opening until January, 1897. The Chief of the Medical Staff, 1894-1911, was Dr. P. D. Hughes. [19]

In November, 1893, the hospital moved to a large two-story brick building at Orchard Street and Tenny Avenue, Kansas City, Kansas, where there was a 45 bed capacity. Six years later a nurses' residence was erected. [20] In the year, 1899-1900, 654 persons were admitted and treated and the total number of workers was now 20, not including medical and surgical staffs. The total receipts from all sources for the year were $15,875.88.[21]

Eleven years later, in 1911, it was reported that a five-and-one-half acre site had been acquired in the heart of Kansas City, Kansas, plans and drawings for a 200 bed hospital to cost $200,000 had been made, and "the foundation is in and paid for." Also, the city was making a park of about nine acres in front of the site at a cost of $125,000.[22] The new building was open on January 18, 1916, but the total cost had grown to $600,000. Another $100,000 went into the adjoining nurses' home dedicated on October 10, 1923.[23]

In a report of 1942 Bethany was an improved, modern institution of 150 beds, accredited by the American College of Surgeons and fully equipped. At that time Bethany Hospital School of Nursing had graduated 536 nurses since its beginning 50 years earlier, and there were 74 enrolled in 1942. They were cooperating with Baker University in a five-and-one-half-year program—B.A. degree and a graduate nurse diploma—in addition to the regular three year course.[24] The patient care unit was completed in 1957 and on July 24, 1966, *The Kansas City Kansan* carried the news of a new wing—extended nursing care and therapy—to be built at a cost of over $3,000,000.

KANSAS CITY NATIONAL TRAINING SCHOOL

Already mentioned in the story of the beginning of Bethany Hospital was the interest of Kansas women in the Deaconess Movement. In the development of Bethany Hospital and the Deaconess Training School in Kansas City, the women as well as some men on both sides of the state line of Kansas and Missouri joined. In the new hospital there was no adequate provision for the Bible training of girls going out as nurse deaconesses wearing an official uniform. Only about three years after Bethany's opening the Woman's Home Missionary Society was considering the founding of a training school in the midwest. At the same time a local group under the leadership of the Rev. J. W. Alderman, was urging the same. After considerable correspondence between Dr. Alderman and Mrs. Jane Bancroft Robinson of the Woman's Home Missionary Society, the Secretary of the Deaconess Bureau, Mrs. Robinson, stopped off in Kansas City on her way to California in the winter of 1899. At this time definite arrangements were made for the founding of a school to be known as "Fisk Bible and Training School" in honor of the national president of the Woman's Home Missionary

Society, Mrs. Clinton B. Fisk.[25]

On October 18, 1899, the school began in two rooms in the home of Mrs. Rogers at 251 Orchard Street, Kansas City, Kansas, under the direction of Miss Mary Pegram. The first gift of supplies was that of Dr. Alderman—six boxes of matches. In January, 1900, the school opened with two students, Lulu King of London Heights Church, Kansas City, Kansas, and Grace Roop of Oakley Church, Kansas City, Missouri. Lectures were provided also for the 18 nurses in Bethany Hospital by the first two part-time teachers, the Rev. Christian F. Reisner, minister of London Heights Church, and Professor W. W. Wallace in music. Although Bethany and Fisk were separate institutions they held their commencements together until 1906.[26]

To take the place of Miss Pegram who resigned in March, 1900, because of ill health, came Miss Winifred Spaulding. During her two-and-a-half years of leadership until she went as a missionary to the Philippines in November, 1902, she made a great contribution. In September of the first year the school moved to 726 Washington Avenue and the enrollment increased to 16. A year later, in 1901, another move took them to 608 Everett. In the class of 1902 was found the person whose leadership would lift the school to new heights —Miss Anna Neiderheiser.[27]

At the national meeting of the Woman's Home Missionary Society in October, 1902, in Grand Avenue Temple, Kansas City, Missouri, Dr. William A. Quayle, pastor, the trustees voted to locate the school in either Kansas City, Missouri or Kansas City, Kansas—in the city which would donate the best site. It was through the influence of Dr. Quayle that a member of Grand Avenue Church, Mr. C. E. Schoellkopf, made a gift of ten acres of land at 15th Street and Denver Streets, Kansas City, Missouri. The gift was accepted and Fisk Hall was built during the latter half of 1904. The school moved to the new location in December of that year and the new building was dedicated, June 4-8, 1905. It was during these times that the name of the school was changed to "Kansas City National Training School for Deaconesses and Missionaries" and the Fisk name retained in the one building.[28]

Before 1910 it was quite evident that another building was needed and collections began; early in 1911 a new building was authorized. A year later came a gift of $25,000 from the brother and nephew of the late Mr. Schoellkopf toward the new building which was given the name "Schoellkopf Hall." It was opened in September, 1913. "Kansas Building" was erected in 1920-21 and it was given its name because of the gift of $25,000 from the Woman's Home Missionary Societies in the three Kansas conferences. It was dedicated May 22, 1922 by Bishop William A. Quayle. At the 25th anniversary, the total property was valued at a half-million dollars with an indebtedness of $40,000.[29]

In the beginning the course of study was two years, but it was extended to three years in 1918. Non-resident part-time teachers did a large part of the work in the early years, but by 1925 three-fourths of the teaching was carried by resident deaconess teachers. In 25 years there were 404 graduates, coming from 34 states, Hawaii, and four foreign countries, who went out to serve in 41 states, the District of Columbia, Alaska and ten foreign countries.[30]

SUCCESSORS TO THE DEACONESS SCHOOL

The unsurpassed leadership of Dr. Anna Neiderheiser continued until her retirement in 1939. Changes were made under the new president, Rev. Lloyd V. Gustafson, 1939-1945, and his successor, Dr. Lewis Carpenter, 1945-1963. The name of the school was changed to "National College for Christian Workers" and then to "National College." After 1939 the program was extended to four years and put on a degree basis; later the school became co-educational.[31] Finally in 1965 the efforts of National College were joined with those of Saint Paul School of Theology Methodist, on a graduate level.

Throughout the school's whole history it has been supported by the women of the entire country, but the local leadership came from Kansas and Missouri women, and others in the middle west region. In the founding of Saint Paul School of Theology Methodist, it was Bishop Dana Dawson of Kansas who furnished the initial leadership. In addition, the first substantial gift to the school, $10,000, was made by the Kansas Conference.

THE METHODIST HOMES FOR THE AGED

TOPEKA—HUTCHINSON

A joint committee composed of nominated representatives of the four Annual Conferences of Kansas met in Topeka, August 2, 1904, to consider a "Home For The Aged" under the direction of the Methodist Episcopal Church in Kansas. They elected a Board of Trustees, authorized the securing of a charter, and chose Topeka as the location of the future home. They recommended to the Annual Conferences, in 1905, that the home be adopted and property be secured. This report was adopted.[32]

It was reported in 1909 that they had rented the old parsonage of First Methodist Church, next to the church on West Sixth Street. More important was the purchase of 24 lots, costing $4,000, but valued at $7,000, in the Lowman Hill District, as a site for a permanent home.[33] For a time the Home was located at 1201 Clay Street. In 1914 the south wing was completed at a cost of $40,000, with accommodations for 24, and a permanent location established. The East and North Wings were built in 1925, which increased the accommodations to 150, at a cost of $165,000 and the West Wing was erected in 1929 for $61,815. In 1930 there were 135 persons in the Home; the property was valued at $300,-000. The north addition was completed, at a cost of more than a million dollars, and opened in August, 1954.[34] In over 60 years of service the Home in Topeka has given a sense of security and Christian fellowship to more than 2,000 worthy, aged people in Kansas.

To the Central Kansas Conference in 1965, came the exciting news of the expansion of the service of the Church to more of the aged or those in retirement. For some time it was obvious that the excellent home in Topeka could not meet the needs of the total state. Therefore, plans for an additional facility, under the control of one board of trustees, incorporated as "The Methodist Homes for the Aged of Kansas," were an-nounced. The location for the new enterprise—Methodist Retirement Center—is at Hutchinson on a site valued at $15,000, made available by Mr. William F. Volkland of Buston. Dr. John Hoon was named as the administrator of the new home. As planned, the Center will care for a total of 182 residents, including 36 in a health care unit. The total cost was estimated at over $2,000,000, and the completion date set for the fall of 1968.[35] The popular name will be "Wesley Towers."

WESLEY HOSPITAL—WICHITA

Without question one of the most important actions of the Southwest Kansas Annual Conference, at its 30th session in Hutchinson, March 13-18, 1912, was the approval of the following report:

Whereas: There is a vast territory of rapidly developing country lying between Kansas City, Missouri, and Denver, Colorado, in which there is no modern Protestant hospital; and whereas, over-tures have been made by reliable business men of Wichita, Kansas, a rapidly growing city of 60,000 people in the midst of a very vigorous and generous Methodist constituency of fully 100,000 people and one-half million Protestants, a city having the neces-sary railroad facilities for reaching this vast territory, and having no Protestant hospital; we believe the time has come when this Conference should take the initial steps necessary to establish a hospital of the Methodist Episcopal Church in the city of Wichita.

Therefore, be it resolved that this Conference elect a hospital Board of trustees consisting of eleven men, for one year, who may receive donations of money, securities and real estate, and any other suitable property, and hold in trust and use the same for the purposes of a hospital of the Methodist Episcopal Church in Wichita:

And furthermore we nominate the following men for this board, viz:

Rev. A. B. Hestwood, J. N. Knapp, A. O. Rohrbaugh, G. D. Fazel, Geo. Cox, J. W. Anderson, J. H. Graham, Rev. W. J. Martindale, G. E. Meeker, W. M. G. Howes, Rev. A. O. Ebright.[36]

Before this action, two men, the Rev. A. O. Ebright and the Rev. A. B. Hestwood, had been urging this move. The former was elected president of the Board of Trustees and the latter became the first superintendent. Later in the year, the board was incorporated and a charter granted on August 28, 1912, to the "Wesley Hospital and Nurse Training School." Soon after they leased for three years a former sanitorium at 1103 North St. Francis Street in Wichita. The owner spent $2,000 on remodelling and the citizens of Wichita furnished it with "the most modern equipment costing more than $5,000." It opened for patients on October 15, 1912, and the first one was admitted the following day.[37]

Two years later attention was drawn to the completion of a new Maternity Home. The figures for this year, 1914-1915, are also revealing: the total value of hospital equipment, $4,560.57; the number of beds, 40; total number of patients during year, 416; income from private and ward patients, $10,564.89; received from Conference collections, $2,566; total indebtedness, $6,382.43.[38]

After eight years at its first location, Wesley moved in 1920 to its present location, Hillside and Central, into the five-story Main Building. The story of $50,000 of that total $125,000 which went into this structure goes back to 1916. Ira T. Foster of Augusta came to the hospital a sick man. After recovery, when he left the hospital, he said, "If I should strike oil on my farm I'll make Wesley a gift for a new building." He struck oil and gave $50,000. Citizens of Wichita raised an additional $75,000.[39] In contrast to the report of 1915, the 1920 figures are amazing: Value of property, $378,935; debts on property, $190,000; income from the hospital, $26,701; number of patients, 955.[40]

Other improvements and buildings were added, the Maternity Building with 86 beds and bassinets in 1948, but the great expansion began in April, 1955, with the West Wing groundbreaking and in 1959 with the Fifth Floor of the West Wing. Thus, in a short period, Wesley had grown from a hospital of 30 beds to an institution with the following 1964 figures: Patients, 21,606; cost of hospital property, less depreciation, $6,140,749; student nurses enrolled, 136; nurses graduated, 1,230; total beds, 543.[41] At the end of 1965 came a thrilling proposal of the Great Wesley Plan, involving $4,650,000.[42]

GRACE HOSPITAL AND SCHOOL OF
NURSING—HUTCHINSON

The forerunner of the present Grace Hospital was the Stewart Hospital, built around 1891 and owned and operated by the two Stewart brothers, medical doctors. In 1915 the Methodists acquired the property and operated it as the Hutchinson Methodist Hospital. To this endeavor the Annual Conference gave its blessing in 1915, but indicated no acceptance of any "present or future financial obligations . . . nor any part of its maintenance. . . ."[43]

Soon after this, Mercy Hospital and the Welch Hospital were taken over and consolidated with the other hospital. In 1922 the Conference voted to take over Grace Hospital upon the fulfillment of certain conditions which included a challenge to the people of Hutchinson in regard to finances. Because of Wesley Hospital's emergency campaign the Hutchinson people postponed their drive.[44] Finally in 1924, when all conditions were fulfilled, Grace Hospital and School of Nursing, Inc., was taken over by the Methodist Episcopal Church as an official institution.[45]

Later that same year the first unit of a five-story plant was begun, to bring the bed capacity to 92 immediately; (the total dream when realized would be a 250 bed hospital) and the nurses home was moved.[46] In 1927 the total value of the property was $221,728.03, and the total number of patients admitted during the year, 2,266. "Grace Hospital was never in better shape financially."[47] The second unit adding 44 beds came in 1929-30, at a cost of $50,000; $417,276 was raised in 1946-47; also the S. P. Rowland Memorial Wing which cost $457,000.[48] The School for Nurses Training was discontinued in 1934, because there were only two student nurses, but it was re-opened in the fall of 1936.[49]

The report of 1963-64 carried the following figures: Patients, 5,477; cost of hospital property, less depreciation, $1,962,961; student nurses enrolled, 58; nurses graduated, 464; total beds, 174.[50]

EPWORTH HOSPITAL—LIBERAL

It was to prevent a six-year-old private hospital from falling into non-Protestant hands that the District Superintendent and a number of people in Liberal and near-by towns, secured an option on the building and equipment in the name of the Methodist Episcopal Church. With the cooperation of the national Methodist Board of Hospitals and Homes, the hospital was acquired on October 1, 1924, subject to the approval of the next Annual Conference, for the purchase price of $50,000, but valued at $85,000. When it was approved, the Conference was in possession of a fairly new property with a capacity of 50 beds.[51]

A great advance came in 1951, when a new wing was opened which included not only 22 patient beds, but also a nursery, operating and delivery rooms, laboratory, pharmacy, dining room and kitchen and staff offices.[52] In 1963 the following was reported: Patients, 3,265; patient beds, 64; cost of property, $353,430.[53]

HOSPITALS IN NORTHWEST KANSAS CONFERENCE

A bold program for hospitals in the Conference was that proposed by a special committee under the chairmanship of President L. B. Bowers, of Kansas Wesleyan University, in 1921:

I. We recommend one conference hospital program to include all the hospitals that may be established under the control of the Methodist Episcopal Church in this Conference.

All hospitals to share pro rata in the funds raised for buildings and maintenance.

II. We recommend, that a 100-bed hospital be located at Salina, Kansas. Salina to furnish site and 1/3 amount necessary to build and equip a standard hospital.

III. That a 50-bed hospital be located at Belleville, Kansas. Belleville to furnish site and 1/3 amount necessary to build and equip a standard hospital.

IV. That a 35-bed hospital be located at Goodland, Kansas. Goodland to furnish 40 percent, including site of the amount necessary to build and equip a standard hospital.

V. That we accept the proposition of Dr. W. C. Lathrop of Norton, Kansas, for cooperation with the Lathrop Hospital at Norton, Kansas which provides that patients sent to this hospital by Methodist authorities shall receive free medical attention and surgical attention at cost, as shown by the books of the hospital.[54]

In the report to the Conference three years later, attention was called to the fact that "we have four well equipped hospitals in operation," Goodland, Belleville, Norton and Salina.[55] The Hays Protestant Hospital, "the last of the Conferences' five hospitals" was dedicated in 1925 and served 99 patients in its first three months of operation.[56]

ASBURY HOSPITAL—SALINA

Methodists in Salina and the surrounding area, have been justly proud of Asbury Hospital. As indicated before, its origin dates back to 1921 when it was accommodated in a large converted residence at the present location. After six years the west wing was finished and occupied. At the time of the union of the Conferences, Asbury had property valued at nearly $200,000 and a school of nursing with 45 girls in training.[57] Two years later, in 1941, the east wing was completed at a cost of $38,000.[58] Another addition, the south wing, came in 1950-51, which brought their property value up to $425,000 and total beds to 102.[59]

In the composite report of 1964 Asbury had the following statistics: Patients admitted, 5,225; total beds, 136; cost of hospital property, $1,229,412; student nurses enrolled, 52; nurses graduated, 401.[60]

HAYS PROTESTANT HOSPITAL

HADLEY MEMORIAL HOSPITAL

A remodelled Methodist Episcopal Church became a small three-story hospital in May, 1925, but it was not until 1942 that it began to be financially stable. This came with the first gift of the Hadley family of a $56,000 addition. In the same year the name was changed to Hadley Memorial Hospital.[61] The next section, started in July, 1949, was dedicated on May 11, 1959. The total gifts from the Hadley family or estate amount to $1,681,500.[62] The statistics for Hadley in 1964 were: Patients admitted, 2,775; total beds, 112; cost of hospital property, $2,117,692.[63]

BOOTHROY MEMORIAL HOSPITAL—GOODLAND

On the western edge of the state in Goodland, was one of those hospitals founded early by the Methodists. It moved along as an effective, but smaller, hospital. In 1944 they reported: Number of patients, 1,205; value of property, $48,569.40; number of beds, 24.[64] In 1947-49, the hospital at Goodland completed a 38 bed annex which brought their total property value to $340,000.[65] Fifteen years later the statistics included the following: Patients admitted, 918; total beds, 49; cost of hospital property, less depreciation, $205,667.[66]

KANSAS METHODIST HOME FOR CHILDREN

METHODIST YOUTHVILLE

Another endeavor of all three of the conferences of Kansas was the Kansas Methodist Home for Children which was first presented to the conferences in 1927. In the first report of the committee, among the proposals were: the selection of the site for the enterprise,

Newton; as to the architecture, the cottage plan; a pay-as-you-go finance plan; the selection of W. V. Burns as superintendent; and

> The organization now has assets amounting to $1,542.51. A substantial offer from the city of Newton consisting of a twenty-acre free site, free school privileges for the children of the Home, and the proceeds of an intensive campaign of their community, which shall be used by the home at its own discretion in furthering the purpose of the home.[67]

By conference time in 1929, the Home reported that the first unit had been built at a cost of $60,000.[68]

In the first five years, 113 children of all ages had been helped by the Home and many had been adopted from the Home. In the last of the five years, 1934, there were 31—17 girls and 14 boys—in the Home. The total amount given by the three conferences, in that year, was over $9,000.[69] In 1939 it was indicated: that 70 children had been in the Home the past year for at least a time; that during the past ten years the ages of the children covered a range from three to eighteen; and the total number of children in any year was between 42 and 46. There were no deaths in the family in the ten year period.[70]

An idea of the program and the expansion of the facilities is caught in the following report of 1942:

> The Home site consists of 307 acres, part of it located within the city limits; two buildings, Libby and Ward Halls; a large modern dairy barn, new hay barn, shelter house and several other farm buildings. The property is out of debt and has been for several years. The farming venture has been very successful as a training school for the boys and a source of fair income.
> Several hundred children have been members of the family and most of them have gone into private homes or graduated and become self-supporting. Fifty-six are at present under the supervision of the Home.[71]

A change in the policy and philosophy of the Home, on the part of the Board of Trustees, came in 1953 and 1954, especially with the coming of the Rev. A. Coyd Taggart, as superintendent. The need for a "well staffed social service department with trained professional people to carry out these placement services" was emphasized, partly due to the prompting of the State Board of Social Welfare in Topeka.[72] Many changes took place in the institution's buildings and professional help was employed; state recognition came during the next year.[73]

By 1957 the program of the Home was largely confined to teen-age youth and it had the distinction of being "the only fully licensed private agency in Kansas to admit teen-age boys and girls for residential care." The income for the Home had doubled and the number of children served had also doubled.[74]

A new name, "Methodist Youthville," first suggested in 1959, was soon accepted. In accord with the new emphasis on decentralization, the "Wichita Group Residence for High School Girls" was begun in 1960, as well as the "Bronco Buster's Boys Ranch and Pioneer Industries" on the Newton campus.[75] In the next year's report appears the "Triple B Ranch," at Dodge City, on which two buildings had already been erected.[76]

IN A THIRD OF A CENTURY

It will be recalled that the state of Kansas was one Conference before 1874. In that year, in the southern part of the state, another Conference, the South Kansas, authorized by the General Conference in 1872, came into being. Another change came in 1883 when the Northwest Kansas Conference, organized out of the Kansas Conference, held its first session. In the same year the South Kansas Conference was divided and the Southwest Kansas Conference became the fourth conference in the state. The number was reduced to three in 1913-14, by authorization of the General Conference of 1912, when the Kansas Conference and the South Kansas Conference united; the first session of the new Conference, the Kansas Conference, was held, March 18-23, 1914, at Chanute, Kansas.[77]

Statistics tell only a part of the story of the life of the Church, but they do reveal something of the external growth or decline. The compilation of figures in the following membership summary indicated the numerical changes of the three Churches: [78]

Membership

Methodist Episcopal	1915	1925
Kansas Conference	70,467	84,713
Northwest Kansas	19,175	24,455
Southwest Kansas	48,491	53,773
Total	138,133	161,941
Methodist Protestant	1,359	1,085
United Brethren 18,915	(1924)	18,749

The above figures reveal that a slow-down in membership had come over the United Brethren. Whereas, in 32 years they had more than doubled in numerical strength from 7,427 in 1882 to 18,915 in 1914, now in the next nine years they were barely holding their own. In regard to the Methodist Protestants, the situation was even more serious. Indeed, the Kansas Conference of this Church declined in membership from 1897 forward. In that early year 36 charges reported a total membership of 3,295, while in 1905 there were 29 charges and 2,147 members. However, in 1930, five years after the final date on the comparative chart the figures show some gain—17 charges and 1,242 members.[79]

In an earlier chapter the action and resolutions of the Methodists in regard to temperance have been related. All through the early decades of the 20th century the annual conferences of the Methodist Episcopal Church in Kansas never failed to express their disapproval of the liquor traffic. In this they were joined by the Methodist Protestants on more than one occasion. For example, in 1911, the Kansas Conference of the Methodist Protestant Church petitioned the Congress to delegate to prohibition states the authority to regulate the shipment of intoxicants into prohibition territory. At the same time they deplored the fact that one member of the President's cabinet had allowed his name to be used as president of the Brewer's Association.[80] For a time each Methodist Protestant minister was required to preach three sermons a year on temperance.[81]

Support of the 18th Amendment and the Volstead Act was a constant emphasis in the three conferences of the Methodist Episcopal Church through the 1920's. The closest any conference came to political involvement was in 1932 when the Kansas Conference urged that "support and confidence be given *only* to those candidates who are definitely committed to the maintenance of the 18th Amendment and the Volstead Act." At the same time they commended the Kansas American Legionaires at the National Convention in Detroit who stood against a resolution favoring the beer trade.[82] Even stronger was the report approved by the Southwest Kansas Conference in the same year, which stated in part:

Senseless and sinister propaganda regarding "the evils of prohibition," adroitly managed, is given out from a legion of sources to the credulous, and "the very elect are deceived." The incredulous are led into fear and confusion by the subtle mashalling of statistics, the vacillations of political candidates, the week-kneed surrender of apostate reformers, the misrepresentation of our economic status, and by the "imposing" spectacle of party-platforms in various stages of saturation. Colossal sums of money are being spent to thwart the enforcement of the Volstead Law, thus tending to discredit all law and bring the Constitution itself to an open shame. Lawlessness has always been a chief characteristic of the liquor traffic, but today there is demonstrated a new aggressiveness as it flaunts its open defiance upon America. And "dry" patriots are painted as buffoons. Much of our hope is in the people! Hence it is imperative that the people recognize the seriousness of our plight.

We deeply regret the stand of the presidential candidates on the two majority tickets. One, standing on his party platform for outright repeal, brazenly sounds the doom of the 18th amendment!

The other, going beyond his party platform, declares for repeal by favoring "state control," on the ground that "an increasing number of states and municipalities are proving themselves unwilling to engage" in enforcement. Such an admission would result in the breakdown of our Democracy: when a nation finds itself unable to enforce the laws it chooses to create, deterioration has begun. "It is not really prohibition that is on trial. Constitutional government is on trial. Law is on trial." [83]

Through the years there was a regular concern for Sabbath observance. That this was an important issue through this period is clearly evident in the action as late as 1931, by the Southwest Kansas Conference:

First: We view with alarm the growing disregard for, and the lack of Sabbath observance. It appears that the day is being increasingly desecrated by the doing of ordinary work, operating and patronizing of picture shows, ball games, golf, swimming pools, etc. In fact, the importance of Sabbath Day observance no longer prevents many, and even professing Christians, from indulging in the foregoing.

Second: We also view with serious concern the failure on the part of the church to protest against Sabbath desecration and to encourage Sabbath observance. We deeply regret that in some quarters men in religious positions not only enter no protest, but actually sanction the indulgence of those things which are contrary to the spirit of the Lord's Day. [84]

Practically all the denominations gave hearty support to the government in the prosecution of our cause in World War I. Here the Kansas Methodists were in the vanguard, especially in the Southwest:

The church to which we belong—that church which in the days of Lincoln and Grant sent more soldiers to the field and more prayers to heaven than any other, should be ready on all proper occasions to declare in most positive terms its attitude towards the desperate conflict whose tramping armies and clashing arms is shaking the earth to its very center. It is the conviction of your committee that the Southwest Kansas Conference should at this time go on record as heartily and loyally supporting the Government in the prosecution of the war. [85]

Of considerable interest is the resolution in regard to war by the Northwest Kansas Conference, in 1927, only nine years after the war:

Whereas, there seems to be concerted effort on the part of certain capitalistic interests and jingoistic parties to embroil the United States of America in war with our national neighbors on the South of us. . . .

First: We are against war and force as international arbiters, since nothing is settled thereby.

Second: We are against military training in our schools.

Third: We favor all effort on the part of individuals and nations who work for the outlawing of war.

Fourth: That we register as our conviction that the United States of America should have no larger army than is needed for policing of our interests.

Fifth: That we pray for the time to come soon when the soul

developments of the world shall be commensurate with the wonderful developments in applied sciences so that we shall be morally fit to be heirs to the ages.[86]

It was a vigorous Methodism that entered the 20th century. That many individual Methodists took determined action on certain issues is assured. Certainly many supported Methodist Governor Henry J. Allen in his problems with the unions that eventuated in the Court of Industrial Relations which existed for a time, 1920-25. A concern over the Ku Klux Klan in the early 1920's occupied the attention of the state. However, the Methodist Church took no official action in regard to either of these serious episodes in the life of Kansas.

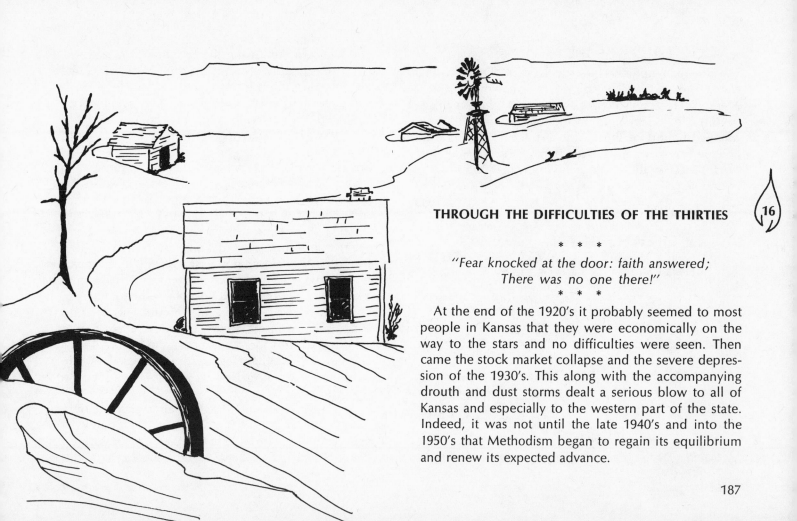

THROUGH THE DIFFICULTIES OF THE THIRTIES

* * *

*"Fear knocked at the door: faith answered;
There was no one there!"*

* * *

At the end of the 1920's it probably seemed to most people in Kansas that they were economically on the way to the stars and no difficulties were seen. Then came the stock market collapse and the severe depression of the 1930's. This along with the accompanying drouth and dust storms dealt a serious blow to all of Kansas and especially to the western part of the state. Indeed, it was not until the late 1940's and into the 1950's that Methodism began to regain its equilibrium and renew its expected advance.

EFFECTS OF THE DEPRESSION

More than numbers are involved in the following chart. The two sets of figures, for each of the three Methodist Episcopal Kansas conferences (two after 1939 in The Methodist Church), indicate the expenditures for the support of the pastor and the total giving to benevolences for a 10 year period, 1930-1939.[1] The drop in each of these categories in the first four years is phenomenal.

Year	Support of Pastor (not including house)			Total Benevolences		
	N.W. Ks.	S.W. Ks.	Kansas	N.W. Ks.	S.W. Ks.	Kansas
1930	$211,291	$356,309	$500,380	$167,254	$373,042	$457,199
1932	149,718	281,207	400,569	105,753	258,481	260,257
1934	125,087	236,294	284,695	62,640	171,644	187,407
1939	116,982	257,723	293,614	58,000	209,177	170,737

To be noted is that from 1930 to 1934 pastoral support declined 44% in the Kansas Conference, 40% in the Northwest Conference and 33% in the Southwest Conference. Even greater was the drop in total benevolent giving in the same period—60% in the Kansas Conference, 60% in the Northwest Conference and 54% in the Southwest Conference.

More surprising are the figures for 1939. Here it will be noted that the giving had not changed appreciably in the five years following the low point of 1934. Indeed, in the Northwest Kansas Conference the giving is slightly lower in both categories while in the Kansas Conference the benevolent giving continued to drop even though the pastoral support had started to climb. The Southwest Conference was up a little in both categories.

Earlier it was suggested that there was more than numbers involved here. Obviously, the decline in the total benevolent giving by the three Kansas Conferences—over $683,000 in four years—had its effect on Methodist work around the world. Missionaries were brought home, foreign and home mission work had to be cut back or closed down, some conference members in detached service had to return to their home conferences and other complications resulted.

Young men just going into the ministry did not find a ready welcome into the crowded conferences. Fewer were received into the conferences during the 1930's and there is a resultant age gap as revealed by the studies and charts prepared by Melvin Booth for the Kansas conference.[2]

In this regard the most dramatic and tragic incident of these years is that at the session of the Southwest Kansas Conference in 1932. In the Executive Session on Friday afternoon, October 7, Question No. 5. "Who have been received on trial?" was taken up.

C. A. Kitch moved that on account of the crowded condition of the Conference no one be received On Trial this year, and the motion prevailed. On motion of S. C. Foster, the Conference requested Bishop Mead to explain to the group of candidates for Admission on Trial why this action was taken and the request was graciously carried out by Bishop Mead.[3]

One of the nine men to be received On Trial at that conference personalized the story later:

After they passed this motion we were invited into the church and marched up to the front seat and all nine of us were in the row. Then Bishop Mead arose to inform us that the Conference had voted to receive no one. Whereupon they marched us right out of the church like a bunch of whipped dogs.[4]

Ray Bressler and some of the others involved in this embarrassing episode were received On Trial the following year, but it was not forgotten. Not all of the nine stayed in the ministry.

THE DUST BOWL

The grasshoppers returned in 1936-37 and again in 1948 but their serious damage was eclipsed by a far greater scourge—dust. The western two-fifths of Kansas became a part of a six-state area designated as the "Dust Bowl." Beginning in 1932 the serious storms continued for seven years. Even by 1934 the Soil Conservation Service estimated that about 300,000,000 tons of soil had been moved by the winds.

THE BLACK BLIZZARD OF HUGOTON—APRIL 14, 1935

To the Southwest Conference in October, 1934, the Dodge City District Superintendent, Everett Freeman, reported:

Emerging from one of the most difficult years in the history of

189

our conference. . . . Never have we seen a more complete consecration and greater determination. Brown fields, barren and parched pastures, starving cattle, and cropless sections have not defeated purpose, but rather challenged positive action.[5]

The most devastating year was 1935. The dust storms were a daily occurrence by April of that year and on April 14th "the sky at noon was as dark as midnight, and people were reported to have lost their way in their own backyards." [6]

William F. Ramsdale, then a pastor in the Dodge City District, recalls two experiences of that same year:

One was when we had to delay a burial for nearly an hour before we were sure we could see the grave sufficiently well so the pallbearers would not misstep and fall into the grave. Another was on the Black Sunday when one of our members coming to choir rehearsal for the Easter Cantata ran into the building before he saw it. . . .[7]

Croplands were abandoned and nearly 15,000 people migrated from the southwestern part of the state between 1934 and 1938. The federal government helped with relief and through the Agricultural Adjustment Administration. The Kansas "rugged" individualists, did not want to become "ragged" individualists, someone said. Even Methodist Republican governor Alfred M. Landon praised this program of the Roosevelt administration.[8]

That Methodists were greatly involved is seen in the vivid descriptions included in the annual report of the District Superintendent of the Liberal District, Jesse C. Fisher, to the Southwest Kansas Conference in 1934:

It would not be fair to our total situation if we did not mention the dust storms and continued drouths. This is our third year of total crop failure in a land that was once the Great Southwest. Each year the farmer has gone forth to sow, only to have the seeds picked up and carried away or to have it come up and give every promise and then gradually wither away, County after county has been left as barren as the hard-surfaced highway. Thousands upon thousands of dollars worth of fine machinery has been without the sound of turning. World capacity elevators have been empty. Long strings of grain cars are standing on the side tracks. Wheat trucks have disappeared off the highways. Rural automobiles are three years old and more. In some places they have been reduced to the chassis and are drawn by horses and mules. Long periods of drouth have dried up the pastures and the stock cattle have been moved out. One of our men was driven to rid himself the other day of 100 shoats that weighed 80 pounds each. The code price was 16 cents per shoat. But they could not be kept for there was no feed. Alfalfa hay went up to $24 per ton and wheat to $1 per bushel but none to sell. The very poor people have been put on relief works and have fared well. The rich have been waiting a better day, trying to hold their belongings intact. But the average family, God only knows what it has faced in these terrible days and long nights. They have borrowed for every crop they have put out 3, 5, 8, and 10 times. No returns. The most of our work is with the average family. When he goes what then?

There has been an increase over last year of more than 10% of all ministerial claims, and of all Missionary offerings. There has been an increase to Southwestern of $736. Epworth Hospital has kept out of the red and settlement made in the interest. The Ladies' Aid Society has brought in $7,327 in egg and quilt money and in some places half of the pastor's salary has been paid by them. The W. F. M. S. and the W. H. M. S. has had an increase this year.[9]

Fisher's report of the next year indicated a more serious condition in the worst area of the state:

And now we have come to the matter of the dust basin. In size it is said by reliable authority to contain 18,000,000 acres. Since we are in the center of the bowl we may be permitted to speak as one on the inside. And since it is a "National Catastrophe," as reported by Governor Landon when he visited this section, you must know our work has been effected, and the outlook right now is far from encouraging. It will rain some time and the dust return to mud and prosperity will come back, but what is to be done until the rain comes? The Federal Government found it necessary to put thousands of dollars into this country to keep people alive. If it had not, a conservative estimate says, three-fourths of the population would have had to have found temporary relief elsewhere, until they could return to their homes. The country was highly developed during the Great War. The world was crying out for wheat, wheat, everywhere wheat, and Southwest Kansas and the Panhandle of Oklahoma answered with some of the best wheat, and the largest number of bushels to the acre, of any state in the Union. During these days the country was prosperous. The people paid for their land, built homes and settled down to carry on the business of agriculture, and to face their responsibility as good citizens. These people came to settle and not to move. They are home loving, church going folk. God does not make better people. They subscribed liberally to Centenary and World Service. Then the war ended, the price of wheat went down below the cost of production, and four years ago came the drouth. The churches have held on hoping that something would happen. The preachers have shared with the people, and many instances, because they would not complain have shared out of all proportion.

I care to speak but briefly of the suffering, the sickness and the fatalities of the dust storms which lasted fifty-four days and with but very little interruption. There could not help but be sickness. The Red Cross sent a doctor and as high as twenty-five Red Cross nurses to work out of Liberal. Emergency hospitals were quickly opened, one in our Church at Ulysses. Measles broke out everywhere. Dust pneumonia raged. People were instructed to wear masks. Ten thousand were sent to Liberal at one time to be distributed to school children in the territory. The mortality rate went up. One pastor conducted ten funerals in eleven days. The dust covered every thing and piled several feet high when obstructed in any way. All houses had to be sealed to prevent choking and in an effort to keep the place habitable. In one place the ceiling of a new church sagged badly when a few people came for the morning service. Before men could get at it, it had burst through and the dust was pouring down. Three tons were taken out. No one attempted to travel any distance except in case of necessity. When they could go it was as between two very close mountains only one could not see the top. The surface of the earth seemed down hill all the time and made one feel he was just about to slip off of something head first. For weeks, and that at the Easter season our churches barely existed. Schools closed most everywhere part of the time and some had to close altogether. But why say more about the storm. It is all over, thank God. We have only had these storms once in the knowledge of man in these parts. We probably will never have them again. You cannot defeat the people of the West. They just will not be defeated.

Pastors salaries are not below that of last year, they are above. The estimates are not below last year, they are above. World Service is not down, it is up. The Woman's Home and the Woman's Foreign Missionary Society are not beating the drums of retreat. They never do. They are marching onward. The Ladies Aid had a better year than last year. The district has been over the top in its number of Christian Advocates for months.[10]

The report of the same man for 1936 showed not much relief:

There has not been a crop in the four years that I have served the District, and the last crop of five years ago sold for less than the cost of production. The enormous expense of putting out one crop after another is staggering. Margins have been wiped out long ago and the country is living on Federal loans. This cannot continue indefinitely. Public programs, such as schools and churches, have been based on days of prosperity. The buildings and equipment are the very best. It is not as in a new country where there never has been plenty. It is the universal belief that the good days will return and bring the greatest joy.[11]

THE COLLEGES IN THE DEPRESSION YEARS

A potentially serious financial situation at Baker in in the beginning of of 1930's was averted by the merger of Missouri Wesleyan College with Baker, 1930-32. Missouri Wesleyan was a descendant of the Cameron Institute, founded at Cameron, Missouri, in 1883. Four years later, in 1887, it was offered to and accepted by the Missouri Annual Conference.

Missouri Wesleyan became a Junior College in 1928 and that fall 25 upper classmen came to Baker; in 1929 there was a total of nine students from Missouri Wesleyan at Baker and the same number in 1930.[12] Meanwhile, a "Joint Commission on the Merger of Missouri Wesleyan College with Baker University, and the Co-operative Educational Enterprise of the Kansas and Missouri Annual Conferences" was at work. Their report to the Kansas Conference in 1931 indicated: that the endowment funds of Missouri Wesleyan had been transferred to Baker; also, all scholastic records had been moved; and that Baker had been adopted as the official college of the Missouri Annual Conference.[13]

In 1930 Baker was in need of $200,000 to obtain from the General Board of Education of New York a pledge of $100,000. The endowment fund of Missouri Wesleyan—$179,500, less the loan of $60,000 Baker had made to them—made possible the full monetary goal needed to satisfy the General Education Board and the payment of $100,000 was received.[14]

The depression brought hardship, however, and the only way to achieve a balanced budget in 1934 was to cut the salaries of all employees at Baker by 25% and then again by 10-25% more. The pain may have been lessened that year by the announcement after re-inspection that Baker was continued on the approved list by the Association of American Universities. This followed an earlier six year term. The school took pride in the fact that it was the only church college in Kansas to have such approval.[15] During the following years, 1936-39, the spectre of indebtedness haunted the school and the annual deficit averaged about $12,000. Total enrollments varied from about 300 to less than 500 students.[16]

Few schools have gone through a more disheartening experience than that of Kansas Wesleyan from about 1930 to 1937. In some respects the situation was not good for two years before that because of operating deficits. In 1930 the school looked good on the surface. There was a total enrollment of approximately 900, including summer school; but only 283 students were in liberal arts and the Business College accounted for nearly half of all students in attendance—427. There were only 9,300 catalogued volumes in the Library.[17]

From the summer of 1931 the financial situation of Kansas Wesleyan worsened rapidly—the debt stood at $87,631 at that time and in February of the next year the payments on bonds could not be met. For the fall of 1933 a professor with a doctorate was hired for room and board and a maximum cash salary of $600. Accreditation of the school was in the balance and was lost. Attempts were made to join with College of Emporia but to no avail.

In the midst of near financial tragedy 132 students petitioned the Board of Trustees in the fall of 1934, as follows:

We, the undersigned, believing the social life on the campus to be lacking in the respect of universal enjoyment to all, petition the Board of Trustees to consider such a policy that will permit dancing at school functions under the supervision of a joint student-faculty committee.[18]

Such a deviation from established practice was met with the following motion by the Board:

That we as members of the Board of Trustees of Kansas Wesleyan University do not place approval upon the dance as part of Kansas Wesleyan University's social program but favor the approval of the traditions of the school in this regard based upon the new

193

advice of the Church, that nothing may be sponsored or approved that cannot be done in the name of the Lord Jesus.[19]

Tragedy struck on December 29, 1936, when the Board of Trustees was informed by President Bowers that the indebtedness stood at $384,000. That evening it was resolved:

That under Section 77-B of the National Bankruptcy Act a petition be filed "for reorganization of the corporation, at the earliest possible date." The schedule of partial payment was generally set lower than that recommended by President Bowers. Final action in the reorganization was taken July 6, 1937.[20]

Only a few months later President Bowers was dead. Truly it was said at the next conference, "we might not have our school at the present time but for the long-time President. . . ." The year, 1938, brought the beginning of a new period but the bankruptcy action cast a cloud over the college for many years.

During the 1930's Southwestern College was fortunate in having the stable administrative leadership of Dr. Frank E. Mossman. All through the period the school was faced with an indebtedness which ranged between $200,000 and $300,000 and the operational budget was always in jeopardy. For example, the total amount in the budget declined in six years, 1927-28 to 1933-34,

from $237,532 to $131,613—the greatest drop was in the last two of these years.[21]

The Conference helped and the city of Winfield contributed $35,000 and the indebtedness was reduced by almost $100,000 but it did not stay down. The campaign to clear the indebtedness began in 1931, but because of poor crops the results were meagre. A renewed effort was made in 1934.[22] There were bright spots, however. At the time of the "Golden Jubilee Year," the fiftieth anniversary, in 1935, the school legitimately boasted that 2,158 persons had received their A.B. degrees and could be found "in every continent and practically every nation of the world." In that year there were 651 students enrolled, including 81 in the School of Fine Arts. Also of importance was the relation of students to the church:

While all the churches of the city shepherd our students, Grace Church is, after all, the college church. The first college prayer meeting had 187 present. The average attendance at the College Epworth League the past year was 150. One hundred sixty-seven have transferred their membership to Grace Church for the present school year. In addition to the students who sing in the various other church choirs in the City, there are enough student members of the Grace Choir to form more than two complete choirs.[23]

The financial condition in 1938 was not as good because of an operational deficit of $30,122.17 and the

194

expectation that the coming year would be no better. Again, the problem was farm income and shortage of income from tuition; the total indebtedness, however, had dropped to $136,700.[24]

WESLEY FOUNDATIONS

Wesley Foundations throughout the country had the misfortune of beginning their work just before the financially perilous days of the 1930's. At the Northwest Kansas Conference of 1929 appreciation was expressed for the work being done at the Kansas State Teacher's College at Hays.[25] In response to the needs of 4,000 Methodist students in the state schools the Methodist Episcopal Kansas Conference in 1929 formulated ambitious plans. During the previous year a study had been made by a committee representing the Wesley Foundation boards at Lawrence, Manhattan, Emporia and Pittsburg. For buildings, endowment, and sustenance they recommended the following: Lawrence—$150,000; Manhattan—$150,000; Emporia—$50,000; Pittsburg—$50,000; $15,000 for campaign expenses; and $25,000 for the church at Baldwin—the income to be used for care of students. Thus, the total amount asked for was $440,000. It was also recommended that "the money for these askings be secured without an intensive campaign through the churches." Also created was a Wesley Foundation Commission, with three members from each Foundation, to coordinate the interests and work of the participating boards. Sustenance for all Foundations to the extent of $8,500 was to be apportioned to the districts.[26]

For the next several years the Kansas Conference urged "a sympathetic interest and substantial support" and commended the work of the Foundations in leadership training, personal counseling and recruitment for the ministry. In light of the economic situation the $440,000 campaign was apparently forgotten and even the sustenance giving was not great—the highest amount received was in 1931 when $4,612 is recorded while two years later it was only $697. In 1938 the amount had risen to $2,091. In the same years gifts for Baker's sustenance were only $3,047, $744 and $2,675.[27]

The educational responsibility of Kansas Methodism for the next fifty years was the subject of a conference of the members of the boards of education of the three annual conferences called by Bishop Mead in March, 1936. Among other things, it was agreed that there were special needs at the Wesley Foundations at Manhattan and Hays.[28] Two years later, the Northwest Kansas Conference recommended that 15% of the $12,000 to be raised among the churches for education sustenance should go to the Hays Wesley Foundation (85% to Kansas Wesleyan) also, "a still hunt" for a total of $100,000 be made—$23,000 to go to the Hays Foundation and the remainder to Kansas Wesleyan.[29]

Early in 1939 three prominent leaders of the three Kansas conferences—Dr. A. E. Henry, Dr. H. J. Root and Dr. C. I. Coldsmith—were appointed as members of a joint committee to study the needs and present a program. Their survey revealed that there were over 4,000 Methodist Students in the State schools—2,100 from Kansas Conference and 1,900 from Central Kansas —and only $8,600 had been made available for this work. In their report, coming out of their meeting on September 5, 1939, they recommended that a total of $25,000 be made available to provide: a full time worker at each of the five foundations (Lawrence, Manhattan, Emporia, Pittsburg and Hays)—$11,000; a full time secretary at Lawrence and Manhattan and a part time secretary at the other three—$3,000; the remaining $8,000 for work conferences, guest speakers, travel expenses, rent, equipment and miscellaneous. An asking of 10¢ per member from all churches was proposed.[30] The first necessity indicated for the future was:

Make the program at all Foundations Christ-centered, spiritual,

dynamic; so that a sane, intellectually respectable and spiritually intense faith in Christ as Savior and Pattern may be the possession of every youth under its influence.[31]

CONCLUSION

That the people of Kansas survived the awful years of the 1930's is to their glory and a tribute to their determination and hope in the future. The reports of the Methodist Annual Conferences of Kansas during these years were not documents of despair and hopelessness but of faith and courageous expectation in the future. Indeed, fear was always knocking but faith answered!

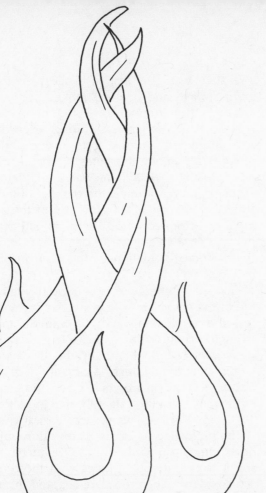

THREE METHODISMS BECOME ONE

The First Twenty-five Years

1939-64

From April 26 to May 10, 1939, Kansas City, Missouri was the scene of the Uniting Conference of the three Methodist Churches—Methodist Protestant Church, Methodist Episcopal Church and Methodist Episcopal Church, South. After much deliberation the vote was finally taken and the union became effective at 8:50 p.m., May 10, 1939.[1] The Methodist Church had come into being.

Another union took place in Kansas in 1939—the joining of the Northwest Kansas Conference and Southwest Kansas Conference. As the result of this merger the Central Kansas Conference came into being, holding its first session in Salina, Kansas, October 5-9, 1939, with Bishop Charles L. Mead presiding.[2] Thus, two former conferences of the Methodist Episcopal Church and a portion of the Kansas Conference of the Methodist Protestant Church became the Central Kansas Conference of The Methodist Church.

CHANGES AND GROWTH
IN THE STATE AND IN METHODISM

In the 25 years following the depression and the dust-bowl days of the 1930's, the state of Kansas changed in a remarkable way. The stimulus of the second world war years gave a new impetus so that Kansas in the late 1950's and the 1960's was more than an agricultural state. Of course, Kansas remained the number one wheat state:

A great transformation has taken place since the Mennonites brought small amounts of hard winter wheat in trunks and sea chests to Kansas from Russia in 1874 to be planted in small allotments.[3]

The state was also first in silage production and in grain storage and in 1960 ranked fourth among the states in the number of cattle. In 1953, however, production from manufacturing exceeded that of agriculture and, surprising to many, Kansas in 1958 ranked fifth among the states in crude oil production. From 1930 to 1960 there was a trend toward larger farms and fewer farmers: the number of farms declined from 166,000 to 115,000; the size of the average farm increased from about 237 acres to 440 acres; and the number of people on farms decreased from about 42% of the total population of the state in 1920 to 20% in 1960.[4]

That all of these changes would vitally affect the life of the church is to be expected and this was manifest in a number of ways. For example, the growth of larger towns and cities made for larger church memberships, which brought about the need for new and larger church buildings. As mentioned in an earlier chapter, this urban growth had a bearing on the decline of the Methodist Protestant Church local congregations, 1920-1939, for these were largely rural churches.

The following chart tells the story of significant developments in Methodism.[5] Of interest is a comparison of some of these figures with those of 1930 in a similar chart in the preceding chapter. In the year 1930 the total amount for Support of Pastor (not including housing) was $500,380 in the Kansas Conference and the combined total for the two other conferences, Southwest and Northwest, was $567,600. After the severe financial collapse of the early 1930's the Kansas Conference dropped to the low figure of $284,695 for pastoral support in 1934; there was no appreciable gain until after 1940. It was not until 1950 that the 1930 figure in this category was again reached. The more rapid recovery of Central Kansas Conference is evidenced by the fact that the 1930 top figure in pastoral support was nearly reached again in 1945. A comparison of benevolence giving before 1940 and the period after that date is not easily determined because in the earlier period more items were included in the benevolence designation.

Year	Support of Pastor (not including house)		World Service and Conf. Benevolences		Buildings and Improvements	
	Central Kansas	Kansas	Central Kansas	Kansas	Central Kansas	Kansas
1940	$ 378,162	$ 281,055	$115,015	$ 73,451	$ 93,499	$ 53,702
1945	528,701	349,332	143,922	100,077	229,221	121,108
1950	800,967	496,480	203,667	151,853	1,103,296	395,561
1955	1,107,928	648,585	285,008	216,001	1,277,747	995,443
1960	1,354,399	841,140	371,467	299,662	1,654,292	1,010,003
1965	1,646,181	1,064,319	978,670	450,089	1,889,330	1,006,901

The period of the war, 1941-45, saw little church building because of lack of materials and man power. Rather, it became a time to pay off debts on property and to set aside money for future building. An indication of the results of the wide-spread debt payment was the report in 1946 that only two of the seven districts of the Central Kansas Conference showed any indebtedness on any church property; the total indebtedness of all churches in one of these two districts was only $3,200.[6]

A breath-taking proposal to the General Conference of 1944 was a program called the "Crusade for Christ." The report began with the sentence: "Christianity is never more creative than in an era of crisis" and then later in the report this striking statement was made:

The tragic and appalling world situation faced by the followers of Jesus Christ at this hour needs no amplification to the members of this General Conference. Never before has so much sorrow, desolation, and utter destruction come to so many peoples. The world awaits the healing touch of Christ upon its misery and desolation.[7]

In the program adopted there were five aspects of the total endeavor: a crusade for world order; a proposal to raise $25 million to relieve suffering and to extend the work of the church around the world as well as at home; spiritual renaissance within the church; an emphasis on stewardship; and a greater concern for the church school.[8]

Surprising to many, the financial goal was quickly surpassed and a dynamic lift was experienced by the whole church. This was the beginning of the quadrennial emphases which became a pattern in The Methodist Church. The conferences in Kansas responded along with the rest of the church. The Kansas Conference in 1945 paid in $219,252 toward the Crusade and $56,750 the next year for a total in two years of $276,902. The contribution of Central Kansas Conference to the same cause was $386,771 in 1945 and $63,030 the following year for a total of $459,801.[9]

In addition to the contribution to the Crusade for Christ, giving to Conference Benevolences and World Service took a decided upturn before 1950. In the ten years, 1945-55, the reports in both conferences indicate more than a 100% increase. Another great upswing in benevolence giving came between 1960 and 1965.

In the building of churches a decided increase took place throughout Kansas Methodism in the decade, 1945-1955. As the chart indicates, the advance in the first five years of this period in Central Kansas was unusual—from $229,221 in 1945 to $1,103,296 in 1950 or an upswing of 480%. The second five years, 1950-55, was the time of the greatest advance in the Kansas Conference but the increase over the ten year period—from $121,108 in 1945 to $995,443 in 1955—was over 800% or 18 times that of 1940. Central Kansas Conference continued an annual increase in church building during the remaining part of this period up to 1965, while the Kansas Conference remained about the same each year, approximately $1 million.

WOMAN'S SOCIETY OF CHRISTIAN SERVICE

One of the new organizations of The Methodist Church after 1939 was the Woman's Society of Christian Service. This society joined the work of the five former organizations—the Woman's Home Missionary Society, the Woman's Foreign Missionary Society and the Ladies Aid Society of the Methodist Episcopal Church and the Missionary Councils of the Methodist Protestant Church and the Methodist Episcopal Church, South.

The first report of this new woman's organization of the Kansas Conference was made to the conference in 1941 by Mrs. H. E. Werner, the first conference president. She called attention to the official purpose of the Society:

The purpose of the W.S.C.S. shall be to unite all women of

the church in Christian living and service; to help develop and support Christian work among women and children around the world; to develop the spiritual life; to study the needs of the world; to take part in such service activities as will strengthen the the local church, improve civic, community and world conditions.[10]

Already, after an organizational year, the Kansas City District reported that all 62 churches had organized a W.S.C.S. and there were only 37 churches in the whole conference without a new society. In the 357 societies of the conference there were 20,138 members and their total giving for the year was $111,351.23.[11] At the end of the quadrennium the women declared their intention of preserving a great tradition:

Kansas as a state has had a great heritage, with a record of producing more missionaries, deaconesses, ministers and other Christian workers than any other state in the Union.[12]

Through the years the women have maintained a high level of activities and financial support. In 1960 the more than 24,000 members in the 329 societies of the Kansas Conference increased their pledge to missions to $114,000 for the year.[13] Mrs. Paul W. Burres, president, in 1964 compared the giving and membership of 1941 and that of 1964: in 1941 there were 18,175 members and the pledge to missions was $36,000; in 1964 the report showed a membership of 23,233 and

an additional 1,645 in the Wesleyan Service Guild, but the pledge to missions for 1965-66 was $145,500.[14]

In the Central Kansas Conference the first W.S.C.S. president was Mrs. Joe T. Rogers of Wichita. The 1941 report indicated a total membership of 28,069 in 442 societies and the total amount sent to their conference treasurer was $52,003. The following year showed an increase of $16,552.[15] The 1948-52 quadrennium was a period of real growth in Central Kansas—an increase of 3,420 members up to a total of 33,223, and a $47,625.35 increase in giving to a total of $168,722.81. Of real pride to Central Kansas Conference was the fact that their Conference Woman's Society continued to lead the South Central Jurisdiction in membership, giving, Youth Fund, Children's Fund, Supplies and in the number of workers on the home and foreign fields.[16]

By 1959 Central Kansas was a "100% organized conference," sharing this unique honor with the New Mexico Conference. Three years later, 1962, the Central Kansas women had pledged $200,000 but were disappointed to discover in a conference study that they were reaching only one third of the women of the church and that there were more members over 70 years of age than there were under 25. In 1965 a loss of membership was reported by President Dorothy

Watson but the payment for missions was $270,093.16, an overpayment of nearly $35,000.[17]

WESLEY FOUNDATIONS

Early in this 25 year period, in 1940, the Inter-Conference Commission was organized to plan and coordinate the work in the state schools. A number of laymen accepted responsibility and gave time and money. The war years brought many complications because of the mixture of civilian and military personnel in the schools. Also, more of the leadership had to be left to the women.[18] Immediately following the war the presence of a much larger number of married students brought a new dimension to the college situation —the same program did not fit the older married group and those coming directly from High School. In 1946 there were more than 7,000 Methodist students on the five state campuses.[19] At Hays the Foundation was faced with a problem altogether different from that of the others—in a town where less than half of the population was Protestant the student body was predominantly Methodist! [20]

Through the years with the growth of the college and university enrollment it was necessary to expand personnel, facilities and support. By 1954 the Kansas Conference was investing $15,000 each year and the Central Kansas Conference $12,500—not quite up to the General Conference minimum standard of 15¢ per member. At Manhattan the first building unit was already outgrown and they were contemplating another unit, to cost $125,000. A new building at Lawrence on the edge of the campus was finished in 1954.[21] Of importance in 1955 was the announcement that all five Wesley Foundations in Kansas had met the standards for official approval by the General Conference Commission on Standards for Wesley Foundations. The next year a broader organization, the Inter-Conference Commission on Student Religious Work, was established. Thereby, a closer relation between religious work at the state schools and that of the Methodist colleges could be achieved and an opening was provided for a new relationship to activities at Washburn College and the University of Wichita.[22] The first State Director of the Kansas Methodist Student Movement, the Rev. Walter S. Nyberg of Hays, was elected in 1957.

Real financial relief was envisaged in the financial campaign approved by the Kansas Conference on June 6, 1957. The total three-year goal was $1,540,000, to be divided as follows: $1,200,000 for Baker ($200,000 for current expenses); $340,000 for Wesley Foundations ($40,000 for current expenses).[23] At the end of the campaign period on May 31, 1961, $674,797.23 had been received; to Baker was allocated a total of $450,-566.65 and to the Wesley Foundations the total amount allocated was $129,343.21.[24]

The following chart suggests something of the situation at the foundations in 1961: [25]

KANSAS WESLEY FOUNDATIONS—1961

Location	Personnel	Methodist Pref. Students	Buildings	Indebt-edness	Expressed Needs
Washburn	1 full time	480	large house	$17,000	
Pittsburg	1 full time	800	large house		new center
Hays	1 full time	2,000	new building	$63,900	staff person
Emporia	1 full time	1,100	small house		new building
	1 part time				total cost—
					$110,000
					$18,000 in
					hand
Wichita United Christian Fellowship	share dir. with other denomina-tions		parsonage		
Lawrence K.U.	2 full time	2,100	adequate building	none	
Manhattan K.S.U.	2 full time	2,600	overcrowded building		an addition— $80,000

At the end of the quadrennium in 1964, Robert Shelton reported on the situation during the past four years: building and budget needs were somewhat alleviated; Emporia and Pittsburg building needs were still to be realized; the number of Methodist preference full-time students on seven campuses had grown to 10,416 (Lawrence and Manhattan accounted for about one-half of these); a total of $54,000 had been contributed by the Kansas Conference alone.[26]

BAKER UNIVERSITY

Baker's financial condition was to improve greatly from 1939 to 1964 but it was not apparent at the beginning of this period. The gifts of Mr. O. Jolliffe and others had made possible the building of a new dormitory for men and the change of Old Science Hall into a student center. On the other hand, in 1940, there was an accumulated operational deficit of $65,000 because of the necessity of annual deficit spending of between $10,000 and $18,000; even on a total budget of only $138,000 (1939).[27]

To all colleges the Second World War brought unusual changes. Enrollment figures of men dropped to a frightening and unparalled low which meant shifts in programs, changes in dormitory usage and financial difficulties due to the loss of tuition. Added to these problems for Baker came the destructive fire of January 3, 1943—the gymnasium, the heating plant and a number of classrooms, all in Taylor Hall, went up in flames.[28]

With enthusiasm the Kansas Conference responded to a campaign for $250,000 under the direction of President Nelson P. Horn but in a few years it was obvious that that amount was inadequate to meet the new needs. Enrollment was going up after the war, especially with returning G.I.'s. The total funds in hand, including insurance, in 1947, amounted to $359,000. Needed expenditures, however, had risen to about $620,000 which meant an indebtedness of $250,000. By 1951 the budget was balanced and enrollment stood at 717.[29]

Growth in the number of buildings in the ten years during the last part of Dr. Horn's administration and that of President William Scarborough are seen in the following: [30]

1956	Rice Memorial Auditorium	$350,000
	Denious Residence Hall for Women	350,000
1958	North Residence Hall for Men	500,000
1959	Student Union	515,000
1961	Baker Library	600,000
1962	West Residence Hall for Women	577,000
	Addition to Student Union	150,000
1964	Administration Building	244,000
1966	Residence Hall for Men	650,000
	Musical Arts Building	363,000

In 1964 Baker's president reported: a total enrollment of 864 from 30 states and eight foreign countries; a gain in plant investment from $1,897,000 in 1958 to $4,430,000 in 1963; and an increase in endowment of $600,000 during the same period to over $2 1/2 million. Like other schools, Baker had Federal Government College Housing Loans which for Baker amounted to nearly $1.7 million.[31]

After more than 100 years of service, Baker was justly proud of its high academic standing and adequate facilities. Its greatest boast was in its graduates—more than 450 ministers (1/3 of the ministers serving in the Kansas Conference were Baker alumni), over 100 missionaries, and countless other business and professional people—serving throughout the world.[32]

KANSAS WESLEYAN UNIVERSITY

In contrast to the despairing days of most of the 1930's, the succeeding years, 1938-1946, for Kansas Wesleyan were encouraging. The coming as president of practical-minded E. K. Morrow, formerly a Wyoming cattleman and a financial man in Missions, brought a needed stability. During his administration there arose the possible merger of Kansas Wesleyan and Southwestern which will be reviewed later in this chapter. Also brought up again was the possible merger with the Presbyterian College of Emporia. Mr. Earl C. Sams, a good friend of Kansas Wesleyan living in New York City, encouraged this possible move and even offered such a united college a gift of $1/2 million. "Willingness to consider such a proposal" for merger was approved by the Annual Conference in 1943 but the Presbyterians were not sufficiently interested.[33]

Like all other colleges Kansas Wesleyan's enrollment dropped during the war. In the fall of 1943 there were fewer than 140 students and in the second semester, 1944-45, there were only 107 students, including 15 special students and 6 nurses—only 22 were male sttudents and 15 of these were freshmen. In President Morrow's last report to the school's Board of Trustees, February, 1946, there was real ground for encouragement. That year there were 353 students; the college was free of debt; endowment stood at $3/4 million and there was almost $1/2 million on hand for new buildings when construction was possible.[34]

Academically the picture was not so ideal. In 1946 Dr. John L. Seaton, prominent educator, conducted a survey of Kansas Wesleyan and Southwestern at the request of the Inter-college Board of the Central Kansas Conference. In his report he had critical words for Kansas Wesleyan University in regard to the ratio of Ph.D.'s in the total faculty membership—it was only 4 to 27. In that year also, the top salary for a faculty member was only $2,400. The next year the top faculty salary was $3,000, the Dean received $3,800 and the President was paid $4,400. The coach, however, received a fourth more than any faculty member.[35]

President H. J. Root's four year tenure was not too eventful except for the student population explosion from the low enrollment of 107 indicated earlier in 1945 to 380 in 1946. After Dr. Root there followed the strenuous years under Dr. A. Stanley Trickett, 1950-54. With money in hand, the Annie Merner Pfeiffer Hall for Women was completed as was the E. C. Sams Hall of Fine Arts. A student apartment building and a faculty apartment were also built. After the academic boom of the late 1940's there was a drop in enrollment.[36]

In an attempt to upgrade the school, salaries were raised, Ph.D.'s were brought in, Dr. Paul Renick was appointed as Dean, the curriculum was revised; but the annual budgets were not balanced. As a result of the latter the indebtedness soon rose to $385,000. Also humiliating during the same years was the failure in the attempt to achieve accreditation. After a requested formal review by the accrediting agency the result was negative.[37]

After 1955 under the leadership of President Arthur Zook and the wise academic guidance of Dean Renick the trend was upward. Accreditation by the North Central Association of Colleges and Secondary Schools was granted in 1958. The gifts of Mr. Glenn L. Martin and the Earl C. Sams Foundation were most helpful. More than all of these was the increased financial undergirding of Kansas Wesleyan, as well as of Southwestern, by the Central Kansas Conference in more than one financial campaign. This story will be told later in this chapter.

SOUTHWESTERN COLLEGE

In 1940 the financial situation was the uppermost concern of President F. E. Mossman and Southwestern because the bonded indebtedness of the school stood at $140,400, and additional obligations amounted to $75,600. Added to this was an accumulated operational deficit of $35,000. The Annual Conference responded with a campaign and in the following two years the total debt was reduced to $109,000 and more payments were to come in.[38]

Naturally there were enrollment difficulties as well as financial problems during the war years. In 1943 there were only 176 college level students but the number began to increase through the efforts of Dean Lyman S. Johnson. Of interest is the dream for the school given by Charles E. Schofield, president only two years, 1942-44, in his report in 1944:

The plans for the development and expansion of the campus and equipment of Southwestern College are moving steadily forward. The program calls for the erection of a new Hall of Science, a new Hall of Fine Arts and Religion, a new Library, the completion of Stewart Gymnasium, with the remodeling of the ground floor, at present occupied by the library, as a Student Social Union, the erection of two quadrangles of dormitory units, the building of a new home for the President, the general landscaping of the campus, and the erection of a stadium and improvement of athletic equipment, including a year-round swimming pool.[39]

Four years later part of this dream was already realized and the prospects were encouraging: 12 new faculty members had been added, the enrollment was the highest in the school's history—772. The new buildings or equipment included: Sonner Stadium, Music Hall, men's dormitory (for 105 men), an addition to Holland Hall for girls, an addition to Stewart Gymnasium, an apartment house, a new heating plant, and a new Student Union. Plans were also underway for a library and the reconstruction of North Hall.[40]

No one was prepared for the events of 1950. President Alvin W. Murray had been in office only one day less than six months when Richardson Hall burned early on the morning of April 16th. Four days later the

FLAMING RICHARDSON HALL

Winfield Chamber of Commerce voted to put on a campaign for $300,000 for rebuilding Richardson Hall and to complete the responsibility of Cowley County for the Memorial Library. A special session of the Central Kansas Conference was called for June 29th to consider "matters pertinent to Southwestern College."[41]

To understand something of the dynamics of this special session of the Central Kansas Conference it is necesssary to go back to at least 1944, or to the time of the merger of the two conferences, Northwest Kansas and Southwest Kansas, into the Central Kansas Conference in 1939. One can and must read between the lines to sense differences in spirit and attitudes which existed among ministers and laymen in the two conferences before and after the merger of the conferences. Therefore, it was not just the interests of the two colleges which were involved in the future struggles.

In the first year of the life of the new conference Southwestern received from the conference $10,074 while Kansas Wesleyan received only $3,272. In 1944 three competent men appointed by the national Board of Education of the Methodist Church reported on a survey of Southwestern and Kansas Wesleyan that they had made on behalf of the national Board of Education. Some of the conclusions were unacceptable to either school but on the whole the report favored Salina as a location for a college. They also recommended that only one school should be encouraged by the conference because a church related college should have the support of at least 60,000 church members—at that time there was a total of 87,471 members in the Central Kansas Conference.[42] Among many, however, there were serious questions as to the adequacy of the data considered in the survey.

The recommendations of the survey team were "prayerfully considered" by the annual conference Board of Education, but it was decided that the two colleges

should continue their functions as creatures of the Central Kansas Conference; that they shall be encouraged to carry on their respective programs as separate and distinct organizations. It also recommended that an Inter-college Board be set up. . . .[43]

The purpose of the new Inter-College Board was: to develop closer correlation between the two schools; to determine possible areas of specialization; to guarantee equality of participation in any campaign for funds; to assist each school in seeking their needed accreditation—Southwestern with Association of American Universities and Kansas Wesleyan with the North Central Association. The total report to the Conference in 1944 was adopted unanimously.[44]

On recommendation of the Inter-College Board a financial campaign for $1/2 million for the two schools was launched in 1946. It was to be a non-apportionment campaign with 60% to go to Southwestern and 40% to Kansas Wesleyan (the contributions of Saline and Cowley Counties were not included in this division).[45] Because of good support and the leadership of Rev. A. E. Henry, the campaign was quite successful, as reported two years later in 1948. There was increased interest in both schools indicated and a total of $218,-000 in cash had been turned over to the colleges. In addition, there was about $100,000 in pledges. Cowley County had raised $75,000 for Southwestern and $127,000 had been pledged by Saline County for Kansas Wesleyan—both of these latter amounts were

to go into libraries for the respective schools. All in all, the total raised in cash and pledges was $564,000.[46]

All of these developments since 1939 were part of the background thinking which Conference members brought to the Special Session in June, 1950. Without question, some were of the opinion that the time to merge the two schools had come. In attendance as a "resource person," invited by Bishop Dana Dawson, was Dr. John O. Gross, a Secretary of the national Board of Education. Immediately following the preliminaries, the president of Southwestern College, Dr. Alvin W. Murray, moved: "that the Million Dollar Building Program as printed in the SOUTHWESTERN COLLEGE FACES THE FUTURE brochure be approved." The motion was seconded by Rev. Raymond E. Dewey.[47] The Million Dollar Program included: Mossman Memorial Science Hall—$250,000; Memorial Library—$150,000; replacement of Richardson Hall—$550,000; grading and paving—$50,000.

A substitute motion was then made by Mr. Ray Streeter that would turn toward the merger of the two schools. After tense discussion and parliamentary maneuvers, the Southwestern cause won the day. As the session closed, the Southwestern A Capella Choir sang "Great and Glorious Is the Name of the Lord." [48]

The next three years was a time for building. When

school opened in the fall of 1953 three new buildings, costing nearly $1 1/2 million, were ready for use. A new $25,000 organ, the gift of Mr. J. P. Sonner, had been installed in the auditorium.[49]

When C. Orville Strohl came as president on January 1, 1954, Southwestern had recovered from its catastrophy of 1950 but there remained a debt of $300,000. In the course of the next ten or eleven years leading up to Southwestern's 80th anniversary in 1965, tremendous strides were made in providing adequate facilities and endowment. For example, endowment funds in 1954 were less than $600,000, whereas in 1965 they were over 2 1/2 million; total assets in 1954 were just over $2.6 million and in 1965 they had reached $7.3 million.

In addition, an ambitious "Master Plan" which involved a demand for academic excellence as well as money was on its way to realization.[50] In this advance the generosity and vision of Mr. Samuel P. Wallingford, a Southwestern graduate and devoted layman, must be noted.

CENTRAL KANSAS CONFERENCE SUPPORT

Few colleges have had greater support by their respective annual conferences than have Kansas Wesleyan and Southwestern. Mention has been made of the campaign for both schools, 1944-46. In more recent years the Christian Higher Education Campaign, or CHECK, launched in 1958, had a goal of $2,212,500: $1 million for Kansas Wesleyan; $1 million for Southwestern; $150,000 for Wesley Foundations in Kansas; and $12,500 for Philander Smith College in Little Rock, Arkansas. In 1960 it was reported by Dr. Raymond Dewey, director, that over $2.3 million had been pledged and over $1/2 million had been paid in. Four years later the total amount realized was just under $1 3/4 million so that each college had received nearly $3/4 million and the Wesley Foundations benefited to the extent of $109,551 and Philander Smith College had received its total promised amount of $12,500.[51]

In the same year, 1964, the "Faith in Action" program for the coming quadrennium was launched. This ambitious Conference Quadrennial Financial Program for the Support of World Service and Annual Conference Benevolences called for giving of over $1 million each year of the coming quadrennium.[52]

AFTER TWENTY-FIVE YEARS

Methodism was much stronger in Kansas in the 1960's than it was at the time of union in 1939. The state was more prosperous and the dread and fear of the 1930's were gone except for an occasional threat of a drouth or dust storm. Tremendous sums of money had been invested in church buildings and in the institutions, especially in the 1950's and 1960's. Ministers were better paid. Certainly, the hospitals, homes and schools were operating on a higher professional and academic level than was possible in the 1930's.

What of the total impact of the Church—its relation to its members, to the people of the communities it was called to serve and what of its wider concern? Was there growth and advance here as well as in the more tangible areas already mentioned?

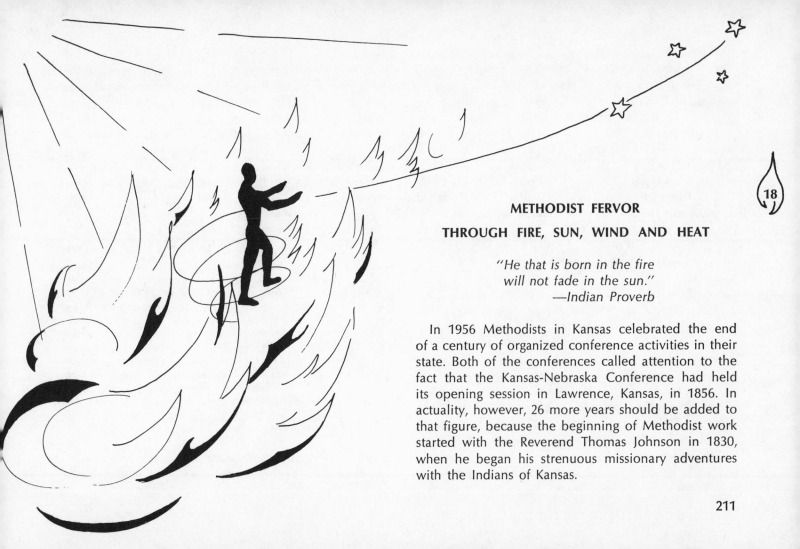

METHODIST FERVOR
THROUGH FIRE, SUN, WIND AND HEAT

*"He that is born in the fire
will not fade in the sun."*
—Indian Proverb

In 1956 Methodists in Kansas celebrated the end of a century of organized conference activities in their state. Both of the conferences called attention to the fact that the Kansas-Nebraska Conference had held its opening session in Lawrence, Kansas, in 1856. In actuality, however, 26 more years should be added to that figure, because the beginning of Methodist work started with the Reverend Thomas Johnson in 1830, when he began his strenuous missionary adventures with the Indians of Kansas.

As we look back from a perspective of about 150 years, we are conscious of the fact that the people of the region which is now Kansas have been subject to a greater variety of experiences than those of nearly any other comparable area in the United States. Early the "cities of gold" drew the ill-fated Coronado on a disappointing, weary journey. Involved in the past history of the area have been well-known explorers and traders, especially from Spain, France and the fledgling United States, in the hopes of building a future empire. For a time it was considered by some to be a part of the great American desert, in which there was no hope of agricultural endeavor, since only buffalos could live in the region. The future State of Kansas was a small part of the vast Louisiana Purchase by the United States in 1803. Thirty years later this region became the designated area to which Indians from the eastern part of the United States could be moved for a "permanent home." It was only a short and passing solution for the Indian problem due to the demand of the whites for new land in the west.

The "impending crisis" of the first half of the 19th Century in the United States, involving the struggle over slavery and state's rights, culminated in civil war. In the settlement of Kansas, many motives were evident: the desire for land; economic betterment and the longing for homes; the escape from responsibility on a new frontier; the opportunity for exploitation by opportunistic renegades, both of the respected and the condemned varieties; an open door for rugged individual initiative; and, finally, a moral and religious crusade for the freedom and redemption of a vital area.

This mixture of motives, the goals sought and the means employed, both good and bad, was partly summed up by Carl Becker in his famous essay, "Kansas," when he said: "Kansas is no mere geographical expression, but a 'state of mind,' a religion and a philosophy is one." Later in the same essay he wrote:

> Now, generally speaking, the men who make the world's frontiers, whether in religion or politics, science, or geographical exploration and territorial settlement, have certain essential and distinguishing qualities. They are primarily men of faith. Having faith in themselves, they are indvidualists. They are idealists because they have faith in the universe, being confident that somehow everything is right at the center of things; they give hostages to the future, are ever inventing God anew, and must be always transforming the world into their ideal of it. They have faith in humanity and in the perfectibility of man, are likely, therefore, to be believers in equality, reformers, intolerant, aiming always to level others up to their own high vantage.[1]

Stout men and even stronger women were needed to stand up to the demands of Kansas life. That it was predominantly an agricultural state made the economy subject to the vagaries of nature—drouth, blizzards, grasshoppers, dust storms, floods. All of these crises affected the price structure and opened the door to political, economic and social turmoil—such as the Populist revolution with its fanatical and creative aspects. Mainly, though, Kansas people were generally conservative. They have responded at times, however, to progressive leadership—of Populism, Governor Henry J. Allen and his Industrial Court, and the final repudiation of the Ku Klux Klan due to the proddings of William Allen White. Witness also the recent response to the leadership of the Menningers in the field of mental health.

GROWTH IN A CENTURY

That Methodists are proud of their growth and service in Kansas is no secret. In 1956 they pointed back to 1856 when their reported total membership was only 840, including 144 Indian members. At that historic conference in Lawrence, there were only nine preachers reporting the work of 11 stations, and there were 17 preachers appointed in 1856. The largest membership reported by a station was that of Wyandotte and Delaware with a total of 118 Indian members.

Then followed: Doniphan with 95 members; Osawatomie with 83 members; and Wolf River and Lawrence each had 80 members. Only three meeting houses were reported—at Lawrence, Wyandotte and Ft. Scott. Not to be forgotten were the 34 local preachers.[2] Contrast these figures with the total membership in the two annual conferences, Kansas and Central Kansas, in 1956 —228,232 with an additional 39,052 preparatory members. In the same year there were nearly 750 preaching places.[3]

In a study made by the National Council of Churches of Christ in the 1950's it was found that:

The Methodist Church not only outranked all other denominations in Kansas, but was also the largest Protestant denomination in 97 of the State's 105 counties.[4]

In a study of religious preferences of Wichita families, in 1958, by the Wichita Council of Churches, the findings indicated the following:

Methodist, 21.0 per cent; Baptist, 18.6 per cent; Roman Catholic, 11.8 per cent; Disciples of Christ, 11.0 per cent; Presbyterian, 7.9 per cent; Lutheran, 3.8 per cent; and a variety of other groups with smaller percentages. The total Protestant was 81.5 in 1958, in contrast to 66.2 per cent in the United States, based on statistics for 1957, one year earlier than the Wichita study.[5]

RIVALRY AND COOPERATION

WITH OTHER CHURCHES

In recent years interdenominational cooperation and ecumenical relations between the denominations have been common and expected. This has not been the pattern throughout Kansas history, although there were early instances of cooperation such as the formation of the Kansas Sunday School Association in 1865. Needless to say, the Protestant denominations joined forces many times against the liquor interests.

There was serious denominational rivalry on this frontier, as there had been earlier east of the Mississippi. These conflicts were intensified by land gift inducements offered by some of the railroads and town associations to the first church in a new settlement. Often the competition was good humored and enjoyed by all and nicknames were not resented too much. Christians or members of the Disciples of Christ were called "Campbellites" and Protestant Episcopalians were nicknamed "Episcolopians."

Difficult to surpass as an amazing example of denominational prejudice was that related to a college in Ottumwa, Kansas. The Methodists of that town raised funds, began work on the foundation and laid the cornerstone with appropriate ceremonies in 1862. The school was known as The Methodist University. During the following year the Ottumwa Christian Church had a significant growth. In 1863, as a result of a vigorous four week evangelistic revival by the Ottumwa Christian Church, all of the leading Methodists were "converted" and joined the Christian Church. Among those who shifted their allegiance were all the members of the board of trustees of the university.[6]

The trustees immediately transferred the school to their new church and renamed it the Western Christian University. Because they did not want to build a Christian school on a Methodist foundation, the walls were torn down and a new foundation laid and then the building was completed. The school opened but had a turbulent career until the end came in 1872. Before this there had been a mortgage foreclosure but it was scheduled to reopen in the fall of 1872. Its educational career closed when the building was set on fire in August. The suspected arsonists were never apprehended.[7]

Regularly, in the annual conference reports through the years, there was noted the danger of the ominous control of the United States by the Roman Catholic Church or the Papacy.[8] A great stir came in 1909 when Governor W. R. Stubbs, a Methodist, appointed Bishop

T. F. Lillis, the Roman Catholic Bishop of the diocese of Leavenworth, Kansas, as a member of the State Commission on text-books for the public schools. Immediately the editor of the *Central Christian Advocate* challenged the appointment in very strong language, although the Bishop was a good native Kansan.[9] The position of the Roman Catholic Church toward public schools was quoted from official sources and it was indicated that the ultimate purpose of this "genial and broadminded gentleman" must be to destroy the schools. The editor therefore urged that he be named commissioner of something else.[10] A week later the editor was happy to report that Bishop Lillis had declined to serve in the position to which he had been appointed without his knowledge or consent; the Bishop thereby cleared up an awkward situation.[11]

Along side of this record of denominational rivalry is the contrasting story of the cooperation between the Protestant churches. Near Lawrence, Kansas, was Bismarck Grove, "the favorite Camp Ground of Kansas," which attracted "Camp Meetings, Temperance Meetings, Jubilee Meetings, Sabbath School Assemblies, School and Society Picnics, Old Settlers Reunions,"[12] for many years beginning in the 1860's. Mention has been made in an earlier chapter of early temperance meetings at Bismarck Grove. It was here in 1865 that the Kansas Sunday School Association was born.

This movement was for the purpose of starting Sunday Schools. It was established as a pioneer movement, functioning outside the churches. Although preachers participated, it was a lay movement. As to accountability, the group was responsible only to themselves.[13]

The first General Secretary was Judge Nelson Case, a Methodist from Oswego, Kansas (later associated with Baker University). He was succeeded by men of other denominations, such as Mr. J. H. Engle, a River Brethren layman from Abilene, and Dr. Frank Richard, a Congregationalist. Under Dr. Richard the movement became more interdenominational and in 1922 it was formed into the Kansas Council of Christian Education. In 1942 came a new reorganization which resulted in the Kansas Council of Churches and Christian Education. The first Executive Secretary of the newly merged organization was the Reverend Ray J. Wonder, a Methodist. He was followed, in the same office, in 1945 by an Evangelical United Brethren minister, Milton R. Vogel. The latter's twelve and a half year tenure "left a positive footprint in the Kansas ecumenical development."[14] Since 1954 the organization has been known as the Kansas Council of Churches. Many Methodists have served as officers or chairmen of the various divisions; Dr. Roy Brady served as president, 1957-59, along with his Methodist pastoral ministry.

RELATIONS WITH NEGROES

Kansas has a spotty record in its relation to Negroes. They were not given the franchise in the Wyandotte Constitution of 1859. Some "Exodusters" came from various areas of the South, in the late 1870's and 1880's, by way of steamboats and railroads. For example, hundreds came to Burlington and to other places on the Katy from Texas and Louisiana, as well as others who came from Tennessee and Mississippi.[15] They often settled together in various areas over the state. Part of the occasion for the Negro movements was the removal of federal troops from the south during those years.

Two events in the 1890's indicate that Negroes were not without their problems in Kansas and that some good Methodists could be blind to them in one instance and vigorously concerned in another. On January 16, 1890, Negroes in Olathe, Kansas, brought suit against the local board of education to compel admission of their children to the public schools. The board was ordered by the court to show cause why they refused the request.[16] Less than three months later, the Kansas Conference, in its annual session at Horton, March 5-10, 1890, in the Report of the Committee on State of the Country, stated in part:

Of the things that are thrusting themselves upon public attention concerning which the voice of the church ought to be heard and heeded by the national administration, your committee will refer but to the following:

First—We call your attention to the terrible wrongs being suffered by our colored brethren in the South. Since the dark day, thirteen years ago, when the government withdrew its protection from the race it had clothed with freedom to save itself from destruction, the black man has endured such wrongs as should make the whole nation blush with shame.[17]

Their eyes were on the South and not on Olathe, in their own midst!

In April, 1893, there was a lynching of a Negro in Salina, Kansas, after he had been sentenced to seven years in prison for slashing a white man with a razor.[18] Eight years later, in 1901, a Negro charged with murdering a young woman, was burned alive by a mob. In commenting on the first, the editor of the *Central Christian Advocate* said:

Will not ministers, and teachers, and editors, and Sunday-school workers join in making common cause against this dreadful policy of mob law? Whether committed in Texas, or Kansas, or Michigan, let there be but one decision registered concerning it— it is a crime against civilization![19]

In regard to the second sad occasion, the editor commented:

A stain has again come upon our land. Almost the last State in the Union which we would expect to see descend to the level of burning a human being alive is Kansas. Kansas, whose star represents about as much of noble meaning as any star in "Old Glory." But it happened in Kansas. Last week a negro, charged with the heinous offense of murdering a young woman, was burned alive. . . .

This Kansas stain will excite the sorrow of all lovers of that noble commonwealth. It is unlike Kansas. We have a pity for the frenzied father and the stricken relatives of the murdered victim: but for those who allowed the majestic laws of a civilized State to be so easily trodden down and betrayed the feelings of all good people will be such as are better not expressed. Can it be that Kansas, the Kansas of Osawatomie and Lawrence, has forever got to bear this stain on its proud escutcheon? [26]

Another incident involved farmers and the Negroes in the area of Nicodemus, in northwest Kansas, where there was an extensive settlement of "Exodusters":

Kansas has 325 locals of Farmers Education and Co-operative Union of America, an organization having 2,000,000 men of the hoe, and particularly strong in the South. Kansas has fifty-one counties organized, with 2,000 members. It has been the custom of Kansas to admit progressive farmers, regardless of color.

At Nicodemus, in north central Kansas, there is a lodge of Negroes. In the same section is one with a Negro preacher as chaplain. The national executive board composed chiefly of Southern men, heard of this and suspended the charter of the Kansas body, nominally for nonpayment of dues. A meeting of the 300 State officers was hastily assembled at Hutchinson, when it developed that the race question was the real one.

The Kansas charter was restored, the old officers permitted to resign, and new ones elected. The latter are not disposed to submit to sectional dictation, have called in their organizers, are taking in no new Negro members, but are not excluding the old ones, and they say they don't intend to. [21]

On a more pleasant note is the story of John Andrew Gregg, a native of Eureka, Kansas. Born in 1877, this

JOHN ANDREW GREGG

Negro boy was converted at the age of 12 and joined the Methodist Episcopal Church at Eureka. His relationships in the church were many—charter member of the Junior Epworth League, member of the church quartette and librarian of the church and Sunday school. After finishing High School and Academy he served in the army, finished his A.B. in 1902, taught school a year then entered the ministry. He received his local preacher's license from his home church in Eureka. He joined the African Methodist Episcopal Church, was a missionary, pastor, president of Wilberforce University and in 1924 was elected a Bishop of the A.M.E. Church. The Methodist Church in Eureka is proud that its first young man to go into the ministry became a Bishop.[22]

The Kansas-Nebraska Act of 1854 was a prelude to the Kansas struggle which was a significant move toward freedom for the Negro. It is interesting that an action of 1954, also involving Kansas, should be another step, although terribly belated, toward the same goal. It was the case of Brown, et. al. vs. Board of Education of Topeka et al. which finally resulted in the famous United Supreme Court decision in regard to desegregation in May, 1954. Thereby, the elementary schools of Topeka, the capitol city of Kansas, were desegregated by court order. Neither the Kansas Conference, which met June 1-6, 1954, nor the Central Kansas Conference, meeting October 5-10, 1954, even noted the historic decision.

It was a great day in the life of each of the Annual Conferences of Kansas in 1963, when all the churches of the Central West Conference of the Central Jurisdiction in Kansas were invited to become a part of the respective conferences of Kansas. In the Central Kansas Conference this included: Quayle Methodist Church, Salina and St. Mark Methodist Church, Wichita. In the Kansas Conference there were: Asbury, Topeka; Coffeyville-Chetopa-Independence; Shepherd Chapel, Manhattan; Mason Memorial, Kansas City, Kansas; Mt. Olive, Topeka; and Parsons-Chanute-Oswego.[23] The desired action was consumated.

CHANGES—IN CHURCH BUILDINGS,
SERVICES AND INSTITUTIONS

Of all the contrasts between the "old days" and today, none could be greater than that of the difference in the church buildings and the services conducted therein. Until well into this century the church was primarily a preaching place or auditorium which served the community. For example, on December 2, 1859, when the Hon. Abraham Lincoln talked in Atchison, Kansas, it was in the Methodist Episcopal Church. (This address at Atchison, if not the same as that given later at the Cooper Institute, was a preview of it.) Although the church boasted of only 30 charter members two years earlier, they built a church to seat 350 people.[24]

METHODIST EPISCOPAL CHURCH —ATCHISON

The earliest meeting places naturally were in homes, such as that of Mrs. Tim Hershey, the wife of the first settler in Abilene, Kansas, and the daughter of a Methodist preacher. To combat the 31 saloons and/or houses of prostitution which because of the fines made Abilene a tax-free city, her home was a "perfect oasis of religion."[25] This was dignified compared to the place of the first services of the Methodist Church of Hays, Kansas. As in several other early towns, these were conducted in a saloon—Tommy Drum's—in 1873.

The preacher, Reverend Leonard Bell, covered the bar with a sheet. Later, they moved to the county court house and then to the school house before they could build a church.[26] Another disturbing element was the presence of guns in the church. In 1875, at the Methodist Church in Ebenezer, the men brought guns because they wanted to be ready for buffalo herds that might pass by. Several services were interrupted by the cry of "buffalo" and the men would go out to replenish their larder with fresh meat.[27]

Often there was an organ problem or the question of the use of musical instruments in the church. This problem was more serious and devisive with the Christians or Disciples of Christ, because some of them questioned the use of anything in the church not mentioned in the Bible. Often this point of view carried over into Methodist thinking. In the Blue Mound Methodist Church, in 1882, a dispute arose when an organ was purchased and used in the church. Some were sure that Satan was in the instrument. Not long after, however, a severe cyclone struck the town, destroying many homes, the school house and the Methodist Church. The church building was in ruins, but two things were saved—the organ and the pulpit Bible. One man was the spokesman for many when he said, "If the good Lord saw fit to save the Organ and

the Holy Bible, I am convinced it is right for use in the church." [28]

From the preaching place or auditorium type of building, churches moved to the Akron plan. This is still very much in evidence. In accordance with this plan, the auditorium with a center pulpit was ringed with Sunday school rooms which could be separated by movable doors or curtains. This was an attempt to keep a large auditorium and yet provide needed rooms for the increasing Sunday school enrollment. The next move by some churches was toward the Sunday school "temple," a separate building. The present "church plant" with its provision for a number of rooms for the present variety of services and activities of the church is quite new.

The importance of the sermon from the beginning seemed to make necessary the center pulpit, no matter what other change was made in the architectural plan. Not until recent years has the divided chancel been thought proper for a Methodist Church. The pulpit garb of the clergy has also been subject to considerable change. Of course, black has been the constant color. Along the way have been the formal long coat, then the Prince Albert coat, to be followed by the cutaway with striped trousers, and finally the pulpit gown or robe. Each change has been ridiculed by some of the former generation.

Today when one visits Baker University at Baldwin, Southwestern College at Winfield and Kansas Wesleyan University at Salina, it seems impossible to believe that these institutions, with all their present buildings and equipment, are the same schools with the humble beginnings of which we have told. Taken separately, each is a story of an early vision, financial hardships, sacrificial leadership on the part of the presidents, faculties, laymen and ministers, and heroic determination to build for the youth and the church of the future. The same statement is just as true of other institutional expressions of the life of the church—hospitals, homes, the Epworth League or M.Y.F., Wesley Foundations, the Campus Ministry and thre Woman's Society of Christian Service.

OUTREACH

Often Kansans have been accused of provincialism and not seeing beyond the borders of their State. At times this has been too true. On the other hand, it is a fact that in spite of its small population, no state has supplied more foreign missionaries for Methodism than Kansas. They have gone to the ends of the earth! One Kansan boasted of this service to the far away lands before a small group. In reply one of his irreverent colleagues said, "That only shows how far some people will go to get away from Kansas!"

Kansas has made other significant contributions to the church at large especially in leadership personnel —laymen, ministers, educators, and bishops. This is true of every one of the churches in the Methodist family—Evangelical United Brethren, Methodist Protestant, Methodist Episcopal Church, South, Methodist Episcopal Church and The Methodist Church. The Reverend E. R. Hendrix, later a bishop of the Methodist Episcopal Church, South, in 1870 was the minister reporting for Leavenworth Station. The story of Bishop William A. Quayle has been told. Among the Evangelical United Brethren the name of Bishop John S. Stamm looms large. This native of Alida, Kansas, was later president of the Federal Council of Churches

1948-50.

In more recent years two bishops of the Methodist Church have been Kansans. Schuyler E. Garth, 1898-1946, born in Saffordville, Kansas, was elected to the episcopacy in 1944 and assigned to the Wisconsin Area. Only two years later he and his wife were killed in an airplane accident in China while on a missionary trip. A native of Cherryvale, Kansas, Eugene M. Frank, had all of his ministry in the Kansas Conference until his election to the episcopacy in 1956. At the time of

SCHUYLER E. GARTH

EUGENE M. FRANK

his election he was the pastor of the First Methodist Church in Topeka, Kansas. With effectiveness Bishop Frank has served as the leader of Methodism in Missouri. In 1967 he was elected to serve as President of the Council of Bishops of the United Methodist Church for the year, 1968-69.

MAINTAINING THE GLOW

What was it that kept the Methodist fervor in Kansas aglow during the more than a century of its witness? What kept the "fire on the prairie" burning? Something of the essence of this is caught in the terse but meaningful phrase of the famous theologian, Dr. Emil Brunner, when he wrote: "The Church exists by mission as a fire exists by burning." The Methodist Church in Kansas was in mission! Both laymen and ministers felt called of God for their task.

One of the great leaders of The Methodist Church during the generation from approximately 1925 to 1960, was Dr. Roy L. Smith—preacher, writer, editor and platform speaker. He was a native of Kansas—born in Nickerson, Kansas, and a graduate of Southwestern College. It was Dr. Smith who was first commissioned by the Kansas conferences to write this history of Methodism of his native state. Only a little had been

ROY L. SMITH

set down when death came, and his earthly work was finished, including this story. This history owes him a debt of gratitude.

On one occasion, he related a poignant story to the Editorial Board concerning Kansas and the ministry of his beloved Church. In January, 1887, there was a terrible blizzard on the Kansas prairie which cut off transportation even in the towns, and the people in the farm areas were nearly buried. On a far removed homestead lived a young couple. The wife was pregnant and about to deliver her first born. The house was cold and the available fuel was soon gone. To keep warm, some of the crude furniture went into the fire. No medical doctor, or even a midwife, was within miles, if either could have gotten there. The young husband

222

served in their stead and a baby boy was delivered, safely for both mother and child. Not long after, as the baby nestled in the arms of the mother, the father placed his hand on the boy's head. Together in prayer the father and mother dedicated the boy to the ministry of Jesus Christ and the Methodist Church. In his conclusion to the story, Dr. Smith said, "Thus, in the first few hours of my life, I was dedicated to God and the ministry of the Methodist Church."

The spiritual glow of that single homestead cabin gathered up into its light great meaning and purpose. Such an experience, however, does not stand alone. Throughout more than a century and a quarter in Kansas there have been not only thousands of persons dedicated to God, but hundreds of others who have risked their lives to carry on the Church in mission. On the altar was also offered a variety of gifts of talent, property and financial support.

All Kansas Methodists in the second century of their history, like other Kansans, are quite conscious that their church and their state have a glorious past. They firmly believe that their state was founded for a purpose and that their church was called by God to a special service.

To be remembered in our day is the admonition of Carl Becker years ago: "The light on the altar must ever be replenished." [29] May the "fire on the prairie" that is Methodism ever be replenished by God to the end that the lordship of Jesus Christ becomes a reality in Kansas and to the end of the earth.

Appendix I—Outline

Annual Conferences

Date, Place of Meeting and Presiding Officer

I-a Methodist Episcopal Church, South
    Kansas Mission Conference—1855-1861
    Western Conference—1870-1905
I-b Methodist Episcopal Church
    Kansas-Nebraska Conference—1856-1860
    Kansas Conference—1861-1939
    South Kansas Conference—1874-1913
    Southwest Kansas Conference—1882-1939
    Northwest Kansas Conference—1882-1939

I-c Methodist Protestant Church—1866-1939
I-d The Methodist Church—1939-1965
    Kansas Conference—1939-1965
    Central Kansas Conference—1939-1965
I-e United Brethren in Christ—1857-1956
I-f Evangelical Association—1865-1922
I-g United Evangelical Church—1902-1922
I-h Evangelical Church—1923-1939
I-i Evangelical United Brethren—1956-1965

Appendix I-a
METHODIST EPISCOPAL CHURCH, SOUTH
KANSAS MISSION CONFERENCE

Date	Place	Presiding Bishop	Total Membership
Oct. 1855	Springfield, Missouri	John Early	Organization
Sept. 1856	Kickapoo, Kansas Territory	George F. Pierce	452 Whites
			1 Colored
			176 Indians
Sept. 1857	Leavenworth City, K.T.	Rev. Nathan Scarritt (elected to preside)	
Sept. 1858	Shawnee, K. T.	John Early	
Sept. 1859	Tecumseh, K.T.	R. Paine	
Sept. 1860	Wyandotte, K.T.	H. N. Kavanaugh	1039 Whites
			5 Colored
			130 Indians
Oct. 1861	Atchison	Rev. Thomas Wallace (elected to preside)	

WESTERN CONFERENCE

Date	Place	Presiding Bishop	Total Membership
Sept. 1870	Leavenworth City	H. N. McTyeire	1,535 Whites
			37 Indians
			134 Colored
Aug. 1871	Council Grove	E. M. Marvin	
Sept. 1872	Nebraska City, Nebraska	George F. Pierce	
Sept. 1873	Atchison	W. M. Wightman	
Sept. 1874	Wyandotte	John C. Keener	
Sept. 1875	Council Grove	E. M. Marvin	
Aug. 1876	Nebraska City, Nebraska	H. N. McTyeire	
Aug. 1877	Atchison	E. M. Marvin	

Date	Place	Presiding Bishop	Total Membership
Sept. 1878	Wyandotte	D. S. Dogget	
Aug. 1879	Council Grove	John C. Keener	
Sept. 1880	Oskaloosa	John C. Keener	3,063
Sept. 1881	Howard City	George F. Pierce	
Sept. 1882	Wyandotte	J. C. Granbery	
Sept. 1883	Fairview	A. W. Wilson	
Sept. 1884	Council Grove	Linus Parker	
Sept. 1885	Wyandotte	J. C. Granbery	
Oct. 1886	Atchison	H. N. McTyeire	
Oct. 1887	Council Grove	Charles B. Galloway	
Aug. 1888	Kansas City, Kansas	E. R. Hendrix	
Aug. 1889	Atchison	E. R. Hendrix	
Sept. 1890	Arrington	Joseph S. Key	3,290
Aug. 1891	Hillsdale	Robert K. Hargrove	
Aug. 1892	Council Grove	E. R. Hendrix	
Aug. 1893	Kansas City, Kansas	Attigus G. Haygood	
Aug. 1894	Arkansas City	E. R. Hendrix	
Sept. 1895	Atchison	R. K. Hargrove	
Sept. 1896	Hillsdale	Wallace W. Duncan	
Aug. 1897	Council Grove	Oscar P. Fitzgerald	
Aug. 1898	Kansas City, Kansas	Warren A. Candler	
Aug. 1899	Elk City	John C. Granbery	
Aug. 1900	Atchison	John C. Granbery	3,003
Aug. 1901	Council Grove	Warren A. Candler	
Sept. 1902	Arkansas City	E. R. Hendrix	
Aug. 1903	Atchison	Charles B. Galloway	
Aug. 1904	Rosedale	E. R. Hendrix	
Aug. 1905	Kansas City, Kansas	E. R. Hendrix	2,575

In 1906 this work became the Western District of the Southwest Missouri Conference.

Appendix I-b
METHODIST EPISCOPAL CHURCH
KANSAS-NEBRASKA CONFERENCE

Date	Place	Presiding Bishop	Total Membership
Oct. 1856	Lawrence, K.T.	O. C. Baker	1,099 (840 in Kansas)
April 1857	Nebraska City, N.T.	E. R. Ames (W. H. Goode presided, except on last day of session.)	
April 1858	Topeka, K.T.	E. S. Janes	
April 1859	Omaha, N.T.	Levi Scott	
March 1860	Leavenworth		3,881 (2,997 in Kansas)

(In the absence of a Bishop, Rev. L. B. Dennis was elected president and presided throughout the whole session.)

KANSAS CONFERENCE

Date	Place	Presiding Bishop	Total Membership
March 1861	Atchison	T. A. Morris	3,932
March 1862	Wyandotte	Matthew Simpson	
March 1863	Lawrence	E. R. Ames	
March 1864	Leavenworth	O. C. Baker	
March 1865	Topeka	Levi Scott	
March 1866	Baldwin	Calvin Kingsley	
March 1867	Manhattan	E. R. Ames	
March 1868	Lawrence	Edward Thompson	
March 1869	Leavenworth	E. S. Janes	
March 1870	Topeka	D. W. Clark	10,290
March 1871	Paola	E. R. Ames	
March 1872	Emporia	Levi Scott	
March 1873	Ottawa	Thomas Bowman	
April 1874	Atchison	E. G. Andrews	
March 1875	Manhattan	S. M. Merrill	
March 1876	Lawrence	J. T. Peck	

Date	Place	Presiding Bishop	Total Membership
March 1877	Holton	Matthew Simpson	
March 1878	Salina	Thomas Bowman	
March 1879	Leavenworth	I. W. Wiley	
March 1880	Topeka	R. S. Foster	15,511
March 1881	Concordia	John F. Hurst	
March 1882	Abilene	H. W. Warren	
March 1883	Hiawatha	W. L. Harris	
March 1884	Topeka	S. M. Merrill	
March 1885	Clay Center	C. H. Fowler	
March 1886	Holton	J. M. Walden	
March 1887	Junction City	E. G. Andrews	
March 1888	Topeka	J. M. Walden	
March 1889	Lawrence	W. X. Ninde	
March 1890	Horton	C. D. Foss	17,957
March 1891	Washington	S. M. Merrill	
March 1892	Kansas City, Kan.	H. W. Warren	
March 1893	Baldwin	Isaac W. Joyce	
March 1894	Abilene	J. H. Vincent	
March 1895	Leavenworth	D. A. Goodsell	
March 1896	Atchison	E. G. Andrews	
March 1897	Manhattan	C. C. McCabe	
March 1898	Lawrence	C. H. Fowler	
March 1899	Hiawatha	J. N. Fitzgerald	
March 1900	Kansas City, Kan.	H. W. Warren	24,858
March 1901	Topeka	S. M. Merrill	
March 1902	Washington	W. F. Mallalieu	
March 1903	Holton	C. D. Foss	
March 1904	Lawrence	J. M. Walden	
March 1905	Junction City	Isaac W. Joyce	
March 1906	Olathe	H. Spellmeyer	
March 1907	Kansas City, Kan.	L. B. Wilson	
March 1908	Topeka	W. F. McDowell	
March 1909	Clay Center	W. A. Quayle	

229

Date	Place	Presiding Bishop	Total Membership
March 1910	Atchison	C. W. Smith	29,675
March 1911	Abilene	David H. Moore	
March 1912	Kansas City, Kan.	C. W. Smith	
March 1913	Lawrence	W. O. Shepard	

(Conference re-organized to include portion of former South Kansas Conference.)

Date	Place	Presiding Bishop	Total Membership
March 1914	Chanute	W. O. Shepard	
March 1915	Topeka	W. O. Shepard	
March 1916	Independence	W. P. Thirkield	
March 1917	Topeka	W. O. Shepard	
March 1918	Pittsburg	W. O. Shepard	
March 1919	Topeka	A. W. Leonard	
March 1920	Atchison	W. O. Shepard	78,167
March 1921	Iola	E. L. Waldorf	
March 1922	Topeka	E. L. Waldorf	
March 1923	Topeka	W. F. Anderson	
March 1924	Topeka	E. L. Waldorf	
March 1925	Independence	F. T. Keeney	
March 1926	Ottawa	E. L. Waldorf	
March 1927	Topeka	F. D. Leete	
March 1928	Manhattan	E. L. Waldorf	
March 1929	Topeka	E. L. Waldorf	
March 1930	Kansas City, Kan.	C. E. Locke	84,765
March 1931	Emporia	E. L. Waldorf	
March 1932	Topeka	W. E. Brown	
March 1933	Lawrence	C. L. Mead	
March 1934	Abilene	C. L. Mead	
March 1935	Parsons	R. S. Cushman	
March 1936	Topeka	C. L. Mead	
March 1937	Pittsburg	C. L. Mead	
March 1938	Ottawa	Titus Lowe	
Sept. 1939	Topeka	C. L. Mead	

SOUTH KANSAS CONFERENCE

Date	Place	Presiding Bishop	Total Membership
March 1874	Fort Scott	E. G. Andrews	9,226
March 1875	Independence	S. M. Merrill	
March 1876	Emporia	J. T. Peck	
March 1877	Wichita	Matthew Simpson	
March 1878	Garnett	Thomas Bowman	
March 1879	Hutchinson	I. W. Wiley	
March 1880	Ottawa	R. S. Foster	17,138
March 1881	Wellington	John F. Hurst	
March 1882	Burlington	H. W. Warren	
March 1883	Oswego	W. L. Harris	
March 1884	Paola	S. M. Merrill	
March 1885	Independence	W. X. Ninde	
March 1886	Parsons	J. M. Walden	
March 1887	Chanute	E. G. Andrews	
March 1888	Fort Scott	Thomas Bowman	
March 1889	Baldwin	J. H. Vincent	
March 1890	Emporia	C. D. Foss	19,281
March 1891	Girard	S. M. Merrill	
March 1892	Ottawa	H. W. Warren	
March 1893	Coffeyville	Isaac W. Joyce	
March 1894	Parsons	W. F. Mallalieu	
March 1895	Burlington	D. A. Goodsell	
March 1896	Baldwin	E. G. Andrews	
March 1897	Pittsburg	C. C. McCabe	
March 1898	Ottawa	Earl Cranston	
March 1899	Columbus	J. N. Fitzgerald	
March 1900	Chanute	J. H. Vincent	23,676
March 1901	Eureka	J. M. Walden	
March 1902	Paola	W. F. Mallalieu	
March 1903	Fort Scott	C. D. Foss	
March 1904	Baldwin	J. W. Hamilton	

Date	Place	Presiding Bishop	Total Membership
March 1905	Iola	Isaac W. Joyce	
March 1906	Neodesha	H. Spellmeyer	
March 1907	Emporia	David H. Moore	
March 1908	Baldwin	W. F. McDowell	
March 1909	Coffeyville	W. A. Quayle	
March 1910	Fort Scott	J. F. Berry	31,501
March 1911	Paola	C. W. Smith	
March 1912	Baldwin	C. W. Smith	
March 1913	Parsons	W. O. Shephard	

SOUTHWEST KANSAS CONFERENCE

Date	Place	Presiding Bishop	Total Membership
March 1882	Burlington	H. W. Warren	
March 1883	Winfield	W. L. Harris	8,307
March 1884	Newton	S. M. Merrill	
March 1885	El Dorado	W. X. Ninde	
March 1886	McPherson	J. M. Walden	
March 1887	Winfield	E. G. Andrews	
March 1888	Wichita	Thomas Bowman	
March 1889	Larned	J. H. Vincent	
March 1890	Hutchinson	C. D. Foss	21,820
March 1891	Newton	S. M. Merrill	
March 1892	Winfield	H. W. Warren	
March 1893	Great Bend	J. F. Hurst	
March 1894	Wellington	W. F. Mallaleiu	
March 1895	Hutchinson	D. S. Goodsell	
March 1896	Wichita	E. G. Andrews	
March 1897	Winfield	C. C. McCabe	
March 1898	Lyons	Earl Cranston	
March 1899	El Dorado	J. N. Fitzgerald	

Date	Place	Presiding Bishop	Total Membership
March 1900	Wichita	J. H. Vincent	24,136
March 1901	Newton	J. M. Walden	
March 1902	Arkansas City	W. F. Mallaleiu	
March 1903	Sterling	C. D. Foss	
March 1904	Wichita	J. W. Hamilton	
March 1905	Peabody	Isaac W. Joyce	
March 1906	Hutchinson	H. Spellmeyer	
April 1907	Wellington	D. H. Moore	
April 1908	Winfield	H. W. Warren	
March 1909	Kingman	J. L. Neulson	
March 1910	Wichita	W. F. McDowell	34,153
March 1911	Great Bend	J. F. Berry	
March 1912	Hutchinson	Robert McIntyre	
March 1913	Wichita	F. M. Bristol	
March 1914	Winfield	W. O. Shepard	
March 1915	Dodge City	W. P. Thirkield	
March 1916	Wichita	W. P. Thirkield	
March 1917	Lyons	W. O. Shepard	
March 1918	Pratt	W. O. Shepard	
March 1919	Newton	W. A. Quayle	
March 1920	Wichita	W. O. Shepard	52,917
March 1921	McPherson	E. L. Waldorf	
March 1922	Liberal	E. L. Waldorf	
March 1923	Wellington	W. F. Anderson	
March 1924	Winfield	E. L. Waldorf	
March 1925	Great Bend	F. F. Keeney	
Oct. 1925	Peabody	E. L. Waldorf	
Oct. 1926	Augusta	E. H. Hughes	
Oct. 1927	Arkansas City	E. L. Waldorf	
Oct. 1928	Dodge City	E. L. Waldorf	
Oct. 1929	McPherson	C. L. Mead	
Oct. 1930	Kingman	E. L. Waldorf	59,068

Date	Place	Presiding Bishop	Total Membership
Oct. 1931 .... El Dorado		E. L. Waldorf	
Oct. 1932 .... Hutchinson		C. L. Mead	
Oct. 1933 .... Wichita		C. L. Mead	
Oct. 1934 .... Wellington		R. S. Cushman	
Oct. 1935 .... Winfield		C. L. Mead	
Oct. 1936 .... Pratt		C. L. Mead	
Oct. 1937 .... Hutchinson		H. Lester Smith	
Oct. 1938 .... Wichita		Titus Lowe	
Oct. 1939 .... Salina		W. C. Martin	66,229

NORTHWEST KANSAS CONFERENCE

Date	Place	Presiding Bishop	Total Membership
March 1883 .... Beloit		W. L. Harris	5,095
March 1884 .... Salina		S. M. Merrill	
March 1885 .... Clyde		W. X. Ninde	
March 1886 .... Kirwin		J. M. Walden	
March 1887 .... Ellsworth		E. G. Andrews	
March 1888 .... Salina		Thomas Bowman	
March 1889 .... Jewell City		J. H. Vincent	
March 1890 .... Minneapolis		C. D. Foss	12,376
March 1891 .... Norton		S. M. Merrill	
March 1892 .... Concordia		H. W. Warren	
March 1893 .... Belleville		John F. Hurst	
March 1894 .... Goodland		W. F. Mallalieu	
April 1895 .... Lincoln		D. A. Goodsell	
April 1896 .... Salina		E. G. Andrews	
March 1897 .... Beloit		C. C. McCabe	
March 1898 .... Minneapolis		Earl Cranston	
March 1899 .... Downs		J. N. Fitzgerald	

Date	Place	Presiding Bishop	Total Membership
March 1900 .... Concordia		H. W. Warren	13,318
April 1901 .... Ellsworth		John M. Walden	
April 1902 .... Osborne		W. F. Mallalieu	
April 1903 .... Stockton		C. D. Foss	
April 1904 .... Salina		J. W. Hamilton	
April 1905 .... Smith Center		Isaac W. Joyce	
March 1906 .... Jewell City		H. Spellmeyer	
March 1907 .... Norton		L. B. Wilson	
March 1908 .... Salina		H. W. Warren	
March 1909 .... Belleville		Edwin H. Hughes	
March 1910 .... Plainville		W. F. McDowell	19,580
March 1911 .... Hays		David H. Moore	
March 1912 .... Salina		John L. Neulson	
March 1913 .... Goodland		Frank M. Bristol	
March 1914 .... Mankato		W. O. Shephard	
March 1915 .... Beloit		W. P. Thirkield	
March 1916 .... Concordia		W. P. Thirkield	
March 1917 .... Ellsworth		W. O. Shepard	
March 1918 .... Downs		W. O. Shepard	
March 1919 .... Lindsborg		W. A. Quayle	
March 1920 .... Hays		W. O. Shepard	22,441
March 1921 .... Salina		E. L. Waldorf	
March 1922 .... Goodland		E. L. Waldorf	
April 1923 .... Concordia		Homer C. Stuntz	
March 1924 .... Salina		E. L. Waldorf	
Oct. 1924 .... Colby		E. L. Waldorf	
Oct. 1925 .... Osborne		F. T. Keeney	
Sept. 1926 .... Oberlin		W. F. Anderson	
Sept. 1927 .... Salina		E. L. Waldorf	
Sept. 1928 .... Plainville		E. L. Waldorf	
Sept. 1929 .... Russell		C. L. Mead	
Sept. 1930 .... Belleville		F. D. Leete	27,492

Date	Place	Presiding Bishop	Total Membership
Sept. 1931	Norton	E. L. Waldorf	
Sept. 1932	Stockton	C. L. Mead	
Sept. 1933	Beloit	C. L. Mead	
Sept. 1934	Colby	C. L. Mead	
Sept. 1935	Salina	Edwin H. Hughes	
Sept. 1936	Concordia	C. L. Mead	
Sept. 1937	Jewell	C. L. Mead	
Sept. 1938	La Crosse	Titus Lowe	
Oct. 1939	Salina	C. L. Mead	27,704

Appendix I-c
METHODIST PROTESTANT CHURCH
KANSAS MISSION CONFERENCE

Date	Place	President	Total Membership
1866	Olathe	Jeremiah Bidison	
1867	Ottawa	Jeremiah Bidison	
1868	Pleasant Valley	M. Jared	
1869	Pleasant Valley	M. Jared	
1870	Xema	F. D. Lay	
1871	Pleasant Valley	F. D. Lay	
1872	Americus	Daniel Young	
1873	Spring Hill	Daniel Wilson	
1874	Louisville	Daniel Young	
1875	Americus	Sullivan Clark	
1876	Canville	Reuben Baker	
1877	Emporia	Sullivan Clark	
1878	Spring Hill	Sullivan Clark	
1879	Shell Rock	Sullivan Clark	
1880	Ottawa	W. M. Woodward	1,737
1881	Emporia	Sullivan Clark	
1882	Whitewater	J. H. Luse	
1883	Fowler's Chapel (near Emporia)	J. H. Luse	
1884	Spring Hill	J. H. Luse	
1885	Ottawa	J. H. Luse	
1886	Spring Creek Church (near Douglas)	J. H. Luse	
1887	Moran	L. C. Onyette	
1888	Neosho Rapids	J. H. Luse	
1889	Haddam	T. J. Shepherd	
1890	Ottawa	T. J. Shepherd	2,244
1891	Neosho Rapids	T. J. Shepherd	

KANSAS CONFERENCE

Date	Place	President	Total Membership
1892	Fort Scott	T. J. Shepherd	
1893	Uniontown	T. J. Shepherd	
1894	Kansas City	W. H. Manary	
1895	Canton	W. H. Manary	
1896	Ottawa	J. R. Daily	
1897	Kansas City	J. R. Daily	
1898	Uniontown	J. E. Rouze	
1899	Neosho Rapids	T. J. Shepherd	3,039
1900	Admire	A. H. Linder	
1901	Kansas City	A. H. Linder	
1902	Moran	A. H. Linder	
1903	Kansas City	W. A. Sprauge	
1904	Haddam	W. A. Sprauge	
1905	LaHarpe	W. A. Sprauge	
1906	Ottawa	B. A. Brooks	
1907	Neosho Rapids	B. A. Brooks	
1908	Centerville	B. A. Brooks	
1909	Kansas City	T. J. Strickler	
1910	Spring Hill	T. J. Strickler	1,975
1911	Centerville	T. J. Strickler	
1912	Kansas City	T. J. Strickler	
1913	Kansas City	T. J. Strickler	
1914	Stanley	B. A. Brooks	
1915	Kansas City	B. A. Brooks	
1916	Kansas City	B. A. Brooks	
1917	Kansas City	B. A. Brooks	
1918	Centerville	B. A. Brooks	
1919	Ash Grove	J. W. Shell	
1920	Kansas City	J. W. Shell	1,137
1921	Neosho Rapids	B. A. Brooks	
1922	Rose Hill	B. A. Brooks	

238

Date	Place	President	Total Membership
1923	Kansas City, Kansas	B. A. Brooks	
1924	Centerville	T. L. Garrison	
1925	Kansas City, Kansas	T. L. Garrison	
1926	Rose Hill	T. L. Garrison	
1927	Pawnee Station (near Anna)	T. L. Garrison	
1928	Kansas City, Kansas	T. L. Garrison	
1929	Kansas City, Kansas	W. M. Snyder	
1930	Kansas City, Kansas	W. M. Snyder	1,242
1931	Haddam	W. M. Snyder	
1932	Rose Hill	W. M. Snyder	
1933	Kansas City, Kansas	W. M. Snyder	
1934	Centerville	B. A. Brooks	
1935	Neosho Rapids	L. E. Dixon	
1936	Kansas City, Kansas	L. E. Dixon	
1937	Rose Hill	L. E. Dixon	
1938	Kansas City, Kansas	L. E. Dixon	
1939	Kansas City, Kansas	L. E. Dixon	1,908

Appendix I-d
THE METHODIST CHURCH
KANSAS CONFERENCE

Date	Place	Presiding Bishop	Total Membership
Sept.-Oct. 1939	Topeka	C. L. Mead	
Oct. 1940	Manhattan	W. C. Martin	83,456
Oct. 1941	Topeka	W. C. Martin	
Sept. 1942	Ottawa	W. C. Martin	
Sept. 1943	Emporia	W. C. Martin	
Oct. 1944	Iola	W. C. Martin	
Oct. 1945	Topeka	W. C. Martin	
Sept. 1946	Coffeyville	W. C. Martin	
Sept. 1947	Topeka	W. C. Martin	
Sept. 1948	Emporia	Dana Dawson	
June 1949	Manhattan	Dana Dawson	
June 1950	Pittsburg	Dana Dawson	78,996
June 1951	Topeka	Dana Dawson	
June 1952	Kansas City, Kan.	Dana Dawson	
june 1953	Independence	Dana Dawson	
June 1954	Ottawa	Dana Dawson	
May 1955	Kansas City, Kan.	Dana Dawson	
June 1956	Lawrence	Dana Dawson	
June 1957	Coffeyville	Dana Dawson	
June 1958	Topeka	Dana Dawson	
June 1959	Manhattan	Dana Dawson	
June 1960	Pittsburg	M. W. Clair, Jr.	106,727
June 1961	Atchison	Eugene Slater	
June 1962	Emporia	Eugene Slater	
June 1963	Kansas City, Kan.	Eugene Slater	
June 1964	Topeka	Eugene Slater	
June 1965	Coffeyville	W. McFerrin Stowe	109,515

CENTRAL KANSAS CONFERENCE

Date	Place	Presiding Bishop	Total Membership
Oct. 1939	Salina	C. L. Mead	97,310
Oct. 1940	Hutchinson	W. C. Martin	97,943
Oct. 1941	Wichita	W. C. Martin	
Oct. 1942	Salina	W. C. Martin	
Oct. 1943	Hutchinson	W. C. Martin	
Oct. 1944	Wichita	W. C. Martin	
Sept. 1945	Salina	W. C. Martin	
Oct. 1946	Hutchinson	W. C. Martin	
Oct. 1947	Wichita	W. C. Martin	
Oct. 1948	Salina	Dana Dawson	
Oct. 1949	Hutchinson	Dana Dawson	
Oct. 1950	Wichita	Dana Dawson	116,704
Oct. 1951	Salina	W. C. Martin	
Oct. 1952	Hutchinson	Dana Dawson	
Oct. 1953	Wichita	Dana Dawson	
Oct. 1954	Salina	Dana Dawson	
Oct. 1955	Hutchinson	Dana Dawson	
Oct. 1956	Wichita	Dana Dawson	
Oct. 1957	Salina	Dana Dawson	
May 1958	Hutchinson	Dana Dawson	
May 1959	Wichita	Dana Dawson	
May 1960	Salina	Glenn Phillips	130,506
May 1961	Hutchinson	Eugene Slater	
May 1962	Wichita	Eugene Slater	
May 1963	Salina	Eugene Slater	
May 1964	Hutchinson	Eugene Slater	
May 1965	Dodge City	W. McFerrin Stowe	137,182

Appendix I-e
"UNITED BRETHREN IN CHRIST"

ONE HUNDRED YEARS IN KANSAS

The first Annual Conference Session of the Church of the United Brethren in Christ, convened on October 30, 1857 at Prairie City, Kansas, eighteen miles south of Lawrence, Kansas, now called Prairie Grove, Kansas.

Dr. A. W. Drury of Dayton, Ohio, church historian (1932) furnished much of the following data. The Religious Telescope file was also searched for dates. The material up to 1956 was compiled by Martin G. Miller.

The following chronological list shows: the year, meeting place, and the presiding officer of each Conference Session held in:

Kansas Conference ....1857 to 1900
Northeast Kansas Conference ....1901 to 1909
North Kansas Conference ....1910 to 1913
Kansas Conference ....1914 to 1956

* * * * *

Date	Place	Presiding Bishop
1857	Prairie City	David Edwards
1858	Tecumseh	David Edwards
1859	Fremont	David Edwards
1860	Mound City	David Edwards
1861	Big Springs	Rev. J. Terrel, Chm.
1862	Prairie City	Rev. J. Terrel, Chm.
1863	Holton	David Edwards
1864	Greeley	David Edwards
1865	Big Springs	David Edwards
1866	Lecompton	David Edwards
1867	Lecompton	David Edwards
1868	Americus	J. Weaver
1869	Lecompton	J. Markwood
1870	Greeley	J. Dickson
1871	Lecompton	J. Dickson

Date	Place	Presiding Bishop
1872	Lecompton	J. Dickson
1873	Topeka	J. J. Glossbrenner
1874	Osage City	J. J. Glossbrenner
1875	Lecompton	J. J. Glossbrenner
1876	May Day	J. J. Glossbrenner
1877	Clifton Circuit	M. Wright
1878	Lecompton	M. Wright
1879	Clifton Circuit	M. Wright
1880	Meriden	M. Wright
1881	Lecompton	E. B. Kephart
1882	Abilene	E. B. Kephart
1883	Lecompton	E. B. Kephart
1884	Robinson	E. B. Kephart
1885	Rusco Church	N. Castle
1886	Lecompton	E. B. Kephart
1887	Lecompton	J. Weaver
1888	Pleasant Grove	J. Dickson
1889	May Day	E. B. Kephart
1890	Lecompton	N. Castle
1891	Whiting	J. Weaver
1892	Lecompton	J. Dickson
1893	McLouth	J. W. Holt
1894	Osage City	J. W. Holt
1895	Meriden	E. B. Kephart
1896	Lecompton	J. S. Mills
1897	Robinson	J. S. Mills
1898	Lecompton	J. S. Mills
1899	Whiting	J. S. Mills
1900	McLouth	J. S. Mills
1901	Topeka	W. M. Weekley
1902	Lecompton	G. M. Mathews
1903	Holton	G. M. Mathews
1904	Lawrence	G. M. Mathews

Date	Place	Presiding Bishop
1905	McLouth	W. M. Weekley
1906	Lecompton	W. M. Weekley
1907	Topeka	W. M. Weekley
1908	Whiting	W. M. Weekley
1909	Holton	W. M. Weekley
1910	Salina	W. M. Weekley
1911	Holton	W. M. Weekley
1912	Concordia	W. M. Weekley
1913	Topeka	C. J. Kephart
1914	Wichita	C. J. Kephart
1915	Lawrence	C. J. Kephart
1916	Concordia	C. J. Kephart
1917	Topeka	C. J. Kephart
1918	Wichita	C. J. Kephart
1919	Topeka	C. J. Kephart
1920	Salina	C. J. Kephart
1921	Iola	C. J. Kephart
1922	Wichita	C. J. Kephart
1923	Kansas City	C. J. Kephart
1924	Concordia	C. J. Kephart
1925	Hutchinson	A. B. Statton
1926	Topeka	A. B. Statton
1927	Wichita	A. B. Statton
1928	Independence	A. B. Statton
1929	Beloit	A. B. Statton
1930	Kansas City	A. B. Statton
1931	Hutchinson	A. B. Statton
1932	Topeka	A. B. Statton
1933	Wichita	A. B. Statton
1934	Iola	A. B. Statton
1935	Salina	A. B. Statton
1936	Coffeyville	A. B. Satton
1937	Hoisington	A. B. Satton

Date	Place	Presiding Bishop
1938	Winfield	V. O. Weidler
1939	Chanute	V. O. Weidler
1940	Wichita	V. O. Weidler
1941	Hutchinson	V. O. Weidler
1942	Coffeyville	V. O. Weidler
1943	Iola	V. O. Weidler
1944	Concordia	V. O. Weidler
1945	Salina	V. O. Weidler
1946	Wichita	V. O. Weidler
1947	Salina	V. O. Weidler
1948	Salina	V. O. Weidler
1949	Salina	V. O. Weidler
1950	Salina	V. O. Weidler
1951	Salina	C. H. Stauffacher
1952	Salina	C. H. Stauffacher
1953	Salina	C. H. Stauffacher
1954	Salina	Rev. D. T. Gregory
1955	Salina	L. L. Baughman
1956	Wichita	L. L. Baughman

Appendix I-f
EVANGELICAL ASSOCIATION

KANSAS CONFERENCE

Date	Place	Presiding Bishop	Total Membership
May 1865	Leavenworth	Joseph Long	176
March 1866	Leavenworth	J. J. Esher (jr. bishop)	
March 1867	Leavenworth	Joseph Long	
March 1868	Nickel's Grove, Mo.	J. J. Esher	
March 1969	Oregon, Mo.	J. J. Esher	
March 1870	Deer Creek	J. G. Pfiefer (elected to preside)	907
March 1871	Cosby, Mo.	J. J. Esher	
March 1872	Nickel's Grove, Mo.	R. Yeakel	
March 1873	Holton	J. G. Pfeifer (elected to preside)	
March 1874	Nemaha, Neb.	J. J. Esher	
March 1875	Deer Creek	R. Yeakel	
March 1876	Leavenworth	R. Dubs	
March 1877	Nickel's Grove, Mo.	J. J. Esher	
March 1878	Willow Springs	Thomas Bowman	
March 1879	Nemaha, Neb.	J. J. Esher	
March 1880	Platte River Circuit, Mo.	R. Dubs	3,087
March 1881	Holton	R. Dubs	
March 1882	Captain Creek	Thomas Bowman	
March 1883	Canada	J. J. Esher	
March 1884	Nemaha, Neb.	R. Dubs	
March 1885	Camp Creek	Thomas Bowman	
March 1886	Willow Springs	J. J. Esher	
March 1887	Jewell City	R. Dubs	
March 1888	Hiawatha	J. J. Esher	
March 1889	Yates Center	Thomas Bowman	
March 1890	Holton	Thomas Bowman	5,701
March 1891	Canada	J. J. Esher	
March 1892	Coal Creek	S. C. Brayfogel	

Date	Place	Presiding Bishop	Total Membership
March 1893	Swede Creek	Wm. Horn	
March 1894	Preston, Neb.	J. J. Esher	
March 1895	Clearfield	S. C. Brayfogel	
March 1896	Cosby, Mo.	J. J. Esher	
March 1897	Yates Center	Wm. Horn	
March 1898	Holton	Thomas Bowman	
March 1899	Leonardville	S. C. Breyfogel	
March 1900	Jewel City	Wm. Horn	6,081
March 1901	Swede Creek	Wm. Horn	
March 1902	Hiawatha	Thomas Bowman	
March 1903	Holton	S. C. Breyfogel	
March 1904	Bern	Wm. Horn	
March 1905	Yates Center	Thomas Bowman	
March 1906	Coal Creek	S. C. Breyfogel	
March 1907	Preston Sta., Neb.	Wm. Horn	
March 1908	Holton	Thomas Bowman	
March 1909	Jewel	Wm. Horn	
March 1910	Yates Center	S. P. Spreng	7,081
March 1911	Kansas City, Mo.	S. C. Breyfogel	
March 1912	St. Joseph, Mo.	Thomas Bowman	
March 1913	Leonardville	Wm. Horn	
March 1914	Newton	S. P. Spreng	7,949
March 1915	Leavenworth	S. C. Breyfogel	
March 1916	Holton	G. Heinmiller	
March 1917	Jewel	S. C. Breyfogel	
March 1918	Kansas City, Mo.	L. H. Seager	
March 1919	Yates Center	S. P. Spreng	
March 1920	Abilene	S. C. Breyfogel	8,356
March 1921	Hutchinson	S. P. Spreng	
March 1922	Yates Center	G. Heinmiller	

Appendix I-g
UNITED EVANGELICAL CHURCH

Date	Place	Presiding Bishop	Total Membership
1902	Longford	W. M. Stanford	
1903	Lincolnville	W. F. Heil	
1904	Ebenezer (Clay Circuit)	H. B. Hartzler	
1905	Lincolnville	W. F. Heil	617
1906	Longford	H. B. Hartzler	
1907	Hiawatha	W. F. Heil	
1908	Mt. Zion	H. B. Hartzler	
1909	Enid, Okla.	W. F. Heil	
1910	Mizpah (Clay Circuit)	H. B. Hartzler	
1911	Richland	W. H. Fouke	
1912	El Reno	U. F. Swengel	
1913	Longford	W. H. Fouke	
1914	Enid, Okla.	U. F. Swengel	
1915	Oklahoma City, Okla.	W. F. Fouke	1,172
1916	Mizpah (Clay Circuit)	U. F. Swengel	
1917	N. Enid, Okla.	W. H. Fouke	
1918	Bellevue	U. F. Swengel	
1919	Oklahoma City, Okla.	M. T. Maze	
1920	Hiawatha	W. F. Heil	876
1921	Enid, Okla.	M. T. Maze	
1922	Longford	W. F. Heil	

Appendix I-h
EVANGELICAL CHURCH

Date	Place	Presiding Bishop	Total Membership
March 1923	Newton	S. C. Breyfogel	9,123
March 1924	Enid, Okla.	M. T. Maze	
March 1925	Falls City, Neb.	S. P. Spreng	
March 1926	Wichita	L. H. Seager	
May 1927	Holton	J. S. Stamm	
May 1928	Kansas City, Mo.	J. S. Stamm	
May 1929	Newton	J. F. Dunlap	
May 1930	Abilene	M. T. Maze	10,258
May 1931	Haiwatha	J. S. Stamm	
May 1932	Enid, Okla.	J. S. Stamm	
May 1933	Jewel	J. S. Stamm	
May 1934	Hutchinson	J. S. Stamm	
May 1935	Leonardville	C. H. Stauffacher	
May 1936	Hesston	C. H. Stauffacher	
May 1937	Topeka	C. H. Stauffacher	
May 1938	Yates Center	C. H. Stauffacher	
May 1939	Holton	C. H. Stauffacher	10,922

Appendix I-i
THE EVANGELICAL UNITED BRETHREN CHURCH
KANSAS CONFERENCE

Date	Place	Presiding Bishop
1956	Wichita	L. L. Baughman
1957	Wichita	L. L. Baughman
1958	Hutchinson	L. L. Baughman
1959	Salina	L. L. Baughman
1960	Salina	L. L. Baughman
1961	Topeka	Paul Milhouse
1962	Topeka	Paul Milhouse
1963	Salina	Paul Milhouse
1964	Topeka	Paul Milhouse
1965	Salina	Paul Milhouse

Appendix II—Outline
GENERAL CONFERENCE DELEGATES
(serving twice or more)

II-a Methodist Episcopal Church, South
      Kansas Mission Conference—1856-1861
      Western Conference—1870-1905
II-b Methodist Episcopal and The Methodist Church
      Kansas-Nebraska Conference—1856-1860
      Kansas Conference—1864-1968
      South Kansas Conference—1876-1912
      Northwest Kansas Conference—1884-1939
      Southwest Kansas Conference—1884-1939
      Central Kansas Conference—1939-1968
II-c Methodist Protestant Church—1887-1939

Appendix II-a
GENERAL CONFERENCE DELEGATES
(serving twice or more)
METHODIST EPISCOPAL CHURCH, SOUTH
KANSAS MISSION CONFERENCE

Ministers
Nathan Scarritt—1858, 1862

WESTERN CONFERENCE

Ministers
Jacob McEwen—1874, 1878
Thomas C. Downs—1878, 1886, 1894, 1902

Lay Representatives

W. S. Chick—1878, 1886

Appendix II-b
GENERAL CONFERENCE DELEGATES
(Serving twice or more)

Methodist Episcopal and The Methodist Church

Ministers   *Lay Representatives*

KANSAS-NEBRASKA CONFERENCE

W. H. Goode—1856, 1860

KANSAS CONFERENCE

Ministers	Lay Representatives
Joseph Dennison—1864, 1880	
Werter R. Davis—1868, 1872, 1880	Ira I. Tabor—1880, 1888
G. S. Dearborn—1872, 1888, 1892	
J. R. Madison—1884, 1900, 1908, 1912	
S. E. Pendleton—1888, 1892	
J. W. Alderman—1892, 1900	D. C. Newcomb—1892, 1900
L. H. Murlin—1900, 1904	
Edwin Locke—1904, 1912, 1916	Miss Viola Troutman—1904, 1912
J. T. McFarland—1908, 1912	
W. C. Hanson—1908, 1912	
J. A. Stavely—1912, 1920	
John Maclean—1916, 1920	J. L. Taylor—1916, 1920, 1924, 1928
George Satterlee—1916, 1920	John Marshall—1916, 1920, 1924, 1928
W. A. Keve—1920, 1924, 1928, 1932	O. G. Markham—1916, 1920, 1924, 1932
Henry O. Holter—1920, 1924	
H. A. Gordon—1920, 1928	
Frank Neff—1924, 1928	Mrs. J. L. McCoy—1924, 1928
S. L. Buckner—1924, 1932	
C. L. Hovgard—1924, 1928, 1932, 1936	
O. E. Allison—1928, 1932, 1963, 1939, 1940, 1944, 1948, 1952	T. O. Cunningham—1928, 1932, 1936, 1939
J. R. McFadden—1928, 1932	R. R. Price—1928, 1932
R. E. Gordon—1932, 1944	John C. Gaede—1932, 1936, 1939, 1940
C. I. Coldsmith—1936, 1940, 1944	Mrs. H. E. Wolfe—1932, 1936
	Jesse D. Bender—1932, 1936

Ministers
Leslie Miller—1940, 1944, 1948

Eugene M. Frank—1952, 1956
Clare J. Hayes—1952, 1956, 1960, 1964, 1966, 1968
Albert F. Bramble—1960, 1964, 1966, 1968
Don W. Holter—1964, 1966, 1968

D. P. Mitchell—1876, 1880
Hugh McBirney—1888, 1892, 1900
C. R. Rice—1884, 1892
H. W. Chaffee—1884, 1892
H. J. Coker—1900, 1904, 1908, 1912

J. H. Lockwood—1884, 1888
M. M. Stolz—1888, 1892
W. H. Sweet—1892, 1896
T. J. Harper Taggart—1900, 1904
L. B. Bowers—1924, 1932

W. J. Martindale—1896, 1908
E. C. Beach—1900, 1904
F. E. Mossman—1908, 1916, 1932, 1936
A. B. Hestwood—1912, 1916
A. E. Kirk— 1916, 1920, 1924, 1928, 1939
I. D. Harris—1924, 1932, 1936, 1939
A. E. Henry—1924, 1928, 1932, 1936

SOUTH KANSAS CONFERENCE

NORTHWEST KANSAS CONFERENCE

SOUTHWEST KANSAS CONFERENCE

Lay Representatives
Mrs. H. E. Werner—1940, 1944
C. A. Byers—1944, 1948
T. Russell Reitz—1948, 1952, 1956
H. L. Collins—1952, 1956
Floyd H. Coffman—1960, 1964, 1966, 1968

E. W. Cunningham—1876, 1892, 1900
Stewart Elliott—1888, 1892

O. G. Markham—1904, 1912
J. Luther Taylor—1908, 1912

J. C. Ruppenthal—1916, 1924
A. H. King—1920, 1928
C. A. Kemp—1928, 1936, 1939
C. E. Rarick—1920, 1932, 1940

James Allison—1896, 1908
Hiram Imboden—1904, 1916
E. R. Burkholder—1908, 1916, 1920

M. M. Southard—1920, 1924
A. O. Rorabaugh—1924, 1928, 1932
Wayne Campbell—1924, 1928
Mrs. C. M. Gray—1928, 1939
Karl Miller—1932, 1936

254

CENTRAL KANSAS CONFERENCE

Ministers

A. E. Kirk—1939, 1940
I. D. Harris—1939, 1940
A. E. Henry—1940, 1944
L. R. Templin—1940, 1944
P. D. Womeldorf—1940, 1944, 1952
H. J. Root—1940, 1944
T. A. Williams—1948, 1952
C. H. Hamm—1948, 1956
J. R. Throckmorton—1948, 1952, 1956
Joseph S. Ploughe—1952, 1960
L. S. Johnson—1956, 1960, 1964, 1966, 1968
George Richards—1956, 1960, 1964, 1966
Clarence J. Borger—1960, 1964, 1966, 1968
Glenn E. Matthew—1964, 1966, 1968
Oren McClure—1964, 1966, 1968

Lay Representatives

C. A. Kemp—1939, 1940, 1948
Mrs. C. M. Gray—1939, 1940

Mrs. Joe T. Rogers—1944, 1948, 1952
Ray Streeter—1944, 1948, 1952

Mrs. George Glenn—1948, 1952
William Becker—1948, 1952

Mrs. Kenneth McGill—1952, 1956

M. K. Snyder—1956, 1960
Mrs. H. L. Georg—1960, 1964, 1966
Mrs. D. E. Watson—1964, 1966, 1968
Marion Livingood—1964, 1966, 1968

GENERAL CONFERENCE DELEGATES
(Serving twice or more)
METHODIST PROTESTANT CHURCH

KANSAS CONFERENCE

Ministers
Eugenia St. John—1892, 1896
B. A. Brooks—1916, 1920, 1924, 1928, 1932

Lay Representatives
Eli Fowler—1896, 1908
A. L. Cook—1912, 1916, 1920, 1924, 1928, 1932, 1936, 1939

CHAPTER NOTES

CHAPTER 1

Gold, Glory and the Gospel

1. W. H. Prescott, *The Conquest of Mexico and History of the Conquest of Peru*, New York, New York: Random House Inc., n.d. pp. 39, 111 f. 147.
2. *Ibid.*, p. 147.
3. *Ibid.*, pp. 723 f.
4. Ray Allen Billington, *Westward Expansion*, a History of the American Frontier, New York, 1960, pp. 422 f.
5. William Frank Zornow, *Kansas, a History of the Jayhawk State*, Norman (University of Oklahoma Press), Copyright 1957, pp. 18 f.
6. *Ibid.*, pp. 21 f.
7. Prescott, *op. cit.*, pp. 964-981.
8. Walter Prescott Webb, *The Great Plains*, New York, 1931, quoted p. 107.
9. *Letter*, October 29, 1962, from Charles C. McCarter, General Counsel, State Corporation Commission, State of Kansas, Topeka.
10. Zornow, *op. cit.*, p. 23.

CHAPTER 2

Builders of Empires

1. Walter Prescott Webb, *The Great Plains*, New York, 1931, pp. 52-68; Ray Allen Billington, *Westward Expansion, A History of the American Frontier*, Second Edition, New York (Macmillan), 1960, pp. 409 f.
2. Billington, *op. cit.*, pp. 463 f.
3. *Ibid.*, pp. 242 ff.; Samuel Eliot Morison and Henry Steele Commager, *The Growth of the American Republic*, Vol. I, New York (Oxford), 1950, pp. 389-392.
4. Billington, *op. cit.*, pp. 446-450.
5. *Ibid.*
6. *Ibid.*
7. Webb, *op. cit.*, p. 156 (quoted from Coues, *Pike*, Vol. II, p. 525).
8. *Ibid.*, p. 156 f. (quoted from "Early Western Travel Series," Vol. XVII, p. 147 f., The Arthur H. Clark Co).

CHAPTER 3

Indians in Transition

1. Isaac McCoy, *History of Baptist Missions,* Washington (W. M. Morrison) New York (H. and S. Raynor), 1840, p. 196 f.
2. Justin A. Smith, *A History of the Baptists in the Western States East of the Mississippi*, Philadelphia (American Baptist Publication Society), 1896, p. 59 f.
3. McCoy, *op. cit.*, pp. 326, 332 f.; Sharp, W. A. Seward, *History of Kansas Baptists*, p. 13 f.
4. Samuel Eliot Morison, and Henry Steele Commager, *The Growth of the American Republic*, New York (Oxford), 1950, Vol. I., p. 412 f.

5. Ray Allen Billington, *Westward Expansion, A History of the American Frontier*, 2nd Edition, New York (Macmillan), 1960, p. 275 f.
6. William T. Hagan, *American Indians*, Chicago (Univ. of Chicago), 1961, p. 88.
7. *Ibid.*, p. 66 f.; Billington, *op. cit.*, p. 469 f.
8. William Frank Zornow, *Kansas, A History of the Jayhawk State*, Norman (Univ. of Oklahoma), 1957, p. 44 f.
9. *Ibid.*, p. 848.
10. *Ibid.*, p. 45.
11. *Christian Advocate*, January 29, 1857, Letter from Bishop O. C. Baker.
12. Zornow, *op. cit.*, p. 54.
13. Morison and Commager, *op. cit.*, Vol. II, p. 114 f.
14. Zornow, *op. cit.*, p. 143 f.
15. Billington, *op. cit.*, p. 655 f.
16. *Ibid.*; Hagan, *op. cit.*, p. 107 f.
17. Billington, *op. cit.*, p. 661 f.
18. *Ibid.*
19. *The World Almanac*, 1968, New York, p. 263.

CHAPTER 4

Indian Missions of Other Churches

1. J. S. Griffing, *MS letter*, December 2, 1854, in the Kansas Conference Methodist Historical Society Library, Baker University, Baldwin, Kansas.
2. Fred Louis Parrish, *The Rise of Methodism in Kansas, 1830-1861, from its Inception to the Opening of the Civil War*, M. A. Thesis, Northwestern University, Evanston, Illinois, 1921-1922, p. 55.
3. J. B. Hill, *The Presbytery of Kansas City*, Kansas City, 1901, p. 100 f.
4. Wm. W. Graves, *The First Protestant Osage Missions, 1820-1837*, Oswego, Kansas, 1949, pp. 25-45; William Brown, *The History of Christian Missions*, London (T. Baker), 1864, Vol. II, p. 145 f.
5. Graves, *op. cit.*, pp. 179-186.
6. *Ibid.*, pp. 186-196.
7. *First Annual Report of the Board of Foreign Missions of the Presbyterian Church in the United States of America*, New York, 1838, p. 13 f.
8. Pryor Plank, "The Iowa, Sac and Fox Indian Mission and Its Missionaries, Rev. Samuel M. Irvin and Wife," *Transactions of the Kansas State Historical Society*, 1907-1908, Vol. X, Topeka, Kansas, 1908, p. 312 f.
9. *Annual Reports of Board of Missions: Eighth, Tenth and Fifteenth Annual Reports*: 1845, p. 7 f.; 1847, p. 9 f.; 1852, p. 12 f.
10. *Ibid.*, 1854; 1860; 1865.
11. *Ibid.*, 1856; 1857; 1860.
12. Peter Beckman, O.S.B., *The Catholic Church on the Kansas Frontier, 1850-1877*, Washington, D.C., 1943, p. 1.
13. *Ibid.*, p. 3; James A. McGonigle, "Right Reverend John B. Miege, S.J. First Catholic Bishop of Kansas," *Transactions of the Kansas State Historical Society*, Vol. IX, 1905-1906, Topeka, 1906, pp. 153-159.
14. Beckman, *op. cit.*, p. 4 .
15. *Ibid.*, p. 7.
16. *Ibid.*, p. 8.

17. *Ibid.*, pp. 12-17.
18. *Ibid.*, p. 18 f.
19. *Ibid.*, p. 28.
20. Isaac McCoy, *History of Baptist Missions,* Washington (W. M. Morison), New York, 1840, pp. 326, 332 f., 404 f.
21. D. C. McMurtrie and A. H. Allen, *'Jotham Meeker, Pioneer Printer of Kansas,'* Chicago (Eyncourt), 1930.
22. *Annual Reports, American Baptist Board of Foreign Missions:* 20th, 1834, p. 28 f.; 22nd 1836, p. 9.
23. *Ibid.,* 23rd, 1847, p. 68 f.
24. *Ibid.,* 48th, 1862, p. 303 f.
24. *Ibid.,* 20th, 1834, p. 31; 23rd, 1837, p. 5 f.; 33rd, 1847, p. 68 f.; 48th, 1862, p. 303 f.; 51st, 1865, p. 79 f.
26. *Ibid.,* 22nd, 1836, p. 10; 23rd, 1837, p. 7; 24th, 1838, p. 20; 41st, 1855, p. 125 f.
27. *Ibid.,* 51st, 1865, p. 79 f.
28. Wilson Hobbs, M.D., "The Friends Establishment in Kansas Territory," *Transactions of the Kansas State Historical Society,* Vol. VIII, pp. 250-271.
29. *Report of the Indian Committee to Indiana Yearly Meeting,* 1862, p. 261 f.; R. W. Kelsey, *Friends and the Indians,* 1655-1917, Philadelphia, 1917, p. 140 f.
30. *Ibid.,* p. 150 f.
31. *Ibid., Transactions of Kansas State Historical Society,* Vol. VIII, pp. 250-271.
32. Kelsey, *op. cit.,* p. 170 f.; 187 f.
33. *Ibid.*

CHAPTER 5

Methodist Missions to the Indians in Kansas

1. Frank Tucker, "The Indian Mission of the Missouri Conference, 1830-1844," *World Parish,* June, 1962, p. 21.
2. *Ibid.,* quoted from Mary Greene, *Life, Three Sermons, and Some Miscellaneous Writings of Rev. Jesse Greene,* by his surviving Companion, Lexington, Mo. (Patterson & Julian), 1852, p. 47 f. See also, J. J. Lutz, "The Methodist Missions Among the Indian Tribes in Kansas, *Transactions of the Kansas State Historical Society,* Vol. IX, 1905-06, Topeka, 1906, p. 162 f.
3. Tucker, *op. cit.,* p. 22.
4. *Ibid.,* p. 23 f.
5. A. T. Andreas, *History of Kansas,* Chicago, 1883, p. 65.
6. *Annals of Shawneee Methodist Mission and Indian Manual Labor School,* Compiled by Martha B. Caldwell, Kansas State Historical Society, Topeka, 1939, p. 10 f.
7. *Ibid.,* p. 13 f.
8. Wade Crawford Barclay, *History of Methodist Missions,* Vol. II, *To Reform the Nation,* New York, 1950, p. 178.
9. *Ibid.,* see note also; *Annals, op. cit.,* p. 23 f.
10. Edith Connelly Ross, "The Old Shawnee Mission," *Collections of the Kansas State Historical Society,* Vol. XVII, p. 421.
11. Lutz, *op. cit.,* p. 174.
12. *Ibid.*
13. *Ibid.;* Fred Louis Parrish, *The Rise of Methodism in Kansas,* M. A. Thesis, Northwestern University, 1921-22, p. 18 f.
14. *Minutes of the Annual Conferences of the Methodist Episcopal Church,* 1773-1880, Three vols., Vol. II, p. 301.
15. Ross, *op. cit.;* Lutz, *op. cit.,* p. 179 f.

16. *Ibid.*
17. William Johnson, Letter, *Christian Advocate and Journal,* July 31, 1835.
18. W. H. Goode, *Outposts of Zion,* with Limnings of Mission Life, Cincinnati (Poe & Hitchcock), 1864, p. 304.
19. Lutz, *op. cit.,* pp. 193-203; William W. Cone, "The First Kaw Indian Mission," *Transactions of the Kansas State Historical Society,* Vol. I & II, p. 276 f.
20. Lutz, *op. cit.,* pp. 203-207; Goode, *op. cit.,* p. 296; *Minutes of the Annual Conferences:* 1832, p. 170; 1833, p. 225; 1844, p. 529.
21. Lutz, *op. cit.,* p. 207 f.; Parrish, *op. cit.,* p. 32 f.; *Minutes of the Annual Conferences.*
22. Parrish, *op. cit.,* p. 34; *Minutes of the Annual Conferences.*
23. Lutz, *op. cit.,* p. 211 f.; *Minutes of the Annual Conferences.*
24. Ida M. Ferris, "The Sauks and Foxes in Franklin and Osage Counties, Kansas," *Collections of the Kansas State Historical Society,* Vol. XI, 1908, p. 355 f.
25. James F. Finley, *Life Among the Indians,* Cincinnati (Cranston Curts) n.d., p. 233 f.
26. *Ibid.*
27. *Ibid.*
28. Barclay, *op. cit.,* Vol. I, p. 203; J. Morse, *Report to the Secretary of War of the U.S.A. on Indian Affairs,* New Haven, 1822, appendix, p. 91.
29. Finley, *op. cit.,* pp. 238-247, 257 f.
30. Barclay, *op. cit.,* Vol. I, p. 204 f.; Vol. II, p. 117.
31. *Ibid.,* Vol. II.
32. James Wheeler, "Removal of the Wyandottes," *Western Christian Advocate,* Vol. X, No. 17, August 11, 1843; Also August 18, September 22, October 6, 1843.
33. Lutz, *op. cit.,* p. 212 f.
34. John Hoon, *The Wyandotte Story and the Persistent Flame of Methodism,* mimeographed address, 1965, p. 7 f.; A. T. Andreas, *History of Kansas,* Chicago, 1883, p. 1226 f.
35. *Ibid.;* Barclay, *op. cit.,* Vol. II, p. 172; Vol. III, p. 344 f.
36. Lutz, *op. cit.,* p. 212 f.; Parrish, *op. cit.,* p. 47.
37. Andreas, *op. cit.,* 1232 f.; Barclay, *op. cit.,* Vol. III, p. 344 f.
38. *Ibid.*
39. Reginald G. Craig, *The Fighting Parson,* Los Angeles (Westernlore Press), 1959. The material on Chivington is largely taken from this book.
40. *Ibid.,* p. 217.

CHAPTER 6

Inheritance

1. *Minutes of Several Conversations between the Rev. Thomas Coke, LL.D. the Rev. Francis Asbury and others,* at a Conference, begun io Baltimore, in the State of Maryland, on Monday, the 27th of December, in the year 1784. Composing a *Form of Discipline for the Ministers, Preachers and other Members of the Methodist Episcopal Church in America,* Philadelphia, (Charles Cist), 1785, p. 3.
2. Frederick C. Gill, ed., *Selected Letters of John Wesley,* New York (Philosophical Library), 1956, p. 157.
3. William Warren Sweet, *Methodism in American History,* New York (Abingdon), 1954, pp. 77, 99.
4. William Warren Sweet, *Religion on the American Frontier,* 1783-1840, Vol. IV, *The Methodists,* A Collection of Source

Materials, Chicago (University of Chicago), 1946, p. 40.

5. *Ibid.*, p. 45 f.

6. *Ibid.*, pp. 38-41.

7. *Ibid.*, pp. 21, 48 f.; 65.

8. *Ibid.*, p. 65.

9. Wade Crawford Barclay, *History of Methodist Missions,* Vol. II, *To Reform the Nation,* New York, 1950, p. 292.

10. Sweet, *The Methodists, op. cit.,* pp. 49 f.

11. Barclay, *op. cit.,* Vol. II, pp. 301-460. (The following material is taken from Barclay.)

12. *Ibid.*, p. 314.

13. *Ibid.*, p. 337.

14. *Ibid.*, p. 372.

15. *Autobiography of Peter Cartwright,* Charles L. Wallis, ed., New York, (Abingdon), 1956, p. 61.

16. William Warren Sweet, *Revivalism in America,* New York, (Scribners), 1945, p. 131 f.; Sweet, *The Methodists, op. cit.,* p. 68 f.

17. Barclay, *op. cit.,* p. 335 f.

18. Samuel Eliot Morison and Henry Steele Commager, *The Growth of the American Republic,* Vol. I, New York (Oxford), 1950, p. 41; Paul Green, "The Epic of Jamestown," *New York Times Magazine,* March 31, 1957, p. 47.

19. *Ibid.*, p. 46; Ina Corrine Brown, *The American Negro,* New York (Friendship), 1957, p. 26 f.

20. William Warren Sweet, *The Story of Religion in America,* New York (Harpers), 1950, p. 34 f.

21. Morison & Commager, *op. cit.,* p. 244 note; Brown, *op. cit.,* p. 27 f.

22. Brown, *op. cit.,* pp. 10 ff.; John R. Spears, *The American Slave Trade,* New York (Ballantine), 1960, pp. 65-70.

23. Brown, *op. cit.,* p. 35.

24. Morison & Commager, *op. cit.,* p. 195 f.; see p. 246 for attitude of Patrick Henry and Jefferson toward slavery. In this regard, the latter wrote, "I tremble for my country when I reflect that God is just; that his justice cannot sleep forever."

25. *Ibid.*, pp. 533-544; Brown, *op. cit.,* pp. 43-46.

26. Morison & Commager, *op. cit.,* pp. 524-533, 244-247.

27. Barclay, *op. cit.,* Vol. II, p. 63 f.

28. Sweet, *op. cit., Methodism in American History,* p. 231.

29. *Minutes . . . ,* 1784. Composing a *Form of Discipline, op. cit.,* pp. 13-15.

30. Barclay, *op. cit.,* Vol. II, pp. 71-86, 104 f.

31. *Ibid.*, p. 85.

32. *Ibid.*, p. 104 f.

33. Sweet, *op. cit., Methodism in American History,* pp. 241-244.

34. *Ibid.*, p. 244 f.; Barclay, *op. cit.,* p. 109.

35. *Ibid.*, p. 109 f.; Sweet, *op. cit., Methodism in American History,* p. 248 f.

CHAPTER 7

Bleeding Kansas

1. A. J. Beveridge, *Abraham Lincoln,* Boston & N.Y.: Houghton Mifflin Co., 1928, II, p. 221 f.

2. *Ibid.*, p. 168.

3. *Ibid.*, p. 301.

4. *Central Christian Advocate,* Vol. VIII, January 7, 1864.

5. *Minutes of the Annual Conferences,* (1848-1850); *Central Christian Advocate,* July 8, 1857.

6. Charles Elliott, *A History of the Methodist Episcopal Church in the South-West, from 1844 to 1864,* Cincinnati, 1868, p. 68 f., 118 f.
7. Wallace Elden Miller, *The Peopling of Kansas,* Columbus, 1906, p. 44.
8. *American Home Missionary Society Collection,* MS Letter, March 10, 1858. Collection is located at Chicago Theological Seminary, Chicago, Illinois.
9. *Ibid.,* MS letter, June, 1856.
10. *Central Christian Advocate,* April 7, 1858, letter from L. B. Dennis.
11. *A. H. M. S. Collection,* MS letter, February, 1855.
12. *Kansas Methodist Historical Society,* MS letter, December 11, 1854. Baker University, Baldwin, Kansas.
13. *Walden Papers,* MS letter, J. M. Walden, Quindaro, April 12, 1858. Collection located at Divinity School Library, University of Chicago.
14. *A. H. M. S. Collection,* MS letter, R. Cordley, Lawrence, March 15, 1858.
15. *Minutes of the Kansas and Nebraska Annual Conference* (Leavenworth, 1860), p. 23.
16. *A. H. M. S. Collection,* MS letter, S. D. Storrs, Quindaro, February 9, 1858.
17. *Ibid.,* MS letter, R. D. Parker, Wyandotte, August 2, 1860.
18. *Walden Papers,* MS Recollections of "Bleeding Kansas"; *A. H. M. S. Collection,* MS letter, Paul Shepherd, Tecumseh, March 1, 1858.
19. *A. H. M. S. Collection,* MS letter, R. D. Parker, Leavenworth, April 26, 1859.
20. *Ibid.,* MS letter, C. E. Blood, Manhattan, April 22, 1859.
21. A. T. Andreas, *History of Kansas,* Chicago, 1883, pp. 178, 253.
22. *A. H. M. S. Collection,* MS letter, R. Cordley, Lawrence, December 10, 1860.
23. W. H. Goode, *Outposts of Zion,* Cincinnati, Poe and Hitch-Cock, 1864, p. 239 f.
24. *Minutes of the Annual Conferences of the Methodist Episcopal Church, 1773-1880,* Three Volumes, New York, Published yearly, (1854), p. 480.
25. *Minutes of the First Session of the Kansas and Nebraska Annual Conference, op. cit.*
26. *Christian Advocate,* January 22, 1857, "Bishop Baker's Trip to Kansas."
27. Joab Spencer, compiler, "The Methodist Episcopal Church, South, in Kansas—1854-1906," *Collections of the Kansas State Historical Society,* Vol. XII, 139 ff.; *MS Minutes, Kansas Mission Conference, Methodist Episcopal Church, South,* pp. 1-6 (manuscript, original hand-written minutes in the Heritage Room, Saint Paul School of Theology Methodist, Kansas City, Missouri.
28. *Ibid.,* p. 37 f.
29. *A. H. M. S. Collection,* MS letter, S. Y. Lum, Lawrence, September 23, 1855.
30. *Ibid.,* MS letter, S. Y. Lum, Lawrence, September 23, 1855.
31. *Ibid.,* MS letter, S. Y. Lum, Plymouth Congregational Church, Lawrence, October 16, 1856.
32. *The Quarterly Journal of the American Unitarian Association,* No. 4; II, 400, 418 f.; III, 541, 552, f.; IV. 476, f., 529; V, 459 f.
33. *Ibid.*
34. *Central Christian Advocate,* April 10, 1861.
35. Horace Greeley, *An Overland Journey,* from New York to San Francisco in the Summer of 1859, N. Y., Alfred A. Knopf, 1964, p. 39.

36. *Minutes of the Annual Conferences,* VI, 1857, 281 f.

37. Peter Beckman, O.S.B., *The Catholic Church on the Kansas Frontier, 1850-1877,* Washington, D.C. (Catholic University of America), 1943, p. 23 f.

38. *Ibid.,* pp. 37 f., 47.

39. *Ibid.,* pp. 32 f., 57.

40. *Ibid.,* pp. 54, 43 f.

41. *A. H. M. S. Collection,* MS letter, R. Cordley, Congregational Church, November 2, 1859.

42. *Central Christian Advocate,* editorial, "The Kansas Conference," April 10, 1861.

CHAPTER 8

Civil War Years

1. *Central Christian Advocate,* June 18, 1863.

2. *Ibid.,* July 20, 1859.

3. *Ibid.,* May 1, 14, July 16, 1863; December 6, 1865.

4. W. M. Leftwich, *Martyrdom in Missouri,* St. Louis (Southwestern Book and Publishing Co.), 1870, Vols. I, II; Charles Elliott, *South-Western Methodism—A History of the M. E. Church in the South-West, from 1844 to 1964,* Cincinnati (Poe and Hitchcock), 1868.

5. Leftwich, *op. cit.*

6. William Warren Sweet, *The Methodist Episcopal Church and The Civil War,* Cincinnati (Methodist Book Concern), 1912, p. 158.

7. *American Home Missionary Society Collection,* MS letter, H. R. Robinson, White Cloud, July 1, 1863 (this collection of letters is at the Chicago Theological Seminary, Chicago, Illinois).

8. *Ibid.,* MS letter, J. Copeland, Clinton, September 1, 1863.

9. A. W. Drury, *History of the Church of the United Brethren in Christ, Dayton,* Ohio (Otterbein Press), 1924, p. 760 f.

10. *A.H.M.S. Collection, op. cit.,* MS letter, G. C. Morse, Emporia, September 25, 1863.

11. *Ibid.,* MS letter, H. P. Robinson, Highland, October 2, 1863.

12. *Ibid.,* MS letter, R. D. Parker, Wyandotte, November 2, 1863.

13. *Ibid.,* MS letter, H. P. Robinson, Highland, September 29, 1864.

14. *Ibid.,* MS letter, G. C. Morse, Emporia, August 8, 1861.

15. *Central Christian Advocate,* May 22, 1861.

16. Martha B. Caldwell, compiler, *Annals of Shawnee Methodist Mission and Indian Manual Labor School,* Kansas State Historical Society, Topeka, Kansas, 1939, p. 108.

17. Kendall E. Bailes, *Rider on the Wind, Jim Lane and Kansas,* Shawnee Mission, Kansas, 1962, pp. 129-142, 158.

18. *A.H.M.S. Collection, op. cit.,* MS letter, J. D. Liggett, Leavenworth, December 3, 1862.

19. *Ibid.,* MS letter, S. D. Storrs, Atchison, July 9, 1863.

20. *Ibid.*

21. *Ibid.,* MS letter, H. P. Robinson, Highland, July 7, 1864.

22. Emory Lindquist, *Kansas, A Centennial Protrait,* reprinted from The Kansas Historical Quarterly, Topeka, Spring, 1961, p. 41.

23. *A.H.M.S. Collection, op. cit.,* MS letter, S. D. Storrs, Quindaro, July 9, 1858.

24. Governor John A. Martin, "Address, Kansas Quarter-Centennial," *Transactions of the Kansas State Historical Society,* Vol. III, Topeka, 1886, p. 377.

25. *A.H.M.S. Collection, op. cit.,* MS letter, R. D. Parker, Wyandotte, February 2, December 11, 1863.

26. *Ibid.,* MS letter, R. Cordley, Lawrence, June 16, 1862, June 26, 1863.

27. *Ibid.,* MS letters, R. Cordley, March 15, June 16, 1862, June 26, 1863.

28. *Central Christian Advocate,* June 12, 1862, letter from L. B. Dennis.

29. A. T. Andreas, *History of Kansas,* Chicago, 1883, p. 328.

30. *Transactions of the Kansas State Historical Society, op. cit.,* Vol. III, p. 377.

31. Pardee Butler, *Personal Recollections,* Cincinnati (Standard Publishing Co.), 1889, p. 232 f.

32. *Minutes of the Kansas Annual Conference,* 1866, p. 21.

33. Bernard L. Cook, *The First Twenty-five Years of the Kansas Conference of the Church of the United Brethren in Christ.* A Thesis, The Bonebrake Theological Seminary, 1942; this is the first section of Cook-Branson-Lehman, *Seedtime & Harvest, A History of the Kansas Conference of the Church of the United Brethren in Christ,* pp. 3-9 (a mimeographed book).

34. *Fifty Years in the Kansas Conference, 1864-1914.* A record of the origin and development of the work of the Evangelical Association in the territory covered by the Kansas Conference, Cleveland (Press of Evangelical Association) n.d.

35. *Minutes of the Annual Conferences of the Methodist Episcopal Church, 1773-1880.* Three Volumes, Vol. III, 1852-1880, New York, 1859, 1860, 1861.

36. *Ibid.,* 1861.

37. *Ibid.,* 1860, 1861.

38. *Ibid.*

39. *Central Christian Advocate,* July 12, 1865, letter, N. Taylor, Circleville, Kansas.

40. *Ibid.,* (1858-65) numerous letters from Kansas.

41. *A.H.M.S. Collection, op. cit.,* MS letter, R. Paine, November 12, 1860; W. H. Ward, March 19, 1860. (See also other letters of the period in the collection.)

CHAPTER 9

Early Educational Endeavors to 1880

1. *The Letters of the Rev. John Wesley, A. M.,* edited by John Telford, London (The Epworth Press), 1931, Vol. III, p. 91.

2. William Lawrence, *Life of Amos A. Lawrence,* Boston and New York (Houghton Mifflin), 1899, p. 115 f.

3. George Frey, "A Century of Education in Kansas," in *Kansas, the First Century,* Editor, John D. Bright (Lewis Historical Publishing Co., Inc.) N.Y., 1956.

4. *Minutes of the First Session of the Kansas and Nebraska Annual Conference,* Omaha City, 1856.

5. *Central Christian Advocate,* April 15, 1857.

6. *Alumni Record of Baker University,* pp. vi-xxxii.

7. *Ibid.;* John Speer, "Patriotism and Education in the Methodist Church," *Transactions of the Kansas State Historical Society,* Vol. VII, p. 499, note.

8. *Central Christian Advocate,* February 15, 1860.

9. J. D. Walters, "The Kansas State Agricultural College," *Transactions of the Kansas State Historical Society,* Vol. VII, 167 f.

10. J. T. Willard, "Blue Mont Central College," *The Kansas Historical Quarterly,* Vol. VIII, May, 1945, Topeka, p. 326 f.

11. *Ibid.*

12. *Central Christian Advocate,* August 13, 1863; March 2, 1859, September 7, 1859.

13. *American Home Missionary Society Collection*, MS letter, S. Y. Lum, Lawrence, June 7, 1859. (Collection in Library, Chicago Theological Seminary, Chicago, Illinois.)
14. F. H. Snow, "The Beginnings of the University of Kansas," *Transactions of the Kansas History Society*, Vol. VI, p. 70 f.
15. A. T. Andreas, *History of Kansas*, p. 487; William E. Connelley, *A Standard History of Kansas and Kansans*, Five Volumes. Vol. II, Chicago and New York; Lewis Publishing Co., 1918; p. 1047 f.
16. *Minutes of the General Association of Congregational Ministers and Churches in Kansas*, 1857, p. 7.
17. *Ibid.*, 1871, p. 36.
18. Connelley, *op. cit.*, p. 1062 f.
19. *Minutes of the Kansas Baptist Convention*, 1860, p. 7.
20. Andreas, *op. cit.*, p. 807.
21. Bernard L. Cook, *The First Twenty-five Years of the Kansas Conference of the Church of the United Brethren*, Thesis, 1942, Bonebrake Theological Seminary, in *Seedtime & Harvest*, p. 41.
22. *Ibid.*, pp. 41-45, for the total story of early days of Lane.
23. James C. Sloan, *A Historical Study of the Ghost Colleges of Kansas*, 1948 Thesis, Kansas State Teachers College, Emporia.
24. Cook, *op. cit.*, p. 43.
25. *Catalogue of the Officers and Students of Lane University*, Lecompton, Kansas, Topeka, Kansas: Kansas Publishing House; Martin, George W. 1877, p. 22. Quoted in James C. Sloan, *A Historical Study of the Ghost Colleges of Kansas*, 1948, Thesis Kansas State Teachers College, Emporia, Kansas, p. 29.
26. *Ibid.*, p. 95 f.
27. Homer Kingsley Ebright, *The History of Baker University*, Baldwin, Kansas, 1951, p. 58 f.
28. *Ibid.*, p. 69.
29. *Ibid.*, p. 74.
30. "*Excerpts of Minutes of Board of Trustees*," believed to have been collected by Prof. S. S. Weatherby, MS, Methodist Historical Society, Baker University, Baldwin, Kansas.
31. Albert R. Robinson, "*Forsan et haec Meminisse juvabit*," MS article, written 1908-09, of his two years in Baker, 1867-69, in Methodist Historical Society, Baker University, Baldwin, Kansas.
32. Ebright, *op. cit.*, p. 84 f.
33. *Christian Advocate*, May 7, 1874, p. 146.
34. *One Hundred Years in Kansas Education*, a book issued as part of the observance of the centennial of the Kansas State Teachers Association, October 1, 1963, pp. 1-12.

CHAPTER 10

The Passing of the Frontier

1. S. E. Morison, and H. S. Commager, *The Growth of the American Republic*, N.Y., Oxford Press, 1950, Vol. II, p. 79.
2. *Eighth United States Census*, Washington, 1864; *Ninth United States Census*, Vol. I, Washington, 1872; *Tenth United States Census*, Washington, 1883.
3. Morison and Commager. *op. cit.*, pp. 105-116.
4. *Ibid.*, p. 112.
5. William Frank Zornow, Kansas, *A History of the Jayhawk State*, Norman, Okla., University of Oklahoma, Copyright 1957, p. 135 f.
6. *A.H.M.S. Collection*, MS letter, J. F. Morgan, Oswego, January 4, 1871.

7. *A.H.M.S. Collection,* MS letter, J. G. Merril, Topeka, 1870.
8. *Eleventh Annual Report of the Board of Home Missions of the Presbyterian Church,* p. 12 f.
9. *A.H.M.S. Collection,* MS Letters from: Highland, April 2, 1866; Manhattan, August 19, 1870; Emporia, May 6, 1870; Topeka, January 5, 1871; Neodosha, March 6, 1871; Leavenworth, May 14, 1870.
10. *The Congregational Record,* June and July, 1864, p. 69; *A.H.M.S. Collection,* MS Report of Special Association of Kansas on Home Evangelization, May, 1867.
11. *Annual Report of the American Baptist Home Mission Society,* 1873, p. 30.
12. *Minutes of the Kansas Baptist State Convention,* 1866, p. 7; *American Baptist Year-Book,* Philadelphia, American Baptist Publication Society, 1881, p. 53 f.
13. *Annual Report of the Board of Domestic Missions of the General Assembly of the Presbyterian Church in the U.S.A.,* 1845, 1856-70.
14. Williston Walker, *A History of the Congregational Churches,* N.Y., Christian Literature Co., 1894, p. 382 f.
15. A. H. Newman, (Ed.), *A Century of Baptist Achievement,* Philadelphia: American Baptist Publication Society, 1901; Morehouse, "The American Baptist Home Mission Society."
16. *Journal of the General Conference,* 1880, p. 594 f.
17. *The Methodist Year-Book,* N.Y., 1880, p. 60; *American Baptist Year-Book,* Philadelphia, 1881, pp. 58 f., 53 f., 60; Green, F. M., *Christian Mission,* St. Louis: J. Burne Publishing Co., 1884, p. 192 f.; *Minutes of the General Assembly,* 1880, p. 457 f.; Woodard, W. S., *Annals of Methodism in Missouri,* p. xlv; *The Congregational Year-Book,* Boston, 1881, pp. 141 f., 103 f., 143 f.
18. *Ibid.,* pp. 432, 500, 629, 882, 804, 715, 1342, 1327, 1457, 1008, 1074, 1121, 1392, 1467, 1475, 1534, 1542.
19. *Ibid.,* p. 1233.
20. *Kansas, A Guide to the Sunflower State,* State of Kansas, Department of Education, The American Guide Series, 1939, p. 57 f.
21. F. W. Giles, *30 Years in Topeka, 1854-1884,* Topeka, 1886, Reprinted, 1960, p. 152 f.; Glen Schwendemann, The "Exodusters" on the Missouri, *Kansas Historical Quarterly,* XXIX, No. 1, Spring, 1968, pp. 25-40.
22. Wallace Elden Miller, *The Peopling of Kansas,* Ph.D. dissertation, Columbia University, Columbus, Ohio, 1906, p. 63 f.
23. *Souvenir Der West Deutschen Konferenz Der Bischoflichen Methodistenkirche (Souvenir of the West German Conference of the Methodist Episcopal Church).* Published on order of the Conference, by Otto E. Kriege, Gustav Becker, Matthaus Hermann and C. L. Korner. Printed by Jennings and Graham, Cincinnati, Ohio, 1906. Portions translated and edited by Wallace Gray. This is the source of much of this early material which follows.
24. *Minutes of Annual Conference,* 1859, 1860, pp. 265; 352.
25. *Souvenir, op. cit.,* p. 30 f.
26. A. T. Andreas, *History of Kansas,* Chicago, Illinois, pp. 233, 549.
27. *Souvenir, op. cit.,* p. 228 f.; p. 52, 53.
28. *Calvary Methodist Church, 85th Anniversary,* May 7, 1961, anniversary brochure, 16 pp.
29. Bernard L. Cook, *The First Twenty-five Years of the Kansas Conference of the Church of the United Brethren in Christ,* a thesis, The Bonebrake Theological Seminary, 1942; his is the first section of Cook—Branson—Lehman, *Seedtime & Harvest, A History of the Kansas Conference of the Church of the United Brethren in Christ* (a mimeographed book).

30. *Ibid.*, pp. 29 f., quotation from Chambers, J. R., *History of the Osage-Neosho Annual Conference, Church of the United Brethren in Christ*, 1870-1901, M.S. in Kansas State Historical Society, p. 7.

31. Cook, *op. cit.*, p. 33; p. 46.

32. *Ibid.*

33. Ancel H. Bassett, *A Concise History of the Methodist Protestant Church From its Origin*, Third Edition, Pittsburgh, Wm. Mc-Cracken, Jr., 1887, p. 387.

34. Edward J. Drinkhouse, *History of Methodist Reform, Synoptical of General Methodism 1703 to 1898, with special and comprehensive reference to his more salient exhibition in the history of the Methodist Episcopal Church.* Board of Publication of the Methodist Protestant Church, Baltimore, Md., two vols., 1899, Vol. II, p. 571.

35. *Ibid.*, pp. 587, 592.

36. R. Yeakel, *History of the Evangelical Association.* 2 vol., Vol. II, Cleveland, Lamb, J. H., 1909, pp. 67 f., 103 f., 106; *Fifty Years In the Kansas Conference, 1864-1914*, A Record of the Origin and Development of the Work of the Evangelical Association, Cleveland, Ohio, pp. 13-30.

37. *Fifty Years, op. cit.*, p. 43.

38. John D. Bright, *Kansas, the First Century*, Vol. II, Lewis Historical Publishing Co., N.Y., p. 367.

39. Bishop Wilson T. Hogue, *History of the Free Methodist Church of North America*, Vol. II., Chicago, 1915, pp. 82-85.

40. Joab Spencer, compiler, "Days of the Missionary. The Methodist Episcopal Church, South, in Kansas—1854 to 1906." *Collections of the Kansas State Historical Society*, Vol. XII, p. 153 f.

41. MS Minutes, *Western Annual Conference*, 1870, First Session, Leavenworth City, Kansas, September 8-11, 1870, pp. 69 ff.

These manuscript minutes are in the Heritage Room, Saint Paul School of Theology Methodist, Kansas City, Missouri.

42. *Ibid.*, p. 76.

43. *Ibid.*, pp. 193 f., 306 f.

44. *The Methodist Almanac*, N.Y. (Lane and Scott) 1873, 1878.

45. *Journal of the General Conference of the Methodist Episcopal Church*, N.Y., 1860, pp. 374-395; 1868, p. 511; 1876, p. 581 f.

46. Anne E. Bingham, "The Grasshopper Plague" in *The Heritage of Kansas*, Everett Rich, (Ed.), Lawrence, Kansas, University of Kansas, 1960, p. 150.

47. Carl Becker, *Kansas*, University of Kansas, reprinted from *Turner Essays in American History*, copyright, 1910, by Henry Holt and Company, p. 10.

48. Cook, *op. cit.*, p. 31 f.

49. *A.H.M.S. Collection*, MS letter, Rev. Harvey Jones, Grasshopper Falls, February 9, 1871.

50. *A.H.M.S. Collection*, MS letter, George A. Beckwith, Manhattan, Kansas, May 27, 1867. See also *Central Christian Advocate*, May 22, 1867, for an account of same revival.

51. *A.H.M.S. Collection*, MS letter, Edwin A. Harlow, Grasshopper Falls, Kansas, July 31, November 1, 1866.

52. *A.H.M.S. Collection*, MS letter, F. T. Ingalls, March 1, 1871.

53. *Central Christian Advocate*, October 31, 1866, letter, John M. Titcomb, Hiawatha, Kansas, October 18, 1866.

54. Cook, *op. cit.*, p. 38 f.

CHAPTER 11

Temperance and Public Morals

1. A. J. Beveridge, *Abraham Lincoln,* New York (Houghton Mifflin), 1928, Volume I, p. 51 f.
2. *Ibid.,* p. 110.
3. *Autobiography of Peter Cartwright,* New York (Abingdon), 1956, p. 145 f.
4. Wade Crawford Barclay, *History of Methodist Missions, Early American Methodism,* Volume II, *To Reform the Nation,* New York (Board of Missions and Church Extension), 1950, p. 27, p. 29, note.
5. *Cyclopedia of Methodism,* edited by Matthew Simpson, Philadelphia (Everts & Stewart), 1878, p. 853.
6. *Ibid.*
7. Otto Frovin Federickson, *The Liquor Question in Kansas before Constitutional Prohibition,* Ph.D. Thesis, University of Kansas, 1931, p. 127.
8. Barclay, *op. cit.,* pp. 30-38.
9. Frederickson, *op. cit.,* p. 53.
10. *Ibid.,* pp. 105-108.
11. *Ibid.,* pp. 156-159, 193, 141-143.
12. *Minutes of the Sessions of the Kansas and Nebraska Conference of the Methodist Episcopal Church,* 1856-1860.
13. Frederickson, *op. cit.,* pp. 244-248.
14. *Ibid.*
15. Barclay, *op. cit.,* volume III, *Widening Horizons,* p. 55.
16. Frederickson, *op. cit.,* quoted, p. 255.
17. H. D. Fisher, *The Gun and the Gospel,* Kansas City, Mo. (Hudson-Kimberly), 1902, p. 227.
18. *Minutes of the Kansas Annual Conference,* Emporia, March 6, 1872, p. 24.
19. *Minutes of the Kansas Annual Conference,* Atchison, April 1-6, 1874, p. 38 f.
20. *Ibid.,* 1878, p. 31.
21. Frderickson, *op. cit.,* pp. 327-330, 293-295.
22. *The Newton Kansan,* the Centennial Edition, January 28, 1961, (quoted in *Historical Society Bulletin,* Central Kansas Conference, April, 1961).
23. Grant W. Harrington, "The Genesis of Prohibition," *Kansas Historical Collections,* Vol. XV (1919-1922), pp. 228-231.
24. Clara Francis, "The Coming of Prohibition to Kansas," *Kansas Historical Collections,* Vol. XV (1919-1922), pp. 204-227.
25. *Minutes of the Twenty-Fifth Session, Kansas Annual Conference M.E. Church,* Topeka, March 10-16, 1880, p. 28.
26. Emory Lindquist, *Kansas: A Centennial Portrait,* reprinted from the *Kansas Historical Quarterly,* Spring, 1961, p. 12.
27. *Minutes of the Twenty-Seventh Session of the Kansas Conference, M. E. Church,* March 4-9, 1882, p. 30.
28. *Minutes of the Fourteenth Session of the South Kansas Conference, Methodist Episcopal Church,* Chanute, March 3-8, 1887.
29. *Central Christian Advocate,* July 23, 1890, p. 9.
30. *Ibid.,* October 8, 1890, p. 1.
31. *Minutes of the Thirty-Seventh Session of the Kansas Conference, Methodist Episcopal Church,* Kansas City, Kansas, March 2-7, 1892, p. 26.
32. *Central Christian Advocate,* January 18, 1893, p. 13.
33. *The Annals of Kansas, 1886-1925,* Volume I., (Kansas State Historical Society), Topeka, p. 284.
34. Herbert Asbury, "Marching As to War," The Story of Carry

Nation, series of articles in *Outlook and Independent*, August 21, 1929, p. 661 f.

35. *Ibid.*, p. 662.

36. *Ibid.*, p. 625; *MS*, private, R.N.M.

37. *Ibid.*; *The Annals of Kansas, op. cit.*, p. 371.

38. Asbury, *op. cit.*, p. 662.

39. *The Annals*, pp. 418, 424, 456, 497.

40. *Ibid.*, p. 167.

41. *Ibid.*, p. 496.

42. Lindquist, *op. cit.*, p. 14.

43. *The Annals of Kansas*, Vol. II, p. 238.

44. *The Annals of Kansas*, Vol. I, pp. 4, 266, 489; Vol. II, p. 121.

CHAPTER 12

Builders of the Fire

1. D. Marquette, *A History of Nebraska Methodism*, p. 29.

2. William H. Goode, *Outposts of Zion*, Cincinnati (Poe & Hitchcock), 1864, p. 40 f.

3. *Ibid.*, p. 254 f.

4. *Ibid.*, p. 276 f.

5. *Ibid.*, p. 324 f.

6. MS Letter, J. S. Griffing to "Augusta," February 19, 1855, in *Methodist Historical Society Collection*, Baker University, Baldwin, Kansas.

7. Goode, *op. cit.*, p. 249, p. 330.

8. *Minutes of the Kansas & Nebraska Annual Conference*, Lawrence City, Kansas Territory, Oct. 23rd A.D., 1865, p. 10.

9. Martin Rist, "Methodism Goes West" a chapter in Vol. II, *The History of American Methodism*, three volumes, E. S. Buck, general editor, N.Y. (Abingdon), 1964, p. 433 f.

10. *Central Christian Advocate*, April 10, 1861, editorial, "The Kansas Conference."

11. *Official Minutes, Forty-fifth Session, Kansas Conference, Methodist Episcopal Church*, Kansas City, Kansas, March 21-26, 1900, p. 38 f.

12. *Official Minutes, Kansas Annual Conference of the Methodist Episcopal Church*, the Thirty-ninth Session, Abilene, March 7-12, 1894, p. 41 f.; H. K. Ebright, *The History of Baker University*, Baldwin, Kansas, 1951, p. 58 ff.

13. *Ibid.*; see also John Speer, "Patriotism and Education in the Methodist Church," *Transactions of Kansas State Historical Society*, Vol. VII, Topeka, 1902, p. 499 (note); *Central Christian Advocate*, July 12, 1893, p. 14.

14. W. H. Sweet, *A History of Methodism in Northwest Kansas*, Kansas Wesleyan University, 1902, pp. 71, 48 f., 62 f.

15. Jeff Jenkins, *The Northern Tier*, or Life Among the Homestead Settlers, Topeka (Kansas Publishing House), 1886; p. 35 f. 97-106, 148-159; *Biographical History of Cloud County, Kansas*, Mrs. E. F. Hollibaugh, Biographer and Historian, N.D., N.P., pp. 80-85.

16. *Biographical History of Cloud County, Kansas, op. cit.*, pp. 244-249; Albert T. Reid, The Man of Mystery of the Lincoln Drama, *Scribner's Magazine*, July 29, 1929, pp. 9-19 *(Historical Facts Concerning the Life of Boston Corbett*, published on the occasion of the dedication of a monument, erected by the Boy Scouts, marking sight of Corbett's dugout house in Cloud County).

17. *Ibid.*

18. MS *Minutes, Kansas Mission Conference, Methodist Episcopal*

Church, South, 1855-1861, p. 1 f. These manuscript minutes are in the Heritage Room, Saint Paul School of Theology Methodist, Kansas City, Missouri.

19. *Ibid.*, pp. 18, 26, 37, 59, 63.
20. *Official Record, Kansas Conference, Methodist Episcopal Church, Seventh Session,* Atchison, Kansas, March 24-29, 1920, p. 436 f.
21. *Ibid.*
22. *Ibid.*
23. M. S. Rice, *William Alfred Quayle,* The Skylark of Methodism, New York (Abingdon), 1928, p. 35 f.
24. *Official Record, Kansas Conference, Methodist Episcopal Church, Sixth Session,* Topeka, March 12-17, 1919, p. 321.
25. Rice, *op. cit.,* pp. 46-55.
26. *Ibid.*, p. 143 f.
27. W. A. Quayle, *The Pastor-Preacher,* New York (Methodist Book Concern), 1910, pp. 130, 131, 127.
28. Rice, *op. cit.,* p. 11.

CHAPTER 13

Growth Amidst Turmoil

1. *Christian Advocate,* April 28, 1870.
2. *Ibid.*
3. *Ibid.*
4. *Ibid.*
5. Raymond Curtis Miller, *The Populist Party in Kansas,* a Ph.D. dissertation, 1928, University of Chicago, p. 22.
6. Arthur Meir Schlesinger, *Political and Social Growth of the American People, 1865-1940,* New York, Macmillan, 1941.
7. Miller, *op. cit.,* pp. 16-25.
8. John D. Hicks, *The Populist Revolt, A History of the Farmers' Alliance and the People's Party,* University of Nebraska, 1961 (originally published by the University of Minnesota, 1931), p. 34.
9. *Ibid.*, pp. 20-35.
10. *Ibid.,* p. 159 (quoted).
11. Miller, *op. cit.,* p. 191 f.
12. Hicks, *op. cit.,* p. 160.
13. Everett Rich, ed., *The Heritage of Kansas, Selected Commentaries on Past Times,* article, "Peffer's Utopia," from the *Kansas City Times,* April 13, 1935, Lawrence, University of Kansas Press, 1960, p. 309.
14. Walter T. K. Nugent, *The Tolerant Populists, Kansas Populism and Nativism,* Chicago, University of Chicago Press, 1963, p. 90.
15. *Christian Advocate,* "Correspondence from Kansas and Indian Territory," by Charles King, January 1, 1874.
16. *Journal, Kansas Conference, Methodist Episcopal Church,* 1890, pp. 45-48.
17. *Central Christian Advocate,* February 22, 1893.
18. *Minutes, Kansas Conference, Methodist Episcopal Church,* 1894, pp. 28-31.
19. *Minutes, South Kansas Conference, Methodist Episcopal Church,* 1894, p. 15.
20. *Minutes, Kansas Conference, Methodist Episcopal Church,* 1875, p. 65; *Minutes, Kansas Conference, The Methodist Church,* 1940, p. 319.
21. *Minutes, Kansas Conference, The Methodist Church,* 1940, *op. cit.*
22. *Minutes, Kansas Conference, Methodist Episcopal Church,*

1886, p. 42; *Minutes, South Kansas Conference, Methodist Episcopal Church,* 1890, p. 51; *Minutes, Kansas Conference, Methodist Episcopal Church,* 1891, p. 39 f.

23. *Ibid.*
24. *Minutes, Northwest Kansas Conference, Methodist Episcopal Church,* 1894, p. 20; 1895, p. 21.
25. *History of the Southwest Kansas Conference,* Volume I, 1869-1931, published by the Conference, pp. 87, 89.
26. *Ibid.,* p. 102.
27. *Central Christian Advocate,* November 21, 1894, Report from E. H. Taylor, Corning, Kansas.
28. *A Kansas Souvenir,* issued by the Kansas Immigration and Information Association, 1896, p. 57.
29. Bernard L. Cooke, *The First Twenty-Five Years of the Kansas Conference of the United Brethren in Christ,* p. 46; Branson, John Erwin, *Ibid.,* Part II, 1883-1914, p. 70, in *Seedtime & Harvest,* 1948.
30. Branson, *Ibid.,* pp. 49, 51, 57.
31. *Ibid.,* p. 57.
32. *Ibid.,* p. 70.
33. MS *Minutes, Western Annual Conference, Methodist Episcopal Church, South,* Vol. II, 1870-1902, pp. 70, 72, 224; Vol. III, 1903-1905, pp. 105, 108. These MS Minutes are in the Heritage Room, Saint Paul School of Theology Methodist, Kansas City, Mo.
34. Ancel H. Bassett, *A Concise History of the Methodist Protestant Church,* Pittsburgh, Pa. (James Robinson), 1877, p. 219.
35. *Minutes, Kansas Conference, Methodist Protestant Church,* Tenth Session, Ottawa, Kansas, October 13-16, 1880, p. 6.
36. *Ibid.;* Bassett, *op. cit.,* Vol. II, p. 592.
37. *Ibid.,* 1881-1887.

38. *Ibid.,* 1899.
39. *Ibid.,* p. 12.
40. *Ibid.,* p. 13.
41. *Ibid.,* 1896, p. 108.
42. *Ibid.,* 1896; 1897, p. 148.
43. *Ibid.,* 1891, p. 19.
44. *Ibid.,* 1900, p. 279.
45. *Ibid.*
46. *Ibid.,* 1891, 1892.
47. *Ibid.,* 1892, 1893.
48. *Ibid.,* 1893, p. 37 f.
49. *Ibid.,* 1895, p. 74.
50. *Historical Society Bulletin,* Central Kansas Conference, Volume III, No. 3, March 1962.
51. *The Annals of Kansas,* January 18, 1890, p. 92.
52. *Central Christian Advocate,* March 21, 1894.
53. MS *Autobiography of A. N. See, DD.,* 80-years Old, by Conference request.
54. William T. Ward, *Pioneering in the Great West,* M.S.
55. *Life of Margaret Baker Meredith,* as told to her son. M.S.
56. *Central Christian Advocate,* March 3, 1897, article by W. A. Spencer, D.D., "Church Growth of Kansas and Missouri"; see also earlier article, *Central Christian Advocate,* March 12, 1890, by the same author.
57. *Central Christian Advocate,* March 11, 1908, "Topeka and Its Methodism," p. 14 f.
58. *Ibid.*
59. *History of the Southwest Kansas Conference of the Methodist Episcopal Church,* Volume I, 1869-1931, published by the Conference.

60. *Central Christian Advocate,* March 24, 1907, "The Churches of Wichita" by Reverend Edwin A. Hoyt, Presiding Elder.
61. *Ibid.*
62. *Ibid.*

CHAPTER 14

The Colleges—The Middle Period
1880 to the Depression

1. *Minutes, Western Annual Conference,* 1870-1881, Twelfth Session, 1881, pp. 317, 319 f.; Thirteenth Session, 1882, p. 24. All of the material on Marvin College comes from these sources. The manuscript minutes of three volumes, 1855-1905, beginning with the Kansas Mission Conference, are in the Heritage Room, Saint Paul School of Theology Methodist, Kansas City, Mo.
2. John Erwin Branson, *Seedtime & Harvest, A History of the Kansas Conference of the Church of the United Brethren in Christ,* Part II, 1883-1914, a thesis, The Bonebrake Theological Seminary, Dayton, Ohio, 1943, p. 61; James C. Sloan, *A Historical Study of the Ghost Colleges of Kansas,* 1948. Thesis, Kansas State Teachers College, Kellogg Library, Emporia, Kansas, p. 53 f.
3. *Ibid.*
4. Sloan, *op. cit.,* p. 55 f.
5. Branson, *op. cit.,* p. 70.
6. Sloan, *op. cit.,* p. 40 f.
7. *Ibid.,* p. 42; Clayton George Lehman, *Seedtime & Harvest, A History of the Kansas Conference of the Church of the United Brethren in Christ,* Part III, 1914-1943, a thesis, The Bonebrake Theological Seminary, Dayton, Ohio, 1944, p. 104 f.
8. Lehman, *Ibid.*
9. Sloan, *op. cit.,* pp. 42 f., 46 f. (figures are taken from the catalogues).
10. *Ibid.,* p. 44.
11. Lehman, *op. cit.,* p. 107 f.
12. *Ibid.,* p. 109.
13. *Minutes, Kansas Annual Conference, Methodist Episcopal Church, Twenty-ninth Session,* Topeka, Kansas, March 26-31, 1884, p. 28.
14. *Minutes of the Kansas Conference, Methodist Episcopal Church, Thirtieth Session,* Clay Center, Kansas, March 12-17, 1885, p. 26.
15. Eleanore Hayes, "Southwestern College," a chapter in *History of the Southwest Kansas Conference of the Methodist Episcopal Church,* Volume I, 1869-1931, Published by the Conference, N.D., p. 263 f.
16. *Ibid.*
17. *Ibid.,* p. 70.
18. *Ibid.,* p. 267 f.
19. Jack Warner VanDerhoof, *The Time Now Past,* Kansas Wesleyan University, 1886-1961, Salina, Kansas Wesleyan University, 1962, p. 8; William Henry Sweet, *A History of Methodism in Northwest Kansas,* Salina, Kansas Wesleyan University, 1920, p. 154 f.; p. 177 f.
20. VanDerhoof, *op. cit.,* pp. 11 f.; John S. Cornett, *Fifty Years of Kansas State Historical Society,* Topeka, Kansas, Vol. I, p. 49.
21. VanDerhoof, *op. cit.,* pp. 15-22.
22. *Ibid.,* p. 27.
23. Cornett, *op. cit.,* pp. 45-50.

24. VanDerhoof, *op. cit.*, pp. 35-38.
25. *The Annals of Kansas*, 1886-1925, In two volumes, volume one, 1886-1910, volume two, 1911-1925, Kirke Mechem, Editor, Kansas State Historical Society, Topeka, Kansas, Vol. I, p. 49.
26. Homer K. Ebright, *The History of Baker University*, Baldwin. 1951, p. 128.
27. *The Annals*, Vol. I, p. 111.
28. Ebright, *op. cit.*, p. 136.
29. *Official Minutes, Kansas Annual Conference, Methodist Episcopal Church, thirty-ninth Session*, Abilene, March 7-12, 1894, p. 31.
30. *The Annals*, Vol. I, p. 183.
31. *Ibid.*, p. 360.
32. *Central Christian Advocate*, March 6, 1907, p. 10.
33. Ebright, *op. cit.*, p. 219.
34. *The Annals*, Vol. I, pp. 310, 337, 338, 516; Vol. II, p. 39; *Official Record, Kansas Conference, Methodist Episcopal Church*, Abilene, March 15-20, 1911, p. 43 f.
35. Ebright, *op. cit.*, p. 183.
36. *Official Record, Kansas Conference, Methodist Episcopal Church, 79th Annual Session*, Abilene, March 7-12, 1934, p. 114.
37. *Ibid.*, p. 115.

CHAPTER 15

New Endeavors in a New Century

1. *The Annals of Kansas*, 1886-1925, in two volumes, Kansas State Historical Society, Topeka, Kansas, Vol. I, 1896, p. 217 f.
2. *Central Christian Advocate*, July 19, 1905, p. 916.
3. *The Annals of Kansas, op. cit.*, Vol. II, March 31, 1915, p. 118.
4. *Ibid.*, January 1, 1912, p. 37.
5. *Ibid.*, July 16, 1913, p. 67.
6. Winfred Ernest Garrison, *The March of Faith*, The Story of Religion in America Since 1865, New York (Harpers), 1933, p. 180 f.
7. *Central Christian Advocate*, July 15, 1909, p. 877.
8. *Ibid.*, July 1, 1903, p. 823 f.
9. *Ibid.*, February 19, 1908, p. 21.
10. *Ibid.*
11. *Ibid.*, June 11, 1910, p. 12.
12. *Minutes, Kansas Conference, Methodist Episcopal Church, 58th session*, Lawrence, Kansas, March 5-10, 1913, p. 45.
13. *Minutes, Southwest Conference, Methodist Episcopal Church*, Fifty-third session, Wellington, Kansas, October 24-29, 1934, p. 318; *Minutes, Kansas Conference, The Methodist Church*, 1st session, Topeka, Kansas, September 29-October 1, 1939, p. 427.
14. Emory Lindquist, *Kansas: A Centennial Portrait*, reprinted from *The Kansas Historical Quarterly*, Topeka, Kansas, Spring, 1961, pp. 21 f.; Martha B. Caldwell, Women's Suffrage Campaign, *The Kansas Historical Quarterly*, Vol. XII, August, 1943, pp. 300-318.
15. Lindquist, *op. cit.*
16. Garrison, *op. cit.*, p. 179.
17. *Central Christian Advocate*, "A New Chapter for our Bethany," November 2, 1910, p. 7.
18. *Minutes, Kansas Conference, Methodist Episcopal Church, 38th session*, Baldwin, Kansas, March 1-6, 1893, p. 33.
19. *The Bethany Visitor*, January, 1942.
20. *Ibid.*
21. *Minutes, Kansas Conference, Methodist Episcopal Church, 45th*

session, Kansas City, Kansas, March 21-26, 1900, p. 32.

22. *Ibid., 56th session,* Abilene, Kansas, March 15-20, 1911.

23. *The Bethany Visitor, op. cit.*

24. *Ibid.*

25. *Kansas City Deaconess,* Vol. XVII, No. 5, Kansas City, Missouri, May, 1925, p. 3.

26. *Ibid.,* pp. 3 f.

27. *Ibid.*

28. Mary F. Smith, Pearle W. Tibbetts, and Minnie Pike, *There Was One Anna,* Kansas City, Missouri, Browne-White-Lowell Press, 1948, pp. 15-20.

29. *Kansas City Deaconess, op. cit.,* pp. 4-6.

30. *Ibid.,* pp. 6-11.

31. Smith, Tibbetts and Pike, *op. cit.,* pp. 97-103.

32. *Minutes, Kansas Conference, Methodist Episcopal Church, 15th session,* Junction City, Kansas, March 15-20, 1905, pp. 31, 53 f.

33. *Ibid., 19th session,* Clay Center, Kansas, March 10-15, 1909, p. 49 f.

34. *House of Happiness,* 1904-1957, 53 years of Service to the Methodists of Kansas, The Methodist Home for the Aged, p. 2 f.; *Official Record, Kansas Conference, Methodist Episcopal Church, 74th session,* Topeka, Kansas, March 5-10, 1929, p. 42 f.; *Ibid., 75th session,* Kansas City, Kansas, March 12-16, 1930, p. 144 f.

35. *Journal, Central Kansas Conference, The Methodist Church, 27th session,* Dodge City, Kansas, May 11-23, 1965, pp. 452-55.

36. *Minutes, Southwest Kansas Conference, Methodist Episcopal Church, 30th session,* Hutchinson, Kansas, March 13-18, 1912, p. 89 f.

37. *Ibid., 31st session,* Wichita, Kansas, March 12-17, 1913, pp. 71 f.;

Thomas O. Faulkner, *Fiftieth Anniversary Commemorative Brochure, Wesley Hospital.*

38. *Ibid., 33rd session,* Dodge City, Kansas, March 17-22, 1915, p. 87 f.

39. Faulkner, *op. cit.,* p. 4.

40. *Minutes, Southwest Kansas Conference, Methodist Episcopal Church, 38th session,* Wichita, March 10-15, 1920, p. 61.

41. *Journal, Central Kansas Conference, The Methodist Church, 26th session,* Hutchinson, Kansas, May 19-24, 1964, p. 163.

42. *The Messenger,* Wesley Medical Center, Wichita, Kansas, Vol. 21, No. 3, December, 1965.

43. *Minutes, Southwest Kansas Conference, Methodist Episcopal Church, 33rd session,* Dodge City, Kansas, March 17-22, 1915, p. 88 f.

44. *Ibid., 41st session,* Wellington, Kansas, March 14-19, 1923, p. 251 f.

45. *Ibid., 42nd session,* Winfield, Kansas, March 11-17, 1924, p. 360 f.

46. *Ibid., 43rd session,* Great Bend, Kansas, March 11-16, 1925, p. 55 f.

47. *Ibid., 46th session,* Arkansas City, Kansas, October 12-16, 1927, p. 385.

48. Grace Hospital and School of Nurses, Hutchinson, Kansas, "50 years of Service," 1915-1965, mimeographed for the Board of Trustees.

49. *Minutes, Southwest Kansas Conference, Methodist Episcopal Church, 55th session,* Pratt, Kansas, October 7-12, 1936, p. 61 f.

50. *Journal, Central Kansas Conference, The Methodist Church, 26th session,* Hutchinson, Kansas, May 19-24, 1964, p. 163.

51. *Minutes, Southwest Kansas Conference, Methodist Episcopal*

Church, 43rd session, Great Bend, Kansas, March 11-16, 1925, p. 56 f.

52. *Journal, Central Kansas Conference, The Methodist Church, 13th session*, Salina, Kansas, October 2-7, 1951, p. 621 f.

53. *Ibid., 25th session*, Salina, Kansas, May 22-26, 1963, p. 805.

54. *Minutes, Northwest Kansas Conference, Methodist Episcopal Church, 39th session*, Salina, Kansas, March 30—April 3, 1921, p. 39.

55. *Ibid., 42nd session*, Salina, Kansas, March 25-30, 1924, p. 312.

56. *Ibid., 44th session*, Osborne, Kansas, October 7-11, 1925, p. 118 f.

57. *Ibid., 58th session*, Salina, Kansas, October 3-9, 1939, p. 269.

58. *Journal, Central Kansas Conference, The Methodist Church, 4th session*, Salina, Kansas, October 7-11, 1942, p. 454.

59. *Ibid., 13th session*, Salina, Kansas, October 2-7, 1951, pp. 619 f., 626.

60. *Ibid., 26th session*, Hutchinson, Kansas, May 19-24, 1964, p. 163.

61. *Ibid., 3rd session*, Wichita, Kansas, September 30—October 5, 1941, p. 287; *40 Years of Service, 1925—1965*, Hadley Memorial Hospital, Hays, Kansas, p. 2.

62. *Ibid., 40 Years of Service, 1925—1965*, Hadley Memorial Hospital, Hays, Kansas, p. 4.

63. *Journal, Central Kansas Conference, The Methodist Church, 26th session*, Hutchinson, Kansas, May 19-24, 1964, p. 163.

64. *Ibid., 6th session*, Wichita, Kansas, October 4-9, 1944, p. 67 f.

65. *Ibid., 11th session*, Hutchinson, Kansas, October 4-9, 1949, pp. 252, 254.

66. *Ibid., 26th session*, Hutchinson, Kansas, May 19-24, 1964, p. 163.

67. *Minutes, Southwest Kansas Conference, Methodist Episcopal Church, 46th session*, Arkansas City, Kansas, October 12-16, 1927, p. 387 f.

68. *Ibid., 48th session*, McPherson, Kansas, October 9-14, 1929, p. 172 f.

69. *Ibid., 53rd session*, Wellington, Kansas, October 24-29, 1934, p. 326 f.

70. *Minutes, Northwest Kansas Conference, Methodist Episcopal Church, 58th session*, Salina, Kansas, October 3-9, 1939, p. 269 f.

71. *Journal, Central Kansas Conference, The Methodist Church, 4th session*, Salina, Kansas, October, 7-11, 1942, p. 459 f.

72. *Ibid., 16th session*, Salina, Kansas, October 5-10, 1954, pp. 551-554.

73. *Ibid., 17th session*, Hutchinson, Kansas, October 4-9, 1955, p. 723 f.

74. *Ibid., 19th session*, Salina, Kansas, October 1-6, 1957, p. 283.

75. *Ibid., 23rd session*, Hutchinson, Kansas, May 23-28, 1961, p. 337.

76. *Ibid., 24th session*, Wichita, Kansas, May 23-27, 1962, p. 567.

77. *Ibid., 4th session*, Salina, Kansas, October 7-11, 1942, p. 493.

78. *Official Record, Kansas Conference, Methodist Episcopal Church, 2nd session*, Topeka, Kansas, March 17-23, 1915; *70th session*, Independence, Kansas, March 4-9, 1925; *Minutes, Northwest Kansas Conference, Methodist Episcopal Church, 33rd session*, Beloit, Kansas, March 24-28, 1915; *44th session*, Osborne Kansas, October 7-11, 1925; *Minutes, Central Kansas Conference, The Methodist Church, 2nd session*, Hutchinson, Kansas, October 9-14, 1940, p. 151; *Official Minutes, Southwest Kansas Conference, Methodist Episcopal Church, 44th session*, Peabody, Kansas, October 14-18, 1925, p. 197; *Kansas Conference, Methodist Protestant Church, 45th session*, Kansas City, Kansas, August 26-29, 1925; Clayton George Lehman, *A History of the Kansas Conference of the Church of the United Brethren*

in Christ (Part III, 1914-1943), Dayton, Ohio, (Bonebrake Theological Seminary) 1942, p. 95.

79. *Kansas Conference, Methodist Protestant Church, 27th session,* Kansas City, Kansas, September 1-4, 1897; *35th session,* La Harpe, Kansas, September 6-9, 1905; *60th session,* Kansas City, Kansas, August 23-26, 1930.

80. *Ibid., 41st session,* Centerville, Kansas, August 30—September 3, 1911, p. 19.

81. *Ibid., 35th session,* La Harpe, Kansas, September 6-9, 1905.

82. *Minutes, Kansas Conference, Methodist Episcopal Church, 77th session,* Topeka, Kansas, March 8-14, 1932, p. 410 f.

83. *Minutes, Southwest Kansas Conference, Methodist Episcopal Church, 51st session,* Hutchinson, Kansas, October 5-10, 1932, p. 70 f.

84. *Ibid., 50th session,* Eldorado, Kansas, October 7-12, 1931, p. 423.

85. *Ibid., 36th session,* Pratt, Kansas, March 6-11, 1918, p. 85 f.

86. *Minutes, Northwest Kansas Conference, Methodist Episcopal Church, 46th session,* Salina, Kansas, September 21-26, 1927, p. 274.

CHAPTER 16

Through the Difficulties of the Thirties

1. *Minutes, Northwest Kansas Conference, Methodist Episcopal Church: 49th Session,* Belleville, Kansas; September 23-28, 1930; *51st Session,* Stockton, Kansas, September 21-25, 1932; *53rd Session,* Colby, Kansas, September 25-30, 1934; *58th Session,* Salina, Kansas, October 3-5, 1939. *Minutes, Southwest Kansas Conference, Methodist Episcopal Church: 49th Session,* King-man, Kansas, October 8-13, 1930; *51st Session,* Hutchinson, Kansas, October 5-10, 1932; *53rd Session,* Wellington, Kansas, October 24-29, 1934; *58th Session,* Salina, Kansas, October 3-9, 1939. *Minutes, Kansas Conference, Methodist Episcopal Church: 75th Session,* Kansas City, Kansas, March 12-16, 1930; *77th Session,* Topeka, Kansas, March 8-14, 1932; *79th Session,* Abilene, Kansas, March 7-12, 1934; *84th Session,* Independence, Kansas, March 7-13, 1939.

2. *Official Record, Kansas Conference, The Methodist Church, 13th Session,* Topeka, Kansas, June 12-17, 1951, p. 714 f.; *18th Session,* Lawrence, Kansas, June 5-10, 1956, p. 127 f.

3. *Minutes Southwest Kansas Conference, Methodist Episcopal Church, 51st Session,* Hutchinson, Kansas, p. 24.

4. *Ray B. Bressler,* Minister, *Personal letter* to Dr. Dale Dunlap, May 31, 1964.

5. *Minutes, Southwest Kansas Conference, Methodist Episcopal Church, 53rd Session,* Wellington, Kansas, October 24-29, 1934, p. 302.

6. William Frank Zornow, *Kansas, A History of the Jayhawk State,* Norman: University of Oklahoma Press, 1957, p. 276 f.

7. William R. Ramsdale, *Personal letter,* August 24, 1967.

8. Zornow, *op. cit.; Ibid.*

9. *Minutes, Southwest Kansas Conference, Methodist Episcopal Church, 53rd Session,* Wellington, Kansas, October 24-29, 1934, p. 308 f.

10. *Ibid., 54th Session,* Winfield, Kansas, October 9-14, 1935, pp. 455-457.

11. *Ibid., 55th Session,* Pratt, Kansas, October 7-12, 1936, p. 46.

12. Homer Kingsley Ebright, *History of Baker University,* Baldwin, Kansas, 1951, p. 219.

13. *Official Record, Kansas Conference, Methodist Episcopal*

Church, *75th Session,* Kansas City, Kansas, March 12-16, 1930, p. 140; *76th Session,* Emporia, Kansas, March 3-8, 1931, pp. 267, 271.

14. *Ibid.,* p. 267.

15. *Ibid., 79th Session,* Abilene, Kansas, March 7-12, 1934, p. 114 f.

16. *Ibid., 85th Session,* Topeka, Kansas, September 26-29, 1939, p. 422 f.

17. Jack Warner Van Derhoof, *The Time Now Past, Kansas Wesleyan University,* 1886-1961, Salina, Kansas, 1962, pp. 35-38.

18. *Ibid.,* p. 44 f.

19. *Ibid.*

20. *Ibid.,* pp. 38-48; *Minutes, Northwest Kansas Conference, Methodist Episcopal Church, 55th Session,* Concordia, Kansas, October 13-18, 1936, p. 29 f.

21. *Minutes, Southwest Kansas Conference, Methodist Episcopal Church, 52nd Session,* Wichita, Kansas, October 10-16, 1933, pp. 179, 182 f.

22. *Ibid., 50th Session to 53rd Session,* 1931-1934.

23. *Ibid., 54th Session,* Winfield, Kansas, October 9-14, 1935, p. 468.

24. *Ibid., 57th Session,* Wichita, Kansas, October 12-16, 1938, p. 318.

25. *Minutes, Northwest Kansas Conference, Methodist Episcopal Church, 48th Session,* Russell, Kansas, September 18-22, 1929, p. 119.

26. *Minutes, Kansas Conference, Methodist Episcopal Church, 74th Session,* Topeka, Kansas, March 5-10, 1929, p. 40 f.

27. *Ibid., 74th to 84th Sessions,* 1929-1939.

28. *Minutes, Northwest Kansas Conference, Methodist Episcopal Church,* 55th Session, Concordia, Kansas, October 13-18, 1936, p. 30.

29. *Ibid., 57th Session,* La Crosse, Kansas, September 27—October 2, 1938, p. 201.

30. *Official Record, Kansas Conference, Methodist Episcopal Church,* 84th Session; Independence, Kansas, March 7-13, 1939; *85th Session,* Topeka, Kansas, September 26-29, 1939; *1st Session, The Methodist Church,* Topeka, Kansas, September 29-October 1, 1939, p. 424.

31. *Ibid.*

CHAPTER 17

Three Methodisms Become One

1. Emory Stevens Bucke, General Editor, *The History of American Methodism,* three volumes, Volume III, pp. 457-476.

2. *Minutes, Central Kansas Conference, The Methodist Church, 1st Session,* Salina, Kansas, October 5-9, 1939.

3. Emory Lindquist, *Kansas: A Centennial Portrait,* Reprinted from the *Kansas Historical Quarterly,* Topeka, Kansas, Spring, 1961, p. 23.

4. *Ibid.,* pp. 22-25.

5. *Official Record, Kansas Conference, The Methodist Church, 2nd Session,* Manhattan, Kansas, October 16-21, 1940; *7th Session,* Topeka, Kansas, October 11-14, 1945; *12th Session,* Pittsburg, Kansas, June 9-14, 1950; *17th Session,* Kansas City, Kansas, May 31-June 5, 1955; *22nd Session,* Pittsburg, Kansas, June 7-12, 1960; *27th Session,* Coffeyville, Kansas, June 1-4, 1965. *Minutes Central Kansas Conference, The Methodist Church, 2nd Session,* Hutchinson, Kansas, October 9-14, 1940; *Journal, 7th Session,* Salina, Kansas, September 26-30, 1945; *12th Session,* Wichita, Kansas, September 26-October 1, 1950; *17th Session,* Hutchinson, Kansas, October 4-9, 1955; *22nd Session,* Salina, Kansas,

May 24-29, 1960; *27th Session,* Dodge City, Kansas, May 18-23, 1965.

6. *Journal, Central Kansas Conference, The Methodist Church, 8th Session,* Hutchinson, Kansas, October 9-13, 1946.

7. Bucke, *op. cit.,* p. 518.

8. *Ibid.,* p. 518 f.

9. *Journal, Central Kansas Conference, The Methodist Church, 8th Session,* Hutchinson, Kansas, October 9-13, 1946; *Official Record, Kansas Conference, The Methodist Church, 8th Session,* Coffeyville, Kansas, September 25-29, 1946.

10. *Official Record, Kansas Conference, The Methodist Church, 3rd Session,* Topeka, Kansas, October 8-12, 1941, p. 273.

11. *Ibid.,* pp. 273-276.

12. *Ibid., 7th Session,* Topeka, Kansas, October 11-14, 1945, p. 270.

13. *Ibid., 22nd Session,* Pittsburg, Kansas, June 7-12, 1960, p. 119.

14. *Ibid., 27th Session,* Coffeyville, Kansas, June 1-4, 1965, p. 348 f.

15. *Journal, Central Kansas Conference, The Methodist Church, 4th Session,* Salina, Kansas, October 7-11, 1942.

16. *Ibid., 14th Session,* Hutchinson, Kansas, October 7-12, 1952, p. 155.

17. *Ibid., 21st Session,* Wichita, Kansas, May 26-31, 1959, p. 651 f.; *Ibid., 24th Session,* Wichita, Kansas, May 23-27, 1962, p. 620 f.; *Ibid., 26th Session,* Hutchinson, Kansas, May 19-24, 1964, p. 230 f.

18. *Official Record, Kansas Conference, 5th Session,* Emporia, Kansas, September 29-October 2, 1943, p. 594 f.

19. *Ibid., 8th Session,* Coffeyville, Kansas, September 25-29, 1946, pp. 404-407.

20. *Ibid., 10th Session,* Emporia, Kansas, September 25-29, 1946, p. 73 f.

21. *Ibid., 16th Session,* Ottawa, Kansas, June 1-6, 1954, pp. 459 f.

22. *Ibid., 17th Session,* Kansas City, Kansas, May 31-June 5, 1955, p. 644; *19th Session,* Coffeyville, Kansas, June 4-7, 1957, p. 259.

23. *Ibid.,* pp. 215, 259.

24. *Ibid., 23rd Session,* Atchison, Kansas, June 6-11, 1961, p. 243.

25. *Ibid.,* pp. 239-241.

26. *Ibid., 26th Session,* Topeka, Kansas, June 1-5, 1964, p. 115.

27. *Ibid., 2nd Session,* Manhattan, Kansas, October 16-21, 1940, p. 62; *Official Record, Kansas Conference, Methodist Episcopal Church, 84th Session,* Independence, Kansas, March 7-13, 1939, p. 294 f.

28. *Ibid., 5th Session,* Emporia, Kansas, September 29-October 2, 1943, pp. 595-597, 602.

29. *Ibid., 6th Session,* Iola, Kansas, October 11-15, 1944, p. 59; *8th Session,* Coffeyville, Kansas, September 25-29, 1946, p. 403 f.; *9th Session,* Topeka, Kansas, September 20-24, 1947, p. 591 f.; *14th Session,* Kansas City, Kansas, June 10-15, 1952, p. 78.

30. *Journal, Kansas Conference, The Methodist Church, 28th Session,* Topeka, Kansas, June 7-10, 1966, p. 489.

31. *Ibid., 26th Session,* Topeka, Kansas, June 1-5, 1964, p. 113.

32. *Ibid., 24th Session,* Emporia, Kansas, June 4-8, 1962, p. 392.

33. *Journal, Central Kansas Conference, The Methodist Church, 5th Session,* Hutchinson, Kansas, October 6-10, 1943, p. 593.

34. *Ibid.,* 8th Session, Hutchinson, Kansas, October 9-13, 1946, p. 327 f.; Jack Warner Van Derhoof, *The Time Now Past, Kansas Wesleyan University, 1886-1961,* Salina, Kansas, 1962, p. 59.

35. *Ibid.,* p. 54 f.

36. *Ibid.,* pp. 64-67.

37. *Ibid.*

38. *Journal, op. cit.,* 4th Session, Salina, Kansas, October 7-11, 1942, p. 447.

39. *Ibid., 6th Session,* Wichita, Kansas, October 4-9, 1944, p. 65.
40. *Ibid., 10th Session,* Salina, Kansas, October 13-17, 1948, p. 75 f.
41. *Ibid., 12th Session,* Wichita, Kansas, September 26-October 1, 1950, p. 413 f.
42. Van Derhoof, *op. cit.,* p. 52 f.
43. *Journal, op cit., 6th Session,* Wichita, Kansas, October 4-9, 1944, p. 61 f.
44. *Ibid.*
45. *Journal, op. cit., 8th Session,* Hutchinson, Kansas, October 9-13, 1946, p. 330 f.
46. *Journal, 12th Session,* Wichita, Kansas, September 26-October 1, 1950, *Appendix, Minutes of the Special Called Session,* Hutchinson, Kansas, June 29, 1950, pp. 505-510.
47. *Ibid.*
48. *Ibid.*
49. *Journal, op. cit., 15th Session,* Wichita, Kansas, October 6-11, 1953, pp. 331-335.
50. *Journal, op. cit., 27th Session,* Dodge City, Kansas, May 18-23, 1965, pp. 434-436, 440; *President's Report, Southwestern College,* March, 1967.
51. *Journal, op. cit., 22nd Session,* Salina, Kansas, May 24-29, 1960, p. 117 f.; *26th Session,* Hutchinson, Kansas, May 19-24, 1964, p. 119 f.
52. *Ibid.,* p. 158.

CHAPTER 18

Methodist Fervor
Through Fire, Sun, Wind and Heat

1. Carl Becker, *Kansas;* Reprinted from "Turner Essays in American History," Henry Holt, 1910, pp. 4, 6.
2. *Minutes, Kansas & Nebraska Annual Conference, Methodist Episcopal Church, 1st Session,* Lawrence, Kansas Territory, October 23-25, 1856, Omaha City, 1856, Reprinted, 1956, pp. 2-5.
3. *Official Record, Kansas Conference, The Methodist Church, 18th Session,* June 5-10, 1956, Lawrence, Kansas; *Official Journal, Central Kansas Conference, The Methodist Church, 18th Session,* October 2-7, 1956, Wichita, Kansas.
4. Emory Lindquist, *Kansas: A Centennial Portrait,* Reprinted from *The Kansas Historical Quarterly,* Topeka, Kansas, Spring, 1961, p. 31.
5. *Ibid.,* p. 32.
6. *The Daily Republican, Fiftieth Anniversary Edition,* 1945, Burlington, Kansas, Volume 88, Section Seven.
7. *Ibid.*
8. *Minutes, Kansas Conference, 35th Session, Methodist Episcopal Church,* Horton, Kansas, March 5-10, 1890, p. 46 f.
9. *Central Christian Advocate, March 17, 1909,* "Should a Roman Catholic Bishop Control the Text Books of the Kansas Public Schools?", p. 5.
10. *Ibid.*
11. *Ibid., March 24, 1909,* "Bishop Lillis Deeclines," p. 1.
12. *Minutes, Kansas Conference, Methodist Episcopal Church, 27th Session,* Abilene, Kansas, March 9-14, 1882—Advertisement.
13. Harold B. Statler, *Executive Secretary's Message to the 1965*

Centennial General Assembly of the Kansas Council of Churches, mimeographed, p. 3.

14. *Ibid.,* p. 4.
15. *The Daily Republican, op. cit.*
16. Robert G. Anderson, *Men, Women and God in Kansas,* Kansas State Printer, 1961, p. 151.
17. *Minutes, Kansas Conference, 35th Session, Methodist Episcopal Church,* Horton, Kansas, March 5-10, 1890, p. 46.
18. *Central Christian Advocate,* April 26, 1893, p. 1.
19. *Ibid.*
20. *Ibid.,* January 23, 1901, p. 105.
21. *Central Christian Advocate,* March 18, 1908, p. 4 f.
22. *History of the First Methodist Church, Eureka, Kansas,* MS Church History, Compiled in 1896 and 1938, Mrs. Fred E. Jones, Historian.
23. *Journal, Central Kansas Conference, Methodist Church, 25th Session,* Salina, Kansas, May 22-26, 1963, p. 708; *Journal, Kansas Conference, Methodist Church, 25th Session,* June 3-7, 1963, p. 511.
24. *100 Years of Methodism in Atchison, Kansas, 1857-1957,* p. 3.
25. Ross Thornton, *Letter,* Minister, First Methodist Church, Abilene, Kansas, July 24, 1962.
26. Leota Motz, *Fort Hays, 1867-1889,* Hays, Kansas, n.d., p. 29.
27. *History of Ebenezer Church, 1873-1958,* n.d. p. 4.
28. *History of the Blue Mound Methodist Church, 1887-1947,* Blue Mound, Kansas, MS mimeographed, p. 1 f.
29. Becker, *op. cit.,* p. 28.

BIBLIOGRAPHY

Manuscripts, Papers, Journals, Letters

American Home Missionary Collection, 1855-1871. Chicago: Chicago Theological Seminary.

Consists of letters and reports written from the home missionary field to the headquarters of the Society in New York. Several thousand of these reports and letters came from the Kansas area. The collection is located at Chicago Theological Seminary in Chicago, Illinois.

Autobiography of A. N. See, D.D.

Manuscript written by See, 80 years old, by conference request, in Historical Society, Central Kansas Conference, Winfield, Kansas.

Kansas Methodist Historical Society. Baker University, Baldwin, Kansas.

Minutes of Board of Trustees, Excerpts, Baker University. Handwritten manuscript "believed to have been collected by Professor S. S. Weatherby."

Griffing, J. S. Manuscript letters: December 2, 1854, December 18, 1854, February 19, 1855.

Robinson, Albert R., *"Forsan et haec Meminisse juvabit."* Manuscript article, written 1908-09, of his two years in Baker, 1867-69.

Minutes—Kansas Mission Conference, Methodist Episcopal Church, South. 1855-1861.

Manuscript handwritten minutes are at Central Methodist Church, Kansas City, Missouri.

Minutes, Western Annual Conference, Methodist Episcopal Church, South. 1870-1905.

Manuscript handwritten minutes are in the Heritage Room, Saint Paul School of Theology Methodist, Kansas City, Missouri.

Walden Papers, 1858. University of Chicago.

The letters, writings, and clippings of J. M. Walden, an editor of a Free-State newspaper in Quindaro, Kansas, during the territorial days; Walden remained in Kansas for only a few years. The collection is located at Divinity School Library, University of Chicago, Chicago, Illinois.

Personal Letters

Bressler, Ray B., minister, to E. Dale Dunlap, May 31, 1964.

McCarter, Charles C., October 29, 1962. State Corporation Commission, State of Kansas, Topeka, Kansas.

Ramsdale, William R., August 24, 1967.

Thornton, Ross, minister, July 24, 1962. Abilene, Kansas.

Reports and Minutes of National Societies and Organizations

American Baptist Year-Book, 1869-1881. Philadelphia: American Baptist Publication Society, 1869-1881.

Annual Reports, American Baptist Board of Foreign Missions.

20th—1834	22nd—1836	23rd—1837	24th—1838
33rd—1847	41st—1855	48th—1862	51st—1865

Annual Report of the American Baptist Home Mission Society, 1873. New York, 1873.

Annual Report of the Board of Domestic Missions of the General Assembly of the Presbyterian Church in the United States of America, 1845, 1856-1870. Philadelphia, 1845, 1856-1870.

Annual Reports of the Board of Missions: Methodist Episcopal Church, 1845, 1847, 1852, 1854, 1856, 1857, 1860, 1865.

Cyclopedia of Methodism. Matthew Simpson (Editor). Philadelphia: Everts & Stewart, 1878.

The Congregational Year-Book, 1881. Boston: Congregational Publishing Society, 1881.

Journal of the General Conference of the Methodist Episcopal Church. 1860, 1868, 1876, 1880, New York, 1860, 1868, 1876, 1880.

The Methodist Almanac. New York: Lane and Scott. 1873, 1878.

The Methodist Year-Book. New York, 1880.

Minutes of the Annual Conferences of the Methodist Episcopal Church 1773-1880. Three volumes. 1773-1840, New York: T. Mason and G. Lane, 1840; 1846-1851, New York: Carlton and Porter, 1856; 1852-1880, published yearly, New York.

Minutes of the General Assembly of the Presbyterian Church in the United States of America.
New York and Philadelphia, 1818-1837.
Old School, Philadelphia, 1838-1869.
New School, New York, 1838-1869.
New York, 1871-1880.

Minutes of the General Association of Congregational Ministers and Churches in Kansas, 1857.

Minutes of Several Conversations between the Rev. Thomas Coke, LL.D., the Rev. Francis Asbury and others, at a conference, begun in Baltimore, in the State of Maryland, on Monday, the 27th of December, in the year 1784. Composing a Form of Discipline for the Ministers, Preachers, and other Members of the Methodist Episcopal Church in America. Philadelphia: Charles Cist, 1785.

Periodicals, Magazines, Newspapers

Central Christian Advocate, 1852-1943 inclusive. St. Louis, Missouri.
   One of the official publications of the Methodist Episcopal Church and the Methodist Church.

Christian Advocate, 1826-1876 inclusive. An official publication of the Methodist Episcopal Church.

Western Christian Advocate, 1834-1934 inclusive. An official publication of the Methodist Episcopal Church.

The Congregational Record, June and July, 1864.
   Published quarterly, under the auspices of the General Association of Congregational Churches and Ministers of Kansas.

The Daily Republican, Fiftieth Anniversary Edition. Volume 88, Section Seven. Burlington, Kansas, 1945.

Outlook and Independent, July 17, 1929.

The Quarterly Journal of the American Unitarian Association. Volumes II-V. Boston: American Unitarian Association, 1855-1858.

Scribner's Magazine, July 29, 1929. "The Man of Mystery of the Lincoln Drama."
   Historical Facts Concerning the Life of Boston Corbett, Published on the occasion of the dedication of a monument, erected by the Boy Scouts, marking the sight of Corbett's dugout house in Cloud County, Kansas.

Minutes, Journals, etc. of State Organizations

Minutes of the Sessions of the Kansas and Nebraska Conference of the Methodist Episcopal Church, 1856-1860.

Minutes of the Kansas Annual Conference of the Methodist Episcopal Church. 1861-1939 inclusive.

Minutes, Kansas Conference of The Methodist Church. 1939-1967.

Minutes, South Kansas Conference of the Methodist Episcopal Church. 1874-1914.

Minutes, Northwest Kansas Conference of the Methodist Episcopal Church. 1883-1939.

Minutes, Southwest Conference of the Methodist Episcopal Church. 1883-1939.

Journal, Central Kansas Conference, The Methodist Church. 1939-1967.

Minutes, Kansas Conference, Methodist Protestant Church. 1868-1939.

Minutes of the Kansas State Baptist Convention. 1860, 1866.

Annals, Autobiographies, Collections

The Annals of Kansas, 1886-1925. Kirke Mechem (editor). 2 volumes, 1886-1910, 1911-1925. Topeka: Kansas State Historical Society, 1954 and 1956.

Annals of Shawnee Methodist Mission and Indian Manual Labor School. Compiled by Martha B. Caldwell. Topeka: Kansas State Historical Society, 1939.

Butler, Pardee. *Personal Recollections.* Cincinnati: Standard Publishing Company, 1889.

Autobiography of Peter Cartwright. Charles L. Wallis (editor). New York: Abingdon, 1956.

Autobiography, William Allen White. New York: Macmillan Co., 1946.

Kansas State Historical Society
   Transactions, Volumes I, II, III, IV.
   Collections, Volumes VII, IX, X, XI, XII, XIII XV, XVI, XVII, XXV, XXVI.
   Kansas Historical Quarterly, VIII, XII, XXIV, XXIX.

Sweet, William Warren. *Circuit-Rider Days Along The Ohio (Being the Journals of the Ohio Conference from its Organization in 1812 to 1826).* New York: The Methodist Book Concern, 1923.

Sweet, William Warren. *Religion on the American Frontier, 1783-1850.*
   The Baptists, Volume I. New York: Henry Holt and Company, 1931.
   The Presbyterians, Volume II. New York: Harpers, 1936.
   The Congregationalists, Volume III. Chicago: University of Chicago, 1939.
   The Methodists, Volume IV. Chicago: University of Chicago, 1946.

United States Census. Eighth, Washington, 1864; Ninth, Volume I. Washington, 1872; Tenth, Washington, 1873.

The World Almanac. New York, 1968.

Books and Other Secondary Material

Anderson, Robert G. *Morning Devotions in the Kansas House of Representatives During Seven Sessions.* "Men, Women & God in Kansas." Published by the State Printer, 1961 (copyright by author).

Andreas, A. T. *History of Kansas.* Chicago, 1883.

Andrews, Charles M. *The Colonial Period of American History.* Volume I, *The Settlements.* New Haven: Yale University, 1934.

Asbury, Herbert. "Marching as to War" The Story of Carry Nation, series of articles in *Outlook and Independent.* August 21, 1929.

Bailes, Kendall E. *Rider on the Wind, Jim Lane and Kansas.* Shawnee Mission, Kansas: The Wagon Wheel Press, 1962.

Baker University, *Fortieth Annual Catalogue.* Baldwin, Kansas, 1898.

Barclay, Wade Crawford. *History of Methodist Missions.* Volume One—*Missionary Motivation and Expansion.* Volume Two—*To Reform a Nation.* New York: The Board of Missions and Church Extension of The Methodist Church, 1950.

Barclay, Wade Crawford. *History of Methodist Missions,* part II.

Volume Three—*Widening Horizons 1845-1895*. New York: The Board of Missions of The Methodist Church, 1957.

Bassett, Ancel H. *A Concise History of the Methodist Protestant Church from Its Origin*. Pittsburgh: William McCracken, Jr., 1887.

Baughman, Robert W. *Kansas in Maps*. Topeka, Kansas: The Kansas State Historical Society, 1961.

Becker, Carl. *Kansas* reprinted from "Turner Essays in American History." New York: Henry Holt & Company, 1910.

Beckman, Peter, O. S. B. *The Catholic Church on the Kansas Frontier, 1850-1877*. Washington D. C., 1943.

The Bethany Visitor, January, 1942.

Beveridge, Albert J. *Abraham Lincoln, 1809-1858*. Volumes I and II. New York & Boston: Houghton Mifflin Company; Cambridge: The Riverside Press, 1928.

Billington, Ray Allen. *Westward Expansion—A History of the American Frontier*. New York: The Macmillan Company, 1960 (second edition).

Bingham, Anne E. "The Grasshopper Plague" *The Heritage of Kansas*. Everett Rich (editor). Lawrence, Kansas: University of Kansas, 1960.

Bowe, Richard J., (editor). *Historical Album of Kansas*. Published by the Editor, Kansas City, Missouri, in cooperation with the Kansas State Historical Society and others. Midway, U. S. A. Centennial of the state of Kansas, 1861-1961.

Branson, John Erwin. *Seedtime & Harvest, A History of the Kansas Conference of the Church of the United Brethren in Christ*. Part II, 1883-1914. A thesis, The Bonebrake Theological Seminary, Dayton, Ohio, 1943.

Bright, John D. *Kansas The First Century*. Volume I and II. New York: Lewis Historical Publishing Company.

Brown, Ina Corinne. *The Story of the American Negro*. New York: Friendship Press, 1936.

Brown, William. *The History of Christian Missions*. Volume II. London: T. Baker, 1864.

Bucke, Emory Stevens (general editor). *The History of American Methodism*. Three volumes. New York and Nashville: Abingdon Press, 1964.

Caldwell, Martha B. "Woman's Suffrage Campaign," *The Kansas Historical Quarterly*. Volume XII, August, 1943.

Calvary Methodist Church, 85th Anniversary. May 7, 1961, anniversary brochure (16 pages).

Castel, Albert. *William Clarke Quantrill: His Life and Times*. Frederick Fell, Inc., 1962.

Cone, William W. "The First Kaw Indian Mission" *Transactions of the Kansas State Historical Society*, Volume I & II.

Connelley, William E. *History of Kansas—State and People*. Volume II. Chicago & New York: The American Historical Society, Inc., 1928.

Connelley, William E. *A Standard History of Kansas and Kansans*. Five volumes. Chicago and New York: Lewis Publishing Company, 1918, Volume II.

Cook, Bernard L. *The First Twenty-five Years of the Kansas Conference of the Church of the United Brethren in Christ*. Part I. A thesis, The Bonebrake Theological Seminary, Dayton, Ohio, 1942.

This is the first section of Cook-Branson-Lehman *Seedtime & Harvest, A History of the Kansas Conference of the Church of the United Brethren in Christ*. A mimeographed book.

Cornett, John S., Ph.D. *Fifty Years of Kansas Wesleyan University 1886-1936*. Padgett's Printing House, 1936.

Craig, Reginald S. *The Fighting Parson—The Biography of Colonel John M. Chivington*. Los Angeles: Westernlore Press, 1959.

Craik, Reginald LeRoy. *A History of the Church of the Brethren in Kansas.* McPherson, Kansas: Published by the author, 1922.

Craven, Avery. *The Coming of the Civil War.* Chicago, Illinois: The University of Chicago Press, 1957. (Originally published by Scribner's, 1942.)

Dick, Everett, Ph.D. *The Sod-House Frontier 1854-1890. A Social History of the Northern Plains from the Creation of Kansas & Nebraska to the Admission of the Dakotas.* Lincoln, Nebraska: Johnsen Publishing Company, 1954.

Drinkhouse, C. Edward J. *History of Methodist Reform, Synoptical of General Methodism 1703 to 1898, With Special and Comprehensive Reference to His More Salient Exhibition in the History of the Methodist Episcopal Church.* Two volumes, Volume II. Baltimore, Maryland: Board of Publication of the Methodist Protestant Church, 1899.

Drury, A. W. *History of the Church of the United Brethren in Christ.* Dayton, Ohio: Otterbein Press, 1924.

Ebright, Homer Kingley, *The History of Baker University,* Baldwin, Kansas, 1951.

Elliott, Charles. *South-Western Methodist—A History of the M. E. Church in the South-West, from 1844 to 1864.* Cincinnati: Poe and Hitchcock, 1868.

Erffmeyer, E. E., historian. *Seventeen Years of History in the Kansas Conference of the Evangelical Church and of the Evangelical United Brethren Church,* n.p. n.d.

Evangelical Association. *Fifty Years in the Kansas Conference, 1864 —1914, a Record of the Origin and Development of the Work of the Evangelical Association, in the territory covered by the Kansas Conference.* Cleveland, Ohio: G. Hauser, Press of the Evangelical Association, n.d.

Evangelical Church. *History of the Kansas Conference of the Evangelical Church.* Volume II, 1914-1939. C. R. Findley, historian.

Faulkner, Thomas O. *Fiftieth Anniversary Commemorative Brochure, Wesley Hospital,* n.p. n.d.

Ferris, Ida M. "The Sauks and Foxes in Franklin and Osage Counties, Kansas," *Collections of the Kansas State Historical Society.* Vol. XI, 1908.

Fifty Years in the Kansas Conference, 1864-1914. A Record of the Origin and Development of the Work of the Evangelical Association in the territory covered by the Kansas Conference. Cleveland: Press of the Evangelical Association, n.d.

50 Years of Service, 1915-1965. Grace Hospital and School of Nurses. Hutchinson, Kansas: mimeographed for the Board of Trustees.

Filler, Louis. *The Crusade Against Slavery 1830-1860.* (The New American Nation Series) New York: Harper & Brothers, 1960.

Finley, James B. *Life Among the Indians.* Cincinnati: Cranston and Curts, n.d.

Fisher, H. D. *The Gun and the Gospel.* Kansas City, Missouri: Hudson-Kimberly, 1902.

Francis, Clara. "The Coming of Prohibition to Kansas," *Kansas State Historical Collections.* Volume XV, 1919-1922.

Frederickson, Otto Frovin. *The Liquor Question in Kansas Before Constitutional Prohibition.* Ph.D. thesis. Lawrence, Kansas: University of Kansas, 1931.

Frogge, Don W. *Co-operation and Denominational Union in the Evangelical United Brethren Church.* New York: Union Theological Seminary, April, 1954. Submitted in partial fulfillment of the Requirements for the Degree of Bachelor of Divinity in the Union Theological Seminary.

Gard, Wayne. *The Chisholm Trail*. Norman, Oklahoma: University of Oklahoma Press, 1954.

Garrison, Winfred Ernest. *The March of Faith, The Story of Religion in America Since 1865*. New York: Harper's, 1933.

Giles, F. W. *30 Years in Topeka, 1854-1884*. Topeka, 1886; reprinted, 1960.

Gill, Frederick C. (editor). *Selected Letters of John Wesley*. New York: Philosophical Library, 1956.

Goode, W. H. *Outposts of Zion—With Limnings of Mission Life*. Cincinnati: Poe & Hitchcock, 1864.

Graves, William W. *The First Protestant Osage Missions 1820-1837*. Oswego, Kansas: The Carpenter Press, 1949.

Gray, Wallace (translator of portions). *Souvenir der West Deutschen Konferenz der Bischoflichen Methodistenkirche. (Souvenir of the West German Conference of the Methodist Episcopal Church.)* Published on order of the Conference, by Otto E. Kriege, Gustav Becker, Matthaus Herrmann and C. L. Korner. Cincinnati: Jennings and Graham, 1906.

Greeley, Horace. *An Overland Journey—from New York to San Francisco in the Summer of 1859*. New York: Saxon, Barker & Company, 1860; New York: Alfred A. Knopf, 1964.

Green, F. M. *Christian Missions*. St. Louis: J. Burne Publishing Company, 1884.

Greene, Mary. *Life, Three Sermons, and Some Miscellaneous Writings of Rev. Jesse Greene*. Lexington, Missouri: Patterson & Julian, 1852.

Green, Paul. "The Epic of Jamestown," *New York Times Magazine*, March 31, 1957.

Gregg, Josiah. *Commerce of the Prairies*. In two volumes. The 1844 edition, unabridged. Philadelphia & New York: J. B. Lippincott Company, 1962.

40 Years of Service, 1925-1965. Hadley Memorial Hospital. Hays, Kansas.

Hagan, William T. "American Indians." *The Chicago History of American Civilization* (Daniel J. Boorstin, editor). Chicago, Illinois: The University of Chicago Press, 1961.

Harrington, Grant W. "The Genesis of Prohibition," *Kansas State Historical Collections*. Volume XV (1919-1922).

Hicks, John D. *The Populist Revolt—A History of the Farmers' Alliance and the People's Party*. University of Nebraska Press, 1961 (A "Bison Book"). Originally published in 1931 by the University of Minnesota Press.

Hill, John B. *The Presbytery of Kansas City & its Predecessors—1821-1901*. Kansas City: The Burd & Fletcher Printing Company, 1901.

Historical Society Bulletin, Central Kansas Conference. Volume III, No. 3, March, 1962.

History of the Blue Mound Methodist Church, 1887-1947. Blue Mound, Kansas, Manuscript mimeographed.

History of Ebenezer Church, 1873-1958. Ebenezer, Kansas, n.d.

History of the First Methodist Church, Eureka, Kansas. Manuscript church history compiled in 1896 and 1938. Mrs. Fred E. Jones, historian.

History of the Southwest Kansas Conference of the Methodist Episcopal Church. Volume One, 1869-1931. Published by the Conference.

Hobbs, Wilson, M.D. "The Friends Establishment in Kansas Territory," *Transactions of the Kansas State Historical Society*. Volume VIII.

Hofstadter, Richard. *The Age of Reform*. Vintage Books, Knopf, Inc. and Random House, Inc., 1955.

Hollibaugh, Mrs. E. F. *Biographical History of Cloud County, Kansas,* n.d. n.p.

Cyrus K. Holliday. Published by the Santa Fe Railroad.
Dedication of the Cyrus K. Holliday Plaque and a brief biographical Sketch, "The Man with the White Hat." Mr. Holliday was one of the founders of Topeka, Kansas, and was the first President of the Atchison, Topeka, and Santa Fe Railroad.

Holter, Don Wendell, *Beginnings of Protestantism in Trans-Missouri,* Ph.D. Dissertation, University of Chicago, 1934.

Honeyman, Bob (editor). *Kansas Pictorial Calendar, 1962.* Arkansas City, Kansas, 1961.

Hoon, John. *The Wyandotte Story and the Persistent Flame of Methodism.* Mimeographed address, 1965.

House of Happiness, 1904-1957. 53 Years of Service to the Methodists of Kansas. The Methodist Home for the Aged. n.p. n.d.

Huber, Camille Bertrand. *The Attitude of the United States Government Toward the Missouri Border "Ruffians," 1854-1861.* Thesis, 1941.

Jackman, Dr. Everett E. *The Nebraska Methodist Story.* Authorized Centennial History of Nebraska Methodism—1854-1954. Published by the Nebraska Conference Methodist Historical Society, 1954.

Jenkins, Jeff. *The Northern Tier of Life Among the Homestead Settlers.* Topeka: Kansas Publishing House, 1886.

Johnson, Charles A. *The Frontier Camp Meeting—Religion's Harvest Time.* Dallas, Texas: Southern Methodist University Press, 1955.

Johnson, Samuel A. *The Battle Cry of Freedom—The New England Emigrant Aid Company in the Kansas Crusade.* Lawrence, Kansas: University of Kansas Press, 1954.

Kansas City Deaconess. Volume XVII, No. 5. Kansas City, Missouri, May, 1925.

A Kansas Souvenir. Issued by the Kansas Immigration and Information Association, 1896.

Kansas, A Guide to the Sunflower State. Harold C. Evans, Chief Editor. The American Guide Series, State of Kansas Department of Education, 1939.

Kelsey, R. W. *Friends and the Indians, 1655-1917.* Philadelphia, 1917.

Laman, Russell. *Manifest Destiny.* Chicago, Illinois: Henry Regnery Company, 1963.

Lawrence, William. *Life of Amos A. Lawrence.* Boston and New York: Houghton Mifflin, 1899.

Leftwich, W. M. *Martyrdom in Missouri.* Volumes I and II. St. Louis: Southwestern Book and Publishing Company, 1870.

Lehman, Clayton George. *Seedtime & Harvest, A History of the Kansas Conference of the Church of the United Brethren in Christ.* Part III, 1914-1943. A thesis, The Bonebrake Theological Seminary. Dayton, Ohio: The Bonebrake Theological Seminary, 1944.

Lewis and Clark. *A Brief Account of their Expedition.* Issued by the Bureau of Land Management under the United States Department of the Interior. May, 1962. Originally issued in 1905 by the General Land Office, a predecessor agency of the Bureau of Land Management.

Lindquist, Emory. *Kansas, A Centennial Portrait,* reprinted from *The Kansas Historical Quarterly.* Topeka, Spring, 1961.

Lutz, J. J. "The Methodist Missions Among the Indian Tribes in Kansas," *Transactions of the Kansas State Historical Society.* Volume IX, 1905-1906. Topeka, 1906.

Malin, James C., Ph.D. *Indian Policy and Westward Expansion.* Bulletin of the University of Kansas, Volume XXII, November 1, 1921, No. 17. Humanistic Studies, Volume II, No. 3. Lawrence, Kansas: University of Kansas, November, 1921.

Marquette, David. *A History of Nebraska Methodism*. Cincinnati: Western Methodist Book Concern, 1904.

Marshall, James. *Santa Fe—The Railroad that Built an Empire*. New York: Random House, 1945.

Martin, Governor John A. "Address, Kansas Quarter-Centennial!" *Transactions of the Kansas State Historical Society*. Volume III. Topeka, 1886.

The Messenger. Wesley Medical Center, Wichita, Kansas. Volume 21, No. 3, December, 1965.

Miller, Raymond Curtis. *The Populist Party in Kansas*. (Dissertation.) Chicago: University of Chicago Library, 1928.

Miller, Wallace Elden. *The Peopling of Kansas*. (Ph.D. Dissertation.) Columbus, 1906.

Morison, Samuel Eliot and Commager, Henry Steele. *The Growth of the American Republic*. Volumes I and II. New York: Oxford, 1950.

Morrow, Ralph E. *Northern Methodism and Reconstruction*. East Lansing, Michigan: Michigan State University Press, 1956.

Morse, J. *Report to the Secretary of War of the U. S. A. on Indian Affairs*. New Haven, 1822.

Motz, Leota. *Fort Hays, 1867-1889*. Hays, Kansas, n.d.

Muller, Herbert J. *The Uses of the Past—Profiles of Former Societies*. New York: Oxford University Press, 1957. (A "Galaxy Book")

McCoy, Isaac. *History of Baptist Missions*. Washington: W. M. Morrison; New York: H. and S. Raynor, 1840.

McGonigle, James A. "Right Reverend John B. Miege, S.J. First Catholic Bishop of Kansas," *Transactions of the Kansas State Historical Society*. Volume IX, 1905-1906. Topeka, Kansas, 1906.

McKitrick, Eric L. (editor). *Slavery Defended: The Views of The Old South*. Prentice-Hall, Inc., 1963. ("A Spectrum Book")

McMurtrie, D. C. and Allen, A. H. *Jotham Meeker, Pioneer Printer of Kansas*. Chicago: Eyncourt, 1930.

McReynolds, Edwin C. *Oklahoma—A History of the Sooner State*. Norman, Oklahoma: University of Oklahoma Press, 1954.

Newman, A. H. (editor). *A Century of Baptist Achievement*. Morehouse, "The American Baptist Home Mission Society." Philadelphia: American Baptist Publication Society, 1901.

The Newton Kansan. The Centennial Edition, January 28, 1961. (quoted in Historical Society Bulletin, Central Kansas Conference, April, 1961.)

Norwood, Frederick A. *History of the North Indiana Conference— 1917-1956. North Indiana Methodism in the Twentieth Century*. Volume II. Published under the auspices of the Conference Historical Society, 1957.

Norwood, John N. *The Schism in the Methodist Church, 1844*. Alfred, New York: Alfred University, 1844.

Nugent, Walter T. K. *The Tolerant Populists, Kansas Populism and Nativism*. Chicago: University of Chicago Press, 1963.

One Hundred Years in Kansas Education. October 1, 1963. A book issued as part of the observance of the centennial of the Kansas State Teachers Association.

100 Years of Methodism in Atchison, Kansas, 1857-1957.

Parrish, Fred Louis. *The Rise of Methodism In Kansas—1830-1861— From its Inception to the Opening of the Civil War*. Northwestern University, for the degree of Master of Arts, 1921-1922.

Plank, Pryor. "The Iowa, Sac and Fox Indian Mission and Its Missionaries, Rev. Samuel M. Irvin and Wife," *Transactions of the Kansas State Historical Society*. Volume X, 1907-1908. Topeka, 1908.

Prescott, W. H. *The Conquest of Mexico and History of the Conquest of Peru*. New York, n.d. Random House, Inc.

Quayle, W. A. *The Pastor-Preacher*. New York: Methodist Book Concern, 1910.

Reid, Albert T. "The Man of Mystery of the Lincoln Drama." *Scribner's Magazine*. July 29, 1929.

  Historical Facts Concerning Life of Boston Corbett, published on the occasion of the dedication of a monument, erected by the Boy Scouts, marking the sight of Corbett's dugout house in Cloud County.

Report of the Indian Committee to Indiana Yearly Meeting. 1862.

Rice, M. S. *William Alfred Quayle, The Skylark of Methodism*. New York: Abingdon, 1928.

Rich, Everett (editor). *The Heritage of Kansas—Selected Commentaries on Past Times*. Lawrence, Kansas: University of Kansas Press, 1960.

Riddle, Kenyon. *Records and Maps of the Old Santa Fe Trail*. Printed by the *Raton Daily Range,* Raton, New Mexico, for the author, 1949.

Rist, Martin. "Methodism Goes West." *The History of American Methodism*. Three volumes, Volume II. E. S. Bucke (general editor). New York: Abingdon, 1964.

Ross, Edith Connelly. "The Old Shawness Mission," *Collections of the Kansas State Historical Society*. Volume XVII.

Sandburg, Carl. *Abraham Lincoln—The Prairie Years and the War Years*. One volume edition. New York: Harcourt, Brace & Company, 1954.

Schlesinger, Arthur Meier. *Political and Social Growth of the American People 1865-1940*. New York: The Macmillan Company, 1941.

Schwendemann, Glen, "The 'Exodusters' on the Missouri," *Kansas Historical Quarterly*, XXIX, No. 1, Spring, 1963, Kansas State Historical Society, Topeka, Kansas, pp. 25-40.

Schwendemann, Glen. "Nicodemus: Negro Haven on the Solomon," *Kansas Historical Quarterly*. Volume XXXIV—Spring, 1968. Topeka, Kansas: Kansas State Historical Society, 1968.

Searle, Robert W. *Author of Liberty*. New York: Friendship Press, 1941.

Shackleton, B. Close. *Handbook on the Frontier Days of Southeast Kansas*. Kansas Centennial, 1861-1961.

Sloan, James C. *A Historical Study of the Ghost Colleges of Kansas*. Thesis; Kellogg Library, Kansas State Teachers College, Emporia, Kansas, 1948.

Smith, Justin A. *A History of the Baptists in the Western States East of the Mississippi*. Philadelphia: American Baptist Publication Society, 1896.

Smith, Mary F.; Tibbetts, Pearle W.; and Pike, Minnie. *There Was One Anna*. Kansas City, Missouri: Browne-White-Lowell Press, 1948.

Smith, Timothy L. *Revivalism and Social Reform in Mid-Nineteenth-Century America*. Nashville & New York: Abingdon Press, 1957.

Snow, F. H. "The Beginnings of the University of Kansas," *Transactions of the Kansas State Historical Society*. Volume VI.

Snow, Florence L. *Pictures on My Wall—A Lifetime in Kansas*. Lawrence, Kansas: University of Kansas Press, 1945.

Southwestern College, President's Report. March, 1967.

Spears, John R. *The American Slave Trade*. New York: Ballatine, 1960.

Speer, John. "Patriotism and Education in the Methodist Church," *Transactions of the Kansas State Historical Society*. Volume VII.

Spencer, Rev. Joab (compiler), "Days of the Missionary—The Methodist Episcopal Church, South, in Kansas—1854-1906." *Collections of the Kansas State Historical Society*. Volume XII, Section IV.

Statler, Harold B. *Executive Secretary's Message to the 1965 Centen-*

nial *General Assembly of the Kansas Council of Churches.* Mimeographed.

Stewart, John. *The Missionary Pioneer or A Brief Memoir of the Life, Labours and Death of John Stewart, Founder Under God of the Mission Among the Wyandotts at Upper Sandusky, Ohio.* New York: John Mitchell, 1827.

Streeter, Floyd Benjamin. *The Kaw—The Heart of a Nation.* Half-title: *The Rivers of America.* New York: Rinehart & Company, Inc., 1941.

Sweet, William Henry. *A History of Methodism in Northwest Kansas.* Salina, Kansas: Kansas Wesleyan University, 1920.

Sweet, William Warren. *Methodism in American History,* (revision of 1953) New York: Abingdon, 1954.

Sweet, William Warren. *The Methodist Episcopal Church and the Civil War.* Cincinnati: Methodist Book Concern, 1912.

Sweet, William Warren. *Revivalism in America.* New York: Scribners, 1945.

Sweet, William Warren. *The Story of Religion in America.* New York: Harpers, 1950.

Sweet, William Warren. *Virginia Methodism—A History.* Richmond, Virginia: Whittet & Shepperson, 1955.

Telford, John. (editor) *The Letters of the Rev. John Wesley, A. M.* Volume III. London: The Epworth Press, 1931.

Thomas, John L. *The Liberator—William Lloyd Garrison.* Boston: Little, Brown & Company, 1963.

Tucker, Frank. "The Indian Mission of the Missouri Conference, 1830-1844." *World Parish.* June, 1962.

Twitchell, Ralph Emerson, Esq. *The Story of the Conquest of Santa Fe, New Mexico, and the Building of Old Fort Marcy, A.D. 1846.* Historical Society of New Mexico Publication, #24.

Utley, Robert M. *Fort Union National Monument, New Mexico.* National Park Service Historical Handbook Series, No. 35. Washington, D.C., 1962.

VanDerhoff, Jack Warner. *The Time . . . Now Past.* (Matthew 14:15) *Kansas Wesleyan University—1886-1961.* Published during the observance of the 75th Anniversary of Kansas Wesleyan University, May, 1962. Salina, Kansas: Arrow Printing Company, 1962.

Versteeg, John M. (editor), Green, John D. (assistant editor), *Methodism: Ohio Area—1812-1962.* Ohio Area Sesquicentennial Commission, 1962.

Walker, Williston. *A History of the Congregational Churches.* New York: Christian Literature Company, 1894.

Walters, J. D. "The Kansas State Agricultural College," *Transactions of the Kansas State Historical Society.* Volume VII.

Waters, L. L. *Steel Trails to Santa Fe.* Lawrence, Kansas: University of Kansas Press, 1950.

Webb, Walter Prescott. *The Great Plains.* New York: Grosset & Dunlap, 1931. Grosset's "Universal Library."

Wheeler, James. "Removal of the Wyandottes," *Western Christian Advocate.* Volume X, No. 17. August 11 and 18, September 22, and October 6, 1843.

Willard, J. T. "Blue Mont Central College," *The Kansas Historical Quarterly.* Volume VIII. Topeka, Kansas, May, 1945.

Woodard, W. S. *Annals of Methodism in Missouri.* Columbia, Missouri: E. W. Stephens, 1893.

Yeakel, R. *History of the Evangelical Association.* Two volumes, Volume II. Cleveland: J. H. Lamb, 1909.

Zornow, William Frank. *Kansas—A History of the Jayhawk State.* Norman, Oklahoma: University of Oklahoma Press, 1957.

Acknowledgements

The author gratefully acknowledges permission to quote from the following sources:

Abingdon Press—WILLIAM ALFRED QUAYLE, by M. S. Rice;
        METHODISM IN AMERICAN HISTORY, by William W. Sweet;
        THE AUTOBIOGRAPHY OF PETER CARTWRIGHT, by Charles L. Wallis;
        THE HISTORY OF AMERICAN METHODISM, Volume III, by Emory S. Bucke;
        THE METHODIST EPISCOPAL CHURCH AND THE CIVIL WAR, by William W. Sweet;
        THE PASTOR-PREACHER, by William Alfred Quayle.

Association of Methodist Historical Societies—WORLD PARISH, "The Indian Mission of the Missouri Conference, 1830-1844," by Frank Tucker, 1962.

Board of Missions of the United Methodist Church—HISTORY OF METHODIST MISSIONS, Volume II, by Wade Crawford Barclay.

The Catholic University of America—THE CATHOLIC CHURCH ON THE KANSAS FRONTIER, 1850-1877, by Rev. Peter Beckman, O.S.B.

Kansas State Teachers College—A HISTORICAL STUDY OF THE GHOST COLLEGES OF KANSAS, by James C. Sloan.

Kansas Wesleyan University—THE TIME NOW PAST, by Jack Warner Van Derhoof.

Alfred A. Knopf & Co.—AN OVERLAND JOURNEY, by Horace Greeley.

Oxford University Press—THE GROWTH OF THE AMERICAN REPUBLIC, Volumes I & II, by Samuel Eliot Morison & Henry Steele Commager.

Philosophical Library—SELECTED LETTERS OF JOHN WESLEY, edited by Frederick C. Gill.

Random House—THE CONQUEST OF MEXICO AND HISTORY OF THE CONQUEST OF PERU, by W. H. Prescott.

The University of Chicago Press—THE TOLERANT POPULISTS, Kansas Populism and Nativism, by Walter T. K. Nugent.

The University of Nebraska—THE POPULIST REVOLT: A HISTORY OF THE FARMER'S ALLIANCE AND THE PEOPLE'S PARTY, by John D. Hicks.

University of Oklahoma Press—KANSAS: A History of the Jayhawk State, by William Frank Zornow.

The University Press of Kansas—THE HERITAGE OF KANSAS, edited by Everett Rich.

INDEX

1856—"The Kansas and Nebraska Conference shall embrace the Kansas and Nebraska Territories, and also that part of the territories of New Mexico and Utah lying east of the Rocky Mountains."

1860—"Kansas Conference shall embrace the State or Territory of Kansas, and the State of Texas, and that portion of New Mexico east of the Rocky Mountains."

1864—"Kansas Conference shall embrace the State of Kansas."

1868—"Kansas Conference shall include the State of Kansas and the Indian Territory."

1872—"Kansas Conference shall include the State of Kansas and so much of the Indian Territory south thereof as lies north of the 36th parallel of north latitude."

1876—"Kansas Conference shall embrace that portion of the State of Kansas lying north of the south line of township 16, including the town of Pomona, which lies south of said line, but shall leave Louisburgh, Ottawa, and Baldwin City, lying north of said line, in the South Kansas Conference. Baldwin City shall belong to the South Kansas Conference after the said Conference in 1877."

1876—"South Kansas Conference shall embrace that portion of the State of Kansas not included in the Kansas Conference, and so much of the Indian Territory south thereof as lies north of the 36th parallel of north latitude."

1880—The only change is that South Kansas Conference leaves off mention of the Indian Territory.

1884—"Kansas Conference shall embrace that portion of the State of Kansas lying east of the sixth principal meridian, and north of the south line of township 16, including the town of Pomona, lying south of said line, but excluding Louis-burgh, Ottawa and Baldwin City lying north of said line, and Soloman City lying east of the sixth meridian, provided that Baldwin City shall remain in the Conference until the next session of the conference."

1884—"North-west Kansas Conference shall include all that part of the State of Kansas north of the south line of township 16 and west of the sixth principal meridian, yet so as to include the Soloman City Circuit."

1884—"South Kansas Conference shall embrace that part of the State of Kansas lying east of the west line of Chautauqua, Elk, Greenwood, and Chase Counties, and south of the south line of township 16, including Louisburgh, Ottawa, and Baldwin City, lying north of said line, and excluding Pomona, lying south of the said line, provided that Baldwin City shall remain in the Kansas Conference until the session of the Conference in 1885."

1884—"South-west Kansas Conference shall include all that part of the State of Kansas lying south of the south line of township 16, and west of a line beginning at the south-east corner of Cowly County, thence north to the south line of Chase County, thence west to the south-west corner of said Chase County, thence north to the south line of township 16."

1888—Kansas Conference remained the same except that Baldwin City is to remain in the South Kansas Conference until its session in 1889.

1888—North-west Kansas Conference changed its southern boundary to "north of the south line of township 17."

1888—"South-west Kansas Conference shall include all that part of the State of Kansas not included in the Kansas, North-west Kansas and South-east (there never was any such conference) Kansas Conference; and also the territory known as No Man's Land."

1892—The only change was that Baldwin City was to be the Kansas Conference until its session in 1893.

1896—"Northwest Kansas Conference shall be bounded on the west and north by the Kansas State line; on the east by the sixth principal meridian, but shall include the Solomon City Circuit; and on the south by the south line of township 17 as far west as to the east line of Lane County, thence north to the north line of said Lane County, thence west to the State Line."

1896—Southwest Kansas Conference changes "No Man's Land" to "Beaver County in the Territory of Oklahoma."

1896—It appears that South Kansas Conference finally got Baldwin to keep.

1900, 1904—No changes

1908—The town of Quenemo is added to the Kansas Conference.

1908—Southwest Kansas Conference included Beaver County in the *State* of Oklahoma.

1912—Southwest Kansas Conference included Beaver, Texas and Cimarron Counties in the State of Oklahoma.

1916—"Kansas Conference shall include that part of the State of Kansas lying east of a line traversing the west boundary of Chautauqua, Elk and Greenwood Counties; thence along the south and west boundary of Chase County to the south and west boundary of Morris County to the south boundary of Dickinson County; thence west to the sixth principal meridian; thence north to the Nebraska State line; excepting the Soloman City Circuit lying east of said line."

1916—South Kansas Conference discontinued.

1920, 24, 28, 32, 36—No Changes

1939—"Central Kansas Conference shall comprise all that part of Kansas not included in the Kansas Conference."

1939—"Kansas Conference shall comprise that part of Kansas lying east of a line traversing the west boundary of Chautauqua, Elk, and Greenwood Counties, thence along the south and west boundary of Chase County to the south and west boundary of Morris County, thence north along the east boundary of Dickinson, Clay and Washington Counties to the Kansas State line."